Indian Economy

Volume I

K.R. Gupta

ATLANTIC
PUBLISHERS & DISTRIBUTORS (P) LTD

Published by
ATLANTIC
PUBLISHERS & DISTRIBUTORS (P) LTD
7/22, Ansari Road, Darya Ganj, New Delhi-110002
Phones : +91-11-40775252, 40775214, 23273880, 23275880
Fax: +91-11-23285873
Web: www.atlanticbooks.com
E-mail: orders@atlanticbooks.com

Printed & bound in India by Atlantic Print Services

Preface

At the time of attainment of independence, our economy was in a bad shape. Centuries of exploitative rule by the British had drained India of its wealth. According to eminent economists Amartya Sen and Jean Drèze, the British had totally destroyed India's self-reliant socio-economic structure. The realization of the need for resurrecting the Indian economy had dawned upon our leaders even before independence. The National Planning Committee (NPC) was set up as early as in 1938 under the inspiration of Jawaharlal Nehru to study various aspects of economic development. After independence, the Planning Commission was set up in 1950 to assess the country's needs of material capital and formulate economic plans. During the initial stages of the planning period which started with the launching of the First Five-Year Plan in 1950-51, the thrust was to develop heavy and basic industries to reduce the country's dependence on import of machinery and equipment, and initiate self-sustained long-term growth. All the key industries, services, mineral resources and utilities were kept in the public sector.

The progress under the Nehru-Mahalanobis model of growth which continued upto the 1980s was slow. The 1990s saw major shifts in Indian economic policies with the introduction of privatization and liberalization in the form of industrial delicensing and opening up of Indian economy to international trade through legislative measures like reduction in tariff, increase in foreign direct investment limit in various sectors, etc. These reforms, together with the adoption of new technologies and building up of infrastructure, have led to a high annual GDP growth rate of over eight per cent for the last three years. Nearly all economic indicators are in the positive zone.

Paradoxically, however, the country is experiencing shortages in amenities, infrastructure and essential services. The basic objectives of alleviation of poverty, generation of adequate employment opportunities and removal of inequalities of income and wealth have not been realized. Growth is, by and large, confined to our urban areas. Transportation, marketing, employment, education, health care and other means of a reasonable socio-economic living are still lacking in large parts of our rural areas.

The Indian economy is, thus, passing through a critical phase. There are several key questions which need to be answered if we are to embark on right policy decisions. Some of these questions are: whether to go for mechanisation in various sectors which will further aggravate unemployment situation, or to adopt labour-intensive methods of production which are slow, and lack quality and precision required to compete in international markets; whether to pursue disinvestments of Public Sector Undertakings (PSUs) which, according to some experts, tantamounts to giving away enterprises established with public money to private hands, or to let them continue with their sluggish growth under public sector; whether to adopt biotechnology in agriculture with its inherent risks of spoiling pure varieties and mass crop failure, or leave our agriculture to old methods and consequent low yield; whether to encourage foreign multinationals to establish their businesses in India which will jeopardise the interests of indigenous companies, or to keep the economy insulated from foreign competition which would deprive us of quality improvement; whether to adopt modern mall culture and Special Economic Zone (SEZ) modes of development, or concentrate on policies which may tackle specific problems like rural poverty and regional imbalances.

The book studies the structure and features of Indian economy and analyses the above key questions. It includes latest facts and figures, besides organising material in such a manner as to facilitate inculcating discussion on the topics covered. The proposals given in the Approach Paper to the Eleventh Plan, approved recently by the Planning Commission, have been incorporated at relevant places. The book will help the economists, government executives, parliamentarians and legislators to frame effective policies. The coverage and treatment of the subject will immensely help students of Economics in various Indian universities and the aspiring candidates of various competitive examinations.

K.R. GUPTA
JANAK RAJ GUPTA

Contents

Economic History of India

1

INDIAN ECONOMY UNDER THE BRITISH RULE INDUSTRIAL DEVELOPMENT

We can discuss the industrial development under the British rule as follows:

I. The East India Company and Early British Rule

Although India has never been an industrialized country in the western sense, or modern sense (large-scale industries, factories, factory laws, division of labour, etc.) yet a large varieties of goods since time immemorial were manufactured in India. Muslin of Dacca, woolen shawls of Kashmir, marble work of Jaipur, perfumes, ivory works, art works, etc. were sold to many foreign traders including European traders. Then there were iron industry like Sanchi Satup or Pillars. Thus in spite of predominantly agricultural character, India produced a large variety of industrial goods.

In fact to begin with the main purpose of East India Company or the Britishers for coming over to India was to trade in those manufactured goods, which were in large demand in European countries. They were not attracted by the natural resources of the country but by the value and variety of her manufactures and crafts. When in 1600, the East India Company (E.I.Co.) obtained a charter (or sought permission) from Queen Elizabeth to trade with East India, it was "to carry the manufactures and commodities of India to Europe". At the end of 17th century cheap and graceful Indian calicoes (cotton fabrics of Calicut), muslin and woolen fabrics found such favour in England that the manufacturers of those fabrics in England were seriously alarmed. Acts were passed in 1700 prohibiting the use of Indian printed or dyed calicoes in England. By a subsequent Act, the wearing of silken fabrics imported from India was also banned and a penalty of £200 was imposed on all persons selling the printed fabrics from India, China and Persia. However, the E.I.Co. was allowed to sell it in other countries. Thus, upto 19th Century, Indian manufacturers were excluded from the British market by law.

The huge amount of wealth exports from India was less by trade and more by plunder. From 1757 (First Battle of Plassey) onward, the direct plunder of Indian economy began to flood the England in ever increasing quantity, which prepared the ground for industrial revolution to occur first in England (around 1760).

But once the revolution began, it changed the whole outlook of England. The manufacturers and traders of England first braked the monopoly of the E.I.Co. in 1813. Then they systematically encouraged the import of manufactured goods into India and the export of raw materials (raw silk, raw cotton, raw jute, coal, etc.) from India. The E.I.Co. had to oblige the English manufacturers even if that meant a decline in the profit of E.I.Co. The manufacturers of England continued their offensive (fight) against E.I.Co. and finally succeeded in breaking its monopoly in 1813.

II. The Early 19th Century

From 1813, when the British manufacturers finally succeeded in destroying the monopoly of E.I.Co. in trade with India, India became suddenly an importing country from an exporting one. And this miracle was performed not on the basis of technical superiority of British industries but on the basis of direct state assistance in the form of one-way forced trade.

Now these millions of ruined artisans and craftsmen, spinners, weavers, potters, etc. from the towns or from the villages had no alternative employment. As the pace of destruction of industries quickened, more and more people fell on agriculture. Whereas in 1872 the total number of dependants on agriculture was 61 per cent of the total population, in 1921 it became 73 per cent. However, foreign capital began to be invested in extracting industries like rubber, tea and coffee plantation. Foreign capital notably from Britain was also invited to build railways. And this foreign capital was assured a return of 5 per cent which was disproportionately higher than the rate of interest at that time.

Progress upto the First World War

Around 1860, a modest beginning of modern Indian industries was made. This period witnessed the establishment of 3 cotton mills in Bombay, 2 jute mills in Bengal, and coal mining industry at Raniganj. While the cotton mills were owned and managed by Indians (who were later on constantly harassed and discriminated), the jute mills and coal mines were owned and managed by the British and the Scottish capitalists. The same period saw the beginning of railways. The first railway line, between Bombay and Thane, was opened in 1853 and the period 1860-70 saw a remarkable growth—5000 miles.

Thus by and large, consumption goods industry predominated the Indian scene. Basic and key industries were perfectly absent. The only important exception was the inauguration of the Tata Iron and Steel Company at Jamshedpur. This commenced its production in 1912. The large organized industries on a stable footing were three in number: the cotton industry of Bombay, the jute industry of Bengal and the coal mining industries of Bihar, Orissa and Bengal.

This period (upto 1914) was marked by two important features — (1) the opposition of the British manufacturers to the starting of new industries in India (2) the spread of Swadeshi Movement in 1905.

Opposition of British Interests

The British manufacturing interests tried their best to destroy the new industries, specially cotton textile industry. When in 1853 cotton textile factories were being started in India, the Manchester Chamber of Commerce insisted that the Government of India should identify themselves "with the cause of civilization, justice and Christianity by helping them to destroy new industry". In December 1894, when financial consideration forced the GOI to impose a general import duty of 5 per cent, a 'countervailing' cotton excise of 5 per cent was imposed upon all Indian mill-made yarn which exempted the imports from Manchester when in 1896, import duty was reduced to 3½ per cent. Similarly, in the last quarter of the century, there was an agitation in Dundee (England) against Indian jute manufacturing. Fortunately for India, Dundee was not as strong as Manchester, and Indian jute manufacturing had been Scottish-owned rather than Indian. The Scots of Calcutta took up the challenge and defeated the sinister move of Dundee. So far as coal industry was concerned, it was actively supported by the Government to enable it to meet the demand from railways.

Swadeshi Movement

The next landmark in the history of Indian industries was the Swadeshi Movement of 1905. From the concluding decades of 19th century the economic backwardness of India began to attract the attention of patriots and economists such as Dadabhai Naoroji and Ranade. The industrial backwardness was rightly held responsible for the recurrent famines and poverty from which the country suffered. The achievements of Japanese Government in bringing their country into the forefront of industrial nations within a very short period, stood in different contrast compared with unsympathetic attitude of the Government in this country. The much hated cotton excise duties confirmed the suspicion of the people that the Government was deliberately hindering the industrial development. Therefore, it is not surprising that the economic discontentment due to the poverty of the masses, and the lack of employment opportunities of the educated middle-class youth began to assume a political colour. The Swadeshi Movement called upon people to buy indigenous foods and to boycott imported goods. This caught the imagination of the people and a great wave of industrial enthusiasm (Indians market establishing more and more industry) spread throughout the country. Between 1890 and 1914, when number of cotton and jute mills increased three-four times, railways (in the hands of British) continued to increase at the rate of 800 miles per annum.

Further, apart from the existing three major industries, numerous factories for the manufacture of pencils, matches, glass, etc. were started. But because of the lack of experience and training these industries had to suffer.

III. The First World War (1914-18)

Upto the First World War, the opposition of the Britishers to industrial development in India was open and unconcealed. But the First World War proved an eye-opener to them. When the war broke out imports from foreign countries, particularly enemy countries were completely stopped. This revealed our miserable dependence on imports even for basic necessities. From strategic military angle this was even more serious. So for the defense of British Empire, India had to be industrialized. Secondly, it was necessary for the foreign rulers to make certain political and economic concessions and promises of concessions to secure cooperation of the Indian people during the war and in the disturbed period following the war. Government announced that in future industrialization will be promoted by all means. Thirdly, foreign competition (notably from Japan) had been affecting British import in India. It was felt that growth of some industries within India was better than foreign competition displacing British imports.

Industrial Commission (1916)

Thus all these considerations resulted in the appointment of the Industrial Commission in 1916, with Sir Thomas Holand as Chairman, "to examine the whole question of industrial development in India, and to indicate new openings for the profitable employment of Indian capital".

Indian Munitions Board

While the report of the Commission was still pending, the Indian Munitions Board was set up, as an emergency measure in 1917 "to control and develop Indian resources with special reference to the needs created by the war, and to apply the manufacturing resources of India to war purposes with the special object of reducing demands on shipping". The Board helped the progress of indigenous industries in various ways such as (i) direct purchase of Indian-made articles and materials of all kinds needed for the army, the civil departments, and the railways; (ii) the diversion of all orders from the U.K. and elsewhere to manufacture in India; (iii) assistance to Indian firms in importing industrial plants or technical experts from abroad. In fact, it gave considerable stimulus to certain established industries, e.g. cotton, jute, iron and steel, leather, etc.

Industrial Progress During the Period

During the war period cotton and jute industries worked at full capacity and thus earning large profits. Steel production increased from 19,000 tonnes in 1913 to 1,24,000 tonnes in 1918 (i.e. 7 times increase). Due to the cutting off of import from abroad, the production of some consumer's goods also developed. A good many articles like chemicals, minerals, acids, cements, fertilizers, cutlery, etc. for which India relied on foreign countries was manufactured for the first time in India. But the lack of basic industries prevented the consumer's goods industries from taking full advantage of the temporary protection accorded by the war to these industries.

It has been rightly observed by Professor Jather and Beri that the success of this new departure of the GOI from the traditional policy of *laissez-faire* showed how much could be done in the sphere of industrial development with the active cooperation of the Government

But once the war and the fear of it on the British Empire was over, the concessions in favour of Indian industries were also withdrawn. The First World War provided only temporary gains to the established industries. And it did nothing to set the country firmly on the road to industrialization.

IV. Inter-War Period (1918-39)

Report of the Industrial Commission

In 1918, the Industrial Commission presented its Report in which it was stressed that, in future, the Government must extend active assistance in industrializing the country with a view to make India self-sufficient. The Report also recognized the fact that the Government cannot do much in this direction unless it is equipped with (i) adequate administrative machinery, and (ii) trained, technical and scientific experts. Therefore, the

Commission recommended, (i) the creation of special industrial and chemical services (ii) the establishment of Board of Industries.

But the elaborate scheme of Indian Industrial Commission for the rapid industrialization of the country came to nothing. Under the GOI Act 1919, "industries became a provincial subject: and following the recommendations of the Industrial Commission, a Provincial Department of Industries was established in each province. The main work of these departments were (i) promotion of technical and industrial education, (ii) supply of industrial intelligence; and (iii) financial assistance to industries and holding of industrial exhibitions for popularizing their products. But nothing substantial was achieved because of lack of funds. The constitutional transfer of industries to the Provinces also handicapped evolution of a comprehensive industrial policy.

Discriminating Protection

The period after the war was over, was followed by a short period of prosperity caused by the rising income and unfulfilled demand of the preceding period. It was a short period of great prosperity for the existing manufacturing industries, such as jute, cotton, iron and steel, etc. But by the middle of 1920, Indian industries were again subjected to the full force of foreign competition, and the long-standing demand for protection of India industries became more powerful and vocal. This eventually led to the appointment of the Fiscal Commission in October 1921. The Commission recommended (1922) a policy of discriminating protection to be administered through an expert body called the Tariff Board. This policy was accepted by the Government in 1923 and a Tariff Board was constituted to examine the claims for protection of several industries. Altogether 13 industries received protection and this enabled a few of them like steel, cotton, sugar, paper and matches to establish themselves in social sector. But the lack of genuine sympathy on the part of the Government, with a view to industrialize the country, hampered the progress of many industries. In fact, protection was given grudgingly and only to face foreign competition. Protection was never used as an instrument of industrialization.

In fact, the triple formula evolved to decide about granting protection was rightly called as discrimination and no protection. Because the Government could refuse protection on any of the 3 grounds (triple formula) mentioned in the formula. These were:

(1) The industry must have natural advantages which would facilitate its growth. These included abundant supply of raw materials, cheap power, a sufficient supply of labour and a large home market.

(2) Then the industry must be such as it is not likely to develop at all, or at least not as rapidly as desirable in the interests of the country, unless it was given protection.

(3) The industry must be one which would ultimately be able to face world competition, without the help of protection.

This triple formula, thus, meant that protection should be temporary, and given only when it was indispensable for the permanent development of an industry. Moreover, this was not a permanent Tariff Board. For each case separate Board was constituted. This resulted into great delays. Lastly, the effectiveness of protection was reduced in some cases by excise duties on the production of sugar, matches, steel, etc. in 1943.

Another noteworthy feature on the front of industrialisation during this period was the institution of 'imperial preferences'.

Export of British Capital to India

During the period following the end of the war, large amount of British capital were exported to India. This was largely encouraged by huge projects earned by the British and Indian firms during and after the war. The total of British capital investment in India which was roughly £400 million just before the war reached £1000 million by 1933. From the Indian share of 11 per cent of the total of British capital investment throughout the world, it reached 25 per cent of the total of British investment. For the Indian industries this was an extremely difficult period. The difficulty was aggravated when the Tariff Board turned down the applications of many vital industries for protection.

Imperial Preference

Imperial preference, a tariff policy, which gave British products an advantage over non-empire products in the Indian markets and Indian products an advantage over non-empire product in the empire market now became the keynote of the tariff system. Though originally proclaimed as a means for promoting Indian industrialization, in reality it was a system which assisted British industry to compete in the Indian market while India got the privilege of reduced rates for the sake of raw materials in the British market. The continuation of this policy of exploitation was naturally opposed by the rising class of industrialists of India. The clash of interests between British and Indian industrialists found expression in the Indian Legislative Assembly when the Trade Agreement between England and India, based on Ottawa Agreement, was defeated. But even in the face of the adverse vote of the Assembly, the Trade Agreement (Imperial Preference) was thrust upon India.

Political Inspiration

Another significant development in the inter-war industrial history of Indian was the Congress's move for industrial planning for India.

Experiences of other countries notably Japan had made it clear to the educated section that with proper guidance of the Government, substantial progress in industrialization can be achieved within a comparatively short time. Remarkable results achieved by the USSR through a system of planning also raised new hopes and strengthened the faith in planning for solving economic problems of poverty and unemployment. The Indian National Congress, which was generally opposed to industrialization particularly large-scale mechanization, also modified its policy in 1938. Under the leadership of Subhash Chander Bose, an ex-Congress President, a Conference of Industries Ministers, from the 'Congress Provinces' was held in October 1938. The Conference came to the conclusion that the problems of poverty and unemployment, of defense and economic development in general could not be generally solved without industrialization. The Conference emphasized the urgency of taking steps to start 'key' industries of national importance, and appointed a National Planning Committee under the Chairmanship of Pandit Jawaharlal Nehru to draw up a comprehensive scheme of national planning. The National Planning Committee appointed 29 sub-committees which submitted their reports. But no concrete action could be taken as the Congress Ministries had to resign in September 1939 following the outbreak of the Second World War. The war and the consequent change in political situation in the country relegated the problems of industrialization to the background.

Industrial Progress during the Period

In spite of the difficulties and obstacles which Indian industries had to face, there was considerable progress in industrial development during the inter-war period. Between 1922 and 1939, the production of cotton piece goods increased two and a half (2½) times, that of steel nearly 8 times, and paper nearly two and a half times. In the case of sugar India became self-sufficient and its production increased nearly 12 times. From a zero-start the cement industry produced nearly 95 per cent of total requirements. The production of matches, glass, soap, vanaspati and a number of engineering industries also recorded large increases. By 1938-39, the manufactures of electric equipment and goods also started. The total number of factories increased 4 times and the number of workers employed in them increased 40 per cent. It means by and large the new industries were small-scale industries.

But in spite of considerable expansion of industrial production during the period, the over-all picture suggested a very slow rate of development. As already said, by and large new establishments were small scale, catering mostly to the demand for consumer goods. Although some protected industries expended considerably and India became independent of foreign countries for the supply of machinery and other capital goods without which the establishment of new industries would be impossible, yet full-fledged industrialization was not still achieved. Even *The Economist*, published from London, in its survey of India's industrialization at the end of 1936 observed, "although India has begun to modernize her industries, it can hardly be said that she is as yet being industrialized".

V. The Second World War (1939-45)

In spite of the life and death situation in which England found herself in the Second World War, the industrialization of India was knowingly discouraged. This was particularly true during the initial years, but the exigencies of war compelled the Government to take up some positive steps for industrialization. Nazi-Germany was threatening the vast Empire of the Britishers. Their ships after ships were being sunk. Near India, Japan had occupied Burma and was threatening to enter India. This revealed the total lack of military base in India. In short, the World War II created a more urgent demand for the rapid growth of 'heavy and key' industries in India than the war of 1914-18.

Further, apart from the needs of the Allies (the forces which constituted to fight Nazi-Germany) for the war purposes, there were other important factors which favoured industrial development during this period.

(1) Drastic curtailment of imports and restrictions on imports created nearly monopoly conditions in the home market.

(2) The assurance given by the Government that industries which are required for war purposes would be given protection after the war is over provided great incentives to start new industries.

(3) In 1940 Board of Scientific and Industrial Research was started at Calcutta. Partly for training war technicians the Board provided training to Indian Technicians. The British also offered stipends for training Indian technicians in British industries. All this greatly increased the supply of skilled labour and technicians (which were hitherto almost negligible so far as Indians were concerned). The Board of Scientific and Industrial Research found a number of indigenous substitutes for import and developed the use of vegetable oil, lubricants, drugs, dyes, plastics, etc.

The Progress of Industries

A number of industries were benefited in different degrees by the conditions created by the war. Existing large and organized industries, such as the iron and steel, jute, cotton, leather and tanning, woolen, sugar, paper and cement industries made considerable progress. Production increased by increasing shifts or by improved methods. Wherever feasible, new plants were also added. Some new large-scale industries also started production for the first time. They were:

(i) Heavy chemical industries like caustic soda, bleaching powder, soda ash, super phosphate, etc.

(ii) Ferrous-alloys (Ferro-manganese) and non-ferrous metals like aluminum, copper-wires, cables, etc.

(iii) New branches of engineering industry including diesel engines, pumps, bicycles, sewing machine tools, etc.

Thus compared with the First World War, new capital and intermediate goods industries also received stimulus. A number of medium and large-scale industries were also established during the World War II compared with small-scale industries during the First World War.

The trend of industrial activity during the war and the major large-scale industries can be studied from their performances. For example, before the War, India was entirely dependent on foreign sources for high grades steel. But during the War production of high grade steel, pig iron, etc. greatly picked up. Fifty-four firms began to manufacture more time tools. Armaments work, explosive plants and small arm factories were greatly expanded. The Hindustan Aircraft Company at Bangalore assembled its first plane in August 1941 from imported parts. Next to those iron and steel industries, consumer goods industries, viz. cotton goods, also recorded a sizeable growth. There was a great demand for clothes from Allies. Japan's competition had been shut. Within one year during 1943-44, production of cotton clothes increased by 30 per cent. So were other industries like sugar and jute. Jute which had depressed earlier established fresh records in production and exports.

Critical Estimate of Progress

As already stated, as far as possible the British Government discouraged the industrialization. The establishment of certain key industries was their war compulsions. The Britishers never wanted to lose India as the supplier of raw materials and the market for British goods. When the Eastern Group Conference was held in New Delhi in October 1940, India was recognized as the leader of the Eastern Group Commonwealth Countries. The main object of the Conference was to make the countries of the Eastern Group, specially India, as far as possible, self-supporting for war purposes. But the recommendations of the Conference were never published in India—the country where the conference was held. When the question of manufacturing aeroplanes came up, it was simply set aside on the ground that it would be a duplication of what other parts of the Empire (viz. Australia) were doing.

Similarly, the American Technical Mission, headed by Dr. Henry Grady, which visited India in April 1942, carried out an investigation into India's war-production possibilities. The Commission recommended the establishment of some new industries for which the country was fully equipped. It also recommended an increase in training facilities. But all its elaborate schemes came to nothing. For safeguarding the interest of British industrialists, the Government avoided the development of key industries even at the risk of losing war. British finance-capital further strengthened its grip over Indian enterprises. The giant British concerns like Lover Brothers, Dunlop, Imperial Chemicals, etc. started their Indian subsidiaries. The number of these 'India Limited' companies was daily growing and within 5 years (period ending 1943-44) their number grew to 108. These limited concerns concentrated in the production of matches, cigarettes, soaps, rubber, chemicals, etc. But the proposal for the establishment of an automobile industry—owned and managed by Indians, was rejected on the ground of difficulties created by war. It was the time when the GOI was placing orders for the import of automobiles from other countries. Australia and Canada were manufacturing aeroplane with the help of England. But when Indian industrialists showed their interest to do so, without any subsidy, the request was turned down. Same was the fate of ship-building industry.

Thus in spite of the extremely favourable environment created by the war and her large metallurgical resources, India still lagged behind in basic and 'key' industries. It is true that she became self-sufficient in respect of something like 90 per cent of her military supplies. But it must also be remembered that the supplies in respect of which India became self-sufficient, consisted mainly of clothing, small ammunition, foodstuffs, tents and blankets. Only those basic and key industries were started for which abundant raw material was available. But not much was done to reverse the shortage of capital and trained personnel.

Adverse Effects

What is worse, the limited industrial progress which was achieved during the war period led to undesirable trends:

(1) As already stated the increase in production was primarily achieved through intensive use of existing machinery, with the result that after the war, the machinery was worn out and needed urgent repair which was neglected.

(2) War time inflation side tracked the economic factors like availability of raw materials, location of industry, proper financial management, etc. These trends were not conducive for long-term industrialization.

(3) During the war, major emphasis was on defence goods industries. Thus consumer goods industries like cotton clothe, cement, sugar, jute, paper, etc. were neglected and hence created huge profits. Thus there was lopsided development in industry.

(4) The shortfall in the production of consumer goods industry compelled the Government to introduce rationing for their equitable distributions. But their continuous price rise made the controls ineffective. This led to corruption and blackmarketing.

Governments' Industrial Policy

While examining the growth of modern industries in India, a question which naturally comes up is what role did the Government play in this regard? The question is relevant because this would verify the claim of the British Government that it did a lot to lay the foundation of modern industries in India.

It is a well known fact that during the E.I.Co.'s tenure (rule) several measures were taken to discourage our industries and to encourage the sale of British goods in India. For example, in 1869, the company's Director ordered the encouragement of production of raw silk in Bengal and discouragement of silk fabrics. In the same year, silk artisans were forced to work in the company's factories under severe punishment in 1813, when the company charter was renewed, the British Parliament enquired into law Indian industrial products could be replaced by the British products. In this regard, the officials of the E.I.Co. readily obliged the British manufacturers.

On the other hand, Indian handicraft products were shut out from England by high import duties varying from 67 per cent and going up to even 400 per cent. Not satisfied with high tariff, there was sometimes a complete ban on the import of Indian goods into England. But the British goods were forced on India free of duty. Thus the process of political injustice was applied to kill Indian handicrafts.

Government attitude changed little under the Crown. At the best, it was a policy of absolute *laissez-faire*. And it served the British interest at the cost of Indian interest. For example, the Famines Commission of 1880 recommended encouragement to industries as the most important remedy for famines, but due to Governments pressure from Manchester, the centre of cotton mills in England, most of the import duties were removed by 1882. Manchester complained that cotton mills in India offered an 'unfair competition' since labour was relatively cheap in India. Consequently, Factory Acts of 1881 and 1891 were forced upon India compelling the cotton manufacturers to provide more facilities to Indian labour and this increased their cost of production.

In December 1894, when financial consideration forced the GOI to impose a general import duty of 5 per cent, under the pressure of Manchester, a 'countervailing' cotton excise of 5 per cent was also imposed on Indian mill cloth when in 1896, import duty was reduced to 3.5 per cent, excise duty was also cut to 3.5 per cent. Thus excise duty greatly harassed the poor consumers demanding coarse clothes. It was only in 1926 that this much-hated 'countervailing' excise duty was removed.

In short, what we needed at that time was protection for our infant industries. But what we received was one way free trade which served the interest of the Britishers at the cost of Indians. It may be mentioned that some provincial governments tried to encourage the establishment of industries, but the European businessmen in India opposed this. Therefore, in 1910 Lord Morley, the Secretary of the State, reversed this policy. The indifference of Government to industrial development in India continued right upto the First World War.

To summarize, it may be reiterated that on the whole the attitude of the British Government towards industrialization in India was negative. It was only under certain compulsions that the British Government had to provide certain industries. But in the heart and heat, the Government tried to retain India as a source of raw material for their industries in England and as a market for their manufacturers.

Indian Industries in the Past and their Decline or Decline of Handicrafts—Causes and Consequences

India was never an industrial country in the modern sense, yet Indian handicrafts before the British era were well known—cotton fabrics, silk fabrics, woolen fabrics, art products, timber (ship industry), metal industries. Even the great iron pillars industries in India testify that even iron (melt) industry was quite developed in India. Broadly, we can divide the Indian industries in three groups:

(1) Village Cottage Industries;

(2) Urban Handicrafts;

(3) Localized Industries.

(1) Village Cottage Industries—There were self-sufficient villages. An army of artisans existed in the village with certain amount of coarse weaving, grinding of grain flour mills, rice milling, sugar making, etc. Their organization was primitive and no division of labour or specialization existed. Often these industries were interwoven with agriculture.

(2) Urban Handicrafts—Urban handicrafts were better organized and confined more or less to higher class of products. These were organized into caste-based guilds. In certain industries, division of labour was practised with same degree of localization. Putting out system was more common.

(3) Localized Industries—Third group of industries, neither urban nor village, was highly localized because of the availability of raw material. Iron industry in Mysore, Chhotanagpur, Central Provinces. Some of these industries were very important to the country. Although not highly developed, products were of fine quality. Their number was not very significant. But they soon decayed because of the unjust tariff and unhelpful attitude of the Government.

Causes of the Decay of Handicraft

Peculiar Nature of Demand—Purely economic, demand declined, artisan, excellence of their product made them luxury goods with growing poverty the demand for their product was declining. The final blow came from the cheap products manufactured in factories in England.

The Kashmiri shawls, cheaply produced in Kashmir and some other parts of the countries (e.g. Amritsar) had been famous for centuries. But by 1850 the industry was rapidly declining and by the end of the century "the industry was already a mere tradition—a memory of the past". The first set-back came in 1830, when a great famine broke out in Kashmir. This along with migration of the Kashmiri population to Punjab towns claimed the extinction of Kashmiri shawls. Some unscrupulous manufacturers started producing low grade shawls.

Around middle of the 19th century, these shawls became very popular in France. The French traders had a monopoly over the shawl traders and asked the artisans to produce shawls to their order (already because of poverty, these artisans preferred to produce on order—putting out system). The French traders introduced the European patterns with the result that artistic merit of the shawls greatly deteriorated. Then came France-German War which completely cut off the exports. This time fashion in France had also changed. To tide over this challenge, the industry adopted cheap dyes and stuff which further reduced the reputation. The final death blow came from cheap factory products.

The gradual decline in demand, along with unfair competition from the side of supply can adequately explain the process of decline and the ultimate death of most of the Indian handicrafts.

Disappearance of Princely Courts

The abolition of native Indian courts also meant stoppage of the main source of demand. For example, the prosperous muslin, cotton and silk industry of Bengal had largely depended on the existence of Great Mughal Empire with courts in Agra, Lahore, Delhi, etc. Break-up of the Mughal empire and hence a decline in demand. Again, e.g. the Nawab of Oudh had patronized the dyeing industry in Lucknow, but after the accession of Oudh, this industry too declined. It is interesting to note that whereas handicrafts were still flourishing in princely states, they were dying out in the British territory. With the gradual extension in the British Empire, the decay of handicrafts further accelerated.

The disappearance of the Indian courts helped the decay of handicrafts in another way. The princes used to hire best craftsmen on fat salary so that he could produce best products not yielding to popular demand for cheaper goods. The stoppage of this patronage made the best artisans subject to popular tasks, not always the best—often cheaper goods.

Hostile Policy of the E.I.Co. and the British Parliament

The E.I.Co. in order to earn profits through trade first gave encouragement to handicrafts. But that meant export of gold and silver from England to India which could not be tolerated. Incidentally, at that time industrial revolution took place in England which necessitated to convert the Indian market into the exporter of raw materials and importer of British factory goods. Tariff policy was changed. There was a prohibition of wearing Indian printed clothes. In short, the British manufacturers employed the arm of political injustice to keep down the Indian handicrafts.

Alien (Foreign) Rule and Consequent Adverse Effects

The English Rule brought in English officers in place of Indian Nawabs and nobles. Naturally they had different (European) tasks. The Indian people started imitating European way of life and suffered from inferiority complex. It became fashion to adopt and wear European designs. Professor Gadgil has gathered from many sources how in Punjab the demand to wear silken clothes was replaced by the demand for European printed clothes.

Of course, apart from slavish mentality and the sense of inferiority, there were other reasons, e.g. Indian petty officials did not want to annoy their English officers by wearing Indian products. Sometimes, there were unwritten conventions and rules not to wear particular type of Indian products, e.g. no Indian could appear before their European officers wearing Indian embroidered shoes. They had to wear cheap factory boots.

Further, the Europeans naturally preferred imported goods from their own country to face this competition; the Indian craftsmen started imitating European designs. Thus blind imitation naturally destroyed the artistic value of handicrafts, e.g. Kashmiri shawls started using cheap dyes and cheap raw materials.

The alien rule affected handicraft in another way. It indirectly weakened the power of the caste-based guilds (because of de-industrialization artisans were fleeing to villages), which had hitherto regulated the quality of the product. This at once led to a decline in their value, both commercial as well as artistic. Further, some arms industries which owned their existence to princely courts and kingdoms had to be closed as people were no longer free to possess arms of their own.

Price Competition from Machine Made Goods

Finally, the most important reason of the decay of Indian handicrafts was that they could not withstand the foreign competition which derived its strength from the Industrial Revolution in England, based on large scale production and minute division of labour. The invention of powerloom in England completed the decline of the Indian textile industry. Though in the matter of quality Indian goods were still superior, in the matter of price they could not face the competition. Development of the means of transport and communication further opened up even the interior part of the country. The construction of Suez Canal further reduced the distance by thousand miles between India and England. This reduced the transport costs of British goods in India. In fact the development of the means of transport and communication was so quick that the urban handicrafts could not bear this sudden attack and disappeared quickly. This explains why some crafts noticed by some English historians in 1878 in Lahore were no more there after an interval of even 10 years.

AGRICULTURE

AGRICULTURE UNDER THE BRITISH RULE

During pre-British days there was a happy blend of agriculture and industry. Even in villages one could see urban handicrafts.

The policy of the Britishers was to turn India into net exporter of raw material for the British industries and net importer for the demand of manufactured goods produced in British factories.

Proportion of population dependent on agriculture increased substantially from 61.7 per cent in 1891 to 73 per cent in 1921.

Even in the face of growing population, the percentage as well as the absolute number of industrial workers declined.

Thus agriculture was the mainstay of the Indian economy—as it is today. But unfortunately, it could not produce enough for its subsistence. Famines were frequent. There were imports of rice from Burma. Vicious circle—growing population—more dependence on agriculture—extension of cultivation through bullocks—more demand for fodder (i.e. there was a competition between man and animal population for subsistence) developed. According to D.R. Gadgil most often the conditions of the Indian farmers deteriorated at the end of the year when he harvested his crops. Later on he fell into moneylender clutches.

For convenience sake we can divide the study of agriculture during British regime in following periods:

1860-80	Period of stagnant agriculture
1880-95	Period of relative prosperity
1895-1914	Period of famines
1914-29	First World War upto the Depression
1929-39	The Depression and after
1939-47	Second World War and its consequences

I. Period of Stagnant Agriculture (1860-80)

Effects of the Permanent Settlement of 1793, began to be felt. Land became a scarce commodity which could be bought and sold. Because of the growing debt the land started flowing from the cultivators into the hands of moneylenders. Because of the decay of urban handicraft even the urban rich were turning to the agricultural sector. The actual cultivators were selling land to the moneylenders who were not agriculturists. The actual cultivators had to work for the moneylenders on share crop basis, i.e. part of the production being paid to the moneylender as the latter's share and partly to pay the interest. According to D.R. Gadgil, the actual cultivator found himself more and more at the mercy of cultivator after the hard work of one year.

Another characteristic of this period was the growing importance of cash crops, viz. jute and cotton. Jute cultivation for exports had already started in around 1833 in Bengal. The development of steamships further accelerated the growth of jute. Cotton cultivation also picked up during this period. Till 1860, America was the chief supplier of raw cotton for the

British mills in England. But the civil war in America interrupted this supply and the British industrialists had to turn towards India. Needless to say that the British Government in India provided the needed facilities to encourage cotton exports. A general prosperity particularly those engaged in cotton cultivation or cotton trade was experienced.

But this prosperity was shortlived since it coincided with the period of revision of revenue assessment. The temporary prosperity was quite mistakenly considered as indicating the ability of the peasants to pay taxes. As a result, the assessment were heavier than what the peasants could bear. There was a sudden crash in cotton trade and prices. Extravagant military expeditions and increasing establishment costs necessitated heavy taxes. All these factors compelled the cultivators to borrow more and more and they fell victim to the moneylenders.

Revolt of the Peasantry

Bewildered by the growing indebtedness and cunningness of the moneylenders actual cultivators revolted. They started killing and looting the moneylenders. Broadly, they were satisfied by destroying the debt bonds. Although this riot was put down easily, this revealed the growing impoverishment of the cultivators. The growing poverty of the cultivators was attributed to the granting of free property right to the tillers who hitherto had not enjoyed it. Legal right was given to moneylenders to recover their loans by attaching the peasant's property. For this reason, the moneylender was very willing to lend money to the cultivators. If good crops—this encouraged the moneylender to lend still more. If bad crops—this compelled the cultivators to borrow more from him.

Dispossession of Land

Moneylenders were not interested in agricultural development. Even agriculturist moneylenders were not better. They tried to alienate and dispossess the peasantry from land.

Famines and its Consequences

During 1860-80 many famines broke out. The effects of prosperity experienced during the American Civil War were shortlived. America soon resumed her cotton supply to Great Britain and the boom in the Indian cotton market came to a sudden end. Secondly, a series of famines, as follows, overtook the decade of seventies:

1865	A mild famine in Madras
1868-69	Rajputana famine
1873-74	Bihar and Bengal famines

Famines increased the distress of farmers who became physically weak and financially they were destroyed. Agricultural progress was checked.

II. Period of relative prosperity (1880-95)

The period between 1880 to 1895 was one of comparative agricultural prosperity. There was a favourable rainfall and consequently absence of any major famines. Of course, local scarcity was there at some places. The relative abundance might have brought down the agricultural prices, but fortunately there was rising demand for Indian agricultural produce—both within and outside the country. However, all categories of farmers were not benefited—only large farmers who had more to sell (i.e. marketable surplus). This period was characterized by:

(1) Expansion of trade—mostly foreign

(2) Extension of cultivation—to meet the needs of growing population

(3) Area under non-food crops which had started earlier picked up. Because of the development of means of transport and communication cash crops, viz. jute, cotton, sugarcane, oilseeds had a wider market.

(4) Greater regional specialization started developing. However, the proportion of area under food crops remained larger than area under non-food or cash or industrial crops.

Practice of Cultivation

Though cultivation remained traditional, yet in certain regions it was greatly developed. Practice of keeping land fallow was abandoned which may be due to poverty. Poverty forced the cultivators to cultivate whatever quality of land was available. He always lacked resources so he could not afford fallow land. For seeds again he had to turn towards moneylenders.

Thus the period of prosperity did not alter his economic condition much.

III. Period of Famines (1895-1914)

The fifteen years of very limited prosperity came to a close. Once more the hands of the clock of agricultural progress were put back; the progress achieved during the previous period was lost throughout the country. The people of the country once more were in the grip of severe famines.

Famines and its Consequences

The famine of 1896-97 was more severe and widespread. The areas hitherto unknown or immune to famines suddenly found themselves in the grip of famines.

The famine of 1899-1900 was of lesser severity. It particularly was confined to cattle. Cattle population was reduced. Consequently, farmers became pauper and resulted into a:

(a) Decline in double cropped area

(b) Displacement of cash crops by food crops

(c) The decline in the total area under cultivation

These two famines—one after the other—inflicted a great misery. They weakened the health of the people and broke their morale. These famines killed whatever small spirit of innovation might have been left.

IV. First World War upto the Depression (1914-29)

Famines continued unabated. The year 1918-19 witnessed very widespread and major famine calamity comparable in extent and severity with that of 1899-1900. Before the people could recover, monsoons failed in 1920-21. Although the famine of 1920-21 was of lesser severity but because of the growing poverty the number of people accepting poor relief multiplied substantially. Although since 1921 agricultural seasons had been, on the whole, good yet periodic failure of monsoons continued to occur coming specifically to the First World War.

First World War and its Effects

The war years (as usual) were marked by rising prices. But increase in agricultural prices was less than the prices of imported foods such as cotton manufactures, metals, sugar, etc. So long as this unequal rise in prices continued agriculture continued to suffer. But by 1926, this disparity in rise in prices disappeared. Agricultural prices as well as manufactures rose by the same rate compared with 1914. But the period was short-lived. Since again in 1929, whereas agricultural prices crashed by 50 per cent prices of manufactured article did not experience the similar declines.

During this period, the continuous competition between man and cattle reduced the area under fodder. Consequently, number of cows and buffaloes declined with severe consequences on the availability of milk.

Growth of Rural Indebtedness and the Agricultural Labourers

Rural indebtedness continued to rise. Land continued to be transferred from the tillers to the moneylenders. During this period, laws were enacted to check this transfer. It was stipulated that only the agriculturalists would be allowed to hold land. But the term agriculturist was too vague.

Subdivision and Fragmentation of Holdings

Declining handicrafts and growing pressure of population on agriculture resulting into subdivision and smaller holdings continued during this period. As a result poverty continued to multiply.

Extension of Irrigation

Some kinds of repair works had begun to revive the dying agricultural economy. Irrigation Commission, during this period recommended the large irrigation projects. However, the other areas continued to be neglected. No attention was paid to private wells with the result that area irrigated through wells declined. However, canal colonies were developed in 1920.

V. The Depression and After (1929-39)

The Depression had twofold effects :

(a) Absolute fall in agricultural prices;

(b) Fall in agricultural prices vis-à-vis non-agricultural prices.

India at that time exported agricultural goods whose prices declined at much sharper rate than the prices of imported good (which were basically manufactured and industrial goods).

The absolute fall in agricultural prices reduced the income of the cultivators. The official data showed that whereas in 1928-29, the value of agricultural crops was Rs. 10,340 million, it fell to Rs. 4,730 million in 1933-34—a fall of more than 50 per cent. Rural indebtedness increased. A notable feature of this period was that in spite of the 50 per cent fall in agricultural income, land revenue demand was dropped by only 9 per cent. The inability to pay land revenue forced the cultivators in many provinces, notably in Bengal and the United Provinces, to surrender their lands.

Thus the total area under cultivation declined by 5 million acres. The decline in area under food crops was even much more (i.e. 5.3 million acres and 0.3 million acres under food crops were shifted to cash crops).

The drop in agricultural income by 50 per cent otherwise meant 50 per cent increase in real debt plus more borrowing. It is estimated through official agencies that rural indebtedness (almost doubled) increased from Rs. 900 crores in 1931 to Rs. 1800 crore in 1937.

Pauperization of peasants continued. Relatively rich farmers were dispossessed of their gold. Gold worth 32 million ounce (more than England had it that time) was exported to England.

VI. Second World War and its Consequences (1939-47)

The agricultural economy of India had become bankrupt was once again revealed during the war. When after the entry of Japan into the war, import of rice was stopped from Burma, the whole country was plunged into famines. Although the shortage was only of a minor proportion (about 5 per cent of the total requirements), mishandling of the situation resulted into a famine-like situation in the country. About 3 million people died in Bengal alone. Rural indebtedness increased—urban areas profiteer and blackmarketers made huge profits. To finance the war there was deficit financing or printing of money. Prices rose still sharper. Economic conditions of the people in general and farmers in particular further deteriorated.

After partition, a major proportion of cultivated area went to Pakistan. Wheat growing canal colonies (developed by the British) even rice growing area went to Pakistan. The proportion of population left in Indian side had greater problem of feeding millions. India was a deficit country—that it remained more or less so till the mid-sixties when Green Revolution era was ushered here.

Pakistan got 23 per cent of territory with wheat-cotton belt, but only 18 per cent of population. Rice-belt of Burma had already gone in 1937 (1st April 1937). India with 77 per cent of territory had to feed 82 per cent of population.

Agricultural Policy of the British Government

In a predominantly agricultural and backward country, Government's agricultural policy has a vital role to play. But under the British rule no concentrated and organized efforts were made in this direction.

I. Period 1860-1880

Limited and Ineffective Action: Up to 1866, the only effort made was to start botanical gardens for introducing new plants or their varieties like tea, potato, etc. Then in 1870 came the Imperial Department of Agriculture, but it was abolished in 1878 on the ground that Provincial Government did not cooperate (in fact Provincial Government had no power at that time). In the same decade some experimental farms were started to evolve new varieties and new methods of production. But this too failed either because these farms were supervised by persons having no knowledge in agriculture. Or also English scientists were limited to lead the experimental stations and the English people had no background of the Indian soil and other environmental conditions. In fact, the Indian peasants had a good knowledge of agricultural technique, what they lacked was irrigation and credit which were completely ignored till that time. The Famine Commission of 1880 recommended that Government should immediately start Agricultural Department and collect agricultural statistics, but nothing was done.

II. Period 1880-95

In this period also there was a similar story of very limited or no action.

Takavi Loans: Acts passed in 1883 and 1884 re-introduced a very old method of encouraging agricultural improvements, i.e. to give small loans to farmers (called takavi loans) who repaid these loans in installment. This measure too did not succeed because the administration was faulty. The collector was made responsible to disburse these loans. These collectors were already overburdened with other administrative works. These loans were quite often untimely and the period of recovery was casually short. Rigidity in the collection of interest and principal further discouraged these loans. Up to 1900 only Rs. 6 crore was lent. However, in certain regions where the collectors were dynamic these loans did make some progress.

In 1889 Dr. Volecker was appointed to suggest agricultural improvements. He toured throughout the country and submitted his report in 1893 but no action was taken on this report till 1900.

III. Period 1895-1914

During this period several beginnings and new type of action were initiated in several directions.

An Inspector-General of Agriculture was appointed in 1901. The Agricultural Research Institute and a few Provincial Agricultural Colleges and Schools were opened. More money was spent on Agricultural Department. But considering the size of Indian subcontinent neither the amount spent on the staff nor for other agricultural activities was sufficient. Therefore, no substantial results were achieved.

To improve the quality of cotton, seed farms were started for producing and distributing better seeds. Research was also conducted in suitable regions for different varieties of wheat. New varieties of rice and groundnut were also introduced. In several parts of India improved implements were introduced, viz. light iron ploughs and small water pumps. Cooperative credit societies were started in 1904 and non-credit societies were formed in 1912.

To sum up, these improvements were limited in scope, wild in nature and did not always reach the farmers.

IV. Period 1914-29

The pace of agricultural improvement done by Government remained slow, and the times of improvement were much the same as before. A large amount of work was done in introducing improved varieties. The major successes were wheat, cotton, jute, groundnut and sugarcane. To spread the knowledge of these varieties special seed farms were started. Arrangements were also made for the production and distribution of better seeds.

However, because of the fact that agricultural prices during this period rose less sharply than the prices of manufactured goods, agricultural sector had to suffer.

V. Period 1929-39

During Depression farmers suffered very severely. Their absolute as well as relative income declined and they had to sell gold to pay off debt and taxes. Gold worth 32 million ounces was exported. India was perhaps the only country in the world in which the Government did very little rather nothing to ameliorate the lot of farmers whereas in most of the countries the Government tried to fight Depression by a positive price policy. However, the Government in India, particularly the Central Government remained the silent spectator.

Provincial Government: By contrast, the Provincial Governments tried to do something. Payment of land revenue was suspended and in certain cases even some remission in land revenue was allowed. But the maximum reduction in land revenue did not exceed 9 per cent compared with more than 50 per cent decline in income. Nothing was done in respect of indebtedness, i.e. the farmer had to pay interest and the principal even in the face of their declining income. In some provinces Acts to regulate moneylenders were passed. In some provinces the Governments also tried to regulate market for the agricultural produce. In 1930s Tenancy Laws were also passed, but the problem of assuring security and justice to the cultivating tenant still remained. In the face of Depression, the Cooperative Movement which was started in 1904 had to face a tough time. Many societies were wound up, recoveries fell and overdue increased. But no help came from the Government's side.

VI. Period 1939-47

War and Food Problem: During the War, food problem was created with high prices and serious food shortages. Import of rice from Burma was cut and famine conditions existed in Bengal. But the Government had no well thought-out policy to execute.

In 1942, the Food Production Conference proposed a plan for increasing food production. 'Grow More Food Campaign' was launched. Then came the Bengal famine in 1943 in which 3 million people lost their lives and the Government was forced to act. A Foodgrain Policy Committee recommended measures for improving the procurement machinery, for extending rationing and food control and for changing the administrative machinery. Consequently, in January 1946, the policy announced was to supply the necessary quantity and quality of foodgrains. High priority was given to increase the yield of food crops. But the implementation was still left to provinces.

Meanwhile, prices continued to rise which necessitated price control and food rationing. By September 1942, there were as much as six Price Control Conferences in quick succession. The last conference recommended the procurement of foodgrains by the Centre. Food was to be procured from the villages for the urban consumers. Rationing at the rate of 1 lb per day per head was introduced. Certain other articles were also provided at fixed prices. In villages also, ration-cards were given to 74.5 million non-producers to buy cheaper foodgrains, but the Government had no obligation to supply them foodgrains.

Several problems because of controls (blackmarketing, profiteer, etc.), did crop up, yet controls tried to keep the prices in check. The basic problem, however, was one of more production and equal distribution.

Consequences

In short the policy of agricultural neglect led to:

(1) Growing pressure on land and its consequences—famines;

(2) Unemployment and poverty;

(3) Export of raw material and import of manufactured goods;

(4) Old village life was broken, i.e. integration of agriculture and industry was no longer followed;

(5) Industrial worker as well as urban population declined.

While in England, in case of the loss of individual independence workers were compensated by the growth of factories. No such thing happened in India.

LAND RELATIONS

Evolution of the Land Tenurial Systems during the British Regime

During the pre-British days in India land was plenty and the rent was static. The main features of land relations were:

(1) Land belonged to the peasant who enjoyed hereditary occupancy right if he was a resident of the village. Rent was fixed and the Zamindars [who were responsible to pay a fixed amount as land revenue to the King (Ruler)] could not raise this revenue beyond the customary level.

(2) Land was not a saleable commodity. No cultivator could be removed from land. But if a cultivator failed to cultivate a given piece of land, his eviction was possible but in that case the evicted land had to be given to another cultivator. In short, land never passed out of the hands of the peasantry.

(3) The Zamindars whose tributes (or revenues) to the ruler were fixed were themselves petty rulers and had to perform the traditional duties of a ruler in relation to the development of agriculture.

CHANGES UNDER THE BRITISH RULE

The Early Phase

According to the legal form of land relations developed under the Mughal Empire, the right of a Zamindar (called tributary feudal landlord) could be obtained by assuring to pay a stipulated sum of revenue to the Emperor. The feudal landlord apart from collecting his share in the total produce, could rule over the entire estate. With the decline in the influence of the emperor in last days of Mughal Rule, this right could be secured from the provincial (States) Governors (Subedars). The first decisive step on the part of the British East India Company was to secure Zamindari rights over 'Calcutta, Gobindapur and Sutanati in the year 1697.

In the prevailing system, apart from collecting revenue, the Zamindars provided social leadership in the villages. But the sole concern of the English Zamindars (or their agents) was money making and with this the land relations in India entered a new phase.

After winning the Battle of Plassey in 1757, the E.I.Co. took a very big step. It threw the Zamindaries to public auction giving out the estate to the highest bidder. The bidders were mostly uprooted Nagar Seths and guilds (because of decline of urban handicrafts) and they turned out to be the Company's Banias. They, in fact, became second-rung robbers next to the E.I.Co. in robbing the actual cultivators. Since the new Zamindars came from the urban rich, they were mostly interested in making money and totally uninterested in agricultural improvement. The traditional rights of the peasants in cultivating the land were completely forgotten and land became a commodity.

Since the revenue hunger of the E.I.Co. was unstable (which cannot be satisfied) the burden of land revenue increased from year to year. In case the actual cultivator could not pay the land revenue it was realized from the Zamindars. If he was in a position to pay, both the Zamindars and the E.I.Co. exploited him. On occasions, he had to flee in order to avoid this reckless burden.

In the wake of this tyranny and plunder came the Bengal famine of 1770 which killed nearly 35 per cent of the entire population. As a result one-third of the cultivable area was laid waste. This figure increased to half in 1776. However, the famine of 1770 was just a beginning. It was quickly followed by famines in 1784, 1787 and 1790.

In certain parts, the cultivators even revolted against the collaborators and the foreign rulers. Although this movement remained localized, it revealed discontentment amongst the peasantry who were crying for a change.

Introduction of Permanent Settlement

Against this background of an acute crisis in agrarian relations leading to periodic revolts of the peasantry, the idea of a Permanent Settlement with Zamindars was thought of and finally acted upon in 1793. The Government demand was permanently fixed and at the time of settlement, it was 10/11 of the rental value. The Zamindars were recognized as the proprietors of land, and actual cultivators were left at the mercy of the new Zamindars. The cultivator lost his traditional status and was reduced to a virtual serf (bonded labour).

The introduction of Permanent Settlement had many objectives:

(1) Stabilization of revenue.

(2) To create the loyal class.

(3) Zamindars would be an enlightened community and thus provides knowledge and sources for agricultural improvement.

(4) Agricultural improvement in return would provide flourishing trade i.e. India as a market for British manufactures and exporter of raw material and agricultural produce.

(5) The next and the most fundamental was the motive to divert permanently the urban capital (accumulated into

the hands of Nagar Seth, i.e. urban rich) into agricultural channels, thereby check the growth of urban industrialization permanently. India was to be made to export raw material and agricultural produce and to import manufactured goods.

(6) Protection against famine: Land revenue being fixed will provide incentives for agricultural improvement, e.g. it is said in Bengal after 1793, there were no major famines.

(7) No-reassessment: The arbitrary power of the revenue officers would be checked.

(8) There will less drain of country's resources, i.e. economical expenditure on reassessment would be avoided.

Abuses of Permanent Settlement

(1) Oppression of Tenants: The system had many disadvantages. It was the Zamindars who benefited from the hard labour of actual tillers. The tenants were oppressed in various ways, until they received some relief from the various Rent Acts from 1859 onwards. As expected by Cornwallis, the Zamindars could not become the 'national leaders' of rural areas. The tenants, therefore, suffered from high rents, evictions (at will), absentee landlordism, unsympathetic agents and many middlemen. Rents, e.g. increased more than threefold between 1793-1903, i.e. within 10 years of 1793.

(2) Unfair Advantage to Rich Class: Contrary, Bengal had to sacrifice all future increase in land revenue. Bengal's income grew nearly four times by 1900, also there was a rapid increase in prices. Consequently, land revenue became a much smaller part of this income. Again, this income had grown not because of any land improvement but from social factors like the growth of population, development of the means of transport and communication, rise in prices, etc. But only the Zamindars, a well-to-do class, benefited from this

development. Further, land resources in other Provinces had been growing, and also other taxes, so rich class in one Province obtained unfair advantage.

(3) A Great Handicap for the Government: At later stage when public expenditure needs of the Government multiplied this necessitated an elastic source of revenue. But land revenue under permanent settlement stood in its way and seriously affected the developmental expenditure in Bengal.

(4) Cost of Re-assessment: While implementing Permanent Settlement it was stipulated that it would reduce the cost of re-assessment again and again, thus check the drain of revenue. But once the land records were completed (as they are now) the cost of reassessment cannot be formidable. Again, while reassessing the land revenue, cost of improvement can be deducted, thereby encouraging land improvement.

It may be mentioned that the Britishers tended to extend the permanent settlement in other parts of the country also. The desire was reinforced by the revolt of 1857 which confirmed the necessity of having dependable allies in the rural areas, i.e. Zamindars. But after 1857, having about 25 years of complete peace, the other considerations (viz. revenue needs) outweighed the above-mentioned one. And in 1883, the idea of permanent settlement was formally abandoned. In the words of R.C. Dutt, "Never has the loyalty of a nation been worse rewarded, never has the peacefulness of a people led more clearly to the withdrawal of a boom proposed in years of trouble and anxiety. It is a bad lesson for a Government to teach and for the people to learn".

Introduction of Ryotwari System

Permanent Settlement was introduced in Bengal, Bihar, Orissa, Banaras and North Madras and in other areas. Temporary Zamindari settlements were made in Uttar Pradesh.

Ryotwari System was introduced in Southern Madras, Bombay, East Punjab, and some portions of Assam and Coorg. Under this type of settlement, the ryot or raiot directly worked under the State, and land revenue is assessed on each separate holding held by the ryot. He is recognized as the proprietor, i.e. he can sublet, mortgage, transfer (by gift or buy/sell) the holding. He cannot be removed so long as he pays the land revenue.

Ryotwari Settlement was a temporary one. The period of Settlement under the British rule varied between 20-40 years—frequent revision were also there.

Although a proprietor, the peasant in the ryotwari area was no better than his counterpart in the Zamindari areas. Generally the rents were high and uncertain. In every successive assessment, they were generally increased on one pretext or the other, say productivity has increased or agricultural prices have risen, etc. The ever-increasing greed of the British rulers ruined the ryots physically and economically. As R.C. Dutt has observerd, "Nature set a limit which the cultivators had not obtained from the moderation of their rulers. Population decreased in Bombay and still more in Central Provinces. Miles of cultivated land became waste. Jungle grew on homesteads, wheat lands and rice lands."

No protection was extended to the ryot against the arbitrary powers of the settlement officers. In 1873 when the High Court of Bombay gave ruling against the settlement queries and in favour of the ryots, subsequently in 1876 a law was enacted to bring the revenue assessments out of the purview of High Court.

Very often the revenue demands were excessive and sometimes were very close to total production. After meeting the cost of production and revenue requirements very little was left in the hands of the ryot to make further improvement in land. Small cultivators were the greatest sufferers. Unable to meet the rising revenue requirements, they transferred their land to moneylenders. Their number declined from 54 per cent in 1891 to 45 per cent in 1900. A Land Alienation Act had to be enacted in 1901 to save the old tribes from a landless existence. The same was the process in other areas also (on land ownership).

Thus the peasant proprietorship was very soon lost to the same elements who had become Zamindars in Bengal, Bihar,

Orissa and in other permanent settlement areas. They were mostly urban rich. The result was that a new class of landlords, as much parasitic as the Zamindars of permanently settled areas, emerged. In the words of Famine Enquiry Commission (1945) "the tenant cultivator was insecure and therefore, had no permanent interest in lands". Further it added, "the absentee landlord earns only for his annual rent and takes no interest in the improvement of his land or the introduction of improved methods of cultivation".

The miseries of the tenant cultivator did not stop here. Taxes like land revenue and over surcharge on land revenue (to be paid by the Zamindars) were shifted onto him. Landlord being monopolist of land capital could succeed in doing this. And even courts upheld this action of the landlords.

The Mahalwari System was the indigenous system. The principles of mahalwari or joint village system was first adopted in Agra and Audh (1833) and later extended to Punjab. Under this scheme, the villages concerned were jointly responsible for the payment of land revenue. The ownership was joint. And these villages or Mahals were directly dealt with for the payment of land revenue. Of course, practically every individual has to pay his share of land revenue but they themselves were responsible for the payment of land revenue on behalf of the other cultivators. If a cultivator failed to pay his share, the other cultivator could acquire his piece of land.

It may be concluded that all these land relationships were new to India. Zamindari system was borrowed from the English pattern. Ryotwari system was copy of the French experience. Mahalwari was a modified form of early land relationship in India (Feudal lords had to pay tributes to the King—they were actually rulers). Whatever the system they adopted, the primary aim was to turn India into an exporter of raw material and agricultural produce. And net importer of food manufactured commodities.

Growth of Tenancy and Tenancy Act

Under the Zamindari system, almost all the lands were cultivated by the tenants. Even under the ryotwari system, tenancy developed and sub-letting of land spread rapidly (through moneylenders). Sometimes there were as many as 50 intermediaries.

Under both the systems, intermediaries took the maximum from the man behind the plough. In certain cases, e.g. Bengal, there were as much as 50 and even more intermediaries. The tiller of the soil was, therefore, not left with anything to feed himself or his family. Even otherwise, the rents were very high and he had no incentive to make improvements. The position was made worse by insecurity of tenure. The tenants were always harmed by the fear of eviction from land. Apart from high rents, sometimes illegal premiums or personal services were obtained (free of charge from the tenants).

Tenancy Acts

Ultimately even the cruel and passive British Government in India had to take some steps and try to improve the position. The first Tenancy Act of 1859 was passed in Bengal—after 66 years of Permanent Settlement. It gave occupancy rights to tenants cultivating the same piece of land for 12 years. Their rents could not be increased except on reasonable and specific grounds. But the Act was ineffective as the Zamindars prevented a tenant from becoming an occupancy tenant cultivating the same piece of land for 12 years. Old tenants were removed, thus rents continued to rise.

Considering the ineffectiveness of the 1859 Act, another Act was passed in 1885 which enabled the tenants to obtain the occupancy rights if he had cultivated any piece of land (not the same piece of land) for 12 years. Even this measure did not succeed, because of the rising land prices, growing pressure on land, transfer of land to non-agricultural classes, growing prestige attached to the ownership of land. Rents continued to rise and the occupancy rights were not honoured.

It was only in 1928 that occupancy holdings became transferable (i.e. tenants could transfer his holding to new tenants or evicted holdings) that the tenants plight was slightly improved. But a lot remained still to be done. And even today, the plight of tenants is not much better than the virtual serfs.

Effects of Tenancy Laws

Tenancy laws instead of improving the lot of tenants, in fact, deteriorated it. The number of occupancy tenants decreased rapidly. And they scrolled the number of landless agricultural labourers. They, therefore, lost all incentives to improve the land or to put in hard work or use better methods. Thus quality of land deteriorated, productivity declined and rents continued to rise. Intermediaries arose even in mahalwari and ryotwari systems. As much a 75 per cent of the land came to be cultivated by tenants.

Provincial Autonomy (1937-39)

Under Provincial Autonomy, popular Governments (democratic) came in power during 1937-39 and they naturally tried to redress the grievances of the tenants. The principal features of these measures were: 3 Fs of Irish land registration:

(1) Fixing of tenure, i.e. no arbitrary removal of tenant;

(2) Fair rents, i.e. limit on rent, without which fixing of tenure would not be of much use;

(3) Freedom of transfer, i.e. making land inheritable and even sometimes transferable.

In addition, tenants were to get benefits for making improvement on land, reduction in rent in case of revision in land revenue and protection against personal service. Thus landlord's privileges were curtailed. But as in the wake of the World War II, majority of the Provincial Governments resigned, therefore many ideas could not be implemented. Even today, in spite of so much tall talk about land reforms and tenancy reforms, the plight of tenants is still miserable. There are a large number of tenants at will or oral tenants.

Commercialization of Agriculture

In the pre-British days, village communities were self-sufficient. Apart from the portion of the output that had to be surrendered or sold in payment of land revenue, agricultural production had been largely for consumption within the village. Under the British Rule, there was a consistent decline in village self-sufficiency. A growing production of output was now for sale in the market. For this reason, there was an important change in the character of agriculture. In the self-sufficient villages agriculture had been a way of life rather than a business enterprise. It now began to be affected by commercial considerations. The growing cultivation of commercial crops, viz. cotton, jute, oilseed, sugarcane, tobacco, tea, indigo, etc. (commercial crops are those which by their very nature, are produced largely for sale and not for the producer's own consumption, like food crops, wheat, rice, maize) indicated a growing trend in this direction. The increased cultivation of such food crops as spices, fruits, vegetables (which were mostly grown now for sale) was another manifestation of this trend. In fact, in course of time, a substantial portion of even foodgrains like wheat came to be sold in the market. The commercialization trend attained its highest level of development from about the middle of the 19th century. Those were large-scale enterprises organized on commercial basis. The production was carried on by employing a large number of wage workers. Almost the entire output was marketed. Thus commercialization was interwoven with the growth of the market economy.

Particularly because of the American Civil War and suspension of supply American cotton to English factories in England that cotton production picked up. There was encouragement of cotton growth and trade in India. Indigo cultivation was traditional item of exports. Cultivation of tea was started later than indigo. In about 1820 after the discovery of tea plant in wild condition in Assam, the cultivation of tea on commercial basis started.

During 1880-95 there was a growth both in internal and external trade in respect of all commercial crops.

Causes of Commercialization

(1) Political unification of the country facilitated the emergence of India as a major market;

(2) Centralized administrative system;

(3) Burden of land revenue (Zamindari, Mahalwari, Ryotwari System) compelled the cultivators to increase the marketed surplus;

(4) Agricultural indebtedness;

(5) Burden of rent;

(6) Replacement of food crops by cash crops;

(7) Unified monetary system;

(8) Development of modern banking;

(9) Growth of organized markets.

However, these causes of commercialization were interwoven with British interests.

1. Political Unification of the Country

Before the British rule India was a divided country. Therefore, different provinces or even villages had to be self-sufficient. But the near total unification of the country within 100 years after the Battle of Plassey, the independent rulers had either been eliminated or were made subordinate to the British Crown. About 75 per cent of the Indian population was directly under the British Crown. In rest of the country, the Indian states were preserved yet they were no longer sovereign or independent states. They had only formal autonomy. British power was supreme.

A high degree of political unification of the country created favourable conditions for the growth of national market which in turn led to specialization of crops and commercialization of agriculture. The continuous wars and conflicts which were so common in the pre-British days came to an end. After the Crown took over the administration of the country (in 1858), for a long time the new regime was highly stable. It maintained peace and order with an iron hand. This situation was conducive to the growth of production, development of transport and communications, removal of physical and fiscal barriers to the movement of goods, creation of a single currency system, introduction and spread of modern banking, expansion of internal and external trade, etc. All this opened the way for market-oriented production both in the agricultural and non-agricultural sectors.

2. Centralized Administrative System

The British Government instituted a highly centralized

administrative system. It altogether ignored and bypassed the village community and directly dealt with the individuals—Zamindars or Ryots (except a few cases of Mahalwari System). The decline and disintegration of the village community reduced the importance of custom. The market forces, viz. demand and supply became more relevant, paving the way for commercialization of agriculture.

3. Burden of Land Revenue

All the agrarian systems, viz. Zamindari, Ryotwari and Mahalwari led to incidence of heavy land revenue (except in case of Permanent Settlement that too in latter years and the rigidity with which it was collected in cash and not in kind) and forced the agriculturists to bring their produce to the market.

In modern development economics, it is accepted that taxation of land and agriculture is a very important instrument in the hands of the State to compel the agriculturists to bring a large enough proportion of their produce to the market. Under the British rule, the stiff land revenue demand, payable in cash played this role.

4. Agricultural Indebtedness

The growth of agricultural indebtedness had a similar impact on production meant for the market. The agriculturist needed cash to meet his interest and repayment obligations. This was another factor that obliged him to produce for the market.

There was an unprecedented and continued growth in agricultural indebtedness under the British rule, due to (i) emergence of private property (ii) rise in land value (iii) eagerness of the moneylender to lend more in order to acquire land (iv) poverty (v) famine (vi) crushing burden of land revenue and rent (vii) extravagance—socio-religious ceremonies (viii) excessive litigation (ix) borrowing sometimes even for productive purpose to buy seed, implements, land, etc.

Indian farmer was born in debt, lived in debt and died in debt. To pay off interest he must sell his produce in the post-harvest season when prices are low (moneylenders were usually the traders so they were clearly benefited by receiving interest and purchase at low prices). But the farmer had to buy again in the off season when prices are generally high. According to D.R. Gadgil, it is not a good sign of commercialization as most of the time, the farmers sell to the moneylenders or traders right in the villages, where prices are not remunerative.

The peasant once fell into indebtedness, found it difficult to come out of it. The interest rates were very high and the debt continued to multiply endlessly because of the compound rate. The same factors which forced the agriculturist into debt prevented him from saving the necessary amount to clear his debt. Not was the moneylender too keen to let the agriculturists debtor win back his freedom. He exploited the latter's helplessness, ignorance and illiteracy and indulged in malpractices. Since the emergence of private property in land, great prestige was attached to the ownership of land. The moneylenders tried to multiply debt by fair or foul means in order to grab the land of the ryots. On the death of the debtor, his obligations were often taken over by his heirs (children, sons and grandsons) who lacking proper consciousness, considered it their religious duty to clear the debt of their forefathers. The ryot was often born in debt, lived in debt, and died in debt. The growing burden of interest charges compelled him to produce increasingly for the market.

5. Burden of Rent

Zamindari System or Permanent Settlement was introduced by Carnwallis in 1793. His expectations about the Zamindars were belied. The actual cultivator was ruthless. He exploited the growing pressure of population and increased rent. If the rent was paid in cash, the tenant himself had to bring the produce in the market. If on the other hand, rent was in kind, the Zamindar sold the produce in the market. In either case, the produce was sold at the cost of actual cultivator who had to suffer.

Things were not better in ryotwari areas. Re-assessment here being higher and uncertain, the cultivator had to borrow money. Once in the grip of moneylender he became the tenant of moneylender who exploited the ryot in totality.

6. Replacement of Food Crops by Cash Crops

Even food crops tended to become cash crops. And regional

specialization of crops took place bidding farewell to self-sufficiency.

7. Unified Monetary System

At the time of British conquest, a large number of currencies operated which discouraged the production on commercial basis. The Mughal rulers at various places issued both gold and silver coins. In addition, the independent and semi-independent rulers issued their own coins to prove their sovereignty. At the time of British conquest, it is estimated that as many as 994 different coins made of gold and silver and of varying weight and quality were in circulation. In such circumstances, no fixed exchange ratio was possible for different coins. The professional money-changers had a thriving business in converting the different coins. They affected trade and commerce greatly.

In 1806, the E.I.Co recognized the silver rupee as the standard coin. But rupees of different weights and qualities continued in circulation. It was in 1835 that for the first time the rupee of fixed weight and prescribed quality (11/12 purity) was declared as the legal tender money (official currency).

Since 1835, the country has had several distinct monetary systems:

1835-93	=	Silver coin system
1893-99	=	Gold exchange standard
1899-1916	=	Wartime breakdown of the gold exchange standard
1916-25	=	Return to gold exchange standard
1925-31	=	Gold exchange standard
1931-47	=	Sterling exchange standard

But all through this period, British India had a single monetary system. It facilitated growth of domestic and foreign trade, fiscal integration, development of modern banking, etc. Without a unified monetary system, the market in general and commercialization in particular would never have grown the way it did.

8. Development of Modern Banking

In the beginning, the East India Company, like other European Trading Companies utilized the indigenous bankers to sell imported goods and to change different type of coins in order to purchase Indian goods, etc. However, after the Battle of Plassey, the English officials and traders set up their European Agency Houses with the help of their accumulated savings. This gave another blow to the indigenous bankers, yet it paved the way for the company to establish its own banks. With the growth of internal and external trade, the financial activities of the banks expanded which further encouraged internal and particularly external trade. External trade in its turn led to the development of commercial production (in fact banking, trade, currency, transport and communication, commercialization all are interrelated).

9. Growth of Organized Market

The growth of organized agricultural produce markets also paved the way for commercialization of agriculture. Agricultural produce was brought from the villages to the town market from where it went to the ports (through well developed railway system) to be exported to England. Thus expansion in the size of the market particularly for cash crop—jute, cotton, tea (export), sugarcane, oilseed (internal) was also responsible for the commercialization.

However, D.R. Gadgil contests this point. According to him, commercialization of agriculture did not mean anything for the cultivator since he continued to sell his produce to the village trader or village moneylender. It was not that he had started producing on commercial lines. Most often the increasing marketed surplus amounted to distress sale in order to pay off rent, interest and the principal. However, it cannot be denied that because of growing market (particularly foreign export) for cash crops notably, tea, jute, cotton, indigo, etc. production on commercial lines had started at the onset of British rule.

Consequences

1. *Evolution of the Market Forces*: Previously there were self-sufficient villages. There was no outside contact. Farmers

were unaware of the demand for different crops. But opening up of the villages and influence of foreign forces made demand and supply factors more dominant, e.g. tea—when export from China to England was stopped, an alternative source of supply was found in India.

2. *Localization or Specialization of Crops:* Based on comparative advantage localization or specialization of crops took place.

Rice	—	Burma
Wheat	—	Punjab
Cotton	—	Maharashtra
Sugarcane	—	Deccan
Jute	—	East Bengal

3. *Growth in Farmer's Income:* Every region did not try to produce its own food. The farmers grew the most profitable crops, sold them for cash and used it to buy food and other agricultural products needed by them. The growing of the most advantageous crops also increased the farmer's income.

4. *Intensive Cultivation:* In fact, important new crops were introduced like potatoes, groundnut, tea, coffee, rubber, etc. With the extension of irrigation, the use of manure, better seeds, etc. became more widespread. The practice of keeping fallow land was abandoned and cropping intensity increased.

Rural Indebtedness

British System of Exploitation: Big cities and ports were the nerve centres of the colonial economy. The products of rural areas first found their way to these cities and ports from where they were exported to foreign countries mostly England.

In the cities and towns and ports along with the expansion of export and import trade there merged new institutions, viz. banking, insurance companies, firms, etc. Although in the initial stages they were mainly manned by the foreign experts, with the passage of time indigenous expertise to grow out of it.

Lower down in the rural areas were the village moneylenders and traders (both mostly combined into one and the same person). Then there were small towns' moneylenders who in order to expand their business penetrated into the rural areas and for considerable time virtually ruled the rural areas. Slowly and steadily they got the land transferred to their names and looted the actual tillers through exorbitant rents and interest rates. In this plunder they were provided protection by law and were most often helped with police force to complete the plunder of the rural economy.

Rural Indebtedness in the Past

It must be understood that the moneylender and debt were not a new phenomenon in the old Indian society. It had existed even before the British rule. What was new was the role assumed by the moneylenders and consequent problems of rural debt under the British rule. In the pre-British Indian society, the peasant could borrow from moneylender only on his personal security. His property (land or the like, houses, animals, implements, etc.) could not be attached to debt. Under these circumstances the business of moneylending was uncertain, often involving great risk. In fact, the trade of moneylending was looked down upon by the society (e.g. according to Islamic laws taking and giving of interest is prohibited). Even in Hindu dominated areas, the village community acted as a check to charge the rate of interest beyond a particular limit. The principle of Damdupat (double money) was a common practice, limiting total interest equal to the total loan.

All these were changed during the British rule. No limit was prescribed for the rate of interest to be charged by the moneylenders. Rather the recovery of interest and principle was ensured through the legal machinery. And in case of default the peasant's land and other property could be attached. Thus while the new economic system cut off the peasants from the seats of power and sources of finances, the moneylender was provided with all the power of police and law. Moneylender thus emerged as the pivotal force in the whole process of exploitation. He provided immoral services, suited to the plunder by the British Government and even collected land revenue on behalf of the British and mostly combined in himself the role of trader and the usurer (living on rate of interest). Often he advanced loans for seeds, implements and other inputs. Being disinterested in agriculture, his sole objective was to exploit the cultivators. It so happened that once the cultivators fell prey to him he had no chances to come out of his clutches. The process according to R.C. Dutt mostly ended with complete alienation of the actual tillers. He became landless labourers or share-croppers attached to the moneylenders. Such was the tragic outcome of the whole process of exploitation by the merchant-cum-usurious capital.

No wonder quite often the exhausted peasants turned against the moneylenders and frequently killed and murdered them. They even looted their property. But because of the widespread power and support of the moneylenders, these rebellions were often crushed.

Growth of Rural Indebtedness

Although indebtedness was not altogether a new thing in India, its increasing magnitude during the British rule owed its origin to direct colonial exploitation. As early as in 1911, Sir Edward Maclagan observed (appointed to examine the rural credit structure particularly Cooperative Credit societies), "It was long been recognized that indebtedness is no new thing in India.... But it is also acknowledged that the indebtedness has risen considerably during our rule, and more specially during the last half century."

As reported in 1880 by the Famine Commission that "the burden of debt had engulfed 2-3rd of the land holding classes. In the subsequent period, specially during the first three decades of the present century, the burden of indebtedness further increased, and there was no evidence to indicate that this growth of debt was in proportion to the growing assets of the people. The fact that the total amount of rural credit increased from Rs. 900 crores in 1931 to Rs.1800 crores in 1937 was really alarming."

Even in the wake of the Second World War, when prices were generally rising, the volume of indebtedness, contrary to expectations, increased for but except the upper class of farmers. The Famine Enquiry Commission of 1945, reached the conclusion that, "As a result of high prices of agricultural produce, there has been a substantial reduction in agricultural indebtedness.

This appears to be particularly of cultivators with large holdings. It appears probable, however, that the indebtedness of small holders may not have been reduced substantially in any parts of the country."

The debt of the landless labourers increased faster than even that of the tenants. It may be added that the majority of rural population was composed of small tenants and agricultural labourers. In Punjab, it was estimated that only 17 per cent of the population was free from debt. Rate of interest being very high they could not come out of debt. In the words of Professor D.R. Gadgil, it has been aptly remarked that the average cultivator in India during the British regime was born in debt, lived in debt and died in debt. Indebtedness, in fact, was hereditary.

Causes

1. *Causes which compel them to borrow:*
   - (a) Poverty;
   - (b) Superfluous, socio-religious expenditure (D.R. Gadgil does not agree to this point. He stressed the point that why in the pre-British days in spite of the rigidity of customs and traditions people were free from debt.);
   - (c) Famines;
   - (d) Crushing burden of land revenue;
   - (e) Excessive litigation (sometimes forced upon by the moneylenders);
   - (f) Sometimes even for production purposes, plantations, seeds, etc.
2. *Causes which enabled the cultivators to borrow more liberally :*
   - (a) Emergence of private property—free purchase and sale of land;
   - (b) Encouragement to the moneylenders to lend liberally in order to acquire land;
   - (c) Rise in land values and ownership of land carried a status symbol.

3. *System of moneylending and recovery of debts (no cooperative or Government credit):*

Rates of interest on private lending were very high which the backward agriculture of India could not bear. They had to be put up, because there was no Government system of easy credit. There was no check on the moneylender. Formerly, the village community acted as a check on the rate of interest. Damdupat (double money) was a common practice, limiting total interest to the amount of the loan. There was to be no transfer of land to the moneylender. Actually he was looked down upon. Under the British, the law gave the moneylender great powers over the debtor. Moneylenders manipulated the accounts and the debtors were cheated.

Consequences

Mostly ended with completed exploitation, i.e. selling of land by the cultivators to the moneylenders. Thus the farmer was completely alleviated from land. In 1860 the process of alleviation started and during Great Depression the total rural debt increased from Rs. 900 crore in 1931 to Rs. 1800 crore in 1937.

The expropriation of farmers followed by indebtedness was universally acknowledged. In the earlier part of the 19th century when land was plentiful relative to labour, the moneylender had no inducement to take over the possession of land. By 1860, this was no longer the case, and land values began to increase. So at about this time there may be the beginning of the process of the alienation of land from the peasants into the hands of the moneylenders.

There is a consensus of opinion that the effects of this process of transference of land had been bad in India. In most parts of the country, the moneylender was not an agriculturist himself, it did not matter either if he was. Because the cultivation was usually carried on by the old cultivator either as a tenant or as share-cropper working for the moneylender and paying over to him rent plus rate of interest which covered a greater proportion of the total produce. The position of the actual tiller thus became more precarious. On the other hand, the transference of land into the hands of the moneylender did not result, as it did in other parts of the world, in consolidation of holdings (Enclosure movement in England) and large-scale production. More striking was the fact that even long leasing of land was discouraged. Thus there emerged a new class of cultivators called tenants-at-will.

It may be emphasized that as early as in 1892, the Deccan Commission on the working of the Agriculturists' Relief Act, which was earlier passed in 1879, observed with great concern, "the transfer of the land in an agricultural country to a body of rack-renting aliens, who do nothing for the improvement of the land". The various Commissions and the Committees appointed by the Government from time to time confirmed the fact that the non-agriculturist moneylender was the sole cause of the growing emergence of landless labourers and tenants. It may be mentioned that although British Government appointed agencies were sincere about their findings about the role of moneylender, yet these Commissions did not go deep to find out the causes (i.e. growing poverty) of growing indebtedness and the role of the Government (in providing all sort of help, i.e. police, law, etc., to the moneylenders to recover their loans).

The world economic crisis of 1930s further deepened the crisis and the amount of indebtedness increased form Rs. 900 crore in 1931 to Rs. 1800 crore in 1937. In the wake of the World War II, when countrywide scarcity of foodgrains and famines were experienced, the rural indebtedness further increased.

Thus the entire outcome of the process of expropriation of the peasantry was a catastrophic worsening of the status of the cultivator. He merely became a wage-labourer. The effects on the efficiency of cultivation were generally adverse; but now it was carried on without the incentive of the ownership of private property. The transfer of lands into the hands of the moneylender had not produced a class of agricultural entrepreneurs, not merely because the professional moneylender was not himself an agriculturist, even when lands were transferred to the agriculturist moneylender, the result was no different.

The growth of agriculturist moneylender was also an important development in Indian agriculture during the British period's later phase. The Rural Credit Survey reported that about 25 per cent of the loans to agriculturists had been supplied by the "agriculturist" moneylenders.

Thus both the agriculturist as well as the non-agriculturist moneylenders failed to emerge as the agricultural entrepreneurs on the Indian scene and semi-moneylender turned out to be as much the exploiter as was the non-agriculturist moneylender. The whole system of land relations during the British opposed the modern (Capitalist) mode of production.

Government Ameliorative Measures or Legislation to Check Indebtedness

I. *Improvement of Civil Law:* Changes in the Civil Procedure Code exempted the debtors from arrest and their cattle and implements from being attached. The debts could be rapid in installments. Under the Usurious Loans Act, 1918, the court could reopen the transaction and reduce the rate of interest if it was too high. But the act did not have much effect, mainly because the initiative was left to the court.

Under the Deccan Agriculturists Relief Act, 1879, arrest or imprisonment for debt was abolished. There was provision for complete insolvency, so that the peasant could start on a clean state. Conciliatory machinery was appointed to settle the accounts. The courts were asked to go behind the contract (as why the cultivator borrowed, how much he actually borrowed, what were the terms and conditions, etc.) and reduce an excessive rate of interest. Creditors (or moneylenders) had to furnish accounts and give receipts for all payments. But the Act was ineffective because no alternative source of credit was available and even harmful as it put constraints on the moneylender and he refused to lend money. If he did, he resorted to certain illegal activities. He gave less but on the deed it was shown more as interest was deduced while lending, etc.— to bypass the law.

II. *Restrictions on Land Transfer:* The right to mortgage and sell land was a cause of increase in debts, which in turn led to land transfer. Therefore, laws were passed to restrict this right in many provinces. Non-agriculturists were not allowed to buy land from agriculturists, or to take it on mortgage for more than 20 years. But this did not cover agriculturist moneylenders. Nor were the debts checked much, as the farmers', need for credit remained unsatisfied. Moneylenders became more cautious and therefore, peasants found it more difficult to get loans.

III. *Supply of Credit (Establishment of Cooperative Credit Societies):* The crux of the problem was to supply loans to the farmer on suitable terms. The Government did try this (Takavi loans of 1883 and 1886). Cooperative Credit Societies were started in 1904 and non-credit societies in 1912, Land Mortgage Bank in 1920 (to provide long-term loans).

The Great Depression and the Provincial Autonomy

During the Great Depression, when prices of agricultural produce fell, indebtedness multiplied which resulted in large numbers of suicides and forced sales of land. But the Central Government did nothing. It was only in 1937 when the Provincial Goverments came into power many Acts were passed to mitigate the evils of rural indebtedness.

Short-term Measures

Some of these were short-term measures which reduced the burden of debt. Interest dues were scaled down, the general principle being 'Damdupat' (double money), i.e. total interest was not to exceed loan. The courts had to reopen the cases and reduce the interest. In certain cases even principal was reduced. Although voluntary reductions of loans were welcomed, wherever necessary even compulsion was also used to reduce the debt burden.

Long-term Measures

Even if the above measures were successful, which they were not, they gave relief only for the time being. Therefore, there would still remain the need for permanent relief through long-term measures. These related to the control over money-lending.

Registration and licensing of moneylenders was made compulsory. They had to maintain accounts and give annual statements to debtors as also receipts for all payments made to them. The debtors were protected against threat and harassment and their property against attachment. Maximum rates of interest were fixed, being higher for unsecured loans. Again, simple rate of interest was higher than compound rate of interest.

But the popular Ministries resigned after about two years in office (1939). They could not do much to ameliorate the lot of moneylenders. The moneylender remained by far the most important source of borrowings. A comprehensive and integrated programme of agricultural reform was urgently required. Since independence various Land Reform Measures, Community Development Programmes, Integrated Area Development Programme, New Agricultural Technology, etc. have been adopted towards this direction.

Population

Since time immemorial, the role of quantity and quality of human power in economic development has been recognized. Both the high growth and low growth of population are considered harmful for economic development. A larger growing size of population apart from producing a growing supply of labour (both for industry and defense), also provides market for consumer goods. But a very high growth rate, i.e. disproportionate with the growth of capital, may retard economic development. With this background in mind, let us study the trends in population in the British India.

The first census in India was taken in 1871 when India's population was estimated at 25.4 crore. Even before 1871, some attempts were made to measure the size of Indian population. But because of the apathy of the people and their suspicions about the British Raj, those estimates are not much reliable. Anyway, from the different factors, viz. birth rate and death rate, affecting population, we can say that the size of Indian population remained stable for a considerable period.

The Table 1.1 would explain the growth of population in the post-census period (i.e. 1871 onwards).

Table 1.1: Rate of Growth of Population in India—The Rhythm, Determined by Famine

Period	Growth per cent	Causes of slow or rapid growth
1871-81	+1.5	Famines 1868-78
1881-91	+9.6	No famines
1891-1901	- 0.2	Famines 1897-98 & 1899-1900
1901-11	+5.7	Hardly any famines
1911-21	- 0.4	World War I, famines 1918-21 & Influenza, 1918
1921-31	+11.0	No famines
1931-41	+13.5	No famines
1941-51	+14.1	At some places, this rate to be lower than that of 1931-41 because of Partition and Famine of Bengal, 1943
1951-61	+21.0	From this year onward the rate of growth of population has been around 2.5 per cent. Thus posing a serious problem.

Causes of Slow Growth prior to 1921

Prior to 1921, the growth of population was not only slow but also fluctuating. In fact, periods of slight increase were followed by periods of actual decline. This is largely explained by recurrent famine and epidemics whose incidence was severe in some decades, but negligible in other. The great Bengal Famine of 1867-68 was followed by a comparatively normal decade, but negligible in other. The great Bengal Famine of 1867-68 was followed by a comparatively normal decades of 1871-81 and 1881-91. Again the decade 1891-1901 saw the recurrence of severe famines in many parts of the country. Then there was an outbreak of plague in Bombay city in 1896, malaria and Kalaazar (black fever) in the eastern part of the country. All these brought about an actual decline in the population of Indian union during the decade 1891-1901. However, the comparatively normal decade of 1901-11 was followed by the great influenza epidemic of 1918. This decreased population by at least 12 to 13 millions. Successive crop failures following the First World War and epidemics of cholera, plague and malaria also contributed in the decline of population during 1911-21. In addition, following factors greatly influenced the population growth:

1. Famines, war, crop failures, etc.;
2. Frequent epidemics (It must be stated that English population was more prone to such epidemics as the Indian population had developed community);
3. Migration to countries like Burma, Mauritius, Ceylon (monthly), Jawa, etc.

Causes of Steady & Accelerating Growth Since 1921

Since 1921, improvement of transport and communication and some extension of irrigation facilities, kept off any widespread famine except for the Bengal Famine of 1943 which involved, on a conservative estimate, a loss of nearly 3 million lives. Similarly, improvements in public health and sanitation have reduced (but not eliminated altogether) the dreadful fall of major epidemics. This resulted into a fairly steady growth of population till 1951. It must be noted that the population growth rate in India never exceeded 1.4 per cent per annum compared with 2 and 3 per cent in other developing countries like Egypt, Ceylon, etc.

Birth & Death Rates

Trends in population growth may be better studied by analyzing the trend in vital rates, i.e. birth rate and the death rate. Although information regarding both is inadequate, Dr. Kindley Davis' estimates which make necessary corrections in the census data, clearly brings out the trends:

Year	Estimated Birth Rate/1000	Estimated Death Rate/1000
1881-91	48.9	41.3
1891-1901	45.8	44.4
1901-11	48.1	42.6
1911-21	49.2	48.6
1921-31	46.4	36.3
1931-41	45.2	31.2
1941-51	39.9	29.4
1951-61	40.0	18.0

The death rate shows a high and little fluctuating trend until 1921, thereafter a continuous fall. Compared with death rates, birth rates show a uniform high level with minor fluctuations. There was some decline during 1941-51 but a further decline in the next decade.

Causes of High Death Rate (Before 1921)

The causes of the high death rate are diseases, lack of proper medical facilities, malnutrition (because of poverty and famine) and infant mortality. The diseases that occurred too often in an epidemic form and created maximum panic were plague, small pox and cholera. But taken together they hardly accounted for 5 to 10 per cent of total deaths. The most important single cause of high mortality in India was malaria which, according to Dr. Gyan Chand, accounted for roughly 20 per cent of all deaths in a year. It was an irony of fate that measures undertaken for famine relief, viz. construction of railways, road, canals, etc. led to breeding places for the mosquitoes and hence malaria). Coale & Hoover put this death estimate at 2 million people per year. Other diseases which account for high mortality in India were, TB, dysentery and diarrhoea, respiratory infection and deficiency diseases due to malnutrition. The heavy incidence of all these diseases is partly due to severe exposure to infection because of unhygienic and unsanitary conditions of living, and partly due to dietary deficiencies and consequent low resistance of the people. In other words, poverty and ignorance are the main causes of high mortality rate. The other disturbing features of Indian mortality are the high infant and child mortality and the high female mortality rate. It has been estimated that before 1921 (during reproductive period) nearly 50 to 60 per cent of children born in India died before reaching the age of 20. Since 1921 loss of life due to infant and child mortality had started declining but still it is very high (i.e. 40 per cent according to 1951 census). This heavy infant and child mortality implies that the country spends a considerable proportion of its resources every year on a batch of newly born population only to lose nearly half of them before they reach the age of 20 when they can be expected to make significant contribution to National Income.

Causes of Declining Death Rate

Although it is generally believed that the decline in death rate is directly associated with economic development, it was not so in case of India. Technological advancement in the sphere of medicine, viz. evolution of DDT, BCG vaccine, sulpha and antibiotic drugs, reduced the mortality rate directly. It is these quick and inexpensive means of fighting diseases which explain why countries like India, Ceylon and Egypt achieved an improvement in the mortality rate in a quarter of a century after the World War II which took some of the advanced countries a long period of economic development. Various welfare measures adopted by the Government, vigorous public health drives including malaria eradication campaign adopted during and after the World War II, etc. reduced the death rate.

Causes of High Birth Rate

(1) Universal marriage; (2) Early marriage; (3) Grinding poverty (children are not liability rather than they are source of income); (4) Religious beliefs (children are the gifts of God), birth is outside the control of human beings; (5) Joint family system (no worry to bring up the children; (6) Inferior social status of women, i.e. women continue to bring up children. Had they been employed and gone outside the families, they would have naturally revolted and compelled the family to have lesser number of children; (7) High death rate particularly, high mortality rate amongst, the children is also responsible for high birth rate. This would ensure that at least some of them would survive and live beyond 20 years (50-60 per cent died before they reached 20 years of age); (8) Finally lack of knowledge about family planning methods.

Forces Retarding (or reducing) Birth Rate

However, in India a large number of forces operated which reduced the birth rate such as:

(1) Prohibition on widow re-marriage;

(2) Poverty and malnutrition of women which reduced their capacity to bear children;

(3) Prolonged lactation period.

Since all these forces now are on the decline widow re-marriage is permissible, artificial feeding of children has replaced lactation and poverty too, to some extent, has been removed. This has naturally affected the birth rate positively. However, at the same time new forces have emerged which have checked the positive impact of these forces. These new forces are urbanization, education and employment of women and consequently a rise in their social status, raising of marriageable age amongst the educated class, and adoption of family planning measure, etc.

Relation between Population and Economic Development

Population and economic growth have always been taken to be interindependent variables, i.e. interrelated. The rapid growth of population in the West was not only an asset but also a cause of economic development. Similarly, a declining trend of population growth is generally considered to be one of the direct causes of a secular tendency towards stagnation in some mature economies.

Effect of Population on Economic Development

The size of population has a direct effect on the per capita income, an important indicator of economic development in a country. The problem of size had attracted Malthus to propound his theory of population. The same problem received more accurate treatment at the hands of optimum theorists, who clearly pointed out that man is not only a consumer but also a "producer", and, therefore, underpopulation also is as serious a problem as overpopulation. However, though this aspect of population is important, the rate of growth is far more important. A rapid growth of population in the West was not only an effect but also a cause of economic expansion. As J.M. Keynes had said, an expanding population will keep up the rate of growth of national income by increasing the effective demand for consumer goods and for houses and public utilities and increasing generally the marginal efficiency of capital. This is more so when the technical developments are leading more and more to capital saving inventions, as a nation becomes richer, its consumption tends to be directed towards these articles of consumption, particularly the services. Because of high MPS capital accumulation goes on increasing. If population fails to increase and new inventions fail to make use of increasing capital accumulation (which will be invariably the case), stagnation would come in. Thus a declining trend of population growth is said to be one of the direct causes of secular stagnation in advanced capitalist countries.

In developing countries the problem is reverse. Such countries are poor and here MPC is very high so that very little is left for savings and investment. Thus increasing population does not match with increasing investment, consequently national income declines.

Effects of an expanding population on the growth of national income, depends, mainly, on the ratio of population to other factors of production like land, capital equipment and level of techniques. Where land is plenty and vast reserves await exploitation, an expanding population can keep up the rate of growth of national income by increasing demand for consumer goods and by encouraging proper division of labour. In this way, underdeveloped, underpopulated countries like Australia and South Africa have attained the present state of development. In such countries immigration was a boon because immigrants were generally able-bodied men of some productive capacity. But in densely populated underdeveloped countries (UDCs) where capital is less and resources fail to keep pace with population increase, an increasing population may aggravate the difficulties of achieving progress. Number of children, i.e. dependent increases, e.g. in India 50-60 per cent of children die before reaching the age of 20. Thus it is a huge wastage of resources. Rising population apart from reducing servings, world also create serious food problem. Huge quantities of foodgrains may have to be imported, leading to loss of precious foreign exchange which otherwise would have been spent on capital imports.

A growing population can assist economic development only when capital accumulation, natural resources and level of technical efficiency can keep pace with population growth. Thus high and rising level of technique and increasing capital accumulation are pre-conditions of economic development. It does not follow, however, that an increasing population is essential for progress. Progress can be achieved even when population is declining, if suitable fiscal policies to stimulate consumption and investment are adopted, and if the state is willing to fill up the gap (Y=C+I) by its own expenditure (G).

Thus, from a narrow economic point of view, "if a growing population has any advantages for the economic system, these can (unless the numbers are very small absolutely) nearly always be achieved by means other than expanding population". On the other hand, the disadvantages of an increasing population in a country already overpopulated are surely many.

Effects of Economic Development on Population

(The Theory of Demographic Transition)

Professor Coale and Hoover's theory of demographic transition is largely based on the experience of the present industrialized countries of the world. It suggests that all countries passing through the process of economic development have to pass through three stages:

(1) The period of stability with rates of births and deaths both very high.

(2) Period of 'population explosion' characterized by declining death rates but stationary or slowly rising birth rates.

(3) The period when birth rates and death rates have both become stable at a low level.

Now, if we look to the demographic evolution historically, we find that the 'mature' industrialized countries of the world have passed through the first two stages and are now in the third stage. So far as India is concerned, it is in the second stage. As the figures of birth rates and death rates show that right up to 1921 both rates were very high because of a number of factors, i.e. reasons for high death rate and reasons for high birth rate. In the post-1921 period while the death rates declined birth rates did not decline much. Consequently, there is said to have occurred population explosion in India. But it must be understood that till recently fall in death rate did not correspond to economic development. It was rather due to the evolution of new technology in medicine, i.e. development of DDT, BCG, anti-cholera vaccine, anti-biotic, etc. Thus our demographic trends, strictly speaking, do not fall in the theory of demographic transition. It was incidental that a decline in death rate was achieved with zero or negative growth rate in national income.

Different Phases of British Rule in India

Before we come to the individual topics like population, decline of handicrafts, growth of agriculture industries, etc. let us have a brief look at the entire period [200 years of British Rule (1757-1947)].

India's size (land area) was 20 times the area of the Great Britain. At the time of World War II, India's colony was the largest colony which constituted more than half of the colonial population at that time. Almost all the European and other colonizing powers had set their great eyes on the Indian wealth. They were making frantic efforts to find out new sea route to India.

Key to British World Supremacy

The conquest of India by the British gave the later immense power and prestige. Britain became the world's largest power to be reckoned with. Behind the success struggle between England over powers—France, Spain, Portugal, Holland, Russia and Germany, India was the main cause. Lord Curzon admitted in 1898 "If the Empire loses any other part of the Domain, we can survive, but if we lose India the sun of our Empire will have set".

Net Outcome of the British Rule

It is generally believed that if a traditional economy comes into contact with advanced country, its outlook is widened, technology is transferred, etc. It is totally incorrect. The British deliberately kept away Indian from new techniques of production. It was a paradox that there was poverty in the amidst of plenty.

Travelers' accounts bore testimony to the fact that there was export surplus, demand of Indian products in foreign countries was huge. There were high natural resources. Even the

American Technical Mission (1942) admitted that there was no proper exploitation of natural resources. There was loot and plunder of Indian economy. With the result poverty increased. Not to speak of clothing or shelter, even two times meals was a luxury. About Bombay Textile worker (923) it is said that their ration was below the jail ration.

What was behind the poverty?

(1) Increase in population—No, the net increase in population was not more than the rate at which population grew in other countries. Eevn famines reduced population.

(2) Social backwardness—No, people were socially so previously also. Further social backwardness mostly follows economic backwardness and not vice versa.

Reason: Destructive Role of India

Whereas previous invaders or rulers settled here and adopted this culture, the English systematically ruined everything—economy, society, social values and relations.

The Drain theory of Dadabhai Naoroji explains everything.

I. Period of Merchant Capital upto 1800 (East India Company)

Destruction of Indian Economy

(1) Direct plunder

(2) Neglect of irrigation and pubic works

(3) Introduction of English land system—private property ownership

(4) Destruction of Indian handicrafts by unjustifiable tariff system.

Original aim of the East India Company was to trade in Indian goods. But the Battle of Plassey changed the scenario in 1757. In 1762 the Nawab of Bengal Mir Kasim complained that the Company agents were forcibly buying goods from the bazars and the peasants by paying just one-fourth of their value. But they were forcing them to pay 5 times of the English goods.

House of Commons (Parliament) condemned in 1784 the tactics adopted by E.I.Co. to loot the Indian people. In 1858 one

British M.P. remarked that, "I do most confidently maintain that no civilized government even existed on the face of this earth which was more corrupt than the Government of the East India Company from 1765 to 1784."

From a letter written by Lord Clive to the Directors of E.I.C. (1765) it becomes clear that the Britishers looted India. The letter reads that the whole amount collected as revenue, one-fourth was sufficient to meet the expenditure needs. One-fourth was spent to please the native princes. Half of it was taken away as investment of his Company. It was a clear drain. The E.I.Co.'s dream was realized to draw wealth without paying for it.

There was complete neglect of irrigation and systematic destruction of industries drove the population to villages. Demand for land increased. There was a reckless collection of land revenue.

More and more demand for revenue led to more exploitation and neglect of land and irrigation led to famines. In 1770, 10 million people died in famine.

II. Period of Industrial Capital

or

The Industrial Devastation

Industrial Revolution in England (Early 19th Century) led to the demand for free trade. Initially there were objections by the East India Company. But other traders (jealous of E.I.Co.) supported free trade. Adam Smith's *Wealth of Nations* (1776) explained the advantages of free trade. International division of labour and the theory of comparative advantages gained momentum.

In 1813, the monopoly of E.I.Co. to trade with India was finally broken.

Tariff Policy of 1813

Before this, Indian goods (particularly cotton, silk fabrics) were selling in England at less than 50-60 per cent of the price of goods produced by English. So tariff rates were increased. In fact the wearing of printed Indian cotton fabric was banned under the law. But there was no tariff duty on British goods while entering India. In 1840 when because of revenue requirement, British cotton goods were imported by paying just 3 per cent. Indian goods were required to pay 10 per cent. Consequently, British cotton export to India increased at a very high rate. By 1850, India which was net exporter of cotton fabrics became the importer and 25 per cent of English cotton clothes were exported to India.

The most questionable part in tariff history is the so-called countervailing duties imposed in 1896. In 1894, revenue requirement of the E.I.Co. further increased. Import duty was increased generally by 50 per cent. There was hue and cry by Manchester industrial capitalists. A countervailing duty on Indian goods was imposed.

Thus political power was used to destroy Indian industries. The number of industrial workers decreased year after year—absolutely as well as relatively. The population of Dacca declined from 1,50,000 to 30,000, i.e. 80 per cent decline.

Effects of De-Industrialization

(1) Decline in industrial workers

(2) Heavy dependence on agriculture

(3) Growing poverty

(4) Export of raw cotton, import of manufactured commodities

(5) Famines were frequent. [While during 1800-1825 one million died, during 1875-1900 15 million died]

(6) Old village before had combination of industries and agriculture. The artisans lost their jobs they became dependent on agriculture.

III. Period of Financial Capital

British investment was a hoax. Resources were raised in India. In the name of home charges Britishers took away huge amount. In 1857 the so-called public debt was £70 million but it took away £150 million charges. So net was in favour of India. But when the British Crown took over from the E.I.Co., it declared a public debt £70 million. Payment of interest, principal, etc. imposed a huge burden on Indian economy.

Public debt further increased by charging to the GOI, every conceivable expenditure. If the Sultan of Turkey was given the reception in England, India had to bear its expenditure. Then expenditure of Embassies was charged to India. Raising of Indian army to defend the Britishers was financed by the Government of India.

When India was opened to private English capitalists, investment started flowing—first in banking industry, transport, plantation—tea, coffee, indigo. It was in no way related to industrial development. Its only purpose was the commercial exploitation of its natural resources.

The extent of financial capital before the World War I was 11 per cent of the total British investment in the world. But in 1933 it increased to 25 per cent.

Up to the World War I, exploitation was open and unconcealed. During the World War it became difficult to import. Besides, the cooperation of nationalities was also required to run the Government. There was growing trend for freedom struggle.

However, this was a shortlived sympathy. The demand of iron and steel industry for protection was not acceded to. Subsidy was withdrawn. The value of the shares of the Tata Iron and Steel Industry fell from Rs. 100 to 10 and the company had to borrow from the Indian market.

During the Depression of thirties value of Indian exports (agricultural goods) fell by 50 per cent. Gold worth 32 million ounces (more than the amount Britishers had it as reserves in England) was exported from Delhi just during 1931-35.

During the War (1943-44) more than 108 foreign (English) business concerns had their branches in India—Dunlop, Lever Brothers, Imperial Chemicals.

1942 (American Technical Mission) observed that in spite of the availability of all natural resources industrialisation did not take place. There was joint venture with Birla Brothers Ltd. and Nuffield Organization to manufacture cars, but only for assembling and under technical supervision of the English.

Import of all spare parts continued. There were workshops for assembling and not for manufacturing.

Progressive Role and Contribution of the British Rule

(1) Education: Modern education particularly foreign education was started in India.

(2) Free press (1835): The English who were used to democracy also popularized it in India.

(3) Means of transport and communication: Roads, railways, steamships, etc. led to the opening of villages and contact with the interaction of new ideas.

(4) Limited industrial development led to the division of labour. Caste system was broken.

(5) New land revenue system led to emergence of the concept of private property. Land became commodity. Collection of land revenue in cash led to more marketable surplus.

(6) Monetization of the rural economy broke the rigidities of barter system.

(7) New administration which was centralized led to the integration of the economy.

An Overview of Indian Economy

2

India has been an important part of the world economy since millennia. The initiatives we took in the early 1990s towards economic liberalisation have not only altered the nature of our interaction with the world, but have also shaped global perceptions of India. They have also altered the manner in which other nations, no matter big or small, relate with us. Today, there is an increasing willingness internationally to work with India and build relationships of mutual benefit and mutual interdependence. This augurs well for our progress, development and security. We have finally able to refute what development planners used to refer to in the 1960s and 1970s as the "external constraint" on growth. A Report released by the IMF's Executive Board in February 2006 noted that the Indian Economy is "continuing to reap the rewards of more than 15 years of reforms". It has even forecasted a growth of over 7.5 per cent for 2006-07. The Board opined that with an acceleration of the reform process, India would be able to achieve sustained economic growth of 8-10 per cent in line with the objectives of the authorities. It is worth recalling here that India has recorded growth at close to 6 per cent per annum for over 20 years. We now have the fourth largest GDP in the world in terms of purchasing power. Looking backwards, we become aware of how limited our horizon of certitude really is. In the mid-1960s, when India was confronted with the threat of widespread famine and was perennially dependent on foreign food aid to feed its people, who amongst the most visionary economists could have estimated/imagined that within such a short period foodgrain production would not only double but even have significant surplus? In 1980, who could anticipate the Personal

Computers revolution that was to follow just two years later? In 1983, when India's total software exports were only $12 million, none would have dreamt of that they would multiply 500 times in 17 years and the country would be recognised across the world as a major IT power? Even a visionary like Microsoft's founder Bill Gates admits that he was unable to grasp the enormous potential of the Internet until it had already spawned a global revolution.

Present Economic Scenario

With the economy booming, India discarded its image as the tortoise of the region and presented itself to the world as an economic powerhouse in 2005. Even the most economic challenged person will find it difficult to disagree that 2005 was the best of the three consecutive years of good growth.

GDP

The Indian economy is on the fulcrum of an ever-increasing growth curve. It grew by an impressive 9.2 per cent during the second quarter (July to September) of 2006-07 taking the first half gross domestic product (GDP) growth to 9.1 per cent. In the first quarter the growth had been only slightly less robust at 8.9 per cent. The GDP growth would have been still higher if agricultural growth had not slumped to 1.7 per cent in the second quarter. Industry and services both have recorded massive improvements during this period at 10.3 per cent and 10.9 per cent. Such high growth has led forecasters to raise GDP projections for the current year 2006-07. Most analysts had earlier estimated that the growth would be lower than the 8.4 per cent growth achieved in 2005-06. The actual growth has exceeded all expectations as yet. It can be well said that the economy had a great year (2005) in terms of the growth in GDP and across the main sectors, and inflation was kept in check. GDP growth in 2005-06 reached 8.4 per cent and it is estimated to reach 9.2 per cent in 2006-07 which are clear indications that India will have three consecutive years of above 7 per cent growth. The oil induced pressures on prices that dominated the economic scene in the latter half of 2004 eased since the beginning of 2005 and inflation was down to 5 per cent by

March end and a little over 4 per cent by end of July 2005. The average inflation rate in India, based on the wholesale price index was 6.3 per cent in July as against 4.1 per cent on a point to point basis, which rose to 6.11 per cent on January 20, 2007. Consumer price inflation remained in the 4.5 per cent range in the first half of 2005. The overall inflation in WPI was recorded 6.7 per cent on February 3, 2007. However, average inflation in the 52 weeks ending on February 3, 2007 remained at 5 per cent. The stock market reached unprecedented heights and India became the hot new destination for foreign investment, both institutional and direct.

Private consumption accounts for 64 per cent of India's gross domestic product. The internal consumption led structure of the Indian economy is rather closer to that of the developed economies of the West and is unlike the structure of East Asian and Chinese economies that are predominantly driven by external investment and trade. In recent years, particularly the year 2005 proved a year in favour of consumers. The salary growth levels were at a record high even as stockmarkets and real estate helped people generate incomes over and above their monthly pay cheques; they even built up record savings in mutual funds and insurance. So far the job opportunity is concerned, it boomed across all levels of corporate hierarchy, both in India and abroad, for educated urban Indians.

Investment

Even the producer's economy remained no less in the pink of health. Companies across different industries enjoyed high sales and higher profit. Two significant changes, however, took place for the first time in a decade. Large manufacturing firms stopped downsizing, with some even increasing its staff, while corporate India made announcement of some large new projects after a decade. It can be inferred from this that private investors now have confidence in the future of the Indian economy and they expect markets for their future products and services. Moreover, for the economy to remain high, and for India to enter a golden period of growth, private investment must continue to rise at an increasing rate for another couple of years.

During 2005-06, the investment grew by over 30 per cent. The rising trend observed during the period accelerated further in 2006-07. As per provisional data available, FDI in April-September 2006 at US$ 4.2 billion was almost twice the investment during the corresponding period in 2005-06. As per the latest data on FDI inflows, there has been a 98.4 per cent jump in the equity investment into India in April-September 2006-07 over the corresponding period. India is undoubtedly on the global radar. Foreign institutional investors pumped in a record $10 billion in 2005-06. Investments and investment intentions are pouring in. As per the report of the Centre for Monitoring Indian Economy, during the quarter that ended in October 2005, 564 projects with investments of Rs. 2,11,054 crore were announced which is the highest ever in a decade.

Undoubtedly, the global environment has never been more conducive for India's economic development than it is today. There is today no external constraint on growth. There is no doubt that several measures have been taken on our part to attract foreign investments. India has one of the most liberal FDI regimes in the world. FDI policies in telecom, publishing, real estate and in asset reconstruction firms have been unshackled. The troublesome Press Note 18 has been done away with. Except for the financial, retailing and coal mining sectors, India is extremely liberal in welcoming FDI. There is much more, however, that can be done to draw on global savings and to tap global markets. India, in fact, needs to be more open to global capital flows and better prepared to take advantage of new markets for goods and services.

The Economic Survey 2006-07 has pointed that "there is a clear need to enhance investment. Higher investment is likely to result in higher imports of basic, intermediate and capital goods and trade and current account deficit." It can be rightly said that policies towards foreign direct investment are extremely important in gaining competitiveness in a globalised world. China's example of the impact of foreign direct investment is relevant in this context since almost 50 per cent of Chinese exports are associated with FDI.

Once again, China's example indicates that we have not exploited the scope for FDI inflow fully, China attracts around $60 billion of FDI whereas FDI in India, on a comparable basis, is about $5 billion. The Chinese economy is three times the size of the Indian economy, which suggests that India should be able to absorb $20 billion. The Common Minimum Programme states that "India needs and has the ability to absorb two to three times the level of FDI than at present." This translates to a target of $15 billion per year, which is a very reasonable target given what China has achieved.

Domestic Savings

There has recently been some improvements in the rate of domestic savings which as a proportion of GDP, have touched a record level of 32.4 per cent in 2005-06. This implies an increase of 5.5 percentage points since 2001-02, before which the rate had remained stagnant and even declined since the mid-1990s. The current savings surge coincides with a massive increase in the pinflow of portfolio FII investment in India's stock and debt markets. Overall, between 2001-02 and 2004-05, while the aggregate savings rate rose by 5.5 percentage points, the household savings rate was stagnant. A close examination of sectoral savings suggests that the sector responsible for the rise in the savings rate is the public sector which has seen a sharp transformation of its dissaving into saving which had been negative until 2002-03, turned to positive for the third consecutive year in 2005-06, contributing a positive savings of Rs. 71,262 crore during the period 2005-06. Thus, the public sector saving rate rose from a negative 2 per cent to a positive 2.2 per cent from 2001-02 to 2005-06 respectively, contributing a remarkable 4.2 percentage points increase to the savings rate.

With a rise in savings and investment rates, reduction in government's deficit and speedy reforms, the country can sustain 8-10 per cent GDP growth. A high level of savings coupled with a buoyant stock market and controlled inflation augur well for the economy.

Foreign Trade

The world is today looking at India with great interest as the saga of our development and rise to prominence on the international stage unfolds. Rare are such moments when a nation suddenly captures the attention of the world. The intensity of India's engagement with other nations was unprecedented in recent history. India moved to do business with other nations. It has taken initiatives to form an Asian bloc along with China, Japan and South Korea in order to ensure a better bargain with the OPEC countries. These countries together account for 55 per cent of the continent's oil consumption.

India's relations with its old enemy China are on the mend. The trade relations between them are booming. They have even made joint bids for oilfields in countries as far flung as Syria and Sudan. OVL and CNPC jointly acquired Petro Canada's stake in a Syrian oilfield as well as a combined stake in the greater Nile oilfield in Sudan. This may even result in a combined effort to fight the so called 'Asian Premium' the two are paying to buy from global suppliers. In the past few years, India has lobbied hard with producers in West Asia to do away with the 'premium' they charge developing nations. Union Petroleum Minister Mani Shankar Aiyar has repeatedly voiced a need for India and China to bid together to get a better deal rather than allowing nations which own fields to enhance their profits ranging in billions of dollars. It is to be mentioned here that India and China are the world's largest buyers and are expected to together account for 35 per cent of future oil consumption. The other joint initiatives includes:

- A bilateral MoV for cooperation in the energy sector in areas such as production, downstream projects, strategic storage and R & D.
- GAIL has joined hands with Sinopec in the area of oil and gas exploration and production in China.
- OVL has signed a MoV to set up a mechanism to exchange information about bidding for third country assets.

- CNOOC and GAIL have agreed to jointly bid for overseas blocks and participate in LNG supply chain.
- There will be now equity participation by GAIL in the LNG project as well as a six per cent stake in China Gas Holdings.

It has been observed by the experts that Indo-China deal is a win-win one for both nations. If the proposed plans fructify, they hold that there will be a tremendous stir in the global market.

Besides establishing cooperation with China, India is also in favour of an Asian Gas Grid—or a network of pipelines, including the proposed Iran-Pakistan-India one and also the Turkmenistan-Afghanistan-Pakistan-India one that will criss-cross Asia.

Globalisation of Indian Economy

Globalisation is the integration of business activities across geographical and organisational boundaries. It is the freedom to conceive, design, buy, produce, distribute and sell products and services in a manner which offers maximum benefit to the firm without regard to the consequences for individual geographic locations or organisational units. The modern world is dominated by the phenomenon of globalisation where commercial networks have become global, transnational corporations operate around the entire world, technology flows are universal and firms have become globalised in terms of marketing, brand names, technology.

Globalisation is fully in India's interests. Although at the outset of globalisation, some persons in India like those in other developing countries perceived it as elite driven and incapable of bringing qualitative change in peoples' lives. This group apprehended that India would lag behind in the race with the advanced countries which would ultimately capture a lion's share in the global market; opening of the markets to foreign corporations would harm local industry and that there would be large-scale privatisation of Public Sector Undertakings (PSUs) resulting in paradigm shift towards capitalism. It was even viewed by many that the consequences of globalisation would be severe, leading to committing of suicide by the farmers as the commodity prices crash, workers going out of jobs as factories close, fair chances of unique and specialised businesses to be driven out of the market because they do not have the advantage of economies of scale etc. To this group, globalisation was just another word for Americanisation.

The present scenario is altogether different. India's apprehensions about globalisation have been removed to some extent. Economic liberalisation has paved way for rapid technological progress for India while globalisation has given its young talent vast employment opportunities in America and Europe. Today, India has become a big market for multinational giants. There is hardly a big name company that is not outsourcing to India. India has developed several hubs of Information technology-enabled services, Business Process Outsourcing, Research & Development, Pharmaceuticals and Telecommunication. On the contrary, the West which kept lecturing us about globalisation is having jitters about it. The advanced countries like the United States are now fearing globalisation because they are losing jobs in the international corporate world to Indian technical experts. European Union (EU) has intentionally created rigid non-tariff barriers so as to forbid India from breaking into their markets. To quote an Italian journalist, "For most Europeans, globalisation only means two kinds of fear. Fear of cheap Chinese goods. And fear of Islamic immigrants." Much the same sort of sentiment spreads across America as well. Even in the pharmaceutical sector, the great drug multinationals have ganged up against Indian pharma companies whenever they have tried to enter the foreign markets. Indian generic drugs firms are finding the going tough due to legal battles and price wars in the United States. The country's second largest drugmaker Ranbaxy, for instance, was mired in an expensive battle with Pfizer, a multinational company, over the cholestered thinning blockbuster drug, Lipitor, which it lost.

It would not be out of place to mention here that in the past few years, India topped the list of countries filing what are called drug master files (DMFs) and Abbreviated New Drug

Applications (ANDAs) in the US, the world's largest drug market. ANDAs are filed with the US Food and Drug Administration (FDA) to establish that the drug's patent is not valid and the new entrant can enter the segment. The first one to get such an ANDAs is called the first filer and gets a 180-day exclusivity marketing period in which no other generics player can launch a similar drug in that country. In order to stall the Indian firms' move, these patent holders like Pfizer, Glaxomithkliae and Merek foiled this strategy. These MNCs have put up aggressive legal defences and have launched their own versions of cheaper authorised generics to prevent marketing exclusivities. Protracted legal Wranglings mean burgeoning costs for the Indian players.

Mittal Steel's bid to take over Arcelor

The most glaring example of the West's changing mindset towards globalisation is its xenophobic reaction to Mittal Steel's $22.7 billion bid to takeover European steel maker, Arcelor. Luxembourg, where the company is registered, is considering legislation to allow the boards of companies to decide on takeover without referral to shareholders which could thwart Mittal's bid. The move is driven by partisanship—in total disregard of commercial considerations which favour Mittal.

Lakshmi Niwas Mittal, who symbolises the entrepreneurial acumen of a new generation of Indians, heads a global conglomerate with plants across the world. He possess astute turnaround skills that have seen him revitalise ailing steel plants in countries like Mexico, Kazakhstan and Poland. Besides, Arcelor's shareholders have understood the benefits of the takeover and would, in all likelihood, approve of it in case of a referral. The rationale for merging is very strong, and Mittal has assured that there will be no job cuts. Once the deal is inked, the Netherlands based Mittal Steel will become the world's first 100 million tons plus steel producer.

Spain opposes the bid, France and Luxembourg find Mittal's bid 'very unfriendly'. Even the WTO Chief, Pascal Lamy, who as European Union Trade Commissioner often criticized developing countries for their reservations about liberalisation, is suddenly talking differently. To justify protectionism in the context of Mittal's bid he alleged that Mittal Steel's governance and its capital are family based, contrary to those of Arcelor. In this regard, a look into the history of Europe reveals that it is used to having family controlled and family influenced companies that have been very successful. Such a contention is, therefore, totally biased and against the EU's claim to champion a free trade regime. Mittal's bid for Arcelor not only indicates the changing mindset of the West but also the materialisation of emerging economies such as India's. It underlines the fact that outsourcing is not the only reason why India is on the world map of globalisation. New Delhi's strong reaction to the developments, telling the Prime Minister of Luxembourg that India will not renew the double taxation treaty with the country, not only attempts to expose the European double standards on globalisation but also symbolises India's confidence about its place among the comity of nations.

The hypocrisy of the developed world with regard to agricultural subsidies also bear testimony to the fact that the Westerners' attitude towards globalisation have considerably changed.

Industry

A distinct improvement has been taking place in the country with the introduction of the New Industrial Policy of deregulation, delicencing and disinvestment in industrial sector. Growing confidence was underlined in business surveys during 2005 about the medium-term prospects for broad-based industrial growth. Growth in the first quarter (April-June) of 2005-06 had risen to above 9 per cent and all indications—corporate profits, bulging order books, increased non-food credit at softened interest rates, and continued growth in exports and imports pointed to continued buoyancy in the latter period.

The industrial sector grew by 9.6 per cent during the year 2005-06. The major driver of this growth is the robust performance in the manufacturing and construction sector. However, a decline has been noticed in the growth rates of mining and electricity sector. The overall situation in the industry sector calls for sustained efforts to remove bottlenecks hindering the productivity of the manufacturing sector. A substantial manufacturing base is essential to absorb the workforce and ensure sustainable growth of the economy. To ensure that the economy grows at least 7-8 per cent per year in a sustained manner even for a decade or more, the industrial production growth rates of around 10 to 12 is essential. While significant progress has been made in the rationalisation of duties, reduction in the rates of taxes and other reforms, including procedural, the reform of the tax system still remains an unfinished task. To be competitive globally, Indian industry needs to be unburdened from the high levels of taxes and the distortive exemptions that provide perverse incentives.

The importance of the Small Scale Industries sector, not only in its contribution to our GDP but also for its stellar performance in exports and in generating employment, cannot be overemphasised. Today, we live in a globalised world where tariff barriers are rapidly coming down. It is, therefore, necessary to examine the implications of this for all enterprises, particularly the small-scale sector and the cottage sectors. It needs to be examined whether the existing provision of protection in the form of reservation of items for production in the SSI sector continues to be an adequate mechanism to enable this sector to thrive as well as protect from international competition. Given the future scenario of trade-driven competition, the efforts need to be made towards enhancing the capabilities of small enterprises. Growth has to be viewed as an organic entities—both small scale and large scale sectors are of considerable importance in achieving the national goal of a dynamic industrial economy.

Energy

Energy is an essential input for economic development and improving the quality of life. The magnitude of consumption per capita is a strong indicator of economic growth of a country or region. India has every reason to be proud of its material achievements since Independence in providing the energy resources required by our country. Yet, there is a long way to go in catching up with levels of consumption of even middle income countries. The availability of adequate, reliable and reasonably priced energy supplies is a *sine qua non* for achieving the growth targets. A rate of growth of 8 per cent can be sustained only if there is a growth in energy supplies as well over 5 per cent per annum. In order to achieve this, India needs to focus not just on basic fuel supplies, and power generation capacities, but also the infrastructure required to deliver the fuel and power to their consumers. This is one of the most important challenges facing our country today and a focused, holistic approach to address the issue is desperately needed.

Among the various forms of energy, electricity is unarguably the most effective energy source for achieving rural transformation and for reducing poverty. The power sector in India has grown considerably in terms of its size, coverage and technological sophistication with the generation capacity growing manifold from 1,360 MW in 1947 to more than 1 lakh MW today. But this growth is still not at par with the growing demand. It must not be forgotten that rural electrification is also linked with GDP growth of a state. It is evident that states that have poor village electrification status have a low per capita GDP as they have a low per capita Net State Domestic Product (NSDP) at current prices. It is a matter of fact that power sector continues to be a cause of major concern for different sectors of the Indian economy. A 12 per cent peak shortage in 2005-06, that could lead to a loss of more than Rs. 30,000 crore to the economy, has been estimated by the Economic Survey of India.

The ongoing reforms and better management of coal and gas supplies to thermal plants could, however, improve the situation. The Indian Government through its National Common Minimum Programme has set a target of complete electrification of all households in the next four years. Under the rural electrification programme nearly 86.2 per cent of the total villages have been electrified. Kutir Jyoti Programme, which was launched for extending single point connection to the household for rural poor families below poverty lines, is also being given priority in the rural electrification schemes. Several other measures are also being adopted by the government for the development and promotion of non-conventional/alternative/new and renewable sources of energy such as solar, wind and bioenergy, etc.

Agriculture

Agriculture is the mainstay of Indian economy, or better say the life blood of our country. The livelihood and economic well-being of its population mainly depend on how agriculture fares. The key to the prosperity of the entire nation depends critically on transforming and rejuvenating Indian agriculture. It has been often observed by many that India lives in two different worlds separated—the reality of a globalised, industrialised India is as true as the reality of the bullock cart and the uneducated farmer. Bridging this gap is the ultimate development challenge of the 21st century.

The importance of agriculture has many dimensions to it. Not only is it a major segment of our economy, contributing nearly 22 per cent of the GDP, but is also the provider of gainful employment and incomes to 65-70 per cent of Indian population. Agriculture accounts for about 14.7 per cent of India's total export earnings, provides raw material to a large number of industries, is a major source of domestic saving and the only source of food security for the nation.

What is alarming, however, is that there seems to have been a neglect of agriculture in the past decade. No one can deny the fact that Indian agriculture has been performing much below its potential in recent years. The agricultural growth has decelerated after the mid-1990s. It had grown at 3.2 per cent from 1980-96. It decelerated to 2.1 per cent during the Ninth Plan which recorded a slightly better growth of 2.3 per cent during the Tenth Plan. During the last three years India has not been able to maintain a consistent growth and has failed to ensure even 1.5 per cent growth rate in agriculture as against the annual target of 4 per cent. It has grown at 6.0 per cent in 2005-06. The agriculture today mainly suffers from low yield, volatility and disparities of productivity. Domestic production of pulses and oilseeds are also below requirements.

The cornerstone of the Tenth Plan has been a reversal of the declining trend in the growth rate of agriculture. Given the recent agricultural growth trend, the country needs to adopt effective measures. The Agriculture Summit held in April 2005 highlighted the need for a Second Green Revolution with an end-to-end approach where production and productivity patterns are tied up with market and end users. It is to be recalled here that the first Green Revolution enabled us to win the war against hunger. From a "ship to mouth" existence it brought the nation to a position to claim that we are not only self-sufficient, but also surplus in food. Owing to the deceleration in agricultural growth after the mid-1990s, the need for Second Green Revolution has been felt as the slippages recorded in the growth rate of agriculture have wide ranging implications for other important economic variables as well. The growth of employment and reduction in poverty, needless to mention, are both intimately linked to growth performance in agriculture.

It has been held by the Economic Survey that minimum support pricing and the public procurement system are preventing farmers from diversifying. It said, "A distinct bias in the agricultural price support policies in favour of foodgrains may have distorted cropping pattern and input usage."

Indian agriculture needs to move from the traditional grain based strategy followed in the past towards diversification, emphasising horticulture, poultry and livestock. Improvement in post-harvest management of agricultural produce is also indispensable. The other constraints that need to be removed are high cost of inputs, dependence of a large number of farmers on informal financial sector for their credit needs, lack of infrastructure and marketing facilities.

Aiming at increasing the returns to investment and the productivity of both land and labour in agriculture, the Second Green Revolution requires the creation of a single market for agriculture products in the country; easy availability of credit to the farmer at minimum possible rates of interest; large investment for irrigation; post-harvest marketing infrastructure including grading, packaging, transportation and storage; processing and value addition for increasing farm incomes and making agriculture and allied sectors internationally competitive.

Some legislative measures also need to be taken in this regard, such as revision of the Agriculture Produce Marketing

Committee (APMC) Act to facilitate greater private sector investment on agriculture and open up contract farming; and bringing forward an Integrated Food Law which will assimilate the myriad legislations that are existing at present. This will streamline decision-making on support prices for various types of crops, framing of proper agriculture marketing policies and efficient distribution of foodgrains through the Public Distribution System (PDS).

The new schemes on dryland farming and micro irrigation can reduce our dependence on rain to sustain our agriculture and cut down the risks involved in the rainfed agriculture. The assured irrigation will improve the productivity of marginal land and enhance cropping intensity. Given the limited availability of land, this is crucial for increasing food production.

Advances in the biotechnology can promote revolutionary changes in agriculture. Genetically modified seeds developed by the Agriculture scientists are now being widely used across the world. Such seeds are capable of repelling pests and cutting down the use of pesticides. Besides, as biotech expert Graham Brookes claims, the use of biotech seeds has led to 14 per cent reduction in environmental hazards during the past decade. In addition, the statistics of earning show that the world over, farmers have earned US$ 27 billion extra income from genetically modified crops.

It is true that biotech farming has been considered unsafe by several world's farming community as it is apprehended that a monoculture of genetically uniform hybrids could lead to natural crop failure, and even diseases could spread faster once the buffer of diversity is removed. Considering such apprehensions as baseless, Brookes has vouched for the objectivity of his studies. The fact remains that the development of drought resistant crops can be of great advantage to the farmers in India where monsoon is neither regular nor evenly distributed. Indian farmers need to be educated to make their own choice in accordance with prevailing conditions.

The Second Green Revolution is the need of the hour. Application of new technologies and modern business practices, product planning in demand driven rather than supply driven mode, awareness of niche markets and export opportunities in line with the new international trade regime opening up through WTO are some of the tips that could help improve the growth rate of Agriculture sector.

Several initiatives are being taken by the government of India to enhance the agricultural produce. Assured irrigation, credit, diversification and creating a market for agricultural products are the thrust areas. The outlay for 2006-07 has been increased to Rs. 7,121 crore from Rs. 4,500 crore in 2005-06 and the Central Government has proposed to increase the level of credit to Rs. 175,000 crore in 2006-07. In addition, Government has decided to ensure that the farmer receives short-term credit at 7 per cent, with an upper limit of Rs. 300,000 on the principal amount. There are also proposals for relief to severely indebted farmers and separate credit windows for self-help groups of tenant farmers. Through the Bharat Nirman development programme, it is envisaged that an additional 1 crore, 10 million hectares would be brought under irrigation. This will certainly help in improving productivity.

Challenges Ahead

No doubt, India's per capita income has doubled over the past twenty years. All the major engines of economic growth have accelerated growth up till now: educational levels are rising rapidly; rates of technological innovation and application are accelerating; cheaper and faster communication is dissolving physical and social barriers, both within the country and internationally; information is being made available in greater quantity and quality than ever before; and globalisation is opening up new markets. The trend of India's economic development have rather undergone a profound change—a paradigm shift—in the recent years. The country's economy is on a much stronger footing. While the software companies like Infosys, Wipro, Reliance, Tata Consultancy Services and a couple of pharmaceutical and biotechnology companies are steadily progressing toward becoming truly globally competitive, the foreign exchange reserves are buoyant. Even the international economic relations have considerably strengthened as is evident, at least to some extent, from the surging business process outsourcing. However, we should not be swayed by the hype and need to have a sense of balance and proportion for a realistic objective assessment of the tectonic forces at work. There are yet persisting problems of fiscal deficit, inflation, extensive unemployment, skewed distribution of income and wealth that need to be addressed. Inflationary pressures have marked the first six months of the current financial year. The point-to-point inflation rate, based on the Wholesale Price Index (WPI) reached a peak of 5.5 per cent in mid-June 2006. Social dimensions like education, health, drinking water and sanitation demand of massive investment—both public and private. Major challenges for India are:

- To bring millions of families above the poverty line.
- Generation of nearly 10 millions of new employment opportunities per annum, especially for those in the lower income groups.
- Eradication of illiteracy.
- Improved public health to reduce infant mortality and child malnutrition.
- Massive investment in power generation, telecommunications and other physical and social infrastructure. Infrastructure, rather, the lack of it, remains a major drag on the economy. To quote Chidambaram, the present Finance Minister (2006), "Weak infrastructure continues to be the Achilles Heel of the Indian economy. Fiscal space needs to be created by cutting down revenue expenditure, including subsidies, to enhance public investment in specified infrastructure where cost recovery is not possible." It is widely accepted that Indian economy is doing fine but it could have made a bigger dent on poverty than actually made. India is in a position to take advantage of the global shift towards services. It needs to consolidate its investment in higher education and by increasing access to quality education so as to address the skills shortage in manufacturing and services. India's savings, at 29 per cent of GDP, should be

mobilised for the creation of both physical and educational infrastructure. In health sector too, the situation is grim. According to the National Family Health Survey-III, 75 per cent of all infants between 6 and 35 months of age are anaemic; over a third of children up to the age of three are stunted and a sixth too thin for their age. As we cannot afford to lose a generation like this, there is a need to make-schools centres of both intellectual and physical nutrition and focus on governance problems in this respect on a war footing.

- Accelerated acquisition of technology capabilities to raise productivity in agriculture, industry and services.
- Becoming a more important player in the world economy in terms of both trade and investments.

With population growth slowing now to about 1.6 per cent per annum, it has been held that a growth rate of the gross domestic product (GDP) of around 9 per cent per annum would be sufficient to quadruple the per capita income by 2020. It has been assumed that if India achieves this quadrupling of per capita income by 2020, it would attain a level of development far higher than where China is today, and on par with upper-middle income countries such as Argentina, Chile, Hungary, Malaysia, Mexico and South Africa. India's progress in the coming years will undoubtedly be intimately linked to events within the region as well as around the world. Both opportunities and challenges will arise as the result of transformations in the regional and global political and security environments. Besides, world trade under WTO will determine access to markets and international competitiveness, particularly after the ascension of China. In addition, the economic growth rates of other regions will influence demand for exports and foreign capital flows. Nevertheless, India will be much more integrated with the global economy and will be a major player in terms of trade, technology and investment. Rising levels of education, employment and income will help stabilise India's internal security and social environment as well.

Features of Indian Economy

3

India is a country with a subcontinental dimension and traits. Its vast and varied geographical features, different climates, cultures, time-zones, races and religions make it subcontinent in true sense of the term. It is for this reason that South Asia is known as Indian subcontinent in world fraternity. Its geo-strategic location, flanked by Indian Ocean in the South, Arabian Sea in the West, Bay of Bengal in the East and the mighty Himalayas acting natural sentinel in the North, makes it important player in international relations.

Endowed with vast and varied natural resources, India is ranked seventh areawise in the world. The country holds second position (after China) in population and third position (after Russia and U.S.A.) in cultivable land. To most Westerners, India is the enchanted country of fakirs and the tigers, a distant land, veiled in mystery.

"To others, it is the Eldorado of philosophers and founders of religions.... India once created some of the world's top-ranking civilizations, its city cultures around the Indus reached their summit at a time when most of Europe was stage in a savage stage and centuries before America was discovered by Columbus. Many an invention and achievement in the development of technology were first conceived in the Indian subcontinent."[1]

India is really a mini-world. Its civilizational heritage and multiculturalism can perhaps act as 'panacea' for all the ills such as terrorism, violence, wars and grinding poverty. As a well-known geographer has put it, "the great Indian peninsula is the keystone of arch formed by the Indian shores. The archmotif recurs within the subcontinent structure. The resistance of massive peninsular block has looped the mountain ranges to north into a sagging inner arch."[2]

A Developing Economy

There are some distinguished features of the Indian economy, which provide it uniqueness. The first and foremost features of Indian economy is that it is a developing economy, with the potentiality of becoming developed one. The average growth rate of 6 to 7 per cent which it has been registering for last five years is expected to be repeated in the subsequent years. And such growth rate is second to China in the comity of nations of the world. This growth rate would make Indian economy a economic power.

However, there are some gray areas like low per capita income, infrastructural bottlenecks, poverty, unemployment, population explosion, increasing regional and sectoral imbalances, increasing current account deficit and poor balance of payment, which merit urgent attention. Particularly, the growing current account deficit is a matter of serious concern. During 2003-04, the current account posted a surplus of $ 14 billion, and in next fiscal of 2004-05 it transformed into a deficit of $ 5.4 billion. During April-September 2005-06, the current account deficit enlarged to around US$ 13.0 billion, which was more than twice the deficit (US$ 5.4 billion) in the whole of 2004-05.

Low per capita Income

Indian economy is characterized by low per capita income. However, it is higher than some least developed countries like Tanzania, Myanmar, Nigeria, Ethopia and other such Afro-Asian countries. When compared with the developed countries, it is very low. According to World Bank, World Development Report, 1986, per capita income of India was $ 40, which was 81 times lower than that of Switzerland, 54 times of Germany, 58 times of USA and 62 times of Japan.

Though per capita income has been increasing over the years, it is still very low as compared to the developed economies. While it changed by 2.5 per cent in 1997-98, per capita income showed the change of 6.8 per cent in 2003-04 and 6.1 per cent in 2004-05 (Table 3.1). Despite the fact that the per capita income differences got narrowed down, the difference between the level of living of the developed countries and developing countries like India is yet significantly large. The main reason for this low per capita income is burgeoning population, which is mitigating the development and growth which has been achieved over the years.

Table 3.1: GDP: Per Capita Income (Constant Prices)

Year	Per capita income (Rs.)	% Change
1997-98	11,569	2.5
1998-99	12,025	3.9
1999-2000	12,650	5.2
2000-01	12,917	2.1
2001-02	13,343	3.3
2002-03	13,655	2.3
2003-04	18,517	6.8
2004-05	19,649	6.1

Source: Monthly Review of the Indian Economy, Oct. 2005, CMIE.

Predominant Agricultural Sector

Another feature of Indian economy is the predominance of agriculture sector. Almost 70 per cent of the population of the country is dependent upon agriculture for their living of which 60 per cent formers own less than 2.5 acres of land. Agriculture contributes 21 per cent to GDP. While in the developed countries the percentage of the population actively engaged in the agriculture ranges from 3 to 11 per cent, it is as high as 30 to 74 per cent in the developing countries. Despite the growth in the urban population, the percentage of the population dependent upon the agriculture has shown slight decrease. What is unique about India is that the predominance of agriculture has remained unaffected, with slight variation of one or two per cent. On the other hand, in the developed countries the percentage of the population actively engaged in agriculture has been decreasing with development and growth. This has not happened in India despite the decades of planning, as it is clear from the Table 3.2.

Table 3.2: Percentage of Active Population Engaged in Agriculture and Industrial Origin of GNP

Country	Active Population Engaged in	Percentage of Distribution of GNP		
		Agriculture	Industrial	Services
USA	4	2	33	65
UK	3	2	42	56
Germany	6	2	51	47
Japan	11	4	45	51
Egypt	46	21	25	54
Pakistan	55	26	24	50
China	74	32	46	21
India	70	32	30	38

Source: World Bank, World Development Report, 1990.

Lack of Capital

Another glaring characteristics of Indian economy is the insufficiency of capital and the use of traditional techniques, both of which keep the output per man-hour very low. The lowness of capital formation is caused by mainly two reasons: the insufficiency of surplus over and above what is necessary to maintain the life of society; and the unproductive consumption of large percentage of the surplus.

The lack of capital also arises due to low saving rate. It is a sort of a vicious circle where low per capita income leads to low saving rate, and this results into lack of capital. Whereas developed countries do not suffer from such shortcomings as their propensity to save is very high. For example, Japan has more than 32 per cent saving of net national product, whereas France has 25 per cent and the USA saves one-fifth of net national income.

Initially, India had very low rate of saving, but in 1980s it picked up to 20 per cent. As country required 10 per cent investment to offset the population growth of 2.5 per cent, and additional 16 per cent was needed to maintain the momentum of economic growth, the lack of capital was major problem.

However, India has managed to attain the gross domestic saving of 29.1 per cent in 2004-05. While the gross domestic saving was 23.1 per cent of GDP in 1997-98, it rose to 26.1 per cent of GDP in 2002-03 which further increased to 28.1 per cent of GDP in next fiscal of 2003-04. Moreover, it has become one of the favourite destination of Foreign Direct Investment (FDI) and Foreign Institutional Investment (FII).

Given the present scenario, when the rate of population growth is 1.93 per cent, India requires as high as 14 per cent level of gross capital formation in order that the nation may cover depreciation and maintain the same level of living. Despite the high rate of capital formation, the present rate is not adequate enough to pave the way for economic growth to improve living standard of the population.

Low Level of Technology

The prevailing condition of technology in a country significantly determines its economy. In other words, a country's economy is based on the technology employed to a great extent. The sharp differences in productivity between developed and developing countries can be traced to a considerable degree to the application of superior techniques by the former.

The Indian economy suffers from the low level of technology which is mainly due to non-availability of adequate skill and fund. No doubt latest technologies are being employed here but majority of the productive units and a major part of the output is produced with the help of primitive techniques which are comparatively much inferior than to those being used in the developed countries. Actually, the absorption of new technology requires two things—availability of capital and training of an adequate number of personnel. India falls short in these two aspects. The vast majority of farmers who are backbone of the nations' economy are largely too poor to buy even the essential inputs like those of improved seeds, fertilisers and insecticides what to talk of expensive producers' goods like tractors, sowing machines etc. Likewise, the small entrepreneurs engaged in manufacturing goods are not able to meet the expenditures required to switch over to latest technology. Thus, deficiency of capital hampers the scrapping off the old techniques and the installation of the latest techniques. Illiteracy and lack of skilled labour force are the other major hurdles in the spread of technology in the Indian economy.

Population Explosion

The Indian economy suffers from the population explosion, which is leading to the diversion of resources for feeding the people. Consequently, investment and capital formation suffer, fueling the vicious circle of poverty and unemployment and putting strain on our economy.

The rate of growth of population which was nearly 1.31 per cent per annum during 1941-50 has risen to 1.93 per cent during 1991-2001.

The rapid growth of population has resulted from the growing disparity between birth and death rates. There has been a steep fall in death rate from 49 per thousand during 1911-20 to 8.1 per thousand in 2002. As compared to this, the birth rate has declined from about 49 per thousand during 1911-20 to 25.0 per thousand in 2002. Thus, while birth rate remains high, the death rate has slowed down due to advancement in medical science and availability of medical facilities. This had led to attendant problems of low per capita income, low saving, low capital formation and accumulation, low marketable surpluses, etc. as the consequence of the rise in requirement of food, clothing, shelter, medicine, education and the like. This has prevented the Indian economy from attaining the desired result.

One can get the fair idea of how rapid population is hampering our economy, when it is compared with Australian economy. While India's national income is one-and-a half times larger, its per capita income is almost 44 times less than that of Australia.

Thus, a growing population imposes greater economic burdens and as a result the society has to make even a much greater effort to initiate the process of growth. In addition, a rising population leads to an increase in the labour force. As per the Tenth Plan, between 2002-07 alone, labour force is estimated to increase by about 1.8 per cent, thereby leading to unemployment as there would be a higher supply of labour than its demand. It is matter of fact that unemployment in rural areas is the result of heavy pressure of population on land and the absence of alternative employment opportunities in villages. Taking the unemployed and underemployed together, they account for 9.21 per cent of the labour force. Thus, the main problem in India is the high level of birth rates coupled with a falling level of death rates.

Low Standard of Living

Indian economy suffers from low level of living. The average Indians lack the basic amenities and facilities which are necessary for the growth of economy. They cannot even afford the minimum requirements of food, clothing and housing.

"The average calories intake of food is only 1990 in India as compared to over 3000 calories per day in most of the developed countries. It is doubtful whether nearly 40 per cent of the population in India lying below poverty line can afford 1800 calories which are required minimum to keep oneself alive. The protein intake is nearly less than half of the level prevalent in the developed countries. Roughly 25 to 40 per cent of Indian population suffers from malnutrition and 60 per cent of the mothers are malnourished.

As regards shelter, the experience is equally bleak. Over 50 per cent of the houses are 'kutcha' and in urban areas nearly 50 per cent of the population live in one-roomed houses with an average of four persons per house. About 31 per cent of the city dwellers live in slums which are abodes of filth and dirt and therefore, unfit for human habitation.[3] The Working Group of the Tenth Plan on Housing has estimated a shortage of 22.45 million houses during the Tenth Plan period, out of which 8.8 million is the shortage of urban housing and 13.5 million of rural housing. It has also been observed that nearly ninety per cent of the housing shortage pertains to weaker sections. "The picture is equally dismal if not worse when it comes to clothing. The annual textiles consumption in India is, though slightly better than some of the South Asian countries, precarious when juxtaposed with Sweden, U.K. or USA whose consumption is nearly more than five times that of India. The precarious consumption of these basic needs is due to overpopulation, poverty and underdevelopment which go together reinforcing each other."[4]

Poor Human Resources

Human capital is the deciding factor in the economic development. The success stories of USA, Japan, Korea, etc., prove this. Indian economy is plagued with poor human resources. While the average population is traditional and lacks scientific temperament, about 33 per cent of population is still illiterate. Illiteracy retards growth as a minimum level of education is indispensable to acquire skill and also to comprehend social problems. Rural areas where illiteracy is maximum, are the centres of superstition, social taboos and conservation. All these ill beliefs are outcome of mass illiteracy. Though literacy rates in India has increased from 18.3 per cent in 1951 to 64.8 per cent in 2001, India is still lagging behind several developing countries in terms of adult literacy and youth literacy rates. Twenty-six per cent of rural households and 8 per cent urban households do not have a single member aged 15 and above who can read or write. Fifty per cent rural homes and 20 per cent urban homes do not have a single literate woman member aged 15 and above.

The poor quality of human resources is a major concern for India. As per Human Development Reports, published annually by United Nations, India ranked 127 in Human Development Index (HDI) in 2002, which is lower than Indonesia (111), China (94), Sri Lanka (96) and other countries like Norway and Australia, which ranked 2nd and 7th respectively in HDI. Though India has improved its ranking from 132 in 1997 to 127 in 2002, a lot of efforts are required in this regard.[5]

Economists have found a connection between the state of family's education and its income. A government survey which was released in December 2006 talks about this relation in the Indian context. According to the survey, for families earning more than Rs. 2,540 per month, the attendance rate in educational institutions is as high as 68 per cent and the literacy rate is 98 per cent. However, for families earning less than Rs. 235 per month, the attendance rate falls below 43 per cent and the literacy rate is just 53 per cent. The national attendance rate is 50 per cent—that is the number of people in the 5-29 age group who attend educational institutions. Those who do not attend these institutes include the ones who have some education but have since dropped out. The National Sample Survey Organisation's Status of Educational and Vocational Training in India has found that attendance is higher in lower age groups and falls dramatically as children reach the age of supplementing family income. From an attendance rate of 821 out of 1,000 children in the age group of 5-14, the number falls to 114 in the 20-24 age group, which means that only 11.4 per cent students reach higher education institutions. Those who do not attend educational institutions have given various reasons for it but a common refrain is "to supplement family income"—about 55 per cent of such people cite this as the main reason for their not attending school or college. For women, the reason is different. Some 30 per cent girls say that they have left school because they are needed at home for "domestic chores". Interestingly, the percentage of such girls is higher in urban areas than in rural areas. In rural areas, 17 per cent of people feel that it is not necessary to educate girls. The study also speaks of poor skills among Indians. It says only two per cent of people above the age of 15 have technical qualification. About eight per cent have received non-formal vocational training. Of the two per cent Indians having technical degrees, diplomas or certificates, the rate is one per cent in rural India and five per cent in urban India.

Only five per cent of the labour force in India in the age group of 20 to 24 is skilled. In actual terms, this means that out of 459 million people in the labour market in this age group, little more than 24.9 million have had any formal training before beginning their careers. This figure is linked to another figure that could easily dampen India's dreams of becoming an economic superpower—the school dropout rate. Out of the 17.5 crore who enroll in Standard I every year, 12.2 crore drop out by the time they reach Standard X. Once the student drops out, he has no alternative but to begin a premature career without training. It is a matter of satisfaction to some extent that the number of out-of-school children has halved to

13.5 million in 2005 from 25 million in 2002. This information was collated from the UNESCO survey, which was commissioned by the government under the Sarva Shiksha Abhiyan.

The Government is however making efforts to divert school dropouts to technical or vocational training streams. A scheme has been formulated through a private-public partnership under which short-term training modules will be conducted. The initial aim of the scheme will be to train a million people over five years. State governments, trade associations and industry representatives will help in its implementation. The Directorate General of Employment and Training has also been roped in. Some of the current schemes that look at helping the youth grab emerging employment opportunities will augment the new scheme. Often, the only training a school dropout gets is on-the-job experience. The ministry has also initiated a scheme to test and certify skills attained informally at the workplace. About 8,400 workers have been tested and certified under this scheme. Seventeen states have also given their assent to it.

The expenditure on education, skill formation, research and improvements in health partly constitute the human capital as these contribute to enhancing productive capacity. Accordingly, there is need to take effective measures in this direction if India is to reach the levels of developed countries in terms of human development index. Incidentally, the Indian public expenditure on primary to higher education and R & D during 1999-2001 was 4.1 per cent of GDP against the 6.0 per cent of GDP in case of the United States.

High Density of Population

The density of population in India is comparatively high, which imposes greater burdens on land and other natural resources. As per the data available, the average density of Indian population was 358 per sq. km in 2003 against 48 per sq. km of the world. The same year in the USA it was 32, Canada and Australia – 3 per sq. km and China – 138 per sq. km. The proportion of children is higher in India than in the advanced countries which results in increasingly dependency load. Thus, the larger lower age group is a constraint on production. However, it favours a higher level of consumption.

To conclude, we can say that despite five decades of efficient planning, India continues to exhibit the basic characteristics of an underdeveloped economy. No doubt, it has progressed substantially in many areas, but we have yet to go a long way to reach the standards of developed countries.

References

1. Borgstorm, George, *The Hungry Planet*, 1917, p. 121.
2. Varughese, K.V., *Indian Economy*, 1993, p. 3.
3. *Ibid.*, p. 8.
4. *Ibid.*
5. UNDP Human Development Report 1999 and 2004.

India's Demography

4

The Censuses

The conduct of population censuses in independent India is based on The Census Act, 1948. The pre-independence censuses were conducted in the years 1872, 1881, 1891, 1901, 1911, 1921, 1931 and 1941. After achieving independence the censuses were undertaken in 1951, 1961, 1971, 1981, 1991 and 2001.

The 2001 Census of India is historic and epoch-making as it is the first census of the third millennium and the twenty-first century. It is also the 14th continuous and uninterrupted census in India. It was conducted between April to September 2000 in different states and union territories as a prelude to the exercise of undertaking the decennial Population Census. The houselisting exercise provided the basis for uniform and precise frame to undertake the population enumeration with the ultimate objective of achieving as full a coverage as is humanly possible without any omission of an area or household. During this Houselisting Operation, data on housing conditions, amenities and assets available to the households were also collected. The second phase of census, *i.e.* Population Enumeration, was undertaken between 9 February to 28 February with a revisional round during 1st to 5th March 2001. The census moment was 00.00 hours of 1st March 2001, the referral time at which the snapshot of the population of the country was taken. This was a departure from the earlier census tradition, as until the 1991 Census, the sunrise of 1st March of the relevant census year was the census moment. The enumeration of houseless population was carried out on the night of February 28, 2001.

In certain inaccessible and snow bound areas of the country, population enumeration was preponed for administrative and technical convenience and carried out non-synchronously. Thus, in Jammu & Kashmir and certain snow bound areas of Himachal Pradesh and Uttaranchal the population enumeration was conducted during 11-30 September 2002 with the revisional round from 1-5 October 2002. In Kinnaur district of Himachal Pradesh, the population enumeration had to be deferred due to flash floods in August, 2000 and was conducted from 12-31 May, 2001 with reference date as 1st June, 2001. In Jammu and Kashmir, due to certain constraints, the enumeration period was extended from 1 October 2000 to 15 November 2000 with a reference date of 16 November 2000 in the six districts, *viz.* Srinagar, Badgam, Anantnag, Baramulla, Kupwara and Pulwama of Kashmir Valley and four blocks namely, Banihal, Ramso, Marwa and Wardwan of Doda district in Jammu Division. It was further extended in Srinagar town and Pulwama district until 15 December 2000 with reference date being 16 December 2000.

Further, due to the devastating earthquake in Gujarat on 26 January 2001, just two weeks prior to the commencement of the nationwide population enumeration, this schedule in the affected areas of Gujarat had to be postponed. These areas included the entire district of Kachchh, the taluk of Morvi, Maliya-Miana and Wankaner in Rajkot district and Jodiya taluka in Jamnagar district. The population enumeration in these areas was undertaken during 9-28 February 2002 with 1 March 2002 as the reference date. Although enumeration in certain areas of the country has been undertaken at different points of time and with different reference dates, no adjustments have been made to the enumerated population so as to bring all of them to the common reference date of 1 March 2001.

The huge task was achieved due to the door to door universal canvassing of the Household Schedule by about two million enumerators and supervisors covering 593 districts, 5,470 sub-districts, 5,161 towns and 638,588 villages. The comprehensive Household Schedule which replaced the individual slip had three parts and two sides A and B. Part I contained the Location Particulars; Part II related to the Individual Particulars and Part III contained questions for Household engaged in

Cultivation/Plantation. The Part II of the Household Schedule had 39 columns and 23 questions all of which were universally canvassed and no sampling was resorted to during enumeration. To facilitate quick tabulation for bringing out Provisional Population Totals, provision for page totalling were made in the schedule itself for a few items, namely population, males, females, population aged 0-6 years by sex, literates and workers and their categories by sex. The Directorates of Census Operations also released provisional data at the district, sub-district and town levels for their respective States or UTs through the publication of Paper I, II and III of Provisional Population Totals. Subsequently, the distribution of population by rural and urban areas and economic activity characteristics of the population by rural and urban areas at district/sub-district/town levels were also released in electronic format at the national level and print form at the state level. All the provisional population totals released so far are also available on census website: http://www.censusindia.net.

Apart from the provisional population totals, the final results of the Houselisting Operations were released in April, 2003 which provided valuable information on the housing stock, amenities and assets available to the household. Houselisting data is available in the hard copy form in 'Tables on Houses, Household Amenities and Assets by India and States.' Similar publications are also available for the Scheduled Caste and the Scheduled Tribe households separately. The Houselisting data is immensely useful to the policy-makers, planners and administrators to improve the quality of life for countrymen as well to the corporate sector for formulating marketing strategies in reaching the rural masses.

Population

As on 1st March 2001, India's population stood at 1,027 million of which 531.3 million were males and 495.7 million females. The overpopulation feature comes to the fore when we see that India accounts for a meagre 2.4 per cent of the world's surface area but supports and sustains 16.7 per cent of the world population. India's population which was 238.4 million at the turn of the 20th century increased to 1,027 million at the dawn of 21st century. The fact leads us to admit that the population control measures have, by and large, failed to cut the ice. The population of our country as recorded at each decennial census since 1901 has grown steadily except for a small decrease during the period 1911-1921, as shown in Table 4.1.

The Table reveals that the decadal growth of population has been uniformly high since 1961. During 1951-61 the population increased by 21.64 per cent. During 1961-71, 1971-81, 1981-91 and 1991-2001 it increased by 24.80 per cent, 24.66 per cent, 23.86 per cent and 21.34 per cent respectively. The annual exponential growth rate is around 2. If we take the population of 1901 as base when the total Indian population was 23.84 crore, we will find that the progressive growth rate over it was whopping 255.03 per cent in 1991 and is as high as 330.80 per cent in 2001. We have the highest rate of growth of population in the world.

Statewise Population and Sex Ratio

Uttar Pradesh remains the most populated state in India with 16.62 crore people, followed by Maharashtra, Bihar, West Bengal and Andhra Pradesh with 9.69 crore, 8.30 crore, 8.02 and 7.62 crore persons respectively. Among the Union Territories, Pondicherry with 9.74 lakh and Chandigarh with 9.01 lakh persons fill the first two slots.

India's sex ratio is 933 which has shown a marginal increase from 927 in 1991. However, there has been a steady decline in the member of females per 1000 males since 1901 when it was 972. The decrease from this level to 933 in 2001 is quite alarming and clearly points towards female foeticide after sex determination tests of expectant mothers despite a ban on such tests. The situation needs stringent policy planning.

Kerala remains the only state with more females, *i.e.* 1,058 per 1000 males. All other states continue to have a negative sex ratio. Haryana, Sikkim and Punjab are the top three states having lowest sex ratio of 861, 875 and 876 females per 1000 males respectively. Among the Union Territories only Pondicherry has a positive sex ratio, *i.e.* 1001. Chandigarh with 777 and Delhi with 821 have very low sex ratio.

The statewise position of total population by sex and sex ratio is given in Table 4.2.

Density of Population

India is a vast country with varied relief features and climates. The density of population, therefore, shows great variation. Its Gangetic plain is in fact the most densely populated area of the world. The number of persons per sq. km. in all the Indian states and Union Territories as per 1991 and 2001 Census is given in Table 4.3.

The Table shows that Delhi had the highest density of population in 1991 and 2001, as 6,352 and 9,294 respectively. The next four positions are taken by Chandigarh, Pondicherry, Lakshadweep and Daman & Diu. Interestingly, the Union Territories show a very high density of population. Andaman and Nicobar by comparison showed a low density of only 34 and 43 during 1991 and 2001 respectively. This may be explainable by its distant location in the Bay of Bengal. The recent Tsunami disaster would prove a further setback to the density of population in these islands.

The data also reveals that Arunachal Pradesh, Mizoram, Sikkim, J & K, Meghalaya, Manipur and Himachal Pradesh have a low density of population. This is because of their difficult terrain and climatic conditions. These places have poor transportation system which makes living more tortuous.

Meghalaya receives very high amount of rainfall which adds to the difficulties of people apart from arduous relief. The valley of Jammu and Kashmir has been under constant threat of terrorism leading to the exodus of a large member of people to other places. The prevailing conditions dwindled the economic opportunities and people migrated to other states for gainful employment.

Population is concentrated in areas where agriculture, the main occupation population of about 70 per cent of the total population flourishes due to favourable weather and proper irrigation facilities. Secondly, the population is dense in the cities where there are high employment opportunities and all modern amenities like education, health care, transportation services and finance. The population-wise number of villages, towns and cities is given in Table 4.4.

The data reveal that the total number of districts in India is 593 and that of sub-districts, 5,470. There are 5,161 towns in India and 6,38,588 villages including census villages. Uttar Pradesh has the highest number of villages of 1,07,452 while Tamil Nadu has the highest number of towns at 832. Andhra Pradesh has the highest number of sub-districts at 1,125 while Uttar Pradesh has as many as 70 districts.

Literacy Rate

In India, 64.8 per cent people are literate. Male literacy is 75.3 per cent against the female literacy of 53.7 per cent. This denotes that roughly one-third of males and half of females are illiterate. High illiteracy is the main cause of socio-economic backwardness of large masses.

Among the states, Kerala has the highest literacy of 90.9 per cent followed by Mizoram—88.8 per cent, Maharashtra—76.9 per cent and Himachal Pradesh—76.5 per cent. Bihar has the lowest literacy of 47 per cent, followed by Jharkhand 53.6 and J & K 55.5 per cent.

Among the Union Territories, Lakshadweep, Goa, Chandigarh and Delhi occupy the top four positions in high literacy rate while Dadra and Nagar Haveli have the lowest literacy. The total number of literates male and female literates, and their respective literacy rates in the Indian Union and in all the States and Union Territories have been shown in the Table 4.5.

The decadal percentages of total literates as well as male and female in the literates from 1951 to 2001 are depicted below:

Census Year	Persons	Males	Females
1951	18.33	27.16	8.86
1961	28.30	40.40	15.35
1971	34.45	45.96	21.97
1981	43.57	56.38	29.76
1991	52.21	64.13	39.29
2001	65.38	75.85	54.16

The figures reveal a steady increase in the literacy percentage. Female literacy is growing at a faster rate although their overall percentage remains lower than males. Increasing literacy bears testimony to the growing educational facilities in India. More and more females are receiving formal education which augurs well for a balanced development of society and equality of women.

Workers and Non-workers

The total population of workers and non-workers in India and their break-up in all Indian states and union territories are given in Table 4.6.

The data reveal that:

(i) Out of the total Indian population of 102.86 crore, 40.22 crore are workers and 62.64 crore are non-workers. The productive population of less than 40 per cent is indicative of low GDP.

(ii) In the traditional Indian family, male is considered the bread-winner of the family. However, out of total male population of 53.22 crore only 27.50 crore, are workers while 25.72 crore are non-workers. Roughly, half the males are non-workers.

Main and Marginal Workers

The total number of workers in India, the main workers and marginal workers out of them and their sex are given in Table 4.7.

The data reveal as under:

(i) Out of the total workers of 40.22 crore, only 31.30 crore are main workers which is approximately 75 per cent of the total number of workers. About 8.92 crore workers are marginal. These are the people who have no fixed employment or occupation. They are drifting population who barely manage to make both ends meet by doing odd jobs in agriculture, labour and seasonal work.

(ii) These marginal workers are nearly 8 per cent of our total population. This is a poor reflection on our employment generation programmes. They are mostly uneducated, unskilled workers who can do only manual work.

The situation calls for intensification of employment schemes among unskilled people, spread of literacy, training facilities and make seasonal employment permanent by supplementary back-up.

(iii) Uttar Pradesh has the largest number of marginal workers, *i.e.* 1.46 crore out of the total workers of 5.40 crore which is over 27 per cent. Bihar, Madhya Pradesh, Jharkhand and Maharashtra have 69.22 lakh, 66.91 lakh, 64.58 lakh and 64.25 lakh marginal workers. These states need to pay special attention regarding the generation of fixed employment and improvement in the existing employment patterns.

(iv) The percentage of females among the main workers is much lower while that of females among the marginal workers quite higher.

This indicates that in matters of fixed employment women in India have much lower contribution. As marginal workers, females get greater opportunities for work as they can do odd jobs from homes while taking care of their households.

The government should tap their potential by developing cottage industries for womenfolk.

Categories of Workers in India

The total workers in India can be divided into four main categories, *i.e.* (i) Cultivators (ii) Agriculture labourers (iii) Household industry workers and (iv) Other workers.

The total position of these categories of workers, their percentage, male-female composition and statewise distribution is given in Table 4.8.

The following facts are revealed by the data:

(i) The cultivators are 12.73 crore, out of which 8.54 crore are males and 4.19 crore are females. In terms of percentage, the cultivators are 31.7 per cent of the total workers.

(ii) Agricultural labourers are 26.5 per cent of the total workers. Out of the total agricultural labourers of 10.67 crore, 5.73 crore are males and 4.94 crore are females. There is no big gap between males and females in this category.

(iii) The household industry workers constitute a meagre 4.2 per cent of the total workers. Out of a total workers of 1.70 crore, 87.44 lakh are males and 82.12 lakh females.

This again is a poor reflection on the development of cottage industries in our country. There are so many traditional occupations in India and a large variety of goods can be made by using locally available resources. There is need to organise this sector and develop marketing infrastructure for its products.

The states of Uttar Pradesh, Bihar, Rajasthan, Madhya Pradesh have large working populations as well as marginal workers. They need to pay special attention to the development of rural artisans.

(iv) Other workers include those engaged in industry, trade and services. This category accounts for 37.6 per cent of the total workers in India. Out of a total of 15.12 crore other workers, 12.35 crore are males and 2.77 crore are females. The contribution of women in this sector is quite low which needs to be looked into.

(v) Himachal Pradesh, Nagaland, Rajasthan, Mizoram and Uttaranchal have more than 50 per cent of their workers engaged in cultivation. But their contribution to food production in India is not noteworthy. This shows their old methods of farming and subsistence agriculture.

In contrast, Punjab has only 22.6 per cent of its working population engaged in cultivation but has a major contribution towards agriculture production. This shows its progressive farming and commercial agriculture.

(vi) The states of Punjab, West Bengal, Gujarat and Haryana have 57.4 per cent, 48.5 per cent, 46.4 per cent and 46.1 per cent respectively of their working population engaged in other work. This shows that their large population is not dependent on agriculture.

Households, Population and Household-size

The Table 4.9 shows the total number of households and their sizes. The figures reveal that there are 19.36 crore households in India for a total population of 102.86 crore. The average household-size is 5.3. Uttar Pradesh not only has the highest population of 16.67 crore but also the highest number of households at 2.57 crore and the highest average household-size at 6.5 persons. J & K also has the same household-size of 6.5 in only 15.69 lakh households. Maharashtra, Andhra Pradesh, West Bengal and Tamil Nadu come next to UP in that order with 1.96 crore, 1.70 crore, 1.59 crore and 1.47 crore households respectively. The states of Rajasthan and Nagaland and the union territory of Lakshadweep have an identical average household-size of 6.1 followed by Bihar at 6.0 persons. All Indian states and UT's have an average household-size of over 4.3.

This calls for stringent measures to put a check on the growth of population especially in the states with high household-size.

Administrative Units

There are 593 districts, 5,470 sub-districts, 5,161 towns and 6,38,588 villages in India.

The data reveal that Uttar Pradesh holds the top position in all the categories of administrative units except sub-districts which Andhra Pradesh has 1,125 and Bihar has 533. It has 70 districts, 300 sub-districts, 704 towns and over one lakh villages. Madhya Pradesh holds the second position with 45 districts, 259 sub-districts, 394 towns and over 55,000 villages.

Growing Urbanisation

In 1901 there were only 25,693 towns in India. There has been a steady rise not only in their number but also the percentage of population residing in them. Table 4.10 shows that the number of towns has risen to 2,83,603 as per 2001 Census. This is indicative of growing urbanisation in India. The number of towns with population of less than 5000 has gone down from 1,572 in 1901 to 772 in 2001. This shows the growth of population in India.

The position of million plus cities is given in Table 4.11. The position taken as per 2001 Census depicts 35 such cities out of which 33 are Urban Agglomeration and 3 are Municipal Corporations. Mumbai, Kolkata, Delhi, Chennai and Bangalore hold the first five positions. As many as six million plus cities are in Uttar Pradesh which shows rising trend of population in the state. There is no million plus city in the northern states of Jammu & Kashmir and Himachal Pradesh and any of the seven north-eastern states.

Age-wise Population of India

Sex-age structure is the most fundamental characteristic of population composition. The population attributes vary with age groups. Age statistics form the basis of population analysis as they provide an insight into the past, a look at the present and forecast future demographic history of the country.

In demography, age is defined as the number of completed years, which have elapsed since the birth of the individual. The census data on age should, therefore, refer to ages of individuals at their last birthday. The sex-age structure is governed by the degree of variations of the immediate preceding and long events that occurred in the society and factors the components of population change, *i.e.* fertility, mortality and migration. Although sex-age structure is a direct reflection of levels and trends of these three factors during the previous decades, yet it is more often the level of the fertility which is the basic factor in determining the age structure of a population over a long period in a closed population. Age structure is a crucial component in demographic analysis as it provides a quick and ready tool for drawing the broad contours of demographic history of a population. The future demographic events are influenced to a large extent by the present sex-age structure, other things being constant.

Age data is also important because most of the socio-demographic analysis is performed according to age and sex variables. Mortality rates fluctuate over a wide range at different ages. The child bearing is associated with only a limited part of the lifespan of women as is the event of marriage. The usefulness of age data is more visible, when it is compared with other demographic and socio-economic characteristics such as marital status, literacy, economic activity etc. While studying population statistics, it becomes clear that many of the aforementioned associated characteristics are unevenly distributed by age. Most of these characteristics become important only when they are observed according to sex and age and that is why the age data becomes an excellent instrument of segregating and identifying the groups of people to be studied.

Analysis of Age-data

Apart from purely demographic concerns, the data on sex-age structure is widely required for a variety of administrative, scientific, technical and commercial purposes. It is of great significance for formulating programmes to raise the standard of living of people. The dependency ratio, which is the ratio of economically active to economically inactive persons in a population, is dependent on the age composition. Many types of schemes, especially, planning of community institutions and services for the children, adolescents, youth and the elderly, require data on age composition. Age is an important variable in measuring mean age at marriage, potential school population, the potential voting population and potential manpower. Projections on the number of households and population, school and college enrolment, labour force, requirement of teachers, health care, food and housing, transportation, problems of economic dependency etc., are some of the key areas in which the sex-age data are of prime importance. Several manufacturing and commercial ventures on consumer goods, leisure and entertainment trade industry, medical and health sector have immense utility of the age data for targeting their products and services. Hence, it is important to know the efforts made in censuses and surveys to collect the information on age.

Age-data in Censuses

A question on age has been regularly canvassed in successive censuses since 1872, but the presentation and tabulation of the same was done on a countrywide scale basis in 1951 to meet certain requirements of the First Five-Year Plan (1951-56). Till 1951, the presentation and tabulation of age data was done mainly to meet the demands of the actuary for the construction of the life tables. In 1951 Census, age data by single year of age for every district, leading to a similar set of figures for the states, zones and the country on a ten per cent sample basis was tabulated. In 1961, there was a further change and tables showing population by single year of age by sex, were formulated for the entire population separately for rural and urban areas on a hundred per cent basis at the state level. In 1971 Census, single year age returns were tabulated at the state level on the basis of a sample of individual slips (*i.e.* 10 per cent in rural and 20 per cent in urban areas). Five-year age groups were also presented at the district level as an appendix of the single year age returns. In 1981, however, separate single year and five-year age-group wise tables at the state level and the district levels respectively, based on 20 per cent sample of enumeration blocks, were presented. In 1991, tabulation of age was done on the basis of 10 per cent sample of Individual Slips at the state as well as district levels.

In 2001 Census, the age-data based on single year and quinquennial age groups by sex and place of residence were tabulated on 100 per cent basis at the state and district levels for all regions of the country. In an identical way, the Sex-age composition for the Scheduled Castes and the Scheduled Tribes, separately, at the national and state levels, was also prepared.

Problems in Data Collection during Censuses

The question on determining age is extremely deceptive and not simple and straightforward as it appears. Generally, two types of approaches are used to ascertain the age of the person, one is based on the question of 'age' and the other is through enquiring the 'date of birth'. The former appears to be very simple to collect but less accurate as compared to the date of birth. The response to question on date of birth is more accurate, but it is not easier to canvass this form of the question on age especially in illiterate populations. United Nations (Population Division) recommends asking the date of birth for children reported as '1 year of age' even if a direct question on age is unconsciously used for the remainder of the populations, to restrict the tendency to deviate and report '1 year of age' for children actually of '0 year of age'. Regarding the quality of reporting of age data, the report on 'Age Tables' based on 1961 Census states that biases in census age returns are present even in the case of statistically advanced countries; but they are of a moderate degree and do not affect their usability so seriously, as they do in the case of countries like India. They are generally due to:

- ignorance of age;
- deliberate misstatement;
- omission in enumeration;
- failure to reckon precise age due to misunderstanding of the question; and
- the faulty manner of obtaining information from the informant.

Conceptually, collection of information on age seems to be a simple item but age returns in the censuses were found to be far from the true ages for a large part of the population. Apart from differential under-enumeration in various ages, the age-data suffers from distortion owing to preferences for certain ages and digits due to social, cultural and legal habits and norms observed in a society. In a country like India, the distortions are naturally greater because precise reporting or determination of age is not considered important in the everyday affairs and laxity is permitted on various grounds of discretion and expediency. Recording of correct age of the population suffers from many typical inaccuracies such as frequent heaping of age ending at 0 and 5, preference for even numbers and certain ages such as 12 and 18. Frequently, the elderly population either does not know its age at all and reports ages in big age approximations such as 50-60, 60-70, 70-80, etc. It is possible that often the enumerator is forced to estimate the age of a person based on physical appearance or hearsay in absence of any reliable proof or information.

In Indian Census there are certain typical shifts upwards and downwards in age reporting but also a tendency among elderly population to record their age a little higher than what possibly it is. In the past, certain persons returned their age much beyond 100 years. There are other two groups for whom recording of age is rather difficult, women being one of them. Although, frequently, women may be in a position to recall when they were married or a child was born to them, it is difficult for them to state their own date or even year of birth unless they are literate. Moreover, assessing age by the enumerator may also be difficult for young women, as in certain sections of this population, they may not be permitted to appear during the enquiry, unless the enumerator is herself a lady. The other group, which may suffer from these inaccuracies are infants and children, particularly those not attending school.

Many reasons are given to explain why recording of age for the Indian population is difficult. There is no proper social, cultural or institutional mechanism, which would allow everyone to know their age every year as celebration of birthdays is not a common phenomenon or ritual in large sections of the population particularly for the rural population. Further, there is no attempt or tendency to discourage even if age, has been incorrectly stated, wherever required in the normal day-to-day life. Frequently, the production of birth certificate, the only legally valid primary document of proof of age is ignored even in important administrative matters such as admission to school, in a criminal case or getting into an electoral roll when attaining the age of 18. Frequently, a question arises in criminal cases if person is adult or not, and even in such matters, instead of insisting only the birth certificates, other methods such as ossification test is used to estimate the age particularly for child offenders or women. Affidavits or a certificate from local elected representatives or village officials is often permitted as proof of age. Of late, many State Governments have introduced pensions for the elderly people and even here, proof of age is based more often on an eye estimate by the Medical Officers or Civil Surgeons. In short, due to lack of conscious efforts on the part of the public and the administration, recording of age at census becomes particularly difficult. This is so because such searching enquiries are made only once in ten years while in day-to-day affairs of the society, it is an exception rather the rule. However, it is felt that in the past few years, the situation throughout the country is changing for the better due to spread of education and mobility of population which force people to carry some identity documents indicating their age. With renewed efforts during training of census enumerators and publicity campaign for raising the awareness level and active participation of the people, it should be possible to make an effort for effecting substantive improvements in recording the age of the Indian population during the next Census of India, *i.e.* in 2011.

Public Involvement for Improved Age-data

To involve the people directly or indirectly in reporting their age correctly, the following approach was conceptualized and implemented during the Census 2001. It is well-known that literacy and enrolment in schools have improved substantially during the last three decades. For persons born after 1975, it was felt that the literacy rates would be very high, possibly upwards by 80 per cent in most parts of the country. This population, therefore, offered a ray of hope for improving the age statistics during Census 2001. Much of the urban adult population had also attended school in the past and with some focused sensitization, it should be possible to record the age of the urban population a little more precisely. Therefore, it was felt that the younger population attending school or college could be sensitized through the Education Department/School authorities and help the census enumerators for recording their ages correctly. To implement this idea, possibilities were explored through the teachers to ensure that every child attending school knew his/her date (year) of birth. The teachers were expected to ask every child to write his/her date of birth (year) and calculate the current age. Such attempts have been made in other countries like USA and Canada for teaching arithmetic through census numbers. For example, if children have to be taught how to write one crore or hundred crores, this can easily be done by quoting the population of India or States. Such illustrative use of population numbers creates awareness among the children about the size of the Indian population. It was thought fit that an active participation in such an important campaign involving the Director of Education and the Principal Census Officers, could be sought by addressing to them through a letter from ORGI and ensuring that each school, government or private, embarks upon such a campaign, so that every child attending school during the educational year 2000-01, knew his/her correct age. It was felt that the movement might be taken forward when the teacher would ask the children to recall the correct ages of other siblings and also those of their parents and grandparents.

Keeping this in mind, separate meetings were convened by the Directors of Census Operations with the State Nodal Officer in-charge of census matters or through the State-level Co-ordination Committee on census and the Director, Primary Education in the States. Thereupon, instructions were issued to all schools both Government and non-Government of their states by the Census directorates and also the Director, Primary Education and the District Collectors. Specific requests were made by the tehsil officers and municipalities to the teachers to make an effort to teach children, the calculation of proper age. It was felt that ultimately the teachers, who worked as census enumerators, would be in a position to easily appreciate the necessity of launching such a movement and convert it into an effective campaign for public awareness.

Instructions to Census Enumerators

In view of the problems in eliciting the accurate age data from the respondents and the effort required to collect the same as accurately as possible, elaborate instructions were laid down and explained in the Instruction Manual for Census Enumerators covering as many situation as possible. Many persons, particularly, in rural areas often do not remember their ages correctly in terms of year and/or date and month. Keeping this in mind, enumerators were instructed and trained to assist such people to arrive at the correct age by stimulating the memory of those persons with reference to any relevant historical event of importance well-known in the local area. In this connection, a list of important historical events relating to the state or union territory of work of the respective enumerators was compiled in advance, discussed and provided to each one of them. Often, the age, if not known, can be ascertained with reasonable accuracy with reference to the age of another person of a known age, who may be living in the same household or in the neighbouring household or that of a well-known person of the village such as Headman of the village. The person then easily recalls, whether she/he was older or younger than such a person and approximately by how many years. The enumerators were advised that this may help them to record the age a little more precisely than the existing situations permitted. They were specifically instructed not to try to assess the age of a person by her/his physical appearance, especially for the elderly, even though the person might ask the enumerator to do so.

In respect of infants, who might not have completed one year by the day of enumeration, the enumerators were instructed that age of those children in completed years must be shown as 'zero'.

Enumerators were advised to give special emphasis for determination of actual age of women, since the age of married women in particular, has a special bearing in demographic analysis. If a woman is not aware about her age and is also unable to report the year of her birth, the enumerators were advised to further probe to estimate her age. One way, provided to the enumerator for such estimation, was to ask her the age of her eldest living son or daughter and her own estimated age at the time, when she gave birth to that child. The sum of these two figures with minor adjustments would provide a fair estimate of her current age. Even if she is not able to tell her age at the time when the first child was born, the enumerator was advised to try to ascertain her age at the time of consummation of her marriage and the interval between her marriage and the birth of her eldest child. Adding these two figures with the age of her eldest child may help in determining her current age. If, she does not know her age at marriage, then the enumerator was advised to find out her age in relation to the age of her husband, whose age might possibly be known a little more precisely.

On mis-reporting of age by individuals, the enumerators were asked to be cautious and they were specifically requested to keep in mind the following:

> 'Very often, there is a tendency on the part of individuals to return 'years running' rather than the 'years completed'. They were instructed to make sure that only the actual number of years completed should be recorded as age. It has also been noticed that people usually tend to return their age with numeric figures ending in '0' and '5'. For example, if the age of the person is 43/46 years, she/he might return her/his age as 45 years or if the age of the person is 39/41 years, one might say, she/he was 40 years old. Another tendency among the elderly people to overstate their age. There is also a tendency among people is to report wrong age to draw some special benefit that accrue with a certain age like right to vote after completing 18 years and superannuation benefits in some states at a certain age. In all such case, careful probing as indicated above should be done in order to closely estimate their age.'

A statement showing the age as on 1st March 2001 and the corresponding year of birth according to English and local calendar for the preceding 100 years was given separately to the enumerators with the intention that it would serve as ready reckoner to quickly and correctly arrive at the exact age, when the respondent was able to give him her/his date and year of birth. In situations, where the respondent gives her/his age, the hundred year ready reckoner could be used to arrive at the year of birth. That would help the enumerator to confirm the correctness of the year of birth worked out by him.

The assumption that the urban and the literate population are able to recall their age correctly is sometimes misplaced. Age heaping frequently results due to the habit of rounding numbers even by the educated population. For example, a person may continue to state his/her age as '35' for railway reservation purposes during ages '32-38' although each of these years his/her age is different. Since the railway authorities do not always insist on the correct age, therefore, it has become habitual for most to round off the age while purchasing tickets. So it was emphasized that while recording ages of the response answers ended with the digit either '0' or '5', additional probing be effected.

Training

Training has always been recognized as one of the most vital inputs for smooth and successful conduct of the census. Nearly two million census enumerators were extensively trained to elicit information on various questions included in the Census Schedule. Special emphasis was laid by the Census Advisors specially appointed for gender training to enumerators on canvassing of the question on age as accurately as possible. Regarding reporting of age by local calendar, a confusion over the reporting of age in accordance with local calendar instead of English calendar exists not only in India but in many countries. In countries like China, Korea, Hong Kong and Singapore, age is reckoned in a still different way, where, at birth, an individual is assigned an age of 1 and he then becomes a year older on each Chinese New Year's day. In 1960 in the census of South Korea, for example, some respondents gave one type of age and the rest, the other type. Since local calendars have some influence in the minds of the people of this country, training was also imparted for consulting the local calendar such as Bengali year, Tamil year or *Vikram Samvat*, and arriving at the correct age by converting the date of birth reported by the above source into English calendar year. This was required, since sometimes date of births are known and reported by local calendars only. The enumerators were sensitized about the quality of age-data recorded and reported in earlier censuses by way of showing different indices used for evaluation of age-data. They were also shown the single year age-data of earlier censuses by way of graphs and tables to give them an idea of the nature of heaping at certain ages, especially, in the ages ending with digits '0' and '5' would result if they were not careful enough.

The age-wise split of population in five-year groups of total population of India as well as the statewise distribution of these groups by sex and residence is given in Table 4.12.

The data reveal as under:

(i) Out of the total population of 102.86 crore, 11.04 crore are in the age group of 0-4 years which is over 10 per cent of the total population. This shows a very high growth rate. In this age group, there are 5.71 crore males and 5.33 crore females which forecasts a trend of better sex ratio in future.

(ii) In the age group of 0-4 years, 8.51 crore live in rural areas and only 2.53 crore live in urban areas. This indicates that the growth of population is higher in rural areas.

The situation calls for creation of awareness and spread of education in villages so that the people know the importance of planning their families.

(iii) Out of the total population of 102.86 crore, 44.27 crore are either below fourteen or above sixty. The dependency ratio of around 43 per cent is quite high. If we add to it the unemployed population, the work participation goes below 50 per cent. This calls for generation of more employment programmes so that all the able-bodied persons contribute towards GDP.

There have been suggestions to reduce the retirement age from 60 to 58 on the plea that it would increase employment by giving these jobs to other people.

But the high dependency ratio and low participation ratio indicate that such a reduction would be counter productive.

(iv) The total number of voters is around 60 crore out of which roughly 40 crore live in rural areas which constitutes two-thirds of the voting population.

The success of democracy is largely dependent on the vigilance of its voters. There is an urgent need to develop our villages fast in terms of education so that the majority that chooses the government brings out capable, clean and devoted people to govern the country.

(v) Out of a total population of 102.86 crore, 25.31 crore are in the age group of 5-14 which is about 25 per cent of the total population. This high number of children need a large number of primary and secondary level schools to give them formal education. As the number of girl children is about half the total children, more girl schools need to be opened.

(vi) The number of children in the age group of 15-19 years is over 10 crore and need more and more senior secondary schools. The population of 8.98 crore in the age group of 20-24 years need a large number of colleges and universities to impart higher education.

Statewise Distribution of Age-groups

The statewise data of five year groups by sex and residence reveal as under:

(i) Uttar Pradesh has the highest number of persons in the 0-4 year age group, *i.e.* 2.07 crore which is over 12.4 per cent of the total population of the state. Bihar has over 13 per cent population in the age group of 0-4 years. This shows a very high rate of growth of population in these states and calls for stringent measures to step up family planning measures and spread overall awareness among people.

(ii) The sex ratio in the lowest age group in these states is higher than the national sex ratio of 933. This indicates that the government's decision to ban pre-birth sex determination tests is paying dividends. People have also begun to understand the equal importance of female child. The cases of female foeticide are declining.

(iii) The dependency ratio in highly populated states is also high. In U.P., out of a total population of 16.66 crore, 8.03 crore persons are either below 14 or above 60. Thus, nearly 50 per cent of the total population is dependent. In Bihar, the total population is 8.30 crore, out of which 4.06 crore is either below 14 or above 60.

Here too, nearly 50 per cent of the population is dependent.

If we look at the fact that there is rampant unemployment and marginal employment, the working participation is reduced to around 40 per cent which is quite low.

(iv) The population in the age group of 5 to 19 in the states of Uttar Pradesh, Maharashtra, Bihar and West Bengal is 6.32 crore, 3.11 crore, 3.12 crore and 2.66 crore respectively. These states need to pay special attention towards opening of sizeable number of schools to spread education in order to improve the quality of life and bring faster development.

NATIONAL POPULATION POLICY 2000

Introduction

The overriding objective of economic and social development is to improve the quality of lives that people lead, to enhance their well-being, and to provide them with opportunities and choices to become productive assets in society.

In 1952, India was the first country in the world to launch a national programme, emphasizing family planning to the extent necessary for reducing birth rates "to stabilize the population at a level consistent with the requirement of national economy". After 1952, sharp declines in death rates were, however, not accompanied by a similar drop in birth rates. The National Health Policy, 1983 stated that replacement levels of total fertility rate (TFR) should be achieved by the year 2000.

On 11 May 2000, India's population reached 1 billion (100 crore), i.e. 16 per cent of the world's population on 2.4 per cent of the globe's land area. If current trends continue, India may overtake China in 2045 to become the most populous country in the world. While global population has increased threefold during the 20th century, from 2 billion to 6 billion, the population of India has increased nearly five times from 238 million (23 crores) to 1 billion in the same period. India's current annual increase in population of 15.5 million is large enough to neutralize efforts to conserve the resource endowment and environment.

India's population in March 1991 and projections to March 2016 are as follows:

Population Projections for India

(in million)

1991	2001	2011	2016
846.3	1012.4	1178.9	1263.5

Source: Technical Group on Population Projections,Planning Commission.

Stabilising population is an essential requirement for promoting sustainable development with more equitable distribution. However, it is as much a function of making reproductive health care accessible and affordable for all, as of increasing the provision and outreach of primary and secondary education, extending basic amenities including sanitation, safe drinking water and housing, besides empowering women and enhancing their employment opportunities, and providing transport and communications.

With a view to achieving these objectives, the Government has formulated the National Population Policy, 2000 (NPP 2000) which provides a policy framework for advancing goals and prioritizing strategies during the next decade, to meet the reproductive and child health needs of the people of India, and to achieve net replacement levels (TFR) by 2010. It is based upon the need to simultaneously address issues of child survival, maternal health, and contraception, while increasing outreach and coverage of a comprehensive package of reproductive and child health services by government, industry and the voluntary non-government sector, working in partnership.

Objectives

The immediate objective of the NPP 2000 is to address the unmet needs for contraception, health care infrastructure, and health personnel, and to provide integrated service delivery for basic reproductive and child health care. The medium-term objective is to bring the TFR to replacement levels by 2010, through vigorous implementation of inter-sectoral operational strategies. The long-term objective is to achieve a stable population by 2045, at a level consistent with the requirements of sustainable economic growth, social development, and environmental protection.

In pursuance of these objectives, the following National Socio-Demographic Goals to be achieved in each case by 2010 are formulated:

National Socio-Demographic Goals for 2010

- Address the unmet needs for basic reproductive and child health services, supplies and infrastructure.
- Make school education up to age 14 free and compulsory, and reduce dropouts at primary and secondary school levels to below 20 per cent for both boys and girls.
- Reduce infant mortality rate to below 30 per 1000 live births.
- Reduce maternal mortality ratio to below 100 per 100,000 live births.
- Achieve universal immunization of children against all vaccine preventable diseases.
- Promote delayed marriage for girls, not earlier than the age of 18 and preferably after 20 years of age.
- Achieve 80 per cent institutional deliveries and 100 per cent deliveries by trained persons.
- Achieve universal access to information/counseling, and services for fertility regulation and contraception with a wide basket of choices.
- Achieve 100 per cent registration of births, deaths, marriage and pregnancy.
- Contain the spread of Acquired Immuno Deficiency Syndrome (AIDS), and promote greater integration between the management of reproductive tract infections (RTI) and sexually transmitted infections (STI) and the National AIDS Control Organisation.
- Prevent and control communicable diseases.

- Integrate Indian Systems of Medicine (ISM) in the provision of reproductive and child health services, and in reaching out to households.
- Promote vigorously the small family norm to achieve replacement levels of TFR.
- Bring about convergence in implementation of related social sector programmes so that family welfare becomes a people-centred programme.

If the NPP 2000 is fully implemented, it is anticipated that the population would be 1,107 million (110 crores) in 2010, instead of 1,162 million (116 crores) projected by the Technical Group on Population Projections:

Anticipated Growth in Population

(in million)

Year	If current trends continue		If TFR 2.1 is achieved by 2010
	Total Population	Increase in Population	Total Population
1991	846.3	–	846.3
1996	934.2	17.6	934.2
1997	949.9	15.7	949.0
2000	996.9	15.7	991.0
2002	1027.6	15.4	1013.0
2010	1162.3	16.8	1107.0

Source: Ministry of Health and Family Welfare.

Similarly, the anticipated reductions in the birth, infant mortality and total fertility rates are as under:

Projections of Crude Birth Rate, Infant Mortality Rate, and TFR, if the NPP 2000 is fully implemented

Year	Crude Birth Rate	Infant Mortality Rate	Total Fertility Rate
1997	27.2	71	3.3
1998	26.4	72	3.3
2002	23.0	50	2.6
2010	21.0	30	2.1

Source: Ministry of Health and Family Welfare.

Causes of Population Growth in India

- **Large size of the population in the reproductive age-group (estimated contribution 58 per cent):** An addition of 417.2 million between 1991 and 2016 is anticipated despite substantial reductions in family size in several states, including those which have already achieved replacement levels of TFR. This momentum of increase in population will continue for some more years because high TFRs in the past have resulted in a large proportion of the population being currently in their reproductive years. It is imperative that the reproductive age group adopts without further delay or exception "small family norm", for the reason that about 45 per cent of population increase is contributed by births above two children per family.
- **Higher fertility due to unmet need for contraception (estimated contribution 20 per cent):** India has 168 million eligible couples, of which just 44 per cent are effectively protected. Urgent steps are currently required to make contraception more widely available, accessible, and affordable. Around 74 per cent of the population lives in rural areas, in about 5.5 lakh villages, many with poor communications and transport. Reproductive health and basic health infrastructure and services often do not reach the villages, and, accordingly, vast numbers of people cannot avail of these services.
- **High wanted fertility due to the high infant mortality rate (IMR) (estimated contribution about 20 per cent):** Repeated child births are seen as an insurance against multiple infant (and child) deaths and accordingly, high infant mortality stymies all efforts at reducing TFR.
- **Under-age marriages of girls:** Over 50 per cent of girls marry below the age of 18, the minimum legal age of marriage, resulting in a typical reproductive pattern of "too early, too frequent, too many". Around 33 per cent births occur at intervals of less than 24 months, which also result in high IMR.

Conclusion

In the new millennium, nations are judged by the well-being of their peoples; by levels of health, nutrition and education; by the civil and political liberties enjoyed by their citizens; by the protection guaranteed to children and by provisions made for the vulnerable and the disadvantaged.

The vast numbers of the people of India can be its greatest asset if they are provided with the means to lead healthy and economically productive lives. Population stabilisation is a multisectoral endeavour requiring constant and effective dialogue among a diversity of stakeholders, and coordination at all levels of the government and society. Spread of literacy and education, increasing availability of affordable reproductive and child health services, convergence of service delivery at village levels, participation of women in the paid workforce, together with a steady, equitable improvement in family incomes, will facilitate early achievement of the socio-demographic goals. Success will be achieved if the Action Plan contained in the NPP 2000 is pursued as a national movement.

Table 4.1: Population 1901-2001

Census years	Population	Decadal growth		Change in decadal growth		Average annual exponential growth rate (per cent)	Progressive growth rate over 1901 (per cent)
		Absolute	Per cent	Absolute	Per cent		
1	2	3	4	5	6	7	8
1901	23,83,96,327	–	–	–	–	–	–
1911	25,20,93,390	1,36,97,063	5.75	–	–	0.56	5.75
1921	25,13,21,213	–7,72,177	–0.31	–1,44,69,240	–6.05	–0.03	5.42
1931	27,89,77,238	2,76,56,025	11.00	2,84,28,202	11.31	1.04	17.02
1941	31,86,60,580	3,96,83,342	14.22	1,20,27,317	3.22	1.33	33.67
1951[1]	36,10,88,090	4,24,27,510	13.31	27,44,168	–0.91	1.25	51.47
1961[1]	43,92,34,771	7,81,46,681	21.64	3,57,19,171	8.33	1.96	84.25
1971	54,81,59,652	10,89,24,881	24.80	3,07,78,200	3.16	2.22	129.94
1981[2]	68,33,29,097	13,51,69,445	24.66	2,62,44,564	–0.14	2.20	186.64
1991[3]	84,64,21,039	16,30,91,942	23.87	2,79,22,497	–0.79	2.14	255.05
2001[4]	1,02,87,37,436	18,23,16,397	21.54	1,92,24,455	–2.33	1.95	331.47

Notes:

1. In working out 'Decadal Growth' and 'Percentage Decadal Growth' for India 1941-51 and 1951-61, the population of Tuensang district for 1951 (7,025) and the population of Tuensang (83,501) and Mon (5,774) districts for 1961 Census of Nagaland state have not been taken into account as the areas went in for census for the first time in 1951 and the same are not comparable.
2. The 1981 Census could not be held owing to disturbances in Assam. Hence, the population figures for 1981 of Assam have been worked out by 'interpolation'.
3. The 1991 Census could not be held owing to disturbances in Jammu and Kashmir. Hence the population figures for 1991 of Jammu and Kashmir have been worked out by 'interpolation' on the basis of 2001 final population.
4. The population figures of 2001 are final and include estimated figures for those of the three sub-divisions, *viz.* Mao Maram, Paomata and Purul of Senapati district of Manipur as population Census 2001 in these three sub-divisions was cancelled due to technical and administrative reasons although a population census was carried out in these sub-divisions also as per schedule.

Table 4.2: Population by Sex and Sex Ratio

State Code	India/State/UT	Population			
		Persons	Males	Females	Sex Ratio
	India@	1,028,610,328	532,156,772	496,453,556	933
01	Jammu & Kashmir	10,143,700	5,360,926	4,782,774	892
02	Himachal Pradesh	6,077,900	3,087,940	2,989,960	968
03	Punjab	24,358,999	12,985,045	11,373,954	876
04	Chandigarh	900,635	506,938	393,697	777
05	Uttaranchal	8,489,349	4,325,924	4,163,425	962
06	Haryana	21,144,564	11,363,953	9,780,611	861
07	Delhi	13,850,507	7,607,234	6,243,273	821
08	Rajasthan	56,507,188	29,420,011	27,087,177	921
09	Uttar Pradesh	166,197,921	87,565,369	78,632,552	898
10	Bihar	82,998,509	43,243,795	39,754,714	919
11	Sikkim	540,851	288,484	252,367	875
12	Arunachal Pradesh	1,097,968	579,941	518,027	893
13	Nagaland	1,990,036	1,047,141	942,895	900
14	Manipur@	2,166,788	1,095,634	1,071,154	978
15	Mizoram	888,573	459,109	429,464	935
16	Tripura	3,199,203	1,642,225	1,556,978	948
17	Meghalaya	2,318,822	1,176,087	1,142,735	972
18	Assam	26,655,528	13,777,037	12,878,491	935
19	West Bengal	80,176,197	41,465,985	38,710,212	934
20	Jharkhand	26,945,829	13,885,037	13,060,792	941
21	Orissa	36,804,660	18,660,570	18,144,090	972
22	Chhattisgarh	20,833,803	10,474,218	10,359,585	989
23	Madhya Pradesh	60,348,023	31,443,652	28,904,371	919
24	Gujarat	50,671,017	26,385,577	24,285,440	920
25	Daman & Diu	158,204	92,512	65,692	710
26	Dadra & Nagar Haveli	220,490	121,666	98,824	812
27	Maharashtra	96,878,627	50,400,596	46,478,031	922
28	Andhra Pradesh	76,210,007	38,527,413	37,682,594	978
29	Karnataka	52,850,562	26,898,918	25,951,644	965
30	Goa	1,347,668	687,248	660,420	961
31	Lakshadweep	60,650	31,131	29,519	948
32	Kerala	31,841,374	15,468,614	16,372,760	1058
33	Tamil Nadu	62,405,679	31,400,909	31,004,770	987
34	Pondicherry	974,345	486,961	487,384	1001
35	A. & N. Islands	356,152	192,972	163,180	846

Note: @ — Excludes Mao-Maram, Paomata and Purul sub-divisions of Senapati district of Manipur. The population of Manipur including the estimated population of the three sub-divisions of Senapati district is 2,291,125 (males 1,161,173 and females 1,129,952).

Table 4.3: Distribution of Population, Sex Ratio, Density and Decadal Growth Rate of Population : 2001

State/ UT Code	India/State/ UT*	Total Population			Sex ratio (females)	Density (per sq.km.)	Decadal growth rate
		Persons	Males	Females			
1	2	3	4	5	6	7	8
	INDIA[1,2]	1,027,015,247	531,277,078	495,738,169	933	324	21.34
1	J&K[2,3]	10,069,917	5,300,574	4,769,34	900	399	29.04
2	Himachal Pradesh[4]	6,077,248	3,085,256	2,991,992	970	109	17.53
3	Punjab	24,289,296	12,963,362	11,325,934	874	482	19.76
4	Chandigarh*	900,914	508,224	392,690	773	7,902	40.33
5	Uttaranchal	8,479,562	4,316,401	4,163,161	964	159	19.20
6	Haryana	21,082,989	11,327,658	9,755,331	861	477	28.06
7	Delhi*	13,782,976	7,570,890	6,212,086	821	9,294	46.31
8	Rajasthan	56,473,122	29,381,657	27,091,465	922	165	28.33
9	Uttar Pradesh	166,052,859	87,466,301	78,586,558	898	689	25.80
10	Bihar	82,878,796	43,153,964	39,724,832	921	880	28.43
11	Sikkim	540,493	288,217	252,276	875	76	32.98
12	Arunachal Pradesh	1,091,117	573,951	517,166	901	13	26.21
13	Nagaland	1,988,636	1,041,686	946,950	909	120	64.41
14	Manipur	2,388,634	1,207,338	1,181,296	978	107	30.02
15	Mizoram	891,058	459,783	431,275	938	42	29.18
16	Tripura	3,191,168	1,636,138	1,555,030	950	304	15.74
17	Meghalaya	2,306,069	1,167,840	1,138,229	975	103	29.94
18	Assam	26,638,407	13,787,799	12,850,608	932	340	18.85
19	West Bengal	80,221,171	41,487,694	38,733,477	934	904	17.84

Contd...

1	2	3	4	5	6	7	8
20	Jharkhand	26,909,428	13,861,277	13,048,151	941	338	23.19
21	Orissa	36,706,920	18,612,340	18,094,580	972	236	15.94
22	Chhattisgarh	20,795,956	10,452,426	10,343,530	990	154	18.06
23	Madhya Pradesh	60,385,118	31,456,873	28,928,245	920	196	24.34
24	Gujarat[5]	50,596,992	26,344,053	24,252,939	921	258	22.48
25	Daman & Diu*	158,059	92,478	65,581	709	1,411	55.59
26	D & N Haveli*	220,451	121,731	98,720	811	449	59.20
27	Maharashtra	96,752,247	50,334,270	46,417,977	922	314	22.57
28	Andhra Pradesh	75,727,541	38,286,811	37,440,730	978	275	13.86
29	Karnataka	52,733,958	26,856,343	25,877,615	964	275	17.25
30	Goa	1,343,998	685,617	658,381	960	363	14.89
31	Lakshadweep*	60,595	31,118	29,477	947	1,894	17.19
32	Kerala	31,838,619	15,468,664	16,369,955	1,058	819	9.42
33	Tamil Nadu	62,110,839	31,268,654	30,842,185	986	478	11.19
34	Pondicherry*	973,829	486,705	487,124	1,001	2,029	20.56
35	A & N Islands*	356,265	192,985	163,280	846	43	26.94

Notes:

1. The population of India includes the estimated population of entire Kachchh district, Morvi, Maliya-Miyana and Wankaner talukas of Rajkot district, Jodiya taluka of Jamnagar district of Gujarat State and entire Kinnaur district of Himachal Pradesh where population enumeration of Census of India 2001 could not be conducted due to natural calamities.
2. For working out the density of India and Jammu & Kashmir the entire area and population of those areas of Jammu & Kashmir which are under illegal occupation of Pakistan and China have not been taken into account.
3. While working out the decadal growth of population of Jammu and Kashmir, the population figures for 1991 have been worked out by interpolation as 1991 Census could not be held in this State owing to disturbed conditions.
4. Figures shown against Himachal Pradesh have been arrived at after including the estimated figures of entire Kinnaur district of Himachal Pradesh where the population enumeration of Census of India 2001 could not be conducted due to natural calamity.
5. Figures shown against Gujarat have been arrived at after including the estimated figures of entire Kachchh district, Morvi, Maliya-Miyana and Wankaner talukas of Rajkot district, Jodiya taluka of Jamnagar district of Gujarat State where the population enumeration of Census of India 2001 could not be conducted due to natural calamity.

Table 4.4: Number of Districts, Sub-Districts, Towns and Villages

State Code	India/State/UT	Number of districts	Number of sub-districts	Number of towns (including census towns)	Number of villages (including uninhabited villages)
	India	593	5,470	5,161	638,588
01	J & K	14	59	75	6,652
02	Himachal Pradesh	12	109	57	20,118
03	Punjab	17	72	157	12,673
04	Chandigarh	1	1	1	24
05	Uttaranchal	13	49	86	16,826
06	Haryana	19	67	106	6,955
07	Delhi	9	27	62	165
08	Rajasthan	32	241	222	41,353
09	Uttar Pradesh	70	300	704	107,452
10	Bihar	37	533	130	45,098
11	Sikkim	4	9	9	452
12	Arunachal Pradesh	13	149	17	4,065
13	Nagaland	8	93	9	1,317
14	Manipur	9	38	33	2,391
15	Mizoram	8	25	22	817
16	Tripura	4	38	23	870
17	Meghalaya	7	32	16	6,026
18	Assam	23	145	125	26,312
19	West Bengal	18	341	375	40,782
20	Jharkhand	18	210	152	32,615
21	Orissa	30	398	138	51,349
22	Chhattisgarh	16	97	97	20,308
23	Madhya Pradesh	45	259	394	55,393
24	Gujarat	25	226	242	18,539
25	Daman & Diu	2	2	2	23
26	D & N Haveli	1	1	2	70
27	Maharashtra	35	353	378	43,711
28	Andhra Pradesh	23	1,125	210	28,123
29	Karnataka	27	175	270	29,406
30	Goa	2	11	44	359
31	Lakshadweep	1	4	3	24
32	Kerala	14	63	159	1,364
33	Tamil Nadu	30	201	832	16,317
34	Pondicherry	4	10	6	92
35	A. & N. Islands	2	7	3	547

Table 4.5: Number of Literates and Literacy Rate by Sex

State Code	India/State/UT	Population			Number of Literates			Literacy Rate		
		Persons	Males	Females	Persons	Males	Females	Persons	Males	Females
1	2	3	4	5	6	7	8	9	10	11
	India@	1,028,610,328	532,156,772	496,453,556	560,687,797	336,533,716	224,154,081	64.8	75.3	53.7
01	Jammu & Kashmir	10,143,700	5,360,926	4,782,774	4,807,286	3,060,628	1,746,658	55.5	66.6	43.0
02	Himachal Pradesh	6,077,900	3,087,940	2,989,960	4,041,621	2,278,386	1,763,235	76.5	85.3	67.4
03	Punjab	24,358,999	2,985,045	11,373,954	14,756,970	8,442,293	6,314,677	69.7	75.2	63.4
04	Chandigarh	900,635	506,938	393,697	643,245	382,686	260,559	81.9	86.1	76.5
05	Uttaranchal	8,489,349	4,325,924	4,163,425	5,105,782	3,008,875	2,096,907	71.6	83.3	59.6
06	Haryana	21,144,564	11,363,953	9,780,611	12,093,677	7,480,209	4,613,468	67.9	78.5	55.7
07	Delhi	13,850,507	7,607,234	6,243,273	9,664,764	5,700,847	3,963,917	81.7	87.3	74.7
08	Rajasthan	56,507,188	29,420,011	27,087,177	27,702,010	18,047,157	9,654,853	60.4	75.7	43.9
09	Uttar Pradesh	166,197,921	87,565,369	78,632,552	75,719,284	48,901,413	26,817,871	56.3	68.8	42.2
10	Bihar	82,998,509	43,243,795	39,754,714	31,109,577	20,644,376	10,465,201	47.0	59.7	33.1
11	Sikkim	540,851	288,484	252,367	318,335	189,060	129,275	68.8	76.0	60.4
12	Arunachal Pradesh	1,097,968	579,941	518,027	484,785	303,281	181,504	54.3	63.8	43.5
13	Nagaland	1,990,036	1,047,141	942,895	1,132,323	640,201	492,122	66.6	71.2	61.5
14	Manipur@	2,166,788	1,095,634	1,071,154	1,310,534	753,466	557,068	70.5	80.3	60.5
15	Mizoram	888,573	459,109	429,464	661,445	350,105	311,340	88.8	90.7	86.7
16	Tripura	3,199,203	1,642,225	1,556,978	2,022,099	1,150,707	871,392	73.2	81.0	64.9
17	Meghalaya	2,318,822	1,176,087	1,142,735	1,157,875	614,272	543,603	62.6	65.4	59.6
18	Assam	26,655,528	13,777,037	12,878,491	14,015,354	8,188,697	5,826,657	63.3	71.3	54.6

Contd...

1	2	3	4	5	6	7	8	9	10	11
19	West Bengal	80,176,197	41,465,985	38,710,212	47,196,401	27,452,426	19,743,975	68.6	77.0	59.6
20	Jharkhand	26,945,829	13,885,037	13,060,792	11,777,201	7,646,857	4,130,344	53.6	67.3	38.9
21	Orissa	36,804,660	18,660,570	18,144,090	19,837,055	11,992,333	7,844,722	63.1	75.3	50.5
22	Chhattisgarh	20,833,803	10,474,218	10,359,585	11,173,149	6,711,395	4,461,754	64.7	77.4	51.9
23	Madhya Pradesh	60,348,023	31,443,652	28,904,371	31,592,563	19,672,274	11,920,289	63.7	76.1	50.3
24	Gujarat	50,671,017	26,385,577	24,285,440	29,827,750	17,833,273	11,994,477	69.1	79.7	57.8
25	Daman & Diu	158,204	92,512	65,692	107,600	70,992	36,608	78.2	86.8	65.6
26	Dadra & Nagar Haveli	220,490	121,666	98,824	103,904	72,149	31,755	57.6	71.2	40.2
27	Maharashtra	96,878,627	50,400,596	46,478,031	63,965,943	37,184,963	26,780,980	76.9	86.0	67.0
28	Andhra Pradesh	76,210,007	38,527,413	37,682,594	39,934,323	23,444,788	16,489,535	60.5	70.3	50.4
29	Karnataka	52,850,562	26,898,918	25,951,644	30,434,962	17,661,211	12,773,751	66.6	76.1	56.9
30	Goa	1,347,668	687,248	660,420	985,562	541,032	444,530	82.0	88.4	75.4
31	Lakshadweep	60,650	31,131	29,519	44,683	24,511	20,172	86.7	92.5	80.5
32	Kerala	31,841,374	15,468,614	16,372,760	25,485,688	12,753,602	12,732,086	90.9	94.2	87.7
33	Tamil Nadu	62,405,679	31,400,909	31,004,770	40,524,545	22,809,662	17,714,883	73.5	82.4	64.4
34	Pondicherry	974,345	486,961	487,384	696,367	378,758	317,609	81.2	88.6	73.9
35	A & N Islands	356,152	192,972	163,180	253,135	146,831	106,304	81.3	86.3	75.2

Note: @ – Excludes Mao-Maram, Paomata and Purul sub-divisions of Senapati district of Manipur.

Table 4.6: Distribution of Population by Workers and Non-workers by Sex

State Code	India/State/UT	Total Population			Total Workers			Total Non-workers		
		Persons	Males	Females	Persons	Males	Females	Persons	Males	Females
1	2	3	4	5	6	7	8	9	10	11
	India@	1,028,610,328	532,156,772	496,453,556	402,234,724	275,014,476	127,220,248	626,375,604	257,142,296	369,233,308
01	Jammu & Kashmir	10,143,700	5,360,926	4,782,774	3,753,815	2,679,941	1,073,874	6,389,885	2,680,985	3,708,900
02	Himachal Pradesh	6,077,900	3,087,940	2,989,960	2,992,461	1,686,658	1,305,803	3,085,439	1,401,282	1,684,157
03	Punjab	24,358,999	12,985,045	11,373,954	9,127,474	6,960,213	2,167,261	15,231,525	6,024,832	9,206,693
04	Chandigarh	900,635	506,938	393,697	340,422	284,419	56,003	560,213	222,519	337,694
05	Uttaranchal	8,489,349	4,325,924	4,163,425	3,134,036	1,996,177	1,137,859	5,355,313	2,329,747	3,025,566
06	Haryana	21,144,564	11,363,953	9,780,611	8,377,466	5,715,526	2,661,940	12,767,098	5,648,427	7,118,671
07	Delhi	13,850,507	7,607,234	6,243,273	4,545,234	3,960,101	585,133	9,305,273	3,647,133	5,658,140
08	Rajasthan	56,507,188	29,420,011	27,087,177	23,766,655	14,695,802	9,070,853	32,740,533	14,724,209	18,016,324
09	Uttar Pradesh	166,197,921	87,565,369	78,632,552	53,983,824	40,981,558	13,002,266	112,214,097	46,583,811	65,630,286
10	Bihar	82,998,509	43,243,795	39,754,714	27,974,606	20,483,003	7,491,603	55,023,903	22,760,792	32,263,111
11	Sikkim	540,851	288,484	252,367	263,043	165,716	97,327	277,808	122,768	155,040
12	Arunachal Pradesh	1,097,968	579,941	518,027	482,902	293,612	189,290	615,066	286,329	328,737
13	Nagaland	1,990,036	1,047,141	942,895	847,796	488,968	358,828	1,142,240	558,173	584,067
14	Manipur@	2,166,788	1,095,634	1,071,154	945,213	527,216	417,997	1,221,575	568,418	653,157
15	Mizoram	888,573	459,109	429,464	467,159	263,008	204,151	421,414	196,101	225,313
16	Tripura	3,199,203	1,642,225	1,556,978	1,159,561	831,346	328,215	2,039,642	810,879	1,228,763
17	Meghalaya	2,318,822	1,176,087	1,142,735	970,146	568,491	401,655	1,348,676	607,596	741,080
18	Assam	26,655,528	13,777,037	12,878,491	9,538,591	6,870,960	2,667,631	17,116,937	6,906,077	10,210,860
19	West Bengal	80,176,197	41,465,985	38,710,212	29,481,690	22,388,044	7,093,646	50,694,507	19,077,941	31,616,566

Contd...

1	2	3	4	5	6	7	8	9	10	11
20	Jharkhand	26,945,829	13,885,037	13,060,792	10,109,030	6,659,856	3,449,174	16,836,799	7,225,181	9,611,618
21	Orissa	36,804,660	18,660,570	18,144,090	14,276,488	9,802,006	4,474,482	22,528,172	8,858,564	13,669,608
22	Chhattisgarh	20,833,803	10,474,218	10,359,585	9,679,871	5,531,859	4,148,012	11,153,932	4,942,359	6,211,573
23	Madhya Pradesh	60,348,023	31,443,652	28,904,371	25,793,519	16,194,368	9,599,151	34,554,504	15,249,284	19,305,220
24	Gujarat	50,671,017	26,385,577	24,285,440	21,255,521	14,477,286	6,778,235	29,415,496	11,908,291	17,507,205
25	Daman & Diu	158,204	92,512	65,692	72,791	60,569	12,222	85,413	31,943	53,470
26	Dadra & Nagar Haveli	220,490	121,666	98,824	114,122	75,835	38,287	106,368	45,831	60,537
27	Maharashtra	96,878,627	50,400,596	46,478,031	41,173,351	26,852,095	14,321,256	55,705,276	23,548,501	32,156,775
28	Andhra Pradesh	76,210,007	38,527,413	37,682,594	34,893,859	21,662,192	13,231,667	41,316,148	16,865,221	24,450,927
29	Karnataka	52,850,562	26,898,918	25,951,644	23,534,791	15,235,355	8,299,436	29,315,771	11,663,563	17,652,208
30	Goa	1,347,668	687,248	660,420	522,855	375,218	147,637	824,813	312,030	512,783
31	Lakshadweep	60,650	31,131	29,519	15,354	13,204	2,150	45,296	17,927	27,369
32	Kerala	31,841,374	15,468,614	16,372,760	10,283,887	7,765,645	2,518,242	21,557,487	7,702,969	13,854,518
33	Tamil Nadu	62,405,679	31,400,909	31,004,770	27,878,282	18,100,397	9,777,885	34,527,397	13,300,512	21,226,885
34	Pondicherry	974,345	486,961	487,384	342,655	258,670	83,985	631,690	228,291	403,399
35	A & N Islands	356,152	192,972	163,180	136,254	109,162	27,092	219,898	83,810	136,088

Source: Primary Census Abstract: Census of India 2001.

Note: @ – Excludes Mao-Maram, Paomata and Purul sub-divisions of Senapati district of Manipur.

Table 4.7: Number of Total Workers, Main and Marginal Workers by Sex

State Code	India/State/UT	Total Workers			Main Workers			Marginal Workers		
		Persons	Males	Females	Persons	Males	Females	Persons	Males	Females
1	2	3	4	5	6	7	8	9	10	11
	India@	402,234,724	275,014,476	127,220,248	313,004,983	240,147,813	72,857,170	89,229,741	34,866,663	54,363,078
01	Jammu & Kashmir	3,753,815	2,679,941	1,073,874	2,608,668	2,226,958	381,710	1,145,147	452,983	692,164
02	Himachal Pradesh	2,992,461	1,686,658	1,305,803	1,963,882	1,333,361	630,521	1,028,579	353,297	675,282
03	Punjab	9,127,474	6,960,213	2,167,261	7,835,732	6,426,028	1,409,704	1,291,742	534,185	757,557
04	Chandigarh	340,422	284,419	56,003	328,989	277,050	51,939	11,433	7,369	4,064
05	Uttaranchal	3,134,036	1,996,177	1,137,859	2,322,347	1,639,242	683,105	811,689	356,935	454,754
06	Haryana	8,377,466	5,715,526	2,661,940	6,241,324	4,933,004	1,308,320	2,136,142	782,522	1,353,620
07	Delhi	4,545,234	3,960,101	585,133	4,317,516	3,794,345	523,171	227,718	165,756	61,962
08	Rajasthan	23,766,655	14,695,802	9,070,853	17,436,888	12,841,318	4,595,570	6,329,767	1,854,484	4,475,283
09	Uttar Pradesh	53,983,824	40,981,558	13,002,266	39,337,649	34,338,260	4,999,389	14,646,175	6,643,298	8,002,877
10	Bihar	27,974,606	20,483,003	7,491,603	21,052,875	17,511,018	3,541,857	6,921,731	2,971,985	3,949,746
11	Sikkim	263,043	165,716	97,327	212,904	146,541	66,363	50,139	19,175	30,964
12	Arunachal Pradesh	482,902	293,612	189,290	415,007	267,384	147,623	67,895	26,228	41,667
13	Nagaland	847,796	488,968	358,828	703,977	424,811	279,166	143,819	64,157	79,662
14	Manipur@	945,213	527,216	417,997	659,364	430,227	229,137	285,849	96,989	188,860
15	Mizoram	467,159	263,008	204,151	362,450	225,428	137,022	104,709	37,580	67,129
16	Tripura	1,159,561	831,346	328,215	912,292	742,054	170,238	247,269	89,292	157,977
17	Meghalaya	970,146	568,491	401,655	757,011	485,694	271,317	213,135	82,797	130,338
18	Assam	9,538,591	6,870,960	2,667,631	7,114,097	5,849,032	1,265,065	2,424,494	1,021,928	1,402,566
19	West Bengal	29,481,690	22,388,044	7,093,646	23,023,583	19,494,971	3,528,612	6,458,107	2,893,073	3,565,034

Contd...

1	2	3	4	5	6	7	8	9	10	11
20	Jharkhand	10,109,030	6,659,856	3,449,174	6,446,782	5,134,067	1,312,715	3,662,248	1,525,789	2,136,459
21	Orissa	14,276,488	9,802,006	4,474,482	9,589,269	8,004,740	1,584,529	4,687,219	1,797,266	2,889,953
22	Chhattisgarh	9,679,871	5,531,859	4,148,012	7,054,595	4,742,935	2,311,660	2,625,276	788,924	1,836,352
23	Madhya Pradesh	25,793,519	16,194,368	9,599,151	19,102,572	14,056,279	5,046,293	6,690,947	2,138,089	4,552,858
24	Gujarat	21,255,521	14,477,286	6,778,235	17,025,074	13,480,566	3,544,508	4,230,447	996,720	3,233,727
25	Daman & Diu	72,791	60,569	12,222	67,522	58,874	8,648	5,269	1,695	3,574
26	Dadra & Nagar Haveli	114,122	75,835	38,287	96,184	71,156	25,028	17,938	4,679	13,259
27	Maharashtra	41,173,351	26,852,095	14,321,256	34,748,053	24,416,295	10,331,758	6,425,298	2,435,800	3,989,498
28	Andhra Pradesh	34,893,859	21,662,192	13,231,667	29,040,873	19,455,492	9,585,381	5,852,986	2,206,700	3,646,286
29	Karnataka	23,534,791	15,235,355	8,299,436	19,364,759	13,896,845	5,467,914	4,170,032	1,338,510	2,831,522
30	Goa	522,855	375,218	147,637	425,305	326,993	98,312	97,550	48,225	49,325
31	Lakshadweep	15,354	13,204	2,150	11,710	10,288	1,422	3,644	2,916	728
32	Kerala	10,283,887	7,765,645	2,518,242	8,236,973	6,460,693	1,776,280	2,046,914	1,304,952	741,962
33	Tamil Nadu	27,878,282	18,100,397	9,777,885	23,757,783	16,303,310	7,454,473	4,120,499	1,797,087	2,323,412
34	Pondicherry	342,655	258,670	83,985	317,367	245,205	72,162	25,288	13,465	11,823
35	A & N Islands	136,254	109,162	27,092	113,607	97,349	16,258	22,647	11,813	10,834

Source: Primary Census Abstract: Census of India 2001.

Note: @ – Excludes Mao-Maram, Paomata and Purul sub-divisions of Senapati district of Manipur.

Table 4.8: Distribution of Workers by Category of Workers
(*e.g.*, Cultivators, Agricultural Labourers, Household Industry Workers and Other Workers by Sex)

StateIndia/State/UT Code				Cultivators		Agricultural Labourers		Household Industry Workers		Other Workers	
			Total Workers	Number	%	Number	%	Number	%	Number	%
1	2	3	4	5	6	7	8	9	10	11	12
00	India@										
		Persons	402,234,724	127,312,851	31.7	106,775,330	26.5	16,956,942	4.2	151,189,601	37.6
		Males	275,014,476	85,416,498	31.1	57,329,100	20.8	8,744,183	3.2	123,524,695	44.9
		Females	127,220,248	41,896,353	32.9	49,446,230	38.9	8,212,759	6.5	27,664,906	21.7
01	Jammu & Kashmir										
		Persons	3,753,815	1,591,514	42.4	246,421	6.6	234,472	6.2	1,681,408	44.8
		Males	2,679,941	1,004,535	37.5	190,339	7.1	126,262	4.7	1,358,805	50.7
		Females	1,073,874	586,979	54.7	56,082	5.2	108,210	10.1	322,603	30.0
02	Himachal Pradesh										
		Persons	2,992,461	1,954,870	65.3	94,171	3.1	52,519	1.8	890,901	29.8
		Males	1,686,658	834,312	49.5	55,658	3.3	34,034	2.0	762,654	45.2
		Females	1,305,803	1,120,558	85.8	38,513	2.9	18,485	1.4	128,247	9.8
03	Punjab										
		Persons	9,127,474	2,065,067	22.6	1,489,861	16.3	333,770	3.7	5,238,776	57.4
		Males	6,960,213	1,762,869	25.3	1,104,140	15.9	178,798	2.6	3,914,406	56.2
		Females	2,167,261	302,198	13.9	385,721	17.8	154,972	7.2	1,324,370	61.1
04	Chandigarh										
		Persons	340,422	2,141	0.6	563	0.2	3,880	1.1	333,838	98.1
		Males	284,419	1,687	0.6	461	0.2	2,504	0.9	279,767	98.4
		Females	56,003	454	0.8	102	0.2	1,376	2.5	54,071	96.6
05	Uttaranchal										
		Persons	3,134,036	1,570,116	50.1	259,683	8.3	72,448	2.3	1,231,789	39.3
		Males	1,99-6,177	684,422	34.3	190,494	9.5	43,744	2.2	1,077,517	54.0
		Females	1,137,859	885,694	77.8	69,189	6.1	28,704	2.5	154,272	13.6

Contd...

1	2	3	4	5	6	7	8	9	10	11	12
06	Haryana										
		Persons	8,377,466	3,018,014	36.0	1,278,821	15.3	214,755	2.6	3,865,876	46.1
		Males	5,715,526	1,855,547	32.5	717,133	12.5	132,069	2.3	3,010,777	52.7
		Females	2,661,940	1,162,467	43.7	561,688	21.1	82,686	3.1	855,099	32.1
07	Delhi										
		Persons	4,545,234	37,431	0.8	15,773	0.3	140,032	3.1	4,351,998	95.7
		Males	3,960,101	26,840	0.7	11,224	0.3	112,522	2.8	3,809,515	96.2
		Females	585,133	10,591	1.8	4,549	0.8	27,510	4.7	542,483	92.7
08	Rajasthan										
		Persons	23,766,655	13,140,066	55.3	2,523,719	10.6	677,991	2.9	7,424,879	31.2
		Males	14,695,802	7,062,726	48.1	1,055,332	7.2	419,528	2.9	6,158,216	41.9
		Females	9,070,853	6,077,340	67.0	1,468,387	16.2	258,463	2.8	1,266,663	14.0
09	Uttar Pradesh										
		Persons	53,983,824	22,167,562	41.1	13,400,911	24.8	3,031,164	5.6	15,384,187	28.5
		Males	40,981,558	17,479,887	42.7	8,245,599	20.1	1,946,545	4.7	13,309,527	32.5
		Females	13,002,266	4,687,675	36.1	5,155,312	39.6	1,084,619	8.3	2,074,660	16.0
10	Bihar										
		Persons	27,974,606	8,193,621	29.3	13,417,744	48.0	1,100,424	3.9	5,262,817	18.8
		Males	20,483,003	6,457,265	31.5	8,730,251	42.6	656,662	3.2	4,638,825	22.6
		Females	7,491,603	1,736,356	23.2	4,687,493	62.6	443,762	5.9	623,992	8.3
11	Sikkim										
		Persons	263,043	131,258	49.9	17,000	6.5	4,219	1.6	110,566	42.0
		Males	165,716	70,107	42.3	8,762	5.3	2,849	1.7	83,998	50.7
		Females	97,327	61,151	62.8	8,238	8.5	1,370	1.4	26,568	27.3
12	Arunachal Pradesh										
		Persons	482,902	279,300	57.8	18,840	3.9	6,043	1.3	178,719	37.0
		Males	293,612	136,336	46.4	10,329	3.5	3,177	1.1	143,770	49.0
		Females	189,290	142,964	75.5	8,511	4.5	2,866	1.5	34,949	18.5

Contd...

1	2	3	4	5	6	7	8	9	10	11	12
13	Nagaland										
		Persons	847,796	548,845	64.7	30,907	3.6	21,873	2.6	246,171	29.0
		Males	488,968	270,927	55.4	15,985	3.3	9,193	1.9	192,863	39.4
		Females	358,828	277,918	77.5	14,922	4.2	12,680	3.5	53,308	14.9
14	Manipur@										
		Persons	945,213	379,705	40.2	113,630	12.0	96,920	10.3	354,958	37.6
		Males	527,216	214,282	40.6	49,928	9.5	20,547	3.9	242,459	46.0
		Females	417,997	165,423	39.6	63,702	15.2	76,373	18.3	112,499	26.9
15	Mizoram										
		Persons	467,159	256,332	54.9	26,783	5.7	7,100	1.5	176,944	37.9
		Males	263,008	130,497	49.6	12,775	4.9	3,476	1.3	116,260	44.2
		Females	204,151	125,835	61.6	14,008	6.9	3,624	1.8	60,684	29.7
16	Tripura										
		Persons	1,159,561	313,300	27.0	276,132	23.8	35,292	3.0	534,837	46.1
		Males	831,346	220,962	26.6	162,640	19.6	14,830	1.8	432,914	52.1
		Females	328,215	92,338	28.1	113,492	34.6	20,462	6.2	101,923	31.1
17	Meghalaya										
		Persons	970,146	467,010	48.1	171,694	17.7	21,225	2.2	310,217	32.0
		Males	568,491	255,018	44.9	90,888	16.0	9,358	1.6	213,227	37.5
		Females	401,655	211,992	52.8	80,806	20.1	11,867	3.0	96,990	24.1
18	Assam										
		Persons	9,538,591	3,730,773	39.1	1,263,532	13.2	344,912	3.6	4,199,374	44.0
		Males	6,870,960	2,634,068	38.3	832,508	12.1	133,902	1.9	3,270,482	47.6
		Females	2,667,631	1,096,705	41.1	431,024	16.2	211,010	7.9	928,892	34.8
19	West Bengal										
		Persons	29,481,690	5,653,922	19.2	7,362,957	25.0	2,172,070	7.4	14,292,741	48.5
		Males	22,388,044	4,655,210	20.8	5,080,236	22.7	917,180	4.1	11,735,418	52.4
		Females	7,093,646	998,712	14.1	2,282,721	32.2	1,254,890	17.7	2,557,323	36.1
20	Jharkhand										
		Persons	10,109,030	3,889,506	38.5	2,851,297	28.2	430,965	4.3	2,937,262	29.1
		Males	6,659,856	2,405,371	36.1	1,485,322	22.3	237,466	3.6	2,531,697	38.0
		Females	3,449,174	1,484,135	43.0	1,365,975	39.6	193,499	5.6	405,565	11.8

Contd...

1	2	3	4	5	6	7	8	9	10	11	12
21	Orissa										
		Persons	14,276,488	4,247,661	29.8	4,999,104	35.0	701,563	4.9	4,328,160	30.3
		Males	9,802,006	3,347,691	34.2	2,587,196	26.4	320,011	3.3	3,547,108	36.2
		Females	4,474,482	899,970	20.1	2,411,908	53.9	381,552	8.5	781,052	17.5
22	Chhattisgarh										
		Persons	9,679,871	4,311,131	44.5	3,091,358	31.9	198,691	2.1	2,078,691	21.5
		Males	5,531,859	2,466,477	44.6	1,262,559	22.8	115,860	2.1	1,686,963	30.5
		Females	4,148,012	1,844,654	44.5	1,828,799	44.1	82,831	2.0	391,728	9.4
23	Madhya Pradesh										
		Persons	25,793,519	11,037,906	42.8	7,400,670	28.7	1,033,313	4.0	6,321,630	24.5
		Males	16,194,368	6,882,776	42.5	3,518,368	21.7	519,127	3.2	5,274,097	32.6
		Females	9,599,151	4,155,130	43.3	3,882,302	40.4	514,186	5.4	1,047,533	10.9
24	Gujarat										
		Persons	21,255,521	5,802,681	27.3	5,161,658	24.3	429,682	2.0	9,861,500	46.4
		Males	14,477,286	3,906,697	27.0	2,509,651	17.3	243,835	1.7	7,817,103	54.0
		Females	6,778,235	1,895,984	28.0	2,652,007	39.1	185,847	2.7	2,044,397	30.2
25	Daman & Diu										
		Persons	72,791	4,034	5.5	1,323	1.8	1,180	1.6	66,254	91.0
		Males	60,569	2,008	3.3	347	0.6	381	0.6	57,833	95.5
		Females	12,222	2,026	16.6	976	8.0	799	6.5	8,421	68.9
26	D & N Haveli										
		Persons	114,122	39,470	34.6	14,715	12.9	850	0.7	59,087	51.8
		Males	75,835	18,072	23.8	5,429	7.2	492	0.6	51,842	68.4
		Females	38,287	21,398	55.9	9,286	24.3	358	0.9	7,245	18.9
27	Maharashtra										
		Persons	41,173,351	11,813,275	28.7	10,815,262	26.3	1,089,318	2.6	17,455,496	42.4
		Males	26,852,095	6,680,696	24.9	4,924,034	18.3	566,861	2.1	14,680,504	54.7
		Females	14,321,256	5,132,579	35.8	5,891,228	41.1	522,457	3.6	2,774,992	19.4

Contd...

1	2	3	4	5	6	7	8	9	10	11	12
28	Andhra Pradesh										
		Persons	34,893,859	7,859,534	22.5	13,832,152	39.6	1,642,105	4.7	11,560,068	33.1
		Males	21,662,192	5,201,564	24.0	6,453,741	29.8	710,222	3.3	9,296,665	42.9
		Females	13,231,667	2,657,970	20.1	7,378,411	55.8	931,883	7.0	2,263,403	17.1
29	Karnataka										
		Persons	23,534,791	6,883,856	29.2	6,226,942	26.5	959,665	4.1	9,464,328	40.2
		Males	15,235,355	4,832,840	31.7	2,620,927	17.2	405,091	2.7	7,376,497	48.4
		Females	8,299,436	2,051,016	24.7	3,606,015	43.4	554,574	6.7	2,087,831	25.2
30	Goa										
		Persons	522,855	50,395	9.6	35,806	6.8	14,746	2.8	421,908	80.7
		Males	375,218	25,708	6.9	15,970	4.3	8,991	2.4	324,549	86.5
		Females	147,637	24,687	16.7	19,836	13.4	5,755	3.9	97,359	65.9
31	Lakshadweep										
		Persons	15,354	0	0.0	0	0.0	902	5.9	14,452	94.1
		Males	13,204	0	0.0	0	0.0	537	4.1	12,667	95.9
		Females	2,150	0	0.0	0	0.0	365	17.0	1,785	83.0
32	Kerala										
		Persons	10,283,887	724,155	7.0	1,620,851	15.8	369,667	3.6	7,569,214	73.6
		Males	7,765,645	602,038	7.8	1,078,354	13.9	191,637	2.5	5,893,616	75.9
		Females	2,518,242	122,117	4.8	542,497	21.5	178,030	7.1	1,675,598	66.5
33	Tamil Nadu										
		Persons	27,878,282	5,116,039	18.4	8,637,630	31.0	1,499,761	5.4	12,624,852	45.3
		Males	18,100,397	3,262,489	18.0	4,256,360	23.5	648,589	3.6	9,932,959	54.9
		Females	9,777,885	1,853,550	19.0	4,381,270	44.8	851,172	8.7	2,691,893	27.5
34	Pondicherry										
		Persons	342,655	10,900	3.2	72,251	21.1	6,339	1.8	253,165	73.9
		Males	258,670	9,637	3.7	42,117	16.3	3,248	1.3	203,668	78.7
		Females	83,985	1,263	1.5	30,134	35.9	3,091	3.7	49,497	58.9
35	A & N Islands										
		Persons	136,254	21,461	15.8	5,169	3.8	7,086	5.2	102,538	75.3
		Males	109,162	14,937	13.7	4,043	3.7	4,655	4.3	85,527	78.3
		Females	27,092	6,524	24.1	1,126	4.2	2,431	9.0	17,011	62.8

Note: @ – Excludes Mao-Maram, Paomata and Purul sub-divisions of Senapati district of Manipur.

Table 4.9: Number of Households, Population and Household Size

State Code	India/State/UT	Number of households	Population	Household size
	India@	19,35,79,954	1,02,86,10,328	5.3
01	J & K	15,68,519	1,01,43,700	6.5
02	Himachal Pradesh	12,21,589	60,77,900	5.0
03	Punjab	43,48,580	2,43,58,999	5.6
04	Chandigarh	2,06,465	9,00,635	4.4
05	Uttaranchal	16,03,242	84,89,349	5.3
06	Haryana	37,12,319	2,11,44,564	5.7
07	Delhi	27,33,383	1,38,50,507	5.1
08	Rajasthan	93,17,675	5,65,07,188	6.1
09	Uttar Pradesh	2,57,57,640	16,61,97,921	6.5
10	Bihar	1,37,44,130	8,29,98,509	6.0
11	Sikkim	114,223	5,40,851	4.7
12	Arunachal Pradesh	215,574	10,97,968	5.1
13	Nagaland	328,057	19,90,036	6.1
14	Manipur@	375,095	21,66,788	5.8
15	Mizoram	176,134	8,88,573	5.0
16	Tripura	664,334	31,99,203	4.8
17	Meghalaya	418,850	23,18,822	5.5
18	Assam	4,914,823	2,66,55,528	5.4
19	West Bengal	15,872,083	8,01,76,197	5.1
20	Jharkhand	4,799,081	2,69,45,829	5.6
21	Orissa	7,738,065	3,68,04,660	4.8
22	Chhattisgarh	4,091,551	2,08,33,803	5.1
23	Madhya Pradesh	10,912,025	6,03,48,023	5.5
24	Gujarat	9,691,362	5,06,71,017	5.2
25	Daman & Diu	35,686	1,58,204	4.4
26	D & N Haveli	45,586	2,20,490	4.8
27	Maharashtra	19,576,736	9,68,78,627	4.9
28	Andhra Pradesh	17,004,305	7,62,10,007	4.5
29	Karnataka	1,04,01,918	5,28,50,562	5.1
30	Goa	2,94,812	13,47,668	4.6
31	Lakshadweep	9,993	60,650	6.1
32	Kerala	67,26,356	3,18,41,374	4.7
33	Tamil Nadu	1,46,65,983	6,24,05,679	4.3
34	Pondicherry	215,538	9,74,345	4.5
35	A & N Islands	78,242	3,56,152	4.6

Note: @ – Excludes Mao-Maram, Paomata and Purul sub-divisions of Senapati district of Manipur.

Table 4.10: Growth of Urbanisation by Class of Town

Class of Town		Population in '000s						
		1901	1951	1961	1971	1981	1991	2001
1		2	3	4	5	6	7	8
I	1,00,000 and above	6,652	27,812	40,518	61,863	95,952	1,40,067	1,76,722
II	50,000 – 99,999	3,011	6,109	8,659	12,108	18,195	23,629	34,098
III	20,000 – 49,999	3,994	9,745	13,154	17,103	21,584	28,688	41,957
IV	10,000 – 19,999	5,281	8,412	9,934	11,861	14,543	17,074	22,307
V	5,000 – 9,999	5,186	7,983	5,449	4,824	5,386	5,640	7,746
VI	Less than 5,000	1,572	1,925	629	496	760	663	772
	All classes	25,696	61,986	78,343	1,08,256	1,56,420	2,15,772	2,83,603
	Urban population as percentage to total population[1]	10.84	17.29	17.97	19.91	23.34	25.70	27.81

Notes:

Excludes figures for Jammu and Kashmir in 1991 where 1991 Census was not conducted owing to disturbances. For comparative purposes, the figures of Jammu and Kashmir have also been excluded for 1901 to 1981.

Excludes figures for Assam in 1981 where census of 1981 was not held.

1. Data include Jammu and Kashmir and Assam.

Table 4.11: Urban Agglomerations/Cities having Population of More than One Million in India

Rank in 2001	Urban Agglomeration/City (1,000,000+population)	Civic Status
1	2	3
1	Greater Mumbai	UA
2	Kolkata	UA
3	Delhi	UA
4	Chennai	UA
5	Bangalore	UA
6	Hyderabad	UA
7	Ahmedabad	UA
8	Pune	UA
9	Surat	UA
10	Kanpur	UA
11	Jaipur	M. Corp.
12	Lucknow	UA
13	Nagpur	UA
14	Patna	UA
15	Indore	UA
16	Vadodara	UA
17	Bhopal	UA
18	Coimbatore	UA
19	Ludhiana	M. Corp.
20	Kochi	UA
21	Visakhapatnam	UA
22	Agra	UA
23	Varanasi	UA
24	Madurai	UA
25	Meerut	UA
26	Nasik	UA
27	Jabalpur	UA
28	Jamshedpur	UA
29	Asansol	UA
30	Dhanbad	UA
31	Faridabad	M. Corp.
32	Allahabad	UA
33	Amritsar	UA
34	Vijayawada	UA
35	Rajkot	UA

Table 4.12: Population in Five Year Age-Group by Residence and Sex

State Code	Area Name	Age-group	Total			Rural			Urban		
			Persons	Males	Females	Persons	Males	Females	Persons	Males	Females
1	2	3	4	5	6	7	8	9	10	11	12
00	India	All Ages	1028610328	532156772	496453556	742490639	381602674	360887965	286119689	150554098	135565591
00	India	0-4	110447164	57119612	53327552	85108410	43857198	41251212	25338754	13262414	12076340
00	India	5-9	128316790	66734833	61581957	98456245	51094698	47361547	29860545	15640135	14220410
00	India	10-14	124846858	65632877	59213981	92382322	48602745	43779577	32464536	17030132	15434404
00	India	15-19	100215890	53939991	46275899	70061823	37748418	32313405	30154067	16191573	13962494
00	India	20-24	89764132	46321150	43442982	61398904	31127482	30271422	28365228	15193668	13171560
00	India	25-29	83422393	41557546	41864847	57685140	28377173	29307967	25737253	13180373	12556880
00	India	30-34	74274044	37361916	36912128	51828879	25688779	26140100	22445165	11673137	10772028
00	India	35-39	70574085	36038727	34535358	48958544	24881624	24076920	21615541	11157103	10458438
00	India	40-44	55738297	29878715	25859582	38565171	20420439	18144732	17173126	9458276	7714850
00	India	45-49	47408976	24867886	22541090	32955002	17023673	15931329	14453974	7844213	6609761
00	India	50-54	36587559	19851608	16735951	25777598	13812691	11964907	10809961	6038917	4771044
00	India	55-59	27653347	13583022	14070325	19971069	9572754	10398315	7682278	4010268	3672010
00	India	60-64	27516779	13586347	13930432	20651969	10146726	10505243	6864810	3439621	3425189
00	India	65-69	19806955	9472103	10334852	14816756	7070706	7746050	4990199	2401397	2588802
00	India	70-74	14708644	7527688	7180956	11129476	5746992	5382484	3579168	1780696	1798472
00	India	75-79	6551225	3263209	3288016	4830140	2412121	2418019	1721085	851088	869997
00	India	80+	8038718	3918980	4119738	6016373	2983060	3033313	2022345	935920	1086425
00	India	Age Not Stated	2738472	1500562	1237910	1896818	1035395	861423	841654	465167	376487
01	J & K	All Ages	10143700	5360926	4782774	7627062	3977652	3649410	2516638	1383274	1133364

Contd...

1	2	3	4	5	6	7	8	9	10	11	12
01	Jammu & Kashmir	0-4	963603	497184	466419	790696	404720	385976	172907	92464	80443
01	Jammu & Kashmir	5-9	1292763	664480	628283	1037354	528918	508436	255409	135562	119847
01	Jammu & Kashmir	10-14	1360659	702837	657822	1063123	546659	516464	297536	156178	141358
01	Jammu & Kashmir	15-19	1147081	592332	554749	866386	444691	421695	280695	147641	133054
01	Jammu & Kashmir	20-24	889969	476469	413500	644484	339507	304977	245485	136962	108523
01	Jammu & Kashmir	25-29	789383	422668	366715	560822	293086	267736	228561	129582	98979
01	Jammu & Kashmir	30-34	697138	378777	318361	488681	257102	231579	208457	121675	86782
01	Jammu & Kashmir	35-39	690105	362578	327527	487492	250371	237121	202613	112207	90406
01	Jammu & Kashmir	40-44	538689	302759	235930	382278	211718	170560	156411	91041	65370
01	Jammu & Kashmir	45-49	458315	245036	213279	325884	170239	155645	132431	74797	57634
01	Jammu & Kashmir	50-54	340304	199297	141007	246091	142146	103945	94213	57151	37062
01	Jammu & Kashmir	55-59	254652	125846	128806	183972	89397	94575	70680	36449	34231
01	Jammu & Kashmir	60-64	243842	137398	106444	184447	104371	80076	59395	33027	26368
01	Jammu & Kashmir	65-69	158118	78254	79864	117146	57981	59165	40972	20273	20699
01	Jammu & Kashmir	70-74	132824	75284	57540	103338	59130	44208	29486	16154	13332
01	Jammu & Kashmir	75-79	58497	30246	28251	44364	22977	21387	14133	7269	6864
01	Jammu & Kashmir	80+	82043	44645	37398	65967	36217	29750	16076	8428	7648
01	Jammu & Kashmir	Age Not Stated	45715	24836	20879	34537	18422	16115	11178	6414	4764
02	Himachal Pradesh	All Ages	6077900	3087940	2989960	5482319	2756073	2726246	595581	331867	263714
02	Himachal Pradesh	0-4	560187	296555	263632	517539	273478	244061	42648	23077	19571
02	Himachal Pradesh	5-9	619164	323058	296106	566404	294317	272087	52760	28741	24019
02	Himachal Pradesh	10-14	705039	361257	343782	644995	329113	315882	60044	32144	27900
02	Himachal Pradesh	15-19	626624	324318	302306	564788	289354	275434	61836	34964	26872
02	Himachal Pradesh	20-24	583029	295703	287326	515945	256218	259727	67084	39485	27599
02	Himachal Pradesh	25-29	517507	256532	260975	458593	224315	234278	58914	32217	26697

Contd...

1	2	3	4	5	6	7	8	9	10	11	12
02	Himachal Pradesh	30-34	432675	215401	217274	381339	187653	193686	51336	27748	23588
02	Himachal Pradesh	35-39	411062	199846	211216	362046	173247	188799	49016	26599	22417
02	Himachal Pradesh	40-44	330669	167405	163264	291109	144391	146718	39560	23014	16546
02	Himachal Pradesh	45-49	302882	151023	151859	270052	131634	138418	32830	19389	13441
02	Himachal Pradesh	50-54	238245	123075	115170	214098	108551	105547	24147	14524	9623
02	Himachal Pradesh	55-59	188537	94721	93816	171610	84952	86658	16927	9769	7158
02	Himachal Pradesh	60-64	174130	86950	87180	161344	80078	81266	12786	6872	5914
02	Himachal Pradesh	65-69	128906	61456	67450	119674	56746	62928	9232	4710	4522
02	Himachal Pradesh	70-74	106707	53486	53221	99721	49780	49941	6986	3706	3280
02	Himachal Pradesh	75-79	56865	29021	27844	53005	27014	25991	3860	2007	1853
02	Himachal Pradesh	80+	80956	39933	41023	76577	37801	38776	4379	2132	2247
02	Himachal Pradesh	Age Not Stated	14716	8200	6516	13480	7431	6049	1236	769	467
03	Punjab	All Ages	24358999	12985045	11373954	16096488	8516596	7579892	8262511	4468449	3794062
03	Punjab	0-4	2128738	1186499	942239	1461660	815187	646473	667078	371312	295766
03	Punjab	5-9	2657368	1458964	1198404	1821911	996513	825398	835457	462451	373006
03	Punjab	10-14	2831770	1522899	1308871	1898684	1014361	884323	933086	508538	424548
03	Punjab	15-19	2555933	1393473	1162460	1662364	898343	764021	893569	495130	398439
03	Punjab	20-24	2339151	1255974	1083177	1497720	794494	703226	841431	461480	379951
03	Punjab	25-29	1945622	1012264	933358	1238921	634986	603935	706701	377278	329423
03	Punjab	30-34	1769154	889759	879395	1142457	564590	577867	626697	325169	301528
03	Punjab	35-39	1725411	892126	833285	1098916	565165	533751	626495	326961	299534
03	Punjab	40-44	1433430	765875	667555	901532	476675	424857	531898	289200	242698
03	Punjab	45-49	1174037	628232	545805	742539	391400	351139	431498	236832	194666
03	Punjab	50-54	895611	503353	392258	582366	324899	257467	313245	178454	134791
03	Punjab	55-59	617179	311595	305584	408416	202529	205887	208763	109066	99697

Contd...

1	2	3	4	5	6	7	8	9	10	11	12
03	Punjab	60-64	669648	323616	346032	470852	226333	244519	198796	97283	101513
03	Punjab	65-69	585810	286101	299709	417243	204653	212590	168567	81448	87119
03	Punjab	70-74	438386	243010	195376	320637	180046	140591	117749	62964	54785
03	Punjab	75-79	199895	103950	95945	145213	75299	69914	54682	28651	26031
03	Punjab	80+	297954	155014	142940	227014	119199	107815	70940	35815	35125
03	Punjab	Age Not Stated	93902	52341	41561	58043	31924	26119	35859	20417	15442
04	Chandigarh	All Ages	900635	506938	393697	92120	56816	35304	808515	450122	358393
04	Chandigarh	0-4	79225	42917	36308	10121	5462	4659	69104	37455	31649
04	Chandigarh	5-9	90190	48915	41275	10091	5442	4649	80099	43473	36626
04	Chandigarh	10-14	91773	49928	41845	8604	4822	3782	83169	45106	38063
04	Chandigarh	15-19	93276	55014	38262	9197	6344	2853	84079	48670	35409
04	Chandigarh	20-24	103533	60442	43091	12799	8508	4291	90734	51934	38800
04	Chandigarh	25-29	93095	52897	40198	12246	7807	4439	80849	45090	35759
04	Chandigarh	30-34	74786	42125	32661	8842	5714	3128	65944	36411	29533
04	Chandigarh	35-39	69529	38557	30972	6762	4328	2434	62767	34229	28538
04	Chandigarh	40-44	55340	31339	24001	4168	2784	1384	51172	28555	22617
04	Chandigarh	45-49	47079	26644	20435	3022	1889	1133	44057	24755	19302
04	Chandigarh	50-54	34370	20475	13895	1957	1223	734	32413	19252	13161
04	Chandigarh	55-59	22227	13201	9026	1259	742	517	20968	12459	8509
04	Chandigarh	60-64	15542	8459	7083	1078	623	455	14464	7836	6628
04	Chandigarh	65-69	11226	5671	5555	706	377	329	10520	5294	5226
04	Chandigarh	70-74	8277	4440	3837	558	327	231	7719	4113	3606
04	Chandigarh	75-79	4659	2507	2152	299	181	118	4360	2326	2034
04	Chandigarh	80+	5208	2667	2541	336	201	135	4872	2466	2406
04	Chandigarh	Age Not Stated	1300	740	560	75	42	33	1225	698	527

1	2	3	4	5	6	7	8	9	10	11	12
05	Uttaranchal	All Ages	8489349	4325924	4163425	6310275	3144590	3165685	2179074	1181334	997740
05	Uttaranchal	0-4	922085	483708	438377	730431	381305	349126	191654	102403	89251
05	Uttaranchal	5-9	1071361	557449	513912	831269	429299	401970	240092	128150	111942
05	Uttaranchal	10-14	1093530	566264	527266	826489	423759	402730	267041	142505	124536
05	Uttaranchal	15-19	929859	485918	443941	686132	350316	335816	243727	135602	108125
05	Uttaranchal	20-24	742540	371700	370840	522608	247495	275113	219932	124205	95727
05	Uttaranchal	25-29	625834	302807	323027	443299	206465	236834	182535	96342	86193
05	Uttaranchal	30-34	547173	267320	279853	385222	182515	202707	161951	84805	77146
05	Uttaranchal	35-39	527314	260250	267064	367681	175724	191957	159633	84526	75107
05	Uttaranchal	40-44	434970	224267	210703	305258	151385	153873	129712	72882	56830
05	Uttaranchal	45-49	375690	189277	186413	268322	129914	138408	107368	59363	48005
05	Uttaranchal	50-54	309198	162143	147055	227896	115147	112749	81302	46996	34306
05	Uttaranchal	55-59	237669	118279	119390	180380	86241	94139	57289	32038	25251
05	Uttaranchal	60-64	229519	113902	115617	183500	89136	94364	46019	24766	21253
05	Uttaranchal	65-69	166863	80695	86168	133057	63774	69283	33806	16921	16885
05	Uttaranchal	70-74	127320	65530	61790	102626	52667	49959	24694	12863	11831
05	Uttaranchal	75-79	60470	31216	29254	48500	25070	23430	11970	6146	5824
05	Uttaranchal	80+	70184	35372	34812	55374	27902	27472	14810	7470	7340
05	Uttaranchal	Age Not Stated	17770	9827	7943	12231	6476	5755	5539	3351	2188
06	Haryana	All Ages	21144564	11363953	9780611	15029260	8052988	6976272	6115304	3310965	2804339
06	Haryana	0-4	2273739	1251155	1022584	1695476	930854	764622	578263	320301	257962
06	Haryana	5-9	2622965	1429636	1193329	1935409	1050913	884496	687556	378723	308833
06	Haryana	10-14	2683276	1436447	1246829	1955460	1042131	913329	727816	394316	333500
06	Haryana	15-19	2256559	1271643	984916	1596808	903241	693567	659751	368402	291349
06	Haryana	20-24	1957303	1075114	882189	1359024	746568	612456	598279	328546	269733

Contd...

1	2	3	4	5	6	7	8	9	10	11	12
06	Haryana	25-29	1733146	911893	821253	1203142	632007	571135	530004	279886	250118
06	Haryana	30-34	1511037	771117	739920	1044343	529149	515194	466694	241968	224726
06	Haryana	35-39	1401762	730882	670880	947267	494058	453209	454495	236824	217671
06	Haryana	40-44	1107196	600693	506503	736335	395603	340732	370861	205090	165771
06	Haryana	45-49	864937	469917	395020	575558	307604	267954	289379	162313	127066
06	Haryana	50-54	631108	351341	279767	429554	235531	194023	201554	115810	85744
06	Haryana	55-59	436948	223135	213813	301459	151400	150059	135489	71735	63754
06	Haryana	60-64	489742	229532	260210	362364	167243	195121	127378	62289	65089
06	Haryana	65-69	440663	214964	225699	333094	163329	169765	107569	51635	55934
06	Haryana	70-74	321755	173911	147844	244178	133938	110240	77577	39973	37604
06	Haryana	75-79	148044	79391	68653	111360	60432	50928	36684	18959	17725
06	Haryana	80+	183885	97585	86300	140819	76508	64311	43066	21077	21989
06	Haryana	Age Not Stated	80499	45597	34902	57610	32479	25131	22889	13118	9771
07	Delhi	All Ages	13850507	7607234	6243273	944727	522087	422640	12905780	7085147	5820633
07	Delhi	0-4	1377861	736982	640879	108382	58456	49926	1269479	678526	590953
07	Delhi	5-9	1552279	829349	722930	120261	64804	55457	1432018	764545	667473
07	Delhi	10-14	1562799	836370	726429	115059	62096	52963	1447740	774274	673466
07	Delhi	15-19	1427979	816497	611482	96102	56303	39799	1331877	760194	571683
07	Delhi	20-24	1426860	814606	612254	93853	53766	40087	1333007	760840	572167
07	Delhi	25-29	1358925	744718	614207	91742	49156	42586	1267183	695562	571621
07	Delhi	30-34	1154976	631361	523615	79518	43438	36080	1075458	587923	487535
07	Delhi	35-39	1056030	579176	476854	68772	39007	29765	987258	540169	447089
07	Delhi	40-44	809408	463374	346034	48821	28409	20412	760587	434965	325622
07	Delhi	45-49	623059	350852	272207	35546	20297	15249	587513	330555	256958
07	Delhi	50-54	448834	257327	191507	24882	14397	10485	423952	242930	181022

Contd...

1	2	3	4	5	6	7	8	9	10	11	12
07	Delhi	55-59	310671	167430	143241	17447	9128	8319	293224	158302	134922
07	Delhi	60-64	258619	131032	127587	15551	7760	7791	243068	123272	119796
07	Delhi	65-69	192294	95854	96440	10784	5477	5307	181510	90377	91133
07	Delhi	70-74	132818	69553	63265	7952	4268	3684	124866	65285	59581
07	Delhi	75-79	65097	34548	30549	3641	1934	1707	61456	32614	28842
07	Delhi	80+	70822	35479	35343	4860	2500	2360	65962	32979	32983
07	Delhi	Age Not Stated	21176	12726	8450	1554	891	663	19622	11835	7787
08	Rajasthan	All Ages	56507188	29420011	27087177	43292813	22426640	20866173	13214375	6993371	6221004
08	Rajasthan	0-4	7233220	3781055	3452165	5832760	3040843	2791917	1400460	740212	660248
08	Rajasthan	5-9	8068070	4242507	3825563	6447827	3383282	3064545	1620243	859225	761018
08	Rajasthan	10-14	7241941	3847418	3394523	5609037	2980214	2628823	1632904	867204	765700
08	Rajasthan	15-19	5490214	2987604	2502610	4059578	2209368	1850210	1430636	778236	652400
08	Rajasthan	20-24	4749366	2470943	2278423	3471786	1778042	1693744	1277580	692901	584679
08	Rajasthan	25-29	4197223	2127889	2069334	3109331	1565375	1543956	1087892	562514	525378
08	Rajasthan	30-34	3821151	1917187	1903964	2852705	1418537	1434168	968446	498650	469796
08	Rajasthan	35-39	3453860	1788941	1664919	2547310	1317474	1229836	906550	471467	435083
08	Rajasthan	40-44	2760275	1476036	1284239	2032679	1076044	956635	727596	399992	327604
08	Rajasthan	45-49	2269651	1183740	1085911	1684446	867014	817432	585205	316726	268479
08	Rajasthan	50-54	1775046	974037	801009	1347261	731953	615308	427785	242084	185701
08	Rajasthan	55-59	1349315	646505	702810	1044977	492815	552162	304338	153690	150648
08	Rajasthan	60-64	1361274	676223	685051	1088341	540598	547743	272933	135625	137308
08	Rajasthan	65-69	982874	457287	525587	774869	358943	415926	208005	98344	109661
08	Rajasthan	70-74	757998	376076	381922	606919	301385	305534	151079	74691	76388
08	Rajasthan	75-79	315930	145849	170081	246599	112754	133845	69331	33095	36236

Contd...

1	2	3	4	5	6	7	8	9	10	11	12
08	Rajasthan	80+	392196	173490	218706	307834	136774	171060	84362	36716	47646
08	Rajasthan	Age Not Stated	287584	147224	140360	228554	115225	113329	59030	31999	27031
09	Uttar Pradesh	All Ages	166197921	87565369	78632552	131658339	69157470	62500869	34539582	18407899	16131683
09	Uttar Pradesh	0-4	20721672	10741471	9980201	17211773	8888667	8323106	3509899	1852804	1657095
09	Uttar Pradesh	5-9	24891226	13144490	11746736	20481968	10808886	9673082	4409258	2335604	2073654
09	Uttar Pradesh	10-14	22310434	11986055	10324379	17623247	9495598	8127649	4687187	2490457	2196730
09	Uttar Pradesh	15-19	16044841	8976423	7068418	12099227	6816726	5282501	3945614	2159697	1785917
09	Uttar Pradesh	20-24	13311974	6974638	6337336	10086238	5184733	4901505	3225736	1789905	1435831
09	Uttar Pradesh	25-29	11792446	5981334	5811112	9188763	4620833	4567930	2603683	1360501	1243182
09	Uttar Pradesh	30-34	10814273	5339396	5474877	8473730	4156074	4317656	2340543	1183322	1157221
09	Uttar Pradesh	35-39	9808560	5076548	4732012	7532499	3910217	3622282	2276061	1166331	1109730
09	Uttar Pradesh	40-44	8047432	4314100	3733332	6158819	3278319	2880500	1888613	1035781	852832
09	Uttar Pradesh	45-49	6639015	3452212	3186803	5098698	2618290	2480408	1540317	833922	706395
09	Uttar Pradesh	50-54	5334446	3013249	2321197	4206702	2363463	1843239	1127744	649786	477958
09	Uttar Pradesh	55-59	4095223	1982803	2112420	3281105	1564083	1717022	814118	418720	395398
09	Uttar Pradesh	60-64	4292319	2263835	2028484	3551153	1877716	1673437	741166	386119	355047
09	Uttar Pradesh	65-69	2906703	1467691	1439012	2390773	1209866	1180907	515930	257825	258105
09	Uttar Pradesh	70-74	2239888	1252699	987189	1861343	1051165	810178	378545	201534	177011
09	Uttar Pradesh	75-79	943157	498182	444975	773747	409902	363845	169410	88280	81130
09	Uttar Pradesh	80+	1267401	692487	574914	1047509	578936	468573	219892	113551	106341
09	Uttar Pradesh	Age Not Stated	736911	407756	329155	591045	323996	267049	145866	83760	62106
10	Bihar	All Ages	82998509	43243795	39754714	74316709	38594996	35721713	8681800	4648799	4033001
10	Bihar	0-4	11006072	5623280	5382792	10083847	5146939	4936908	922225	476341	445884
10	Bihar	5-9	12804302	6705263	6099039	11662465	6105814	5556651	1141837	599449	542388
10	Bihar	10-14	11063777	5970201	5093576	9879727	5336752	4542975	1184050	633449	550601
10	Bihar	15-19	7190188	4028643	3161545	6263105	3508252	2754853	927083	520391	406692

Contd...

1	2	3	4	5	6	7	8	9	10	11	12
10	Bihar	20-24	6323193	3180063	3143130	5560017	2753122	2806895	763176	426941	336235
10	Bihar	25-29	5908308	2894706	3013602	5255133	2551836	2703297	653175	342870	310305
10	Bihar	30-34	5549787	2713871	2835916	4960310	2411088	2549222	589477	302783	286694
10	Bihar	35-39	5077935	2576089	2501846	4512838	2285108	2227730	565097	290981	274116
10	Bihar	40-44	4153203	2213770	1939433	3685237	1956198	1729039	467966	257572	210394
10	Bihar	45-49	3461664	1778368	1683296	3063371	1562074	1501297	398293	216294	181999
10	Bihar	50-54	2711041	1543620	1167421	2412224	1368429	1043795	298817	175191	123626
10	Bihar	55-59	2069940	990011	1079929	1849794	874482	975312	220146	115529	104617
10	Bihar	60-64	2103909	1120743	983166	1904233	1015297	888936	199676	105446	94230
10	Bihar	65-69	1354937	683656	671281	1218312	613260	605052	136625	70396	66229
10	Bihar	70-74	1029921	571438	458483	930722	517763	412959	99199	53675	45524
10	Bihar	75-79	446860	233961	212899	403029	211000	192029	43831	22961	20870
10	Bihar	80+	565647	312207	253440	509628	282999	226629	56019	29208	26811
10	Bihar	Age Not Stated	177825	103905	73920	162717	94583	68134	15108	9322	5786
11	Sikkim	All Ages	540851	288484	252367	480981	255774	225207	59870	32710	27160
11	Sikkim	0-4	52269	26789	25480	48083	24593	23490	4186	2196	1990
11	Sikkim	5-9	64970	32655	32315	59576	29890	29686	5394	2765	2629
11	Sikkim	10-14	71668	36516	35152	64562	32933	31629	7106	3583	3523
11	Sikkim	15-19	63444	32639	30805	55792	28607	27185	7652	4032	3620
11	Sikkim	20-24	55171	29567	25604	48077	25574	22503	7094	3993	3101
11	Sikkim	25-29	47552	24964	22588	41121	21539	19582	6431	3425	3006
11	Sikkim	30-34	39153	21650	17503	33960	18809	15151	5193	2841	2352
11	Sikkim	35-39	36384	20383	16001	31446	17620	13826	4938	2763	2175
11	Sikkim	40-44	28129	16214	11915	24523	14050	10473	3606	2164	1442
11	Sikkim	45-49	22177	12832	9345	19282	11037	8245	2895	1795	1100

Contd...

1	2	3	4	5	6	7	8	9	10	11	12
11	Sikkim	50-54	16919	9771	7148	15141	8659	6482	1778	1112	666
11	Sikkim	55-59	12037	7071	4966	10852	6344	4508	1185	727	458
11	Sikkim	60-64	10469	5812	4657	9585	5317	4268	884	495	389
11	Sikkim	65-69	7593	4250	3343	7000	3939	3061	593	311	282
11	Sikkim	70-74	5523	3233	2290	5119	3015	2104	404	218	186
11	Sikkim	75-79	2749	1552	1197	2509	1429	1080	240	123	117
11	Sikkim	80+	2706	1544	1162	2486	1417	1069	220	127	93
11	Sikkim	Age Not Stated	1938	1042	896	1867	1002	865	71	40	31
12	Arunachal Pradesh	All Ages	1097968	579941	518027	870087	454680	415407	227881	125261	102620
12	Arunachal Pradesh	0-4	137843	69791	68052	113140	57403	55737	24703	12388	12315
12	Arunachal Pradesh	5-9	162176	83243	78933	131962	67757	64205	30214	15486	14728
12	Arunachal Pradesh	10-14	142806	72764	70042	113324	58005	55319	29482	14759	14723
12	Arunachal Pradesh	15-19	110561	57558	53003	84622	43815	40807	25939	13743	12196
12	Arunachal Pradesh	20-24	86033	44512	41521	65121	33182	31939	20912	11330	9582
12	Arunachal Pradesh	25-29	92902	46972	45930	69645	35086	34559	23257	11886	11371
12	Arunachal Pradesh	30-34	77342	41772	35570	57326	30276	27050	20016	11496	8520
12	Arunachal Pradesh	35-39	77268	42957	34311	57819	31319	26500	19449	11638	7811
12	Arunachal Pradesh	40-44	54374	31603	22771	42392	23665	18727	11982	7938	4044
12	Arunachal Pradesh	45-49	46844	26700	20144	38027	20847	17180	8817	5853	2964
12	Arunachal Pradesh	50-54	35083	21181	13902	29387	17105	12282	5696	4076	1620
12	Arunachal Pradesh	55-59	23710	13762	9948	20506	11425	9081	3204	2337	867
12	Arunachal Pradesh	60-64	20000	10707	9293	18275	9722	8553	1725	985	740
12	Arunachal Pradesh	65-69	11871	6173	5698	10945	5672	5273	926	501	425
12	Arunachal Pradesh	70-74	8295	4404	3891	7695	4097	3598	600	307	293
12	Arunachal Pradesh	75-79	4101	2160	1941	3837	2025	1812	264	135	129

Contd...

1	2	3	4	5	6	7	8	9	10	11	12
12	Arunachal Pradesh	80+	5649	2973	2676	5221	2747	2474	428	226	202
12	Arunachal Pradesh	Age Not Stated	1110	709	401	843	532	311	267	177	90
13	Nagaland	All Ages	1990036	1047141	942895	1647249	859716	787533	342787	187425	155362
13	Nagaland	0-4	187660	94857	92803	155066	78096	76970	32594	16761	15833
13	Nagaland	5-9	257530	133580	123950	216649	112272	104377	40881	21308	19573
13	Nagaland	10-14	283219	147721	135498	236195	123436	112759	47024	24285	22739
13	Nagaland	15-19	266104	139923	126181	221953	116545	105408	44151	23378	20773
13	Nagaland	20-24	209930	110221	99709	173437	90914	82523	36493	19307	17186
13	Nagaland	25-29	163442	83129	80313	130546	66055	64491	32896	17074	15822
13	Nagaland	30-34	122907	64536	58371	96447	49555	46892	26460	14981	11479
13	Nagaland	35-39	122224	63725	58499	96633	48865	47768	25591	14860	10731
13	Nagaland	40-44	94984	50914	44070	77289	40186	37103	17695	10728	6967
13	Nagaland	45-49	87263	47494	39769	72989	38687	34302	14274	8807	5467
13	Nagaland	50-54	59972	35162	24810	50114	28489	21625	9858	6673	3185
13	Nagaland	55-59	39734	22543	17191	34700	19164	15536	5034	3379	1655
13	Nagaland	60-64	31747	18067	13680	28259	15815	12444	3488	2252	1236
13	Nagaland	65-69	20957	11610	9347	18946	10397	8549	2011	1213	798
13	Nagaland	70-74	14881	8348	6533	13425	7484	5941	1456	864	592
13	Nagaland	75-79	9127	5001	4126	8337	4545	3792	790	456	334
13	Nagaland	80+	13611	7710	5901	12327	7059	5268	1284	651	633
13	Nagaland	Age Not Stated	4744	2600	2144	3937	2152	1785	807	448	359
14	Manipur	All Ages	2166788	1095634	1071154	1590820	808953	781867	575968	286681	289287
14	Manipur	0-4	205280	104863	100417	154900	79260	75640	50380	25603	24777
14	Manipur	5-9	242917	124006	118911	185100	94581	90519	57817	29425	28392
14	Manipur	10-14	258508	131998	126510	194283	99482	94801	64225	32516	31709

Contd...

1	2	3	4	5	6	7	8	9	10	11	12
14	Manipur	15-19	237976	118535	119441	177651	88784	88867	60325	29751	30574
14	Manipur	20-24	222484	110393	112091	162899	81395	81504	59585	28998	30587
14	Manipur	25-29	193882	95097	98785	140987	69565	71422	52895	25532	27363
14	Manipur	30-34	159016	80757	78259	114486	58860	55626	44530	21897	22633
14	Manipur	35-39	147041	74098	72943	106062	54072	51990	40979	20026	20953
14	Manipur	40-44	116885	59858	57027	83387	42935	40452	33498	16923	16575
14	Manipur	45-49	98549	50241	48308	70784	36213	34571	27765	14028	13737
14	Manipur	50-54	78474	41206	37268	55360	29213	26147	23114	11993	11121
14	Manipur	55-59	55773	28929	26844	39738	20634	19104	16035	8295	7740
14	Manipur	60-64	48133	24343	23790	34517	17654	16863	13616	6689	6927
14	Manipur	65-69	35897	17990	17907	25501	12921	12580	10396	5069	5327
14	Manipur	70-74	28806	14561	14245	19905	10271	9634	8901	4290	4611
14	Manipur	75-79	15459	7894	7565	10527	5487	5040	4932	2407	2525
14	Manipur	80+	17175	8445	8730	11597	5939	5658	5578	2506	3072
14	Manipur	Age Not Stated	4533	2420	2113	3136	1687	1449	1397	733	664
15	Mizoram	All Ages	888573	459109	429464	447567	232726	214841	441006	226383	214623
15	Mizoram	0-4	100812	51097	49715	56323	28454	27869	44489	22643	21846
15	Mizoram	5-9	104232	53201	51031	57435	29464	27971	46797	23737	23060
15	Mizoram	10-14	108692	55242	53450	57594	29479	28115	51098	25763	25335
15	Mizoram	15-19	98632	49922	48710	47014	24207	22807	51618	25715	25903
15	Mizoram	20-24	93686	48172	45514	43022	22185	20837	50664	25987	24677
15	Mizoram	25-29	79266	41468	37798	36956	19576	17380	42310	21892	20418
15	Mizoram	30-34	60182	31930	28252	27557	14630	12927	32625	17300	15325
15	Mizoram	35-39	58829	31376	27453	27645	14872	12773	31184	16504	14680
15	Mizoram	40-44	47026	24723	22303	22895	11959	10936	24131	12764	11367

Contd...

1	2	3	4	5	6	7	8	9	10	11	12
15	Mizoram	45-49	36304	19297	17007	18618	10004	8614	17686	9293	8393
15	Mizoram	50-54	30956	16609	14347	15719	8503	7216	15237	8106	7131
15	Mizoram	55-59	20157	10829	9328	10702	5838	4864	9455	4991	4464
15	Mizoram	60-64	16561	8507	8054	8855	4655	4200	7706	3852	3854
15	Mizoram	65-69	12371	6344	6027	6434	3390	3044	5937	2954	2983
15	Mizoram	70-74	9381	4832	4549	4803	2536	2267	4578	2296	2282
15	Mizoram	75-79	5402	2687	2715	2772	1408	1364	2630	1279	1351
15	Mizoram	80+	5308	2430	2878	2819	1333	1486	2489	1097	1392
15	Mizoram	Age Not Stated	776	443	333	404	233	171	372	210	162
16	Tripura	All Ages	3199203	1642225	1556978	2653453	1363638	1289815	545750	278587	267163
16	Tripura	0-4	294460	149741	144719	257771	130914	126857	36689	18827	17862
16	Tripura	5-9	362924	185024	177900	319397	162751	156646	43527	22273	21254
16	Tripura	10-14	418168	214033	204135	360673	185049	175624	57495	28984	28511
16	Tripura	15-19	339439	174314	165125	282734	146090	136644	56705	28224	28481
16	Tripura	20-24	274087	135058	139029	223826	110615	113211	50261	24443	25818
16	Tripura	25-29	278984	136617	142367	226888	111729	115159	52096	24888	27208
16	Tripura	30-34	243142	126049	117093	194686	101055	93631	48456	24994	23462
16	Tripura	35-39	245388	129677	115711	196082	104473	91609	49306	25204	24102
16	Tripura	40-44	171319	94513	76806	134914	74459	60455	36405	20054	16351
16	Tripura	45-49	149769	81560	68209	117208	63216	53992	32561	18344	14217
16	Tripura	50-54	106263	59390	46873	83292	46199	37093	22971	13191	9780
16	Tripura	55-59	77906	40798	37108	61473	31741	29732	16433	9057	7376
16	Tripura	60-64	72848	36201	36647	59630	29640	29990	13218	6561	6657
16	Tripura	65-69	53253	25895	27358	42917	20953	21964	10336	4942	5394
16	Tripura	70-74	46459	22721	23738	38235	18946	19289	8224	3775	4449

Contd...

1	2	3	4	5	6	7	8	9	10	11	12
16	Tripura	75-79	24745	12036	12709	20249	9992	10257	4496	2044	2452
16	Tripura	80+	35244	15803	19441	29470	13492	15978	5774	2311	3463
16	Tripura	Age Not Stated	4805	2795	2010	4008	2324	1684	797	471	326
17	Meghalaya	All Ages	2318822	1176087	1142735	1864711	946999	917712	454111	229088	225023
17	Meghalaya	0-4	324566	164343	160223	278681	140957	137724	45885	23386	22499
17	Meghalaya	5-9	337157	170722	166435	283481	143775	139706	53676	26947	26729
17	Meghalaya	10-14	319154	161632	157522	259432	131816	127616	59722	29816	29906
17	Meghalaya	15-19	249780	126857	122923	192206	98865	93341	57574	27992	29582
17	Meghalaya	20-24	195187	94446	100741	148138	71292	76846	47049	23154	23895
17	Meghalaya	25-29	184137	87233	96904	143692	67755	75937	40445	19478	20967
17	Meghalaya	30-34	147732	74672	73060	114984	58150	56834	32748	16522	16226
17	Meghalaya	35-39	151079	78859	72220	118946	61963	56983	32133	16896	15237
17	Meghalaya	40-44	103535	55573	47962	81013	43292	37721	22522	12281	10241
17	Meghalaya	45-49	90705	48622	42083	71584	38246	33338	19121	10376	8745
17	Meghalaya	50-54	63787	34715	29072	49784	26951	22833	14003	7764	6239
17	Meghalaya	55-59	43117	22596	20521	34332	17764	16568	8785	4832	3953
17	Meghalaya	60-64	39326	20448	18878	32280	16950	15330	7046	3498	3548
17	Meghalaya	65-69	26664	13611	13053	21652	11248	10404	5012	2363	2649
17	Meghalaya	70-74	18797	9525	9272	15145	7868	7277	3652	1657	1995
17	Meghalaya	75-79	9696	4948	4748	7653	4030	3623	2043	918	1125
17	Meghalaya	80+	11243	5484	5759	8988	4537	4451	2255	947	1308
17	Meghalaya	Age Not Stated	3160	1801	1359	2720	1540	1180	440	261	179
18	Assam	All Ages	26655528	13777037	12878491	23216288	11939945	11276343	3439240	1837092	1602148
18	Assam	0-4	3033998	1539293	1494705	2767570	1402617	1364953	266428	136676	129752
18	Assam	5-9	3603701	1838233	1765468	3271972	1667026	1604946	331729	171207	160522

Contd...

1	2	3	4	5	6	7	8	9	10	11	12
18	Assam	10-14	3332643	1717969	1614674	2952353	1523864	1428489	380290	194105	186185
18	Assam	15-19	2610793	1368367	1242426	2270735	1192131	1078604	340058	176236	163822
18	Assam	20-24	2315138	1157866	1157272	1971154	976886	994268	343984	180980	163004
18	Assam	25-29	2315931	1125381	1190550	1967157	948411	1018746	348774	176970	171804
18	Assam	30-34	1978201	1006114	972087	1671602	842485	829117	306599	163629	142970
18	Assam	35-39	1921570	1020991	900579	1622394	857239	765155	299176	163752	135424
18	Assam	40-44	1369116	765738	603378	1152454	637304	515150	216662	128434	88228
18	Assam	45-49	1142350	633848	508502	961756	527911	433845	180594	105937	74657
18	Assam	50-54	843595	467765	375830	712821	389360	323461	130774	78405	52369
18	Assam	55-59	599152	317679	281473	509480	264655	244825	89672	53024	36648
18	Assam	60-64	577084	288977	288107	504403	250253	254150	72681	38724	33957
18	Assam	65-69	382083	191204	190879	330498	164467	166031	51585	26737	24848
18	Assam	70-74	296029	157066	138963	259696	138008	121688	36333	19058	17275
18	Assam	75-79	135531	75158	60373	117167	65226	51941	18364	9932	8432
18	Assam	80+	169639	88180	81459	149483	78248	71235	20156	9932	10224
18	Assam	Age Not Stated	28974	17208	11766	23593	13854	9739	5381	3354	2027
19	West Bengal	All Ages	80176197	41465985	38710212	57748946	29616009	28132937	22427251	11849976	10577275
19	West Bengal	0-4	7616261	3874439	3741822	6085921	3092818	2993103	1530340	781621	748719
19	West Bengal	5-9	9490608	4851125	4639483	7520374	3833023	3687351	1970234	1018102	952132
19	West Bengal	10-14	9538536	4914752	4623784	7246017	3728805	3517212	2292519	1185947	1106572
19	West Bengal	15-19	7633878	4069305	3564573	5460196	2923195	2537001	2173682	1146110	1027572
19	West Bengal	20-24	7066173	3570800	3495373	4968144	2467427	2500717	2098029	1103373	994656
19	West Bengal	25-29	7051603	3487173	3564430	4986327	2433556	2552771	2065276	1053617	1011659
19	West Bengal	30-34	6247678	3224082	3023596	4372794	2243149	2129645	1874884	980933	893951
19	West Bengal	35-39	6020467	3153170	2867297	4146870	2176412	1970458	1873597	976758	896839

Contd...

1	2	3	4	5	6	7	8	9	10	11	12
19	West Bengal	40-44	4598048	2552521	2045527	3084358	1699943	1384415	1513690	852578	661112
19	West Bengal	45-49	3964137	2171113	1793024	2624640	1417102	1207538	1339497	754011	585486
19	West Bengal	50-54	2865721	1555475	1310246	1861985	980082	881903	1003736	575393	428343
19	West Bengal	55-59	2271271	1194984	1076287	1509400	764431	744969	761871	430553	331318
19	West Bengal	60-64	1957889	963542	994347	1323204	628838	694366	634685	334704	299981
19	West Bengal	65-69	1469768	702927	766841	985413	458271	527142	484355	244656	239699
19	West Bengal	70-74	1066622	529068	537554	713899	346977	366922	352723	182091	170632
19	West Bengal	75-79	535936	268959	266977	351017	173656	177361	184919	95303	89616
19	West Bengal	80+	669884	319995	349889	434742	207815	226927	235142	112180	122962
19	West Bengal	Age Not Stated	111717	62555	49162	73645	40509	33136	38072	22046	16026
20	Jharkhand	All Ages	26945829	13885037	13060792	20952088	10679596	10272492	5993741	3205441	2788300
20	Jharkhand	0-4	3269645	1655097	1614548	2710437	1366574	1343863	559208	288523	270685
20	Jharkhand	5-9	3904096	2001345	1902751	3198507	1634584	1563923	705589	366761	338828
20	Jharkhand	10-14	3534953	1852228	1682725	2755312	1443226	1312086	779641	409002	370639
20	Jharkhand	15-19	2499650	1351313	1148337	1815202	976911	838291	684448	374402	310046
20	Jharkhand	20-24	2149707	1086951	1062756	1580950	773759	807191	568757	313192	255565
20	Jharkhand	25-29	2031648	1011956	1019692	1545726	756779	788947	485922	255177	230745
20	Jharkhand	30-34	1882378	930481	951897	1457192	708304	748888	425186	222177	203009
20	Jharkhand	35-39	1770077	912149	857928	1356155	696514	659641	413922	215635	198287
20	Jharkhand	40-44	1416919	746852	670067	1072041	560374	511667	344878	186478	158400
20	Jharkhand	45-49	1232946	653169	579777	916931	478200	438731	316015	174969	141046
20	Jharkhand	50-54	929297	511522	417775	697266	373503	323763	232031	138019	94012
20	Jharkhand	55-59	712543	363852	348691	546941	266069	280872	165602	97783	67819
20	Jharkhand	60-64	626146	311884	314262	510410	250017	260393	115736	61867	53869
20	Jharkhand	65-69	399356	191041	208315	321779	151650	170129	77577	39391	38186

Contd...

1	2	3	4	5	6	7	8	9	10	11	12
20	Jharkhand	70-74	283615	145095	138520	230526	117642	112884	53089	27453	25636
20	Jharkhand	75-79	121585	61011	60574	96378	48010	48368	25207	13001	12206
20	Jharkhand	80+	147960	78203	69757	115897	61904	53993	32063	16299	15764
20	Jharkhand	Age Not Stated	33308	20888	12420	24438	15576	8862	8870	5312	3558
21	Orissa	All Ages	36804660	18660570	18144090	31287422	15748970	15538452	5517238	2911600	2605638
21	Orissa	0-4	3573657	1823878	1749779	3131603	1595977	1535626	442054	227901	214153
21	Orissa	5-9	4377605	2240896	2136709	3820552	1952710	1867842	557053	288186	268867
21	Orissa	10-14	4256610	2171099	2085511	3640344	1853494	1786850	616266	317605	298661
21	Orissa	15-19	3531384	1760391	1770993	2945866	1452934	1492932	585518	307457	278061
21	Orissa	20-24	3190193	1600793	1589400	2629115	1301093	1328022	561078	299700	261378
21	Orissa	25-29	3108955	1518820	1590135	2587377	1252683	1334694	521578	266137	255441
21	Orissa	30-34	2761000	1376140	1384860	2307105	1138311	1168794	453895	237829	216066
21	Orissa	35-39	2663984	1368317	1295667	2228738	1140014	1088724	435246	228303	206943
21	Orissa	40-44	2062636	1104313	958323	1722995	911463	811532	339641	192850	146791
21	Orissa	45-49	1755849	926189	829660	1474053	768235	705818	281796	157954	123842
21	Orissa	50-54	1344141	708873	635268	1135788	590322	545466	208353	118551	89802
21	Orissa	55-59	1077484	523752	553732	927986	441283	486703	149498	82469	67029
21	Orissa	60-64	1104140	543006	561134	973151	474591	498560	130989	68415	62574
21	Orissa	65-69	768141	363846	404295	683570	321836	361734	84571	42010	42561
21	Orissa	70-74	615357	309442	305915	546921	274970	271951	68436	34472	33964
21	Orissa	75-79	258189	131458	126731	227207	115821	111386	30982	15637	15345
21	Orissa	80+	293273	154978	138295	253637	134915	118722	39636	20063	19573
21	Orissa	Age Not Stated	62062	34379	27683	51414	28318	23096	10648	6061	4587
22	Chhattisgarh	All Ages	20833803	10474218	10359585	16648056	8307443	8340613	4185747	2166775	2018972
22	Chhattisgarh	0-4	2452954	1241636	1211318	2042755	1030310	1012445	410199	211326	198873

Contd...

1	2	3	4	5	6	7	8	9	10	11	12
22	Chhattisgarh	5-9	2634363	1331008	1303355	2176215	1095843	1080372	458148	235165	222983
22	Chhattisgarh	10-14	2605337	1332937	1272400	2100483	1074605	1025878	504854	258332	246522
22	Chhattisgarh	15-19	1931724	1008441	923283	1487415	773358	714057	444309	235083	209226
22	Chhattisgarh	20-24	1671488	827776	843712	1268540	616462	652078	402948	211314	191634
22	Chhattisgarh	25-29	1636950	814809	822141	1265273	627523	637750	371677	187286	184391
22	Chhattisgarh	30-34	1542280	755721	786559	1204248	582456	621792	338032	173265	164767
22	Chhattisgarh	35-39	1424842	729700	695142	1110871	568062	542809	313971	161638	152333
22	Chhattisgarh	40-44	1096145	565191	530954	852879	433152	419727	243266	132039	111227
22	Chhattisgarh	45-49	946009	482637	463372	744757	374941	369816	201252	107696	93556
22	Chhattisgarh	50-54	748558	384446	364112	600178	302842	297336	148380	81604	66776
22	Chhattisgarh	55-59	610688	294489	316199	500681	237384	263297	110007	57105	52902
22	Chhattisgarh	60-64	568926	263949	304977	476198	218813	257385	92728	45136	47592
22	Chhattisgarh	65-69	402092	181311	220781	338410	150885	187525	63682	30426	33256
22	Chhattisgarh	70-74	275341	127203	148138	234988	107679	127309	40353	19524	20829
22	Chhattisgarh	75-79	122719	55014	67705	105181	46606	58575	17538	8408	9130
22	Chhattisgarh	80+	135305	62208	73097	115901	53546	62355	19404	8662	10742
22	Chhattisgarh	Age Not Stated	28082	15742	12340	23083	12976	10107	4999	2766	2233
23	Madhya Pradesh	All Ages	60348023	31443652	28904371	44380878	23031093	21349785	15967145	8412559	7554586
23	Madhya Pradesh	0-4	7368736	3801712	3567024	5776585	2969769	2806816	1592151	831943	760208
23	Madhya Pradesh	5-9	8114671	4198430	3916241	6249858	3222812	3027046	1864813	975618	889195
23	Madhya Pradesh	10-14	7769009	4123794	3645215	5783834	3073349	2710485	1985175	1050445	934730
23	Madhya Pradesh	15-19	5690617	3155715	2534902	3975497	2217629	1757868	1715120	938086	777034
23	Madhya Pradesh	20-24	5168016	2693698	2474318	3633948	1862686	1771262	1534068	831012	703056
23	Madhya Pradesh	25-29	4664502	2364315	2300187	3338674	1689802	1648872	1325828	674513	651315
23	Madhya Pradesh	30-34	4348461	2189149	2159312	3133954	1567973	1565981	1214507	621176	593331

Contd...

1	2	3	4	5	6	7	8	9	10	11	12
23	Madhya Pradesh	35-39	3927208	2062808	1864400	2771848	1464861	1306987	1155360	597947	557413
23	Madhya Pradesh	40-44	3016434	1635980	1380454	2122388	1138061	984327	894046	497919	396127
23	Madhya Pradesh	45-49	2437191	1281601	1155590	1726760	897520	829240	710431	384081	326350
23	Madhya Pradesh	50-54	1890978	1035226	855752	1366303	740408	625895	524675	294818	229857
23	Madhya Pradesh	55-59	1511753	723319	788434	1118938	523221	595717	392815	200098	192717
23	Madhya Pradesh	60-64	1572796	778022	794774	1206420	598278	608142	366376	179744	186632
23	Madhya Pradesh	65-69	1102622	523430	579192	838754	397151	441603	263868	126279	137589
23	Madhya Pradesh	70-74	816977	414281	402696	626008	319504	306504	190969	94777	96192
23	Madhya Pradesh	75-79	352761	168501	184260	265610	126534	139076	87151	41967	45184
23	Madhya Pradesh	80+	435768	207559	228209	328393	158588	169805	107375	48971	58404
23	Madhya Pradesh	Age Not Stated	159523	86112	73411	117106	62947	54159	42417	23165	19252
24	Gujarat	All Ages	50671017	26385577	24285440	31740767	16317771	15422996	18930250	10067806	8862444
24	Gujarat	0-4	5268670	2789888	2478782	3576413	1871793	1704620	1692257	918095	774162
24	Gujarat	5-9	5682022	3010278	2671744	3791256	1987480	1803776	1890766	1022798	867968
24	Gujarat	10-14	5673476	3014422	2659054	3623780	1919246	1704534	2049696	1095176	954520
24	Gujarat	15-19	5183754	2756478	2427276	3152829	1644102	1508727	2030925	1112376	918549
24	Gujarat	20-24	4839265	2538544	2300721	2871801	1470791	1401010	1967464	1067753	899711
24	Gujarat	25-29	4224871	2182059	2042812	2511297	1287160	1224137	1713574	894899	818675
24	Gujarat	30-34	3985565	2027533	1958032	2406237	1204983	1201254	1579328	822550	756778
24	Gujarat	35-39	3630780	1901397	1729383	2163571	1133808	1029763	1467209	767589	699620
24	Gujarat	40-44	3013173	1585745	1427428	1799007	926415	872592	1214166	659330	554836
24	Gujarat	45-49	2421061	1277531	1143530	1473030	766483	706547	948031	511048	436983
24	Gujarat	50-54	1851667	988925	862742	1150542	601702	548840	701125	387223	313902
24	Gujarat	55-59	1350413	657563	692850	876878	416917	459961	473535	240646	232889
24	Gujarat	60-64	1297301	625662	671639	862383	412250	450133	434918	213412	221506

Contd...

1	2	3	4	5	6	7	8	9	10	11	12
24	Gujarat	65-69	892465	418028	474437	585605	271612	313993	306860	146416	160444
24	Gujarat	70-74	650698	303145	347553	433701	201498	232203	216997	101647	115350
24	Gujarat	75-79	284362	126396	157966	184383	80871	103512	99979	45525	54454
24	Gujarat	80+	374237	155243	218994	252879	106029	146850	121358	49214	72144
24	Gujarat	Age Not Stated	47237	26740	20497	25175	14631	10544	22062	12109	9953
25	Daman & Diu	All Ages	158204	92512	65692	100856	63606	37250	57348	28906	28442
25	Daman & Diu	0-4	14957	7777	7180	9788	5124	4664	5169	2653	2516
25	Daman & Diu	5-9	14261	7376	6885	8856	4572	4284	5405	2804	2601
25	Daman & Diu	10-14	13976	7341	6635	8633	4594	4039	5343	2747	2596
25	Daman & Diu	15-19	17679	11117	6562	11856	8138	3718	5823	2979	2844
25	Daman & Diu	20-24	24834	17610	7224	18432	14233	4199	6402	3377	3025
25	Daman & Diu	25-29	19974	12969	7005	13635	9647	3988	6339	3322	3017
25	Daman & Diu	30-34	13437	8288	5149	8449	5583	2866	4988	2705	2283
25	Daman & Diu	35-39	10433	6034	4399	6383	3966	2417	4050	2068	1982
25	Daman & Diu	40-44	7105	4022	3083	4062	2432	1630	3043	1590	1453
25	Daman & Diu	45-49	5722	2910	2812	3096	1722	1374	2626	1188	1438
25	Daman & Diu	50-54	4363	2182	2181	2191	1155	1036	2172	1027	1145
25	Daman & Diu	55-59	3350	1519	1831	1652	778	874	1698	741	957
25	Daman & Diu	60-64	3033	1326	1707	1524	685	839	1509	641	868
25	Daman & Diu	65-69	2080	876	1204	991	445	546	1089	431	658
25	Daman & Diu	70-74	1379	552	827	628	240	388	751	312	439
25	Daman & Diu	75-79	739	287	452	308	130	178	431	157	274
25	Daman & Diu	80+	811	281	530	319	129	190	492	152	340
25	Daman & Diu	Age Not Stated	71	45	26	53	33	20	18	12	6

Contd...

1	2	3	4	5	6	7	8	9	10	11	12
26	D & N Haveli	All Ages	220490	121666	98824	170027	91832	78195	50463	29834	20629
26	D & N Haveli	0-4	29421	14861	14560	23842	11920	11922	5579	2941	2638
26	D & N Haveli	5-9	25573	12904	12669	20556	10296	10260	5017	2608	2409
26	D & N Haveli	10-14	22764	11935	10829	18608	9723	8885	4156	2212	1944
26	D & N Haveli	15-19	19967	11313	8654	15581	8552	7029	4386	2761	1625
26	D & N Haveli	20-24	27032	16762	10270	19799	12081	7718	7233	4681	2552
26	D & N Haveli	25-29	25146	15557	9589	17500	10798	6702	7646	4759	2887
26	D & N Haveli	30-34	18006	10441	7565	12761	7158	5603	5245	3283	1962
26	D & N Haveli	35-39	14739	8418	6321	11011	6093	4918	3728	2325	1403
26	D & N Haveli	40-44	10351	5702	4649	7981	4232	3749	2370	1470	900
26	D & N Haveli	45-49	8327	4534	3793	6704	3569	3135	1623	965	658
26	D & N Haveli	50-54	5682	3034	2648	4539	2391	2148	1143	643	500
26	D & N Haveli	55-59	4564	2270	2294	3782	1855	1927	782	415	367
26	D & N Haveli	60-64	3702	1623	2079	3119	1315	1804	583	308	275
26	D & N Haveli	65-69	2495	1160	1335	2115	964	1151	380	196	184
26	D & N Haveli	70-74	1427	590	837	1145	459	686	282	131	151
26	D & N Haveli	75-79	579	255	324	441	200	241	138	55	83
26	D & N Haveli	80+	611	254	357	469	190	279	142	64	78
26	D & N Haveli	Age Not Stated	104	53	51	74	36	38	30	17	13
27	Maharashtra	All Ages	96878627	50400596	46478031	55777647	28458677	27318970	41100980	21941919	19159061
27	Maharashtra	0-4	9532843	4983885	4548958	5873107	3068305	2804802	3659736	1915580	1744156
27	Maharashtra	5-9	10230090	5302533	4927557	6228773	3215898	3012875	4001317	2086635	1914682
27	Maharashtra	10-14	11337442	5945917	5391525	6870566	3591211	3279355	4466876	2354706	2112170
27	Maharashtra	15-19	9570648	5262931	4307717	5370972	2940496	2430476	4199676	2322435	1877241
27	Maharashtra	20-24	8856660	4781322	4075338	4574262	2401727	2172535	4282398	2379595	1902803
27	Maharashtra	25-29	8218364	4187247	4031117	4239973	2082403	2157570	3978391	2104844	1873547

Contd...

1	2	3	4	5	6	7	8	9	10	11	12
27	Maharashtra	30-34	7392720	3800551	3592169	3944147	1944710	1999437	3448573	1855841	1592732
27	Maharashtra	35-39	6958360	3540148	3418212	3802015	1880140	1921875	3156345	1660008	1496337
27	Maharashtra	40-44	5546231	3010446	2535785	3050529	1605215	1445314	2495702	1405231	1090471
27	Maharashtra	45-49	4543209	2404222	2138987	2514164	1299683	1214481	2029045	1104539	924506
27	Maharashtra	50-54	3446336	1863428	1582908	1916435	1003404	913031	1529901	860024	669877
27	Maharashtra	55-59	2672981	1320060	1352921	1603426	753956	849470	1069555	566104	503451
27	Maharashtra	60-64	2730791	1204117	1526674	1788719	747802	1040917	942072	456315	485757
27	Maharashtra	65-69	2632665	1229605	1403060	1840697	861255	979442	791968	368350	423618
27	Maharashtra	70-74	1629333	813846	815487	1117798	566264	551534	511535	247582	263953
27	Maharashtra	75-79	682773	333393	349380	442428	216615	225813	240345	116778	123567
27	Maharashtra	80+	779098	351240	427858	519488	235507	283981	259610	115733	143877
27	Maharashtra	Age Not Stated	118083	65705	52378	80148	44086	36062	37935	21619	16316
28	Andhra Pradesh	All Ages	76210007	38527413	37682594	55401067	27937204	27463863	20808940	10590209	10218731
28	Andhra Pradesh	0-4	6684361	3402214	3282147	5012932	2548446	2464486	1671429	853768	817661
28	Andhra Pradesh	5-9	8980791	4571152	4409639	6772164	3444395	3327769	2208627	1126757	1081870
28	Andhra Pradesh	10-14	8732973	4507721	4225252	6369389	3303807	3065582	2363584	1203914	1159670
28	Andhra Pradesh	15-19	7579964	3954124	3625840	5263858	2778306	2485552	2316106	1175818	1140288
28	Andhra Pradesh	20-24	6936897	3478288	3458609	4796962	2396915	2400047	2139935	1081373	1058562
28	Andhra Pradesh	25-29	6762271	3229258	3533013	4779944	2272443	2507501	1982327	956815	1025512
28	Andhra Pradesh	30-34	5625505	2857197	2768308	4020132	2026502	1993630	1605373	830695	774678
28	Andhra Pradesh	35-39	5652711	2800929	2851782	4035189	1992437	2042752	1617522	808492	809030
28	Andhra Pradesh	40-44	4353961	2344256	2009705	3137235	1673937	1463298	1216726	670319	546407
28	Andhra Pradesh	45-49	3804932	1961920	1843012	2760190	1400021	1360169	1044742	561899	482843
28	Andhra Pradesh	50-54	3064827	1607693	1457134	2272256	1176748	1095508	792571	430945	361626
28	Andhra Pradesh	55-59	2109286	980830	1128456	1596098	727068	869030	513188	253762	259426

Contd...

1	2	3	4	5	6	7	8	9	10	11	12
28	Andhra Pradesh	60-64	2337506	1122341	1215165	1813468	868599	944869	524038	253742	270296
28	Andhra Pradesh	65-69	1371770	621812	749958	1070345	482166	588179	301425	139646	161779
28	Andhra Pradesh	70-74	1160623	580811	579812	918723	465731	452992	241900	115080	126820
28	Andhra Pradesh	75-79	413869	204959	208910	317166	158218	158948	96703	46741	49962
28	Andhra Pradesh	80+	504310	227665	276645	386032	177404	208628	118278	50261	68017
28	Andhra Pradesh	Age Not Stated	133450	74243	59207	78984	44061	34923	54466	30182	24284
29	Karnataka	All Ages	52850562	26898918	25951644	34889033	17648958	17240075	17961529	9249960	8711569
29	Karnataka	0-4	4942594	2537476	2405118	3397862	1742354	1655508	1544732	795122	749610
29	Karnataka	5-9	5681431	2893477	2787954	3904587	1984925	1919662	1776844	908552	868292
29	Karnataka	10-14	6221576	3189233	3032343	4251140	2177833	2073307	1970436	1011400	959036
29	Karnataka	15-19	5381672	2840330	2541342	3484228	1852678	1631550	1897444	987652	909792
29	Karnataka	20-24	4886225	2541933	2344292	2985560	1546091	1439469	1900665	995842	904823
29	Karnataka	25-29	4578219	2216303	2361916	2848720	1359926	1488794	1729499	856377	873122
29	Karnataka	30-34	3821205	1917602	1903603	2430733	1198795	1231938	1390472	718807	671665
29	Karnataka	35-39	3918079	1926776	1991303	2530832	1228241	1302591	1387247	698535	688712
29	Karnataka	40-44	3058456	1636842	1421614	1997708	1058414	939294	1060748	578428	482320
29	Karnataka	45-49	2713842	1434271	1279571	1774819	928804	846015	939023	505467	433556
29	Karnataka	50-54	2109655	1117489	992166	1399820	733108	666712	709835	384381	325454
29	Karnataka	55-59	1423742	694759	728983	959486	458153	501333	464256	236606	227650
29	Karnataka	60-64	1498909	728997	769912	1059747	510997	548750	439162	218000	221162
29	Karnataka	65-69	953187	441373	511814	669806	307599	362207	283381	133774	149607
29	Karnataka	70-74	799497	382616	416881	579970	276687	303283	219527	105929	113598
29	Karnataka	75-79	353230	168279	184951	247996	117686	130310	105234	50593	54641
29	Karnataka	80+	457199	202465	254734	332075	147877	184198	125124	54588	70536
29	Karnataka	Age Not Stated	51844	28697	23147	33944	18790	15154	17900	9907	7993

Contd...

1	2	3	4	5	6	7	8	9	10	11	12
30	Goa	All Ages	1347668	687248	660420	677091	340545	336546	670577	346703	323874
30	Goa	0-4	103823	53624	50199	51505	26426	25079	52318	27198	25120
30	Goa	5-9	107390	54996	52394	51047	26108	24939	56343	28888	27455
30	Goa	10-14	120013	61304	58709	59453	30234	29219	60560	31070	29490
30	Goa	15-19	125031	64970	60061	64091	32570	31521	60940	32400	28540
30	Goa	20-24	142016	75652	66364	72435	37803	34632	69581	37849	31732
30	Goa	25-29	138614	70745	67869	69748	35778	33970	68866	34967	33899
30	Goa	30-34	117544	61304	56240	57642	30168	27474	59902	31136	28766
30	Goa	35-39	104565	53245	51320	50703	25637	25066	53862	27608	26254
30	Goa	40-44	82539	44065	38474	40079	21026	19053	42460	23039	19421
30	Goa	45-49	75632	38066	37566	37570	18549	19021	38062	19517	18545
30	Goa	50-54	64311	32882	31429	31947	15678	16269	32364	17204	15160
30	Goa	55-59	46905	23063	23842	24471	11370	13101	22434	11693	10741
30	Goa	60-64	42394	19972	22422	23093	10591	12502	19301	9381	9920
30	Goa	65-69	28168	12501	15667	15502	6718	8784	12666	5783	6883
30	Goa	70-74	20484	8650	11834	11429	4761	6668	9055	3889	5166
30	Goa	75-79	10315	4279	6036	5583	2275	3308	4732	2004	2728
30	Goa	80+	10912	4274	6638	5866	2287	3579	5046	1987	3059
30	Goa	Age Not Stated	7012	3656	3356	4927	2566	2361	2085	1090	995
31	Lakshadweep	All Ages	60650	31131	29519	33683	17191	16492	26967	13940	13027
31	Lakshadweep	0-4	6468	3289	3179	3971	1974	1997	2497	1315	1182
31	Lakshadweep	5-9	6625	3415	3210	3846	1969	1877	2779	1446	1333
31	Lakshadweep	10-14	7641	3983	3658	4240	2149	2091	3401	1834	1567
31	Lakshadweep	15-19	6230	3203	3027	3510	1787	1723	2720	1416	1304
31	Lakshadweep	20-24	5634	2769	2865	3161	1554	1607	2473	1215	1258

Contd...

1	2	3	4	5	6	7	8	9	10	11	12
31	Lakshadweep	25-29	5160	2597	2563	2812	1448	1364	2348	1149	1199
31	Lakshadweep	30-34	4358	2245	2113	2348	1258	1090	2010	987	1023
31	Lakshadweep	35-39	4105	2040	2065	2235	1123	1112	1870	917	953
31	Lakshadweep	40-44	3003	1603	1400	1595	849	746	1408	754	654
31	Lakshadweep	45-49	3253	1669	1584	1733	873	860	1520	796	724
31	Lakshadweep	50-54	2287	1263	1024	1179	638	541	1108	625	483
31	Lakshadweep	55-59	2104	1140	964	1116	611	505	988	529	459
31	Lakshadweep	60-64	1487	761	726	802	396	406	685	365	320
31	Lakshadweep	65-69	955	487	468	504	260	244	451	227	224
31	Lakshadweep	70-74	639	309	330	314	141	173	325	168	157
31	Lakshadweep	75-79	267	152	115	127	70	57	140	82	58
31	Lakshadweep	80+	381	175	206	156	73	83	225	102	123
31	Lakshadweep	Age Not Stated	53	31	22	34	18	16	19	13	6
32	Kerala	All Ages	31841374	15468614	16372760	23574449	11451282	12123167	8266925	4017332	4249593
32	Kerala	0-4	2765164	1409487	1355677	2085053	1062041	1023012	680111	347446	332665
32	Kerala	5-9	2544181	1295679	1248502	1910571	972851	937720	633610	322828	310782
32	Kerala	10-14	2987200	1523842	1463358	2250970	1148380	1102590	736230	375462	360768
32	Kerala	15-19	2984506	1484586	1499920	2236959	1113279	1123680	747547	371307	376240
32	Kerala	20-24	2983990	1440467	1543523	2214417	1070197	1144220	769573	370270	399303
32	Kerala	25-29	2786195	1296905	1489290	2050842	952190	1098652	735353	344715	390638
32	Kerala	30-34	2516463	1185807	1330656	1835928	862361	973567	680535	323446	357089
32	Kerala	35-39	2466354	1154778	1311576	1810725	845679	965046	655629	309099	346530
32	Kerala	40-44	1951284	960397	990887	1415848	695536	720312	535436	264861	270575
32	Kerala	45-49	1926144	952021	974123	1405506	692508	712998	520638	259513	261125
32	Kerala	50-54	1437520	724701	712819	1033889	520811	513078	403631	203890	199741

Contd...

1	2	3	4	5	6	7	8	9	10	11	12
32	Kerala	55-59	1130244	541668	588576	825769	395076	430693	304475	146592	157883
32	Kerala	60-64	1032136	480345	551791	760831	353980	406851	271305	126365	144940
32	Kerala	65-69	902015	399671	502344	669045	297855	371190	232970	101816	131154
32	Kerala	70-74	613422	273293	340129	454667	204841	249826	158755	68452	90303
32	Kerala	75-79	399089	173558	225531	298225	131384	166841	100864	42174	58690
32	Kerala	80+	389013	157345	231668	296344	122269	174075	92669	35076	57593
32	Kerala	Age Not Stated	26454	14064	12390	18860	10044	8816	7594	4020	3574
33	Tamil Nadu	All Ages	62405679	31400909	31004770	34921681	17531494	17390187	27483998	13869415	13614583
33	Tamil Nadu	0-4	5098462	2619883	2478579	2999803	1548451	1451352	2098659	1071432	1027227
33	Tamil Nadu	5-9	5600086	2875394	2724692	3305549	1704477	1601072	2294537	1170917	1123620
33	Tamil Nadu	10-14	6012326	3086803	2925523	3476580	1791785	1684795	2535746	1295018	1240728
33	Tamil Nadu	15-19	6183767	3135595	3048172	3477060	1771011	1706049	2706707	1364584	1342123
33	Tamil Nadu	20-24	5801384	2872914	2928470	3104691	1551058	1553633	2696693	1321856	1374837
33	Tamil Nadu	25-29	5719070	2732907	2986163	3053491	1452229	1601262	2665579	1280678	1384901
33	Tamil Nadu	30-34	4687799	2344412	2343387	2463318	1214333	1248985	2224481	1130079	1094402
33	Tamil Nadu	35-39	4919080	2396927	2522153	2698598	1290675	1407923	2220482	1106252	1114230
33	Tamil Nadu	40-44	3786341	1978669	1807672	2059525	1062501	997024	1726816	916168	810648
33	Tamil Nadu	45-49	3610873	1842970	1767903	2024247	1013197	1011050	1586626	829773	756853
33	Tamil Nadu	50-54	2817473	1452890	1364583	1577965	798431	779534	1239508	654459	585049
33	Tamil Nadu	55-59	2232676	1101957	1130719	1295258	632403	662855	937418	469554	467864
33	Tamil Nadu	60-64	2049791	1019088	1030703	1215578	603028	612550	834213	416060	418153
33	Tamil Nadu	65-69	1374926	663631	711295	804288	389510	414778	570638	274121	296517
33	Tamil Nadu	70-74	1030919	520254	510665	609388	313218	296170	421531	207036	214495
33	Tamil Nadu	75-79	498560	261694	236866	281505	151331	130174	217055	110363	106692

Contd...

1	2	3	4	5	6	7	8	9	10	11	12
33	Tamil Nadu	80+	553204	271133	282071	311989	158757	153232	241215	112376	128839
33	Tamil Nadu	Age Not Stated	428942	223788	205154	162848	85099	77749	266094	138689	127405
34	Pondicherry	All Ages	974345	486961	487384	325726	163703	162023	648619	323258	325361
34	Pondicherry	0-4	84617	42930	41687	30538	15500	15038	54079	27430	26649
34	Pondicherry	5-9	83653	42740	40913	29496	15098	14398	54157	27642	26515
34	Pondicherry	10-14	94416	48091	46325	33108	16820	16288	61308	31271	30037
34	Pondicherry	15-19	97688	49398	48290	34015	17358	16657	63673	32040	31633
34	Pondicherry	20-24	97694	48028	49666	32112	16083	16029	65582	31945	33637
34	Pondicherry	25-29	96515	45974	50541	31345	15007	16338	65170	30967	34203
34	Pondicherry	30-34	81221	41258	39963	25333	13042	12291	55888	28216	27672
34	Pondicherry	35-39	78419	39641	38778	25541	12929	12612	52878	26712	26166
34	Pondicherry	40-44	59082	31637	27445	18308	9834	8474	40774	21803	18971
34	Pondicherry	45-49	50482	26101	24381	16365	8349	8016	34117	17752	16365
34	Pondicherry	50-54	38842	20077	18765	12234	6154	6080	26608	13923	12685
34	Pondicherry	55-59	29887	14143	15744	10283	4742	5541	19604	9401	10203
34	Pondicherry	60-64	28624	13170	15454	9875	4594	5281	18749	8576	10173
34	Pondicherry	65-69	20479	9039	11440	6854	3120	3734	13625	5919	7706
34	Pondicherry	70-74	15263	6762	8501	5056	2398	2658	10207	4364	5843
34	Pondicherry	75-79	8434	3838	4596	2560	1311	1249	5874	2527	3347
34	Pondicherry	80+	8216	3652	4564	2531	1257	1274	5685	2395	3290
34	Pondicherry	Age Not Stated	813	482	331	172	107	65	641	375	266
35	A & N Islands	All Ages	356152	192972	163180	239954	128961	110993	116198	64011	52187
35	A & N Islands	0-4	31241	15956	15285	22076	11211	10865	9165	4745	4420
35	A & N Islands	5-9	34049	17310	16739	23507	11953	11554	10542	5357	5185
35	A & N Islands	10-14	38754	19924	18830	27024	13915	13109	11730	6009	5721

Contd...

1	2	3	4	5	6	7	8	9	10	11	12
35	A & N Islands	15-19	38448	20801	17647	26294	14132	12162	12154	6669	5485
35	A & N Islands	20-24	38290	20956	17334	24427	13026	11401	13863	7930	5933
35	A & N Islands	25-29	36751	19383	17368	23472	12219	11253	13279	7164	6115
35	A & N Islands	30-34	28599	15911	12688	18363	10013	8350	10236	5898	4338
35	A & N Islands	35-39	28531	15191	13340	18649	9911	8738	9882	5280	4602
35	A & N Islands	40-44	20609	11720	8889	13530	7679	5851	7079	4041	3038
35	A & N Islands	45-49	19077	11067	8010	12751	7401	5350	6326	3666	2660
35	A & N Islands	50-54	12649	7786	4863	8432	5096	3336	4217	2690	1527
35	A & N Islands	55-59	9509	5921	3588	6702	4103	2599	2807	1818	989
35	A & N Islands	60-64	6496	3790	2706	4780	2791	1989	1716	999	717
35	A & N Islands	65-69	4688	2659	2029	3527	2016	1511	1161	643	518
35	A & N Islands	70-74	2983	1654	1329	2298	1288	1010	685	366	319
35	A & N Islands	75-79	1534	869	665	1217	698	519	317	171	146
35	A & N Islands	80+	1665	862	803	1346	704	642	319	158	161
35	A & N Islands	Age Not Stated	2279	1212	1067	1559	805	754	720	407	313

National Income

5

National income reflects the macro flows of goods and services, and the economic structure of the economy. To quote National Income Committee, 1951, "National Income statistics provide a wide view of the country's entire economy, as well as of the various groups in the population who participate as producers and income receivers, and that, if available over a substantial period, they reveal clearly the basic changes in the country's economy in the past and suggest, if not fully reveal, trends for the future." A total of national income measures the flow of final goods and services in an economy over a particular period of time, usually a year. Contrary to the national wealth that measures the stock of commodities held by the nationals of a country, national income measures the productive power of economy. It is defined as the sum of incomes accruing to factors of production, supplied by normal residents of the country before deduction of direct taxes. It is identically equal to net national product at factor cost. Thus, there are several aggregates that constitute the national income of the country:

1. Gross Product

The Gross Domestic Product (GDP) is the measure in monetary terms, of all goods and services produced in the economy. The GDP at constant prices, which is also termed as the real GDP, depicts the growth of the economy in real terms, as it excludes the effect of price changes over the years. It is also considered to be the most comprehensive single measure of aggregate economic output of the country, since it encompasses the performance of all economic activities during the period of reference. Gross National Product (GNP) measures the total domestic and foreign output claimed by residents of a country.

2. Net Product

Net Domestic Product (NDP) is the GDP minus depreciation, i.e. reduction in the value of assets through wear and tear. Net National Product (NNP) is GNP minus depreciation. NNP, when calculated at factor cost, is called National Income. Estimates of NDP and NNP are made at market prices. The market prices constitute costs of production, indirect taxes and subsidies. While the indirect taxes are added to the costs of production, the subsidies are subtracted from them. When the indirect taxes are deducted and subsidies added to the various estimates, the resulting value will equal the cost of producing goods and services. Thus, there are two types of estimates: at market prices and at factor cost.

3. Per Capita Product/Income

Per capita income refers to the average income of the country. It is calculated by dividing the national income of a country by its population. Per capita income serve as an index of welfare of the people as its increase indicates a rise in the availability of goods and services.

Estimation of National Product

In order to estimate the national product, the producing sectors are identified and then the products of such sectors are evaluated at market prices. To the value of products of these sectors is added the net income from abroad to get at the estimate of national product.

Both the output and the income methods are applied for the valuation of the products. While the output method has been used largely in the commodity producing sectors like manufacturing and agriculture, the income method is used in the tertiary or service sector like trade, public administration and defence, etc. Besides, this method is also applied to those segments of commodity sectors where there is absence of output data. The third method—experimental method—is used in a very limited way to such sectors like Kaccha construction.

The output method involves "value-added" approach. The term "value-added" implies the value of goods minus the cost of production. The output method determines the net contribution of a producing unit to national income. The sum total of value added by all the producing units in the commodity sector is the value of this sector's contribution to national income. The estimation is made by evaluating the value of goods at ex-factory prices and deducting from it the value or the costs of inputs supplied by other enterprises, and the estimated value of depreciation (or capital consumption).

The income method involves the procedure of finding out the number of people working or the workforce in a profession as well as average per head earnings. Thereafter, both the figures so derived are multiplied and its product is the value of income contributed by the profession.

The expenditure method involves estimation of spending or disposition of income on final goods and services.

So far the data for these methods are concerned, they are furnished by government agencies like those of ministries, departments and directorates. The National Sample Survey Organisations (NSSO), set up in 1950, is responsible for conducting large scale sample surveys to meet the data needs of the country for the estimation of national income and other aggregates. Reports of the Rural Credit Survey, Indian Rural Debt and Investment and the like also form the sources of data for the calculation of national income. Similarly, censuses of population have also been made use of to estimate the workforce in the absence of comprehensive employment statistics in various professions. Arbitrary imputations are made in respect of certain goods and services if there is need of data related to those goods and services. Data for the income method are made available through various indicators. For instance, the index of trading activity is indicator for trade while the index number of average daily wages of rural skilled labour in agriculture is used as an indicator for the non-agricultural sector. To put it in a nutshell, various devices have been applied for various sectors to get the data as required by the income method.

Estimates of National Income during Pre-Independence Period

During the pre-independence period eminent estimators like Dadabhai Naoroji, Wadia and Joshi, Shah and Khambatta estimated the value of the output of the agricultural sector and thereafter added a certain percentage as the income of the non-agricultural sector. Since their assumptions were mostly arbitrary, the estimates were devoid of any scientific basis. Besides, the estimates of national income during the British rule were based on statistics from the agricultural sector which were highly undependable. Growth rate of Indian economy for the period 1860-1945 at 1970-71 prices is as give in Table 5.1 below:

Table 5.1: Growth Rate of Indian Economy for the Period 1860-1945

Period	Rate of Growth
1860-1885	1.1
1885-1905	-0.3
1905-1925	1.3
1925-1950	-0.1
1860-1945	0.5

Source : J.R. Hicks, M. Mukherjee and S.K. Ghosh, *The Framework of Indian Economy*, 1984, p. 217.

The Table clearly indicates that during the British rule the Indian economy was more or less stagnant over a long period with a growth rate of 0.5 per cent for 1860-1945.

Estimates of National Income during Post-Independence Period

The National Income Committee was appointed by the Government of India in August 1949. It was entrusted with the responsibility of compilation of authoritative estimates of national income. The first report of the National Income Committee came in 1951 and the final report in 1954. It was for the first time that the report provided a comprehensive data of national income for the whole of India. The main features of this report were as under:

(1) Agriculture, including animal husbandry, forestry and fisheries, contributed nearly 50 per cent of the national income during 1950-51.

(2) One-sixth of the total national income was contributed by the mining, manufacturing and hand trades.

(3) Commerce, transport and communications also

accounted for more than one-sixth of the total national income.

(4) Fifteen per cent of national income was contributed by the other services such as professions and liberal arts, administrative services, domestic services, house property, etc.

(5) Two-thirds of the national income was contributed by the commodity production that included material production derived from agriculture, mining, factory establishments, etc.

(6) Services sector comprising commerce, transport and communications, administrative services, liberal arts, etc., accounted for about one-third of the total national income.

(7) The share of government sector in net domestic product and in national expenditure during 1950-51 was 7.6 per cent and 8.2 per cent, respectively.

National Income Series

For examining the performance of the economy in real terms through the macro-economic aggregates like Gross Domestic Product (GDP), national income, consumption expenditure, capital formation, etc. estimates of the aggregates are prepared at the prices of selected year known as base year. The estimates at the prevailing prices of the current year are termed as "at current prices", while those prepared at base year prices are termed "at constant prices". The measure of real growth is obtained from the comparison of the estimates at constant prices, i.e. in real terms. The base year of the national accounts is changed periodically to take into account the structural changes which take place in the economy and to depict a true picture of the economy through macro aggregates mentioned above.

As mentioned earlier, the first official estimates of national income was prepared by the Central Statistical Organisation with base year 1948-49 for the estimates at constant prices. These estimates at constant (1948-49) prices along with the corresponding estimates at current prices and the accounts of Public Authorities were published in the publication, *Estimates of National Income,* in 1956. With the gradual improvement in the availability of basic data over the years, a comprehensive review of methodology for national accounts statistics has constantly been undertaken with a view to updating the database and shifting the base year to a more recent year. As a result, base years of the National Accounts Statistics series have been shifted from 1948-49 to 1960-61 in August 1967, from 1960-61 to 1970-71 in January 1978, from 1970-71 to 1980-81 in February 1988, and from 1980-81 to 1993-94 in February 1999.

In the past National Accounts Statistics were revised decennially changing the base to a year, which ends with 1. It was primarily because in the base year estimates, the information on working force has played an important role and working force estimates were obtained from the Population Census, which are conducted decennially in the years ending with 1. In this sequence, the previous series of National Account Statistics should have been with the base year 1990-91. At that time, it was observed that data on worker participation rate (WPR) was captured by the NSSO better than that through the Population Census. Accordingly, the CSO used the workforce estimates based on NSS workforce participation rates from the NSS 1993-94 (50th round) survey results, and revised the base year of national accounts to 1993-94.

In continuation with this practice thus we have in addition to the conventional series—income data at current prices and at 1948-49 prices for the period 1948-49 to 1964-65 involving the Net Output Method and Net Income Method discussed earlier, the other national income series estimates detailed below for the post-Independence period. To begin with, the 1960-61 series provide national income data at current prices and at 1960-61 prices for the period of 1960-61 to 1975-76. In 1970-71 another series was started with 1970-71 as base year instead of 1960-61. It is to be noted here that magnitudes in estimates for different base years show variation which is due to differences in weights used for the series. After the 1970-71 series, another series came with 1980-81 as its base year. Thereafter, the Central Statistical Organisation (CSO) revised the base year to 1993-94 and introduced a new series of National Accounts Statistics. With this series the coverage of GDP was extended, for instance under agriculture and allied activities, several horticultural and floricultural crops have been included. Likewise, in mining and manufacturing too, estimation of income from unregistered manufacturing activities and use of quick estimates of Annual Survey of Industries for 1996-97 and 1997-98 have been included. In the other services sector, estimation of income from unorganised service activities on the basis of new NSS Employment Survey Results, private consumption services, private activities under TV and radio and the high value activities like software consultancy, and business services have been included. The extension in coverage has no doubt reduced the under-reporting of GDP.

At present, the base year for estimation of national income is 1999-2000. The year 1999-2000 has been chosen as the base year by the CSO as it coincides with the NSS 55th round (1999-2000) Quinquennial survey year on employment and unemployment. The CSO released the New Series of national accounts statistics with base year 1999-2000 on 31-1-2006, along with the Quick Estimates of National Income and related aggregates for the year 2004-05. The new series included (a) latest available results of long-term surveys; (b) several improvements in terms of coverage; and (c) some important procedural changes. The important procedural changes made in the new series are:

(i) using the production data provided by the National Horticulture Board (NHB) for all horticultural crops (with the exception of those covered under principal crops) and using the price data provided by the State Directorates of Economics and Statistics (State DESs) for all crops;

(ii) introduction of a new basic material, 'fixtures and fittings' in the construction sector in addition to the existing four basic materials for estimating the value of output of construction sector;

(iii) getting the retained reserves and dividends paid from the property income of mutual funds, for the purpose of estimating the output of banking sector;

(iv) aligning the estimates of capital formation by industry with the estimates of capital formation by institutions namely, public and private;

(v) adjusting for reinvested earnings in India of foreign companies in the estimates of saving of private corporate sector and the consequential changes in the external transactions account;

(vi) including in the gross fixed capital formation of the private corporate sector, the domestic consumption of software (net of public sector purchases), and the expenditures of new companies under construction (in the absence of coverage of such companies in the present corporate finance studies, provisional estimates of capital formation have been added to the corporate sector's capital formation based on these studies); and

(vii) treating the operating losses of departmental commercial undertakings as imputed subsidies, in line with the practice currently followed for irrigation departments.

It would not be out of place to mention here that when the base year of national accounts statistics is changed, there is some change in the levels of GDP estimates, which is mainly due to the widening of coverage and inclusion of long-term survey results.

The Table 5.2 below illustrates the changes in the levels of GDP due to the introduction of the new series of national accounts. The increase in the level of GDP in the new series ranges from zero to 1.7 per cent during 1999-2000 to 2004-05.

There are no major changes in the overall growth rates of GDP at constant (1999-2000) prices with the change in the base year, although there are changes in growth rates at sectoral level. The major change is in the year 2004-05 Quick Estimates, which is due to the availability of detailed data at sectoral level, whereas the earlier estimates were based on indicators.

Table 5.2: Gross Domestic Product (At Current Prices) (Rs. Crore)

Year	New Series (Base Year 1999-2000)	Old Series (Base Year 1993-94)	Percentage Difference
1999-2000	17,92,292	17,61,838	1.7
2000-01	19,30,184	19,02,999	1.4
2001-02	20,97,446	20,81,474	0.8
2002-03	22,55,574	22,54,888	0
2003-04	25,43,396	25,19,785	0.9
2004-05	28,43,897	28,30,465	0.5

The growth rates in the new and old series are shown in the Table 5.3.

Table 5.3: Growth Rates in the New and Old Series

Year	New Series	Old Series	Growth Rates	
			(Base Year 1999-2000)	(Base Year 1993-94)
1999-2000	17,92,292	11,48,367		
2000-01	18,70,387	11,98,592	4.4	4.4
2001-02	19,78,055	12,67,945	5.8	5.8
2002-03	20,52,586	13,18,362	3.8	4
2003-04	22,26,041	14,30,548	8.5	8.5
2004-05	23,93,671	15,29,408	7.5	6.9

The weighting pattern of various sectors in the GDP in the old and new series for the year 1999-2000 is presented in the Table 5.4.

Table 5.4: Weighting Pattern in the GDP in New and Old Series

	Industry	New Series (Base Year 1999-2000)	Old Series (Base Year 1993-94)
1	Agriculture, forestry and fishing	25.3	26.2
1.1	Agriculture	23.2	24
1.2	Forestry and logging	1.1	1.1
1.3	Fishing	1.1	1.1
2	Mining and quarrying	2.3	2.3
3	Manufacturing	14.7	15.1

Contd...

3.1	Registered	9.7	9.7
3.2	Unregistered	5.1	5.4
4	Elect. Gas and water supply	2.5	2.4
5	Construction	5.9	6
6	Trade, hotels and restaurant	14.2	14
6.1	Trade	12.9	13
6.2	Hotels and restaurants	1.2	1
7	Transport, storage and communication	7.4	7.1
7.1	Railways	1.1	0.9
7.2	Transport by other means	4.6	4.6
7.3	Storage	0.1	0.1
7.4	Communication	1.6	1.5
8	Financing, insurance, real estate and business services	13	12.5
8.1	Banking and insurance	5.9	6.8
8.2	Real estate, ownership of dwellings and business services	7.1	5.8
9	Community, social and personal services	14.7	14.4
9.1	Public administration and defence	6.7	6.6
9.2	Other Services	8.1	7.8
10	Gross domestic product at Factor cost (1 to 9)	100	100

Source: PIB Press Releases.

Trends in National Income Growth Performance

A careful study of trends in national income is indispensable to understand the impact of planning in India. More importantly, for a low-income economy like India, a significant indicator of its economic performance is the increase in the national income and per capita income over a period of time. Hence, it would be preferable if the trend in national income and changes in the structure of national product are analysed over the last fifty years of planning. Thereafter, a critical evaluation of the various aspects of these trends would be made so as to trace the causes of unsatisfactory performance of the economy on the one hand and the factors that are responsible for the fast growth in the recent years on the other. This would enable to suggest measures to improve upon the growth performance of the economy.

(a) Trends in Net National Product

During the thirty-year period, i.e. 1950-51 to 1980-81, the annual rates of growth of net national product was of the order of 8.9 per cent and that of per capita income was 6.6 per cent. However, such increase in NNP at current prices indicates only a monetary increase consequent upon a sharp increase in prices particularly after the Third Plan period. If the data provided in the Table 4.4, is further split into three period, it can be observed that during the first ten years of planning, i.e. 1950-51 to 1960-61, net national product increased at the annual rate of 3.8 per cent while the performance of the economy has been on deterioration henceforth. During the second break-up, i.e. the period between 1960-61 to 1970-71, the rate of growth of NNP declined to 3.5 per cent and that of per capita NNP to 1.2 per cent per annum. During 1970-71 to 1980-81, the rate of growth of Net National Product was 3.0 per cent and that of per capita Net National Product declined to 0.7 per cent per annum.

Improvement in growth rate of NNP is perceptible during the eighties. During 1980-81 to 1990-91, it was 5.4 per cent per annum and the per capita NNP grown on an average 3.2 per cent per annum at 1993-94 prices. Thereafter, during 1990-91 to 2000-01, the annual average rate of growth of NNP at 1993-94 prices was just of the order 5.5 per cent per annum and that of NNP per capita was 3.4 per cent. Owing to the high growth in agriculture, manufacturing, electricity, construction, transport excluding railways and communication, trade and hotels, there has been a sharp growth during 1993-94 to 1997-98. During this period, the growth rate of NNP was 7.0 per cent on the average and of per capita NNP at 5.1 per cent. Overall, in the last two decades, i.e. 1980-81 to 2000-01, the average annual growth of NNP was 5.5 per cent and that of per capita NNP was 3.3 per cent. Comparatively, the performance of economy during these two decades has been better than in the previous three decades (See Table 5.5).

Table 5.5: Rate of Growth of Net National Product at Factor Cost and Per Capita NNP

Period	NNP	Per Capita NNP	NNP	Per Capita NNP
	(At 1993-94 Prices)		(At Current Prices)	
1950-51 to 1960-61	3.8	1.8	5.2	3.2
1960-61 to 1970-71	3.5	1.2	9.9	7.5
1970-71 to 1980-81	3.0	0.7	11.7	9.2
1980-81 to 1990-91	5.4	3.1	14.2	11.6
1990-91 to 2000-01	5.5	3.5	14.2	12.0
2001-02	6.2	4.3	9.6	7.7
2002-03	4.2	2.4	8.7	6.8
2003-04*	9.0	7.1	12.1	10.2
1950-51 to 1980-81	3.4	1.2	8.9	6.6
1980-81 to 2000-01	5.5	3.3	14.3	12.0

* Quick estimates.

Source: CSO, National Accounts Statistics (2004).

(b) Growth Rate During the Five-Year Plans

The annual average growth rate of NNP during the First Plan (1951-56) at 1993-94 prices was 3.6 per cent. This rate improved during the Second Plan (1956-61) rising to 4.1 per cent. During the Third Plan (1961-66) rate again slumped down to 2.5 per cent, which was only sufficient to neutralise the growth of population. This decline was a consequence of a serious drought in 1965-66. However, after 1967-68 the economy improved and the growth rate showed an uptrend. During the Fourth Plan (1969-74), the country witnessed a setback in the economy as the annual rate of growth of national income declined to 3.3 per cent and that of real per capita income 1.0 per cent per annum. The main factors responsible for such decline during the Fourth Plan were firstly, the sharp increase in prices during 1972-73 and 1973-74 and secondly, shortfalls in production owing to lower utilisation of capacity. The performance of the economy during the Fifth Plan is considered satisfactory as the average annual increase in national income was of the order of 5.0 per cent.

During the Sixth Plan (1980-85), the annual growth rate of NNP was 5.4 per cent while during the Seventh Plan (1985-90) it improved to 5.8 per cent per annum. This was seen as a remarkable development as it achieved its target of 5 per cent growth rate of NNP. During the Eighth Plan (1992-97), NNP growth rate of 6.7 per cent was achieved while it was 5.5 per cent during the Ninth Plan (1997-2002). So far the present Tenth Plan is concerned (2002-07), the NNP at factor cost during 2001-02, 2002-03, 2003-04, 2004-05 has been respectively as 6.2, 4.2, 9.0 and 7.5 per cent. The Table 5.6 below gives a quick review of annual growth rates of NNP during the Five-Year Plans.

Table 5.6: Annual Average Growth Rate in Various Plans at 1993-94 Prices

Plan	NNP at Factor Cost	Per Capita NNP
First Plan (1951-56)	3.6	1.8
Second Plan (1956-61)	4.1	2.0
Third Plan (1961-66)	2.5	0.2
Annual Plans (1966-69)	3.8	1.5
Fourth Plan (1969-74)	3.3	1.0
Fifth Plan (1974-79)	5.0	2.7
Annual Plans (1979-80)	-6.0	-8.3
Sixth Plan (1980-85)	5.4	3.2
Seventh Plan (1985-90)	5.8	3.6
Annual Plans (1990-91)	5.4	3.3
Annual Plans (1991-92)	0.5	-1.5
Eighth Plan (1992-97)	6.7	4.6
Ninth Plan (1997-2002)	5.5	3.6
2001-02	6.2	4.3
2002-03	4.2	2.4
2003-04	9.0	7.1

Source : CSO, National Accounts Statistics, 2001 and 2004.

(c) Trends in Per capita Income

The growth rate of per capita income since 1950 has been of the order of about 2 per cent annum. In the three decades since 1950, the growth rate was dismally low due to the slow growth of national income and a fast increase in population. In the 1980s, the growth rate was relatively higher at an average of over 3 per cent. The rate increased further in the 1990s and moved on an average of about 4 per cent. When calculated in absolute terms, the per capita income rose slowly during 1950 to 1980 from Rs. 3,688 in 1950 to Rs. 5,353 in 1980. However, the rise in per capita income has been quite significant since 1980—from Rs. 7,322 in 1990-91 to Rs. 11,799 (quick estimate) in 2003-04. The per capita income of the country in 2005-06 stands at Rs. 25,788 at current prices, and at Rs. 20,813 at constant (1999-2000) prices, respectively showing growth rates of 11.0 per cent and 5.9 per cent.

(d) Trends in Distribution of National Income by Industrial Origin

(i) *Primary Sector:* The share of primary sector that includes agriculture, forestry and fishery in GDP, if studied since Independence, has declined from 57.7 per cent in 1950-51 to 23.9 per cent in 2001-02. Since agriculture dominates the primary sector, it is the agricultural output that determines the share of the primary sector in GDP. The Table 5.7 below gives the share of components in the GDP by industry of origin.

Table 5.7: Share of GDP by Industrial Origin

	Distribution in per cent		
	1950-51	1980-81	2001-02
I. Agriculture etc.	57.7	39.7	23.9
1. Agriculture	50.2	35.8	21.9
2. Forestry	6.7	3.0	1.1
3. Fishing	0.9	1.0	1.0
II. Mining. Manufacturing etc.	14.8	23.7	26.6
1. Mining & Quarrying	1.5	2.1	2.2
2. Manufacturing	8.9	13.8	16.8
a. Registered	4.4	8.1	11.1
b. Unregistered	4.5	5.8	5.8
3. Electricity, gas & water supply	0.3	1.7	2.5
4. Construction	4.1	6.1	5.1
III. Transport, Communication & Trade etc.	11.9	18.4	23.5
IV. Finance and Real Estate	6.7	6.5	12.5

Contd...

V. Community and Personal Services	9.4	11.7	13.5
A. Commodity Sector (I+II)	72.0	63.0	50.5
B. Service Sector (III+IV+V)	28.0	36.6	49.5
Total	100.0	100.0	100.0

Source: National Accounts Statistics of India (1950-51 to 2002-03).

(ii) Secondary Sector: Manufacturing industries and construction are the two major components of the secondary sector. The other components of this sector include: mining, manufacturing, construction, electricity, gas and water supply. The secondary sector overall has shown a steady growth from 16.1 per cent of GDP in 1950-51 to 26.6 per cent in 2001-02. So far the performance during the Tenth Plan (2002-07) is concerned, there has been a distinct improvement in the manufacturing field. The target growth of industry during the Tenth Plan was put at 10 per cent consistent with an overall GDP growth of 8 per cent. However, there has been deceleration in the growth of mining and electricity sector, thereby adding pressure on manufacturing sector to maintain overall industrial buoyancy. The Table 5.8 below gives the yearly growth of industrial production in major sectors of the industry during the Tenth Plan.

Table 5.8: Annual Growth of Industrial Production in Major Sectors

(Base 1993-94 = 100) (per cent)

Period	Mining and Quarrying	Manufacturing	Electricity	Overall
2002-03	5.8	6.0	3.2	5.7
2003-04	5.2	7.4	5.1	7.0
2004-05	4.4	9.2	5.2	8.4
2005-06	1.0	9.1	5.2	8.2
2006-07*	3.8	11.5	7.3	10.6

* (April-December)

Source: Central Statistical Organisation.

It is to be noted here that manufacturing industries are grouped under registered and unregistered units. While the share of registered units grew sharply from 4.4 per cent in 1950-51 to 11.1 per cent in 2001-02, there was a marginal increase in the share of unregistered units during the corresponding period, i.e. from 4.5 per cent of GDP to 5.8 per cent. Likewise, there has been a slight improvement in the construction sector—from 4.1 per cent in 1950-51 to 5.1 per cent in 2001-02. During 2003-04 to 2005-06, the construction growth has been in double digits in each of the three years, i.e. 7.7 per cent in 2002-03, 10.9 per cent in 2003-04, 12.5 per cent in 2004-05 (Quick estimates) and 12.1 per cent in 2005-06 (Advance estimates).

(iii) *Tertiary Sector*: The tertiary sector includes trade, transport, storage, communications, banking, insurance, personal services, real estate and community. The share of this sector has also increased from 28.0 per cent in 1950-51 to about 4905 per cent in 2001-02. The two prominent components of this sector—community and persona services—together has shown an increase in its share from 9.4 per cent in GDP in 1950-51 to 13.5 per cent in 2001-02. The share of transport, communications and trade improved from 12 per cent in 1950-51 to 23.5 per cent in 2001-02. On the contrary, the share of finance and real estate which includes banking and insurance declined from 6.7 per cent in 1950-51 to 6.5 per cent in 1980-81. However, it improved to 12.5 per cent in 2001-02. Indeed, since the beginning of the Tenth Plan in 2002-03, on average services with a share of 52.0 per cent of GDP, contributed 65.0 per cent of GDP growth, and increased its share in GDP from 49.8 per cent to 54.1 per cent. Services sector growth has been broad-based. For the three consecutive years during the Tenth Plan, the three sub-sectors of services—trade, hotels, transport and communication continued to lead by growing at double digit rates while growth in financial services after dipping in 2003-04 bounced back in 2004-05. The Table 5.9 below clearly indicates the real growth rates in GDP of Services Sector at factor cost 1999-2000 prices during the Tenth Five-Year Plan:

Table 5.9: Growth Rates in GDP at Factor Cost of Service Sector (1999-2000 prices)

Services	Percentage change over the previous year			
	2002-03	2003-04 (P)	2004-05(Q)	2005-06(A)
Trade, Hotels, Transport and Communication	9.1	12.0	10.6	11.1
Financial Services	8.0	4.5	9.2	9.5
Community, Social and Personal Services	3.8	5.4	9.2	7.9

Note: P: Provisional Q: Quick Estimates A: Advance Estimates

Source: Central Statistical Organisation.

(e) Trends in the Share of the Public Sector

Decade-wise, the share of public sector in gross domestic product was 14.9 per cent in 1970-71, 19.7 per cent in 1980-81 and 24.4 per cent in 2001-02. The setting up of new industries, nationalisation of coal mining companies, banks and insurance etc., expansion of existing enterprises and merger of private electricity companies into electric boards have led to the increase in the share of GDP of the public sector. During the Tenth Plan, the percentage share of public sector in GDP has been 24.7 and 23.2 in 2002-03 and 2003-04, respectively.

(f) Urban and Rural Income Break-up

As per the National Accounts Statistics, the rural sector in 1970-71 contributed 62.4 per cent of the total NDP but declined to 54.3 per cent in 1993-94. On the other hand, the share of the urban sector in NDP improved from 37.6 per cent to 45.7 per cent in the corresponding period.

Share of Organised and Unorganised Sector in NDP

According to the CSO, Organised enterprises are those that are within the preview of any of the Acts and maintain annual accounts and balance sheets. While the unorganised enterprises mainly refer to unincorporated enterprises and household industries lacking in annual accounts and balance sheets. As per the CSO, the share of the organised sector has risen since

1980-81 by approximately 7 per cent. Consequently, the value of the unorganised sector has declined by same proportion, i.e. from 70 per cent to 63.2 per cent during the corresponding period.

Limitations of National Income Estimation

While making an estimate of national income millions of economic quantities have to be added up, which requires of to be kept in mind the basic judgments and social criteria based on the mores and traditions of a society. Accordingly, there are many limitations of national income estimation which have a particular relevance in India. Some of the limitations are listed below:

(i) The general assumption while calculating national output is that the major share of the commodities and services produced are exchanged for money. But India being an agrarian economy, hire the bulk of the agricultural output that come to the market is not meant for sale rather it is consumed by the producers themselves or is bartered away with other producers in exchange for other goods and services. If this portion of the output is ignored, the national output would considerably reduce. In brief, one of the limitations of national income estimation is that there is no objective method of finding out the imputed value of the produce of the non-monetised sector and add it to the value of the monetised sector.

(ii) In India there is non-availability of data about the income of small producers or entrepreneurs, mainly because they are either illiterate and so unable to maintain accounts or they do not feel the necessity of keeping such account on a regular basis. Consequently, there is a tinge of guesswork in National Income estimation. As the high proportion of the economy is in the unorganised sector, the chances of error in estimation cannot be overlooked.

(iii) National Income estimation suffers from the absence of data on income distribution. The National Accounts

Statistics do not generate any data on income distribution of households or persons.

(iv) In India a considerable part of the economy operates as hidden economy and the income generated in it remains unrecorded. Professionals like teachers, doctors, lawyers, chartered accountants never wish to reveal their income or earnings. It is a dark reality that the magnitude of the black economy is increasing and so also the error in estimation of national income. Thus, national income estimates to some extent are underestimates.

Critical Evaluation of Trends in National and Per Capita Income

An in-depth study of trends in national and per capita income shows both the positive and the negative features.

When viewed in overall terms, the trend exhibits a persistent rise both in the national income and the per capita income. Despite the years of poor performance, the rise has been modest and sizeable, although the upcurve is not a consistent one. Even the per capita income has been on the rise, although not significantly.

It is quite obvious that the service sector has become the leading sector in the composition of the gross domestic product owing to its faster growth as compared to that of industry and agriculture. Its share in the national product at 30 per cent in 1950 rose sharply to 48 per cent. From this data it can be inferred that Indian economy is moving the way the developed countries had moved in the past. Today, the country is no longer dependent on agriculture, rather its economy is being led by the industry and services sectors.

Indian economy has built up some inherent strength to spring back or rebound after going through a difficult phase. Experiences of the 1980s are one of the evidences. During the Sixth Plan, the growth rate was over 5 per cent, which is yet held to be good in the light of drought of 1979-80, the deterioration in the functioning of infrastructure, a 17 per cent drop in the production of food grains and unfavourable weather in 1982-83, etc. Likewise, despite the worst drought in 1987-88,

1990s, the fixed capital formation, which adds to the capital stock of a country, reached around 22-23 per cent of the gross domestic product. The Table 5.10 gives the data of fixed capital formation in terms of percentage of GDP.

From the Table 5.10 it is quite apparent that India's capital formation still lags behind the actual need for a reasonable growth of domestic product. Unfortunately, it is even lower than that attained by countries like China (35 per cent), Indonesia (31 per cent), and Sri Lanka (27 per cent).

It is mainly the public sector investment that has been responsible for the small output growth. Since 1951, except for few years, capital formation in public sector has always been low than the private sector. As per the latest data available, during 2004-05 public sector capital formation accounted for 6.7 per cent of GDP while the private sector correspondingly accounted for 19.1 per cent.

Table 5.10: Gross Fixed Capital Formation (As per cent of GDP)

Year	Gross fixed Capital Formation (1993-94 series)
1950-51	8.9
1960-61	12.7
1970-71	14.0
1980-81	18.5
1990-91	22.9
	Base year (1999-2000)
1999-2000	23.3
2000-01	22.7
2001-02	23.1
2002-03	24.1
2003-04	24.7
2004-05 (Q)	25.9

Q-Quick Estimates

(c) **High Capital-Output Ratio:** The high capital-output ratio is another major factor that has led to slow growth of national income. Despite the increase in

following the prior four consecutive poor monsoons, a growth rate of over 5 per cent was achieved during the Seventh Plan (1985-90) which is no less remarkable. Even during the 1990s, when the country suffered East Asian crisis in 1997, post-Pokhran economic sanctions by developed countries like the USA, effects of Kargil War of 1999, the average growth rate of economy at 7 per cent is appreciating. Thus it can be well said that Indian economy has acquired some resilience against difficult situations. The nation has undoubtedly seen some definite growth in national income.

Contrary to these obvious positive performance, there has been certain weaknesses in the growth trend of national income. Firstly, the size of growth rate has been less than desirable as indicated by the targets of the various plans. For instance, the targets of growth in national income were not fulfilled in the Seconds, Third and Fourth and Ninth Plans. The shortfalls during these plans were as under:

Plan	Target	Actual Growth	Shortfall
Second Plan	4.2%	4.0%	0.2%
Third Plan	5.6%	2.3%	3.3%
Fourth Plan	5.7%	3.3%	2.4%
Ninth Plan	6.5%	5.35%	1.1%

However, the targets exceeded in the First, the Fifth and Eighth Plans while the Sixth and Seventh Plan fulfilled the targets at over 5 per cent. So far the Tenth Plan is concerned, against the annual growth rate of 8.0 per cent envisaged in the Tenth Plan, the average rate is estimated to have been 7.0 per cent in the first four years ending in 2005-06. It has been estimated that maintenance of growth at or above 8 per cent in 2006-07 will yield a plan period annual average growth rate of at least 7.2 per cent.

Apart from such mixed performances, India's growth performance in comparison to China, one of the developing countries, has been unsatisfactyory. Over the past five years, i.e. during 2000-05, China has grown at an annual rate of 9.7 per cent to become the world's fourth largest economy today; while

India, though picking up pace, has managed to grow at an average of 8 per cent a year. However, in respect of other developing countries like Indonesia, Pakistan, Sri Lanka, Bangladesh, etc. India has performed better except for one or two plan periods.

India's economic growth exhibits fluctuation in character, mainly in agricultural sector. Factor responsible for fluctuation in agriculture sector is mainly the uncertain weather conditions. This significantly affects agriculture and agro-economies, which is turn affect the growth in other sectors.

For instance, a year of drought results in a chair of adverse reactions in the country's economy. First and foremost, the agricultural produce gets reduced which consequently causes cut in raw materials for industries, as also food grains for consumption. This in turn badly affect the industrial output. A reduction in industrial output leads to rise in prices and reduction in income. Thus, the unstable growth of economy ultimately weakens the motivations to invest, innovate and to take risks.

Since the total income is very small in relative to population, even a meagre downturn causes much hardship. On the contrary, a small rise in income hardly makes impact on living standards owing to the vast population. In nutshell, the fluctuating character of—the growth—performance is one of the serious weaknesses of India's economic development.

The low growth of commodity sectors is yet another dismal aspect that affects the national income. The commodity sectors —agriculture and industry—has not yet made the desired progress. Since 1950 agricultural production has grown at around 2.7 per cent only. So is the case of the industrial sector which overall grew at the rate of 6 per cent. If power generation and mining are not included, the growth in the manufacturing sector is not an impressive one. It is to be noted here that manufacturing sector is the most dynamic part of the industrial sector, accounting for over 79 per cent of weight in the index of industrial production. The slow growth in the commodity sector has prevented a faster growth of the economy due to the weak

impulses emanating from this sector. Besides, the me exports have also not risen fast due to this very fast.

The slow growth in national income is another w remains as yet a big handicap is raising the consum of the vast masses. With growth less than targeted in mentioned three Five-Year Plans, and the excess n the other Plans, the growth in consumption has be only a little. For the large many years since 1950-51 rate in the per capita consumption was 1.1 per ce prevailing low levels of consumption, this marg could not improve much the living standards of th a great mass is yet below the poverty line. As th inequalities of assets and a significant portion of deprived of full-employment for the whole year, income of the poorer sections is relatively much all-India average. Consequently, the per capita c the large number is still smaller.

Factors Influencing Growth of National Incon

Since the growth of an economy is a res variables interacting upon one another, it is of to enlist distinct causes. However, some of the r been discussed below:

(a) **Rapid Population Growth**: The larg its continuous rapid growth have signi the growth of national income. Th have been multifaceted. The resourc could not rise proportionately for lo of national income continued to con goods. Similarly, stockpiling ma consumer goods and as such lesser to the raising of fixed capital forn several schemes for employment large subsidies, thereby reducing r capacities for more production. national income has been little an the large remains as yet.

(b) **Low Investment:** The growth r India has been relatively low si

Note

capital formation, though not appreciating, the increase in capital has not been accompanied with substantial increase in output. In other words, additions to output with additional capital has remained low for many years.

(d) **Low Agricultural and Industrial Growth:** Evidently, national income is determined by trends in agriculture and industrial production. As mentioned earlier, the production of agricultural and industrial goods has been relatively low and so also the growth curve of national income. While the growth rate of agricultural production, accounting to 2.7 per cent, has been just little above the population growth; the industrial growth has been around 6 per cent which too is not very highly impressive.

Keeping in view the above factors determining and influencing the national income, some measures for raising growth performance can be suggested. *First and foremost*, production structure needs to be reshaped is a manner that it become compatible with our resources. In this respect the assessment of our resources and the use as well as development of most advanced technologies would be the most viable measures. Resources include energy, land, water, essential minerals, ecology and environment, which determine the potential for growth. Technology on the other hand can argument the resources by raising their productivity. Thus, a rationalized production-structure will best cater with the domestic as well as foreign demands, thereby rising substantially the growth rate.

For the adequate production structure—we need to promote labour intensive industries, as because India is facing massive unemployment and hence labour in abundance is available at much lower wage rate. This will reduce unemployment and consequently the per capita income will improve. Likewise, the use of advanced technology will require more capital which means that production would become capital intensive. In other words, the production growth needs to be labour-intensive in the first phase and capital-intensive in the second phase. Above all, agriculture and other land-based activities need to be developed on priority. Agriculture-based activities like dryland farming in the rainfed areas; agro-processing and agro-business; aquaculture, animal husbandry need to be significantly promoted.

Secondly, appropriate strategies need to be adopted to curb the population growth. It is a matter of fact that projected rise in the per capita income of many of the plans have gone wrong only because the population projections have gone wrong. The growing population adversely affect the savings both in the private and public sectors. Reduction in population growth would mean reduction in consumption and larger resources for investment which in turn would lead to growth in terms of national income.

Thirdly, creation of capacity and adequate and proper maintenance of the already created capacity are indispensable for the growth of national income. Thus, policy needs to be formulated to step-up the rate of fixed capital formation and eliminate the unnecessary increase in stocks. In the Indian economy, a large part of the economy's capacity remains unutilized which amounts to waste of resources. This results mainly from lack of demand both for consumer goods as well as capital goods. While the former requires income generation among people, the latter requires an increase in investments.

Fourthly, increase in productivity in many sectors need to be attained. For instance, agricultural output is much less than is possible with existing resources. So is the case with many industries where optimum production is not being realised. A proper allocation of resources and better management of productive units would give positive result. By proper allocation of resources it is meant that dispersal of resources among different lines should be such that it balance demand for and supply of output of different producing units. As a matter of fact, the inadequacy in balancing investments in the related sectors has been mainly responsible for the inefficient use of the existing capacity. To illustrate, the Command Area Development Programme involves irrigation on which much investment is being made while little investment is made on the construction of field channels that supply water to land, irrespective of fact that the former is of little use without the latter. Thus, the need of the hour is to ensure a balance between investment in the creation of new capacities and investment in the complementary sectors.

Equally necessary is the better management of producing units which can be achieved through efficient management personnel. Besides, a greater autonomy for decision-making to the managements in respect of matters like investments for modernization and replacement. Choice and pricing of products etc., would prove beneficial is stepping up the efficiency of the economy.

Fifthly, workers' optimum cooperation must be sought, as their cooperation determines productivity. To ensure maximum output, it is essential to obtain uninterrupted operation of the plants. The contributed of labour can markedly increase if they acquire a stake or share in the producing units as this will reduce absenteeism and loss of working days.

Lastly, competition needs to be more vigorous as our country is basically market dominated. Accordingly, competition will bring rise in output, reduction in costs and improvement in the quality of products, which will ultimately add to the national income.

To conclude, India's national income, despite some unsatisfactory features, has been development oriented and holds out a great promise for the future.

Domestic Saving

6

In a country, the capital formation or investment as well as the productive capacity largely depend on the domestic saving for finance. Thus, the significance of adequate saving cannot be overemphasised.

Trends of Domestic Saving

It would be advantageous to discuss the sources of domestic saving before entering into the study of trends of the saving behaviour of the Indian economy. In India domestic savings originate from three principal sectors, namely (i) household sector (ii) the private corporate sector and (iii) Public sector.

The Household Sector constitutes individuals non-government; non-corporate entities in agriculture, trade and industry; and non-profit organisations or private collectives like trusts, charitable and religious institutions. The saving of this sector comprises the surplus income after meeting the consumption expenditure. A part of the saving of this sector is in the form of physical assets, like construction of well, ponds etc.

The Private Corporate Sector includes the non-government corporate sector and cooperative sector. The saving of this sector is the retained profits obtained after meeting up the expenses of the business including dividends distributed as corporate tax to the government.

The Public Sector includes the government administration, government's departmental and non-departmental undertakings. The saving of this sector includes the surplus current revenue over current expenditure of the government and the profits of the undertakings. Accordingly, the saving of this sector relates to the budgetary surplus on current account of the central government, state government, local authorities, the current surplus of various government departments and retained projects of government undertakings. Since 1950s there has been a remarkable rise in the domestic saving from 8.9 per cent of gross domestic product in 1950-51 to 32.4 per cent in 2005-06. However, the rise in saving has not been a smooth one. While, the first two decades of the post-Independence era observed the increase by five percentage points, the next three decades witnessed the shoot by about 10 percentage points. In addition, for many years there have been year-to-year fluctuations with either increases or decreases over the previous years which is clearly evident in the Table 6.1 below:

Table 6.1: Gross Domestic Savings by Institutional Sectors

(Rs. in crore)

Sectors	At 1993-94 Series			At 1999-2000 series		
	1950-51	1960-61	1970-71	1980-81	1990-91	2000-01
1. Household	612	1254	4634	19868	109897	458215
As per cent of GDP	6.2	7.3	10.1	13.8	19.3	21.2
2. Private Corporate Sector	93	281	672	2339	15164	87017
As per cent of GDP	0.9	1.6	1.5	1.6	2.7	4.1
3. Public Sector	182	454	1343	4929	6279	-37062
As per cent of GDP	1.8	2.6	2.9	3.4	1.1	-1.8

Source: Economic Survey, 2005-06.

The ongoing Tenth Five-Year Plan (2002-07) has as yet witnessed a significant improvement in the rates of savings. Savings rate, which is gross domestic savings as a proportion of GDP at current market prices increased from 26.4 per cent in 2002-03 to 32.4 per cent in 2005-06. Further improvements in savings came in 2003-04 to which accounted to 29.7 per cent and thence touched a record level of 31.1 per cent in 2004-05. This record level implies an increase of 5.5 percentage points since 2001-02, before which the rate had remained stagnant and even declined since the mid-1990s.

The recent revision of the weighting system and revision of the base year from 1993-94 to 1999-2000 has made a difference to the savings rate estimates for individual years. However, the trend remains broadly the same. The initial rise in the savings rate was captured by the old series and provisional estimates from the new series for the year 2004-05 suggest that the trend has continued (See Table 6.2 below).

Table 6.2: Gross Domestic Savings (At current prices)
(Base Year 1999-2000)

(Rs. in crore)

Sectors	2001-02	2002-03	2003-04	2004-05
Household	502674	565408	648634	687079
As per cent of GDP	22.0	23.1	23.5	22
Private Corporate Sector	81669	99767	120052	150947
As per cent of GDP	3.6	4.1	4.4	4.8
Public Sector	-43677	-16181	28026	69390
As per cent of GDP	-2.0	-0.7	1.0	2.2

Source: Economic Survey, 2005-06

A careful study of Tables 6.1 and 6.2 above clearly shows that of the three saving sectors, the major contributions have been that of the household sector. For most of the years since 1950-51, its share has been around 70-75 per cent in the domestic saving and even more. It would not be wrong to say that the trend in this sector has actually influenced the rise and fall in the domestic saving. On the second position has been the private corporate sector in contributing to the grass domestic saving. Till the 1980s its contribution ranged between 10 to 12 per cent while in the later 10 years its share increased remarkably. The contributions of public sector have been mixed. Until 1980s its contributions were greater than the private corporate sector but thereafter it declined more so in the 1990s when it was even negative. Thus, in brief it can be said that overall there has been a substantial increase in the saving. More importantly, the rise in the savings rates during 2002-05 has coincided with an increase in the rate of growth of GDP over the corresponding period, suggesting that the economy is transiting to a sustainable higher growth trajectory.

The question thus arises as to what are the factors that have been mainly responsible for the rise in savings? Whether the sudden increase in the recent years is more statistical than actual?

Owing to the current savings surge coinciding with a massive increase in the inflow of portfolio FII investment in India's stock and debt markets, it has been often argued that some of this capital may have been lodged with the banks and got wrongly recorded as household savings invested in financial assets. *A priori* this is indeed a possibility. As said earlier, savings are estimated by classifying the savers into the public sector, the private corporate sector and the household sector. While public sector saving is computed from budgetary data and captures the excess of government expenditure at both levels—Centre and State—over revenue expenditure, the private corporate sector savings in the form of retained earnings are obtained from company balance-sheet data. The household savings are estimated in two parts: firstly household financial savings which is estimated using data on the assets and liabilities of the financial sector, adjusted for its outstanding positions with the public and private corporate sector. Secondly, household savings in financial assets, which is the excess of aggregate of capital formation estimated by the product flow method over the estimated capital formation in the public and private corporate sectors based on budgetary data and company balance sheets. It is to be noted here that if funds transferred by FIIs for investment purposes are parked in bank deposits or other financial investments before being invested in corporate equity and bonds, there is a possibility of their being attributed to the household sector.

Likewise, if aggregate capital formation obtained through the product flow method is overestimated, there would be an overestimation of "physical savings" in the household sector.

Apart from these issues of relevance, there are two other features in the sectoral savings that need to be noted: firstly, during 2000-01 and 2003-04, the gross savings rate increased by 5.4 percentage points, against which it remained

2.3 percentage points in the household sector. Secondly, during 2004-05 the household savings grew at 5.9 per cent—slower than the GDP growth rate—and made a negative contribution by coming down as a proportion of GDP. The above data reveal that the movements in household sector savings account for much less than half of the increase in the aggregate savings rate in the recent years. Overall, during 2001-02 and 2004-05, the aggregate savings rate rose by 5.5 percentage points while the household savings rate remained stagnant. The composition of the household savings rate has not changed significantly in favour of financial instruments. The Figure 6.1 below shows the distribution of household savings:

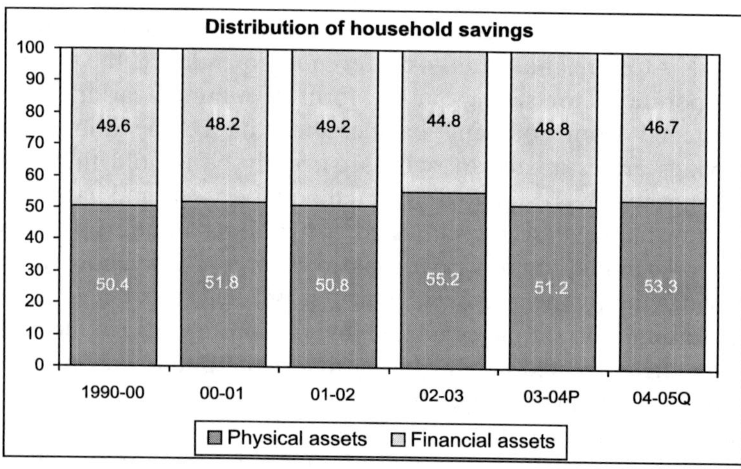

P- Provisional Q- Quick Estimates

Figure 6.1

A close examination of sectoral savings trends suggests that it is the public sector which has seen a sharp transformation of its dissaving into saving during 2001-02 and 2004-05, when its saving rate rose from a negative 2 per cent to a positive 2.2 per cent, contributing a remarkable 4.2 percentage points increase to the savings rate.

Thus, together with a small contribution from the private corporate sector, public sector has been primarily responsible for the statistically recorded savings surge. Of its three

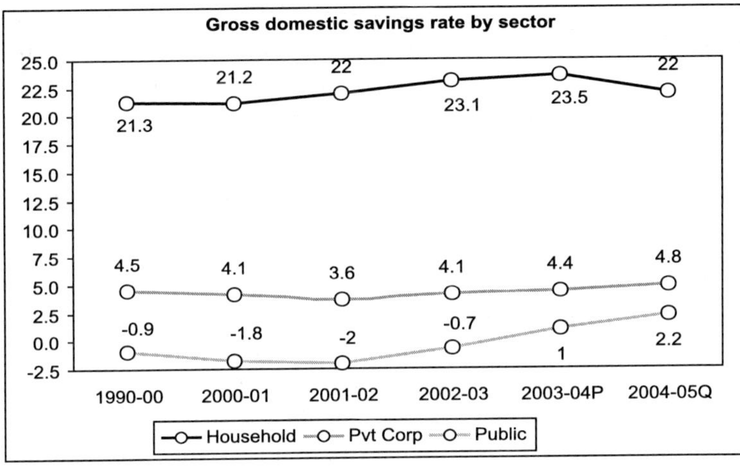

P- Provisional Q- Quick Estimates

Figure 6.2

sub-sectors—government administration; departmental enterprises and non-departmental enterprises—the non-departmental public enterprises have largely contributed to reduced dissaving or the increase in saving. This has become possible because of the liberalisation of public sector pricing practices (See Figure 6.3 below).

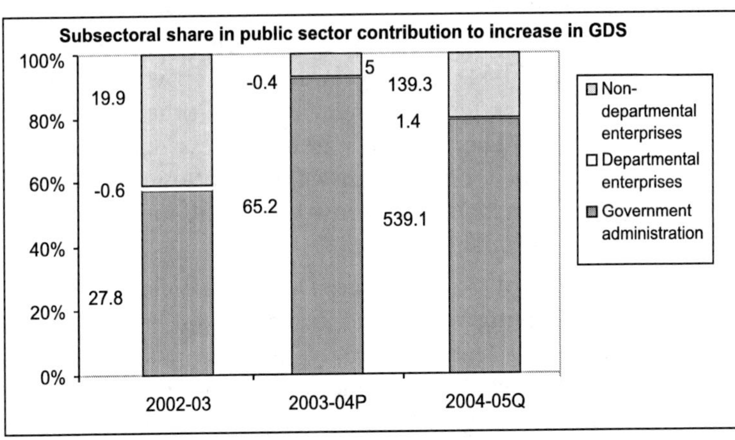

P- Provisional Q- Quick

Figure 6.3

The reduced dissaving in government administration also substantially accounts for the estimated improvement in the savings rate. The contribution of this sub-sector to the increases in the savings rate in 2002-03, 2003-04 and 2004-05 has respectively been 60, 90 and 80 per cent.

Factors Responsible for Improvement in Public Savings

The factors that are mainly responsible for improvement in public savings may be noted as under:

(i) A stagnation and decline in government expenditures and a significant improvement in government revenues apparently delivered the reduction in net dissaving of the administrative departments of government.

(ii) A growing curtailment of public employment, which is no way appreciating given the massive deficit in public services, especially in rural areas.

(iii) Improved customs duty collections despite reduced tariffs, because of an increase in the quantum of imports and the steep increases in oil prices.

(iv) Contribution of special dividends from to-be-privatised entities and receipts from disinvestment and privatisation to government revenues.

Assessment of the Performance of Domestic Savings

(1) **Significant Achievement:** The rise in the rate of saving since 1950-51 is fairly large. The growth in saving has been better here than in many other developing countries. This growth has led to less dependence of the country on foreign capital inflow, which has generally remained at a low level of about 2-3 per cent of the national product.

(2) **Inconsistent Performance:** Despite a considerable rise in the saving rate, it continues to suffer from some disquieting features. Firstly, the rise has not been a smooth one. During some financial years, the rate has often been stagnant. For instance, during 1976 to 1981 it remained around 19 per cent except for 22 per cent in 1978-79, while during 1982 to 1987 it moved

around 17-19 per cent. The tendency of the falling rate is evidenced during 1978-79 to 1984-85 when the rate fell from 22 per cent to 19 per cent.

Secondly, the saving rate, in spite of being high in comparison to the rate until 1950s, is not satisfactory in the sense that India has not as yet become self-reliant in the sense of elimination of dependence on foreign aid or financial loans on concessional and easy terms.

(3) **Unsatisfactory Performance of Private and Public Sector:** The role of the two sub-sectors, namely Public Sector and Private Corporate Sector, cannot be overemphasised. The economy of a developing country like India is largely determined by the role of these two sub-sectors, particularly when the objective is to step up the rate of capital formation. Unfortunately, performance of these two sub-sectors have been far from satisfactory. Despite its small size, the private corporate sector could have done better provided its unnecessary expenditures like those of excessive advertising were curtailed and resources were efficiently utilised. Likewise, public sector need improvement on both fronts—income and expenditure. The saving capacity of the government has been mainly eroded by the increasing growth in the non-plan or non-productive expenditure.

(4) **Inadequate Distribution:** The inadequate distribution or deployment of domestic saving has significantly affected the performance of the economy. It is commonly evident that a large proportion of the total saving is allocated to the new projects in comparison to the amount earmarked for the maintenance and promotion of existing capital assets and their replacements. This has led to fast deterioration of these assets which in turn result in higher capital-output ratio. It has been noticed that the Planning Commission, in general, uses the concept of gross domestic saving and ignores the estimation of the consumption of capital or depreciation that gives the net investment. As a result, there has

been a tendency to use up as much as possible the available financial resources for financing new projects all though the successive plans. However, the estimation of capital consumption to arrive at net investment can never be absolutely correct as it is estimated under diverse assumptions of the life of assets and the replacement cost of assets. Whatever might be the approach of the Planning Commission to the estimation of net investment, the need of the hour is the efficient allocation of saving.

To conclude, the saving profile of the economy is marked with substantial rise although not a remarkable one. While the household sector significantly contributed to the domestic saving, the private corporate sector logged behind and the performance of the public sector remained simply far from what was actually required and expected.

Suggested Measures for Raising Saving

Some measures need to be adopted to ensure rise in the rate of saving and sustaining the same at a higher level as well. *Firstly*, adequacy of the financial institutions such as banks, insurance agencies, stock exchanges, etc. is to be sought as these institutions serve as intermediaries between the savers and the investors on the one hand and cater with the varying incomes, needs and temperaments of the people on the other.

Secondly, since the most powerful incentive for the savers is the interest, its rate should be reasonable so that it attracts adequate saving. Furthermore, it should be continuously adjusted with the changes in the price level. It has even been generally suggested by the economists that the rate of interest must correspond to the rise in prices if stability in the return on saving is to be ensured. It is a matter of fact that people save for monetary motives. Hence, in determining a reasonable rate of interest, the important factor is not merely its level rather its real worth. As in India, the inflation has for long been on the rise, increase in the rate of interest appears to be indispensable. Unfortunately, the interest rate has seldomly aligned with the price level. There is no denying that savings have improved but an attractive rate of interest can bring forth a much larger saving in India the propensity to save is quite high.

Thirdly, income distribution has a significant influence on domestic saving. Savings are considered to be a proportion of national accruing to the owners of property. Larger the proportion of income going to this section, larger the saving, because the high income group has a higher propensity to save as compared to wage earners whose income is largely consumed. If viewed from this perspective, income inequalities are justified. But, for India such policy would not be appreciating as the corporate sector is comparatively very small. Accordingly, given an income distribution favourable to it, the corporate sector may not by itself be a determining factor in influencing the trend in total saving. So far the population of the high income group is concerned, the income distribution has prove advantageous to it as is evident from the widening inequalities in income and wealth, and a large proportion of population lying below the poverty line. However, their large proportion of income account for black money and so it hardly make a significant impact on saving on account of this factor of income distribution. It follows that a more equitable distribution of income if promoted would bear fruitful result.

Fourthly, savings heavily depend on inflation. Hence, if it remains within the limit, saving can be improved because analyses show that saving rate moves inversely with the index of price level. The middle and the lower classes are able to save less during the phase of rapidly rising prices as they find their purchasing power being eroded. On the contrary, the higher income groups are benefited from inflation. But their income have not contributed significantly to substantial increase of saving owing to their large expenses on ostentatious living. Their extravagance rather encourage the middle and low income group toward expenses on luxuries thereby resulting in dissaving. Thus, theoretically it may appear that inflation increases saving on the ground that a rise in prices causes a shift in real income, this is not the case with India where under inflationary conditions there is a slow rise and often a fall in the rate of saving. Only a stable and mildly rising price level can bring a rapid and continuous increase in real saving in India.

Fifthly, some effective steps need to be taken in the household sector to ensure larger saving. Although several saving schemes have been started by the government like those of National Saving Certificates (NSC), Units of Unit Trust of India (UTI), etc. schemes of saving yet need to be evolved so as to better cater with the need of the small savers, particularly those engaged with unorganised sector and in agriculture. While the most preferred financial instruments like deposits, provident and pension funds, life insurance and claims on government need to be popularised, it is essential to evolve techniques so as to divert people more and more towards shares and debentures and thereby strengthen the sources of risk capital for the industrial development. At the same time saving in the physical form must also be promoted. The physical assets like wells, water channels, storage etc. are of immense value as they help raising output in several ways, particularly in agriculture.

Sixthly, the share of the private corporate sector in the saving has to be raised substantially. For this the expenses on large and lavish perks for the personnel and entertainment allowances etc. need to be curtailed while the loopholes in the law need to be removed so as to eliminate extravagant expenses on excessive advertisements, unfair commissions etc. Not only the big ones rather the small enterprises must also be allowed to make larger profits, provided a considerable proportion of these profits is used for the creation of capital assets. Furthermore, a reduction in cost of production and increase in efficiency will raise the capacity of the enterprises of secondary and tertiary sectors whose share has not reached its potential as yet.

Measures like upgradation of technology, use of modern methods of inventory control, availability of infrastructural services, avoidance of slackening in demand and thereby removing underutilization of large capacity etc. would facilitate raising earning capacity. Above all, the structure of the corporate tax needs to be designed such that liberal tax concessions (investment rebates), tax holidays etc. are given under the condition that a major share of the profits is ploughed to the capital accumulation.

These measures will undoubtedly promote the expansion of the capitalist sector which is one of the prerequisites for obtaining large domestic saving like those of developed countries.

Seventhly, increase in current revenue—which constitute both direct and indirect taxes as well as non-tax revenue, and a reasonable limit on the current expenditure are to be sought. The scope for raising tax revenue is fairly large in India. Being an agrarian economy, agriculture accounts for over one-fourth of India's national income. As this sector is yet exempted from tax and since there are large inequalities of income and land holdings in villages, revenues can be remarkably raised by making tax obligatory for the richer sections of the rural population. Likewise, those in the unroganised sector can be made liable to pay tax who do not do so by extending the tax net.

In the public sector there is need to reduce the level of underutilised capacity which to some extent, however, is caused by general slackening of investment in the economy, low demand for this products, etc. The savings of the public sector enterprises as for the non-tax revenue have been relatively low. This can be improved by lowering the present high expense ratio, i.e. between the net sales turnover and cost of sales including depreciation but excluding interest. Close to this requirement is the need of evolving a rational price policy so as to enable these enterprises to meet their costs and to generate a reasonable surplus on the capital employed. Simultaneously, the current expenditure needs to be restrained from rising unduly. In the recent years the non-development expenditure like those of defence, civil administration, subsidies on food and fertilizer, interest on public debt etc. has relatively increased which restrain the growth of saving on revenue account.

Lastly, the fiscal policy has to be modified. In relation to saving, the fiscal factor is of great importance. Taxes if not adequately devised adversely affect the saving potential of the economy. For instance, when tax rate is fairly high, it affects the incentive for work leading to reduction in income and savings. Furthermore, taxes add to the price hike thereby reducing the household saving. Consequently, the next benefit to the economy in terms of higher government saving may thus be less. The other aspects of the fiscal policy, i.e. government expenditure, needs to be so determined that may bring about increase surpluses on revenue account. The expenditure pattern ought to be such that it raises the productivity capacity of the people which then would increase the saving.

Domestic Savings in the Approach Paper to Eleventh Plan

It has been envisaged in the Approach Paper to Eleventh Plan that the total domestic savings rate must increase from 27.1 per cent to 32.3 per cent provided the current account deficit could be kept below 3 per cent. The growth of household and corporate savings will be determined by behavioural parameters, given the growth of income and GDP. A significant portion of the needed increase in domestic savings will have come to from an improvement in Government savings. The Table 6.3 below suggests a turnaround in government savings of around 2.5 percentage points of GDP for a growth rate between 8 and 9 per cent. It follows that the government both at Centre and State levels will have to ensure strong budgetary discipline.

Table 6.3: Alternative Scenarios for the Eleventh Plan

(%)

Target Growth Rate in 11th plan	7.0	8.0	9.0
Average Investment Rate	29.1	32.0	35.1
Average CAD as percentage of GDP	2.0	2.4	2.8
Domestic Savings Rate :	27.1	29.6	32.3
(a) Household	20.1	20.5	21.0
(b) Corporate	5.0	5.5	6.1
(c) PSEs	3.1	3.1	2.8
(d) Government	-1.1	0.5	2.4

Source: An Approach to the Eleventh Five-Year Plan, Planning Commission, GOI, 2006.

Agriculture

7

Agriculture is the mainstay of the Indian economy. The agriculture sector has overall recorded satisfactory growth due to improved technology, irrigation, inputs and pricing policies. Livestock, poultry, fisheries and horticulture are surging ahead in production growth in recent years and are expected to have greater demand in the future. However, industrial and service sectors have expanded faster than agriculture sector resulting in declining share of agriculture in national accounts. Despite the structural change, agriculture still remains a key sector, providing both employment and livelihood opportunities to around 65 per cent of the total workforce in the country. Besides, it sizeably contributes to the domestic product as also to exports. The importance of agriculture and allied sectors in the national economy can be best studied by analysing the role of agriculture under separate headings:

1. Large Share of Agriculture in National Income

The all-pervading influence of agriculture can be gauged from its contribution to the nation's gross domestic product (GDP). Agriculture and allied sectors contribute nearly 22 per cent of GDP.

Table 7.1 shows the share of agriculture decade-wise in total GDP at factor cost since 1950-51.

Table 7.1: Share of Agricultural Sector in Total GDP at Factor Cost

(At 1993-94 prices) (Rs. crore)

Year	GDP at Factor Cost	Agriculture	Percentage of GDP
1950-51	1,40,470	83,150	55.4
1970-71	2,96,280	1,42,580	44.5
1990-91	6,92,870	2,42,010	30.9
2003-04	14,30,550	3,43,810	24.1

Note: Agriculture includes agriculture, forestry and fishing.

* Quick Estimates.

Source: Compiled from *Economic Survey* 2004-05.

As per the Table 7.1 and figures provided by the CSO, the share of agriculture in GDP between 1950-51 to 1970-71 showed a declining trend, although the range of share was respectable, *i.e.* 55 to 44 per cent. In the later years, because of the liberalisation and industrialisation policy of the country that gave momentum to the economic growth, the share of agriculture indicated a sharp decline and reached a level of 24 per cent in 2003-04. Despite the declining trend, however, the agriculture sector continues to contribute a major share to the national income in India. In terms of quantity, its standing in the economy will continue to be quite significant.

2. Source of Large Employment and Support for many Activities

Since agricultural sector is the source of largest number of commodities in the country, it provides employment and livelihood to a very high proportion of working population in India. As per the data provided by the Census of India, agriculture provided employment in absolute terms to 97 million persons in 1951 which has raised to 402 million in 2001 (Table 7.2).

In addition to those dependent on agriculture directly, a large number of people earn their living by working in occupations dependent upon agriculture, like storage, processing, and trade and transport of agricultural products. While in villages people earn from cultivation and allied agro-industries,

Table 7.2: Employment of Main Workers in Agriculture

(in million)

	1951	2001
Total Population	361	1027
Rural Population	299	742
Cultivators	70	128
Agricultural Labourers	27	107
Other Workers	43	167
Total Working Population	40	402

Source: Agricultural Statistics at a Glance (2002).

a major part of entire labour force in towns and cities also finds jobs in marketing, export and other activities linked with agriculture.

3. Source of Large Supplies of Food and Fodder

Needless to mention, agricultural sector meets the need of food of the country's entire population. No doubt, imports of foodgrains have played a significant role in meeting the growing needs of rising population, but the fact remains that the proportion of such imports has always been small. Except for 1966 and 1967, when food imports were higher than 10 per cent of the net availability of foodgrains in the country, in most of the years it was on an average less than 5 per cent. Yet in other years there were in fact exports of foodgrains.

The importance of agriculture in providing fodder to sustain livestock cannot be overemphasized. The various products of the livestock are the sources of nourishing food like milk, eggs, meat etc. as well as commercial products like wool and hides.

4. Significant Role of Agriculture in the Foreign Trade

Agriculture contributes a considerable part to exports and is also an important segment of imports of the country. Since 1970s the exports of agricultural products have been quite large and rising. Agricultural products like tea, sugar, oilseeds, tobacco, spices, etc. constitute the main items of exports. These exports at present constitute 15 to 20 per cent of the total exports of the country. The Tenth Plan estimates 14.7 per cent of contribution by agriculture to the total export earnings. This earning is of significance, for increased exports help the country to pay for the increased imports of machinery and raw materials. The entire earnings may be made use of in the import of non-agricultural development goods as agriculture itself requires marginal imports as its input. Imports of agricultural products contribute mere 5 to 7 per cent of country's total imports. The important import items include pulses, oilseeds, animal and vegetable oil and fats, agricultural machinery and implements, etc.

5. Significant Role of Agriculture in Economic Planning

Agricultural sector being the largest private sector, its significant role in nation's economic planning cannot be overstated. This sector determines the success or failure of other sectors. For instance, transport sector is directly dependent on agriculture since the railways and roadways secure majority of their business from the transaction of agricultural goods. Similarly, agriculture constitutes a significant part of the industrial profile of the country as many industries are engaged in the processing of agricultural products or in manufacturing agricultural products into finished goods like those of cotton textiles, jute manufactures, vanaspati, etc. Moreover, good harvest implies large purchasing power with the farmers which in turn leads to greater demand for manufactures, and therefore, better prices. Thus, prosperity of the farmers is also the prosperity of industries. There is no denying the fact that the failure in the agriculture sector has in past led to failure of economic planning in the corresponding periods. The Second and Third Plan periods and more recently the financial year 2002-03 may be cited when failure of the agricultural sector spelt disaster to the entire planning process. In addition, services like banking, storage, etc. receive no less support from the large operations in the agricultural sector.

Likewise both the Centre and the State Budgets have been considerably influenced by land revenue and tax income on the one hand and the expenditure on its development on the other. The massive expenditure for agricultural development and related purposes has increased from plan to plan. It would not be out of place to mention that a considerable part of the productive capacity of the country is in the form of agricultural assets like irrigation facilities, storage capacity, ploughs to name a few. It follows that in respect of investment too, agricultural sector occupies an important place. Besides these, agricultural growth has direct impact on poverty eradication. It is also a determining factor in causing inflation, raising agricultural wages and for employment generation.

Thus, it is quite evident that despite low per capita productivity in comparison to industry, agriculture is truly the backbone of the Indian economy. However, some economists of developing economies consider this a weak point as in their view so long as the Indian economy is dominated by agricultural activity, the country would not be able to obtain the necessary and desirable per capita income.

Need for Agricultural Development

There remains no doubt from the above discussion that agriculture has an important role to play in the economic development of the country. Accordingly, agricultural development is indispensable for economic growth, because:

(i) industrialization requires such set of motives and values which India's agrarian economy cannot supply,

(ii) increasing industrialization calls for considerable increase in the marketable agricultural surplus so as to meet the demand of growing urban population as well as the requirement of raw materials by industries,

(iii) incapability of industrial and services sectors to provide adequate employment, no matter however fast they may be growing, to the ever-growing population of the country, and

(iv) above all, the agricultural sector maintains food security and in the process national security as well. Also, in order to maintain the ecological balance, the sustainable and balanced development of the agriculture and allied sectors are to be achieved.

These are some of the major factors that necessitate the development of agricultural sector. There is a need to create new employment opportunities in agriculture and allied industries and this could be made possible only if the agricultural sector is promoted or developed.

Features of Indian Agriculture

(a) Dependence on Nature

Indian agriculture still remains dependent on nature, although the influence of monsoon has been moderated by the initiation of various development programmes. Weather is the single largest factor responsible for as much as fifty per cent variations in crop yields which occur from year to year. For irrigation, majority of the farmers continue to depend on uncertain rains excess of which generally result in flood or its skewed distribution causes drought. In India rainfall is grossly inadequate, highly irregular and very unevenly distributed among regions. Consequently, agriculture becomes an uncertain occupation.

(b) Production of Multiple Variety of Crops

The climate of India as well as its soil condition enable the farmers to produce a large variety of crops. Multiplicity of crops is in fact a boon for India as it helps meet the needs of different types of food and raw materials and also the diverse demands of exports. In about seventy per cent of the land under cultivation, food crops are grown while the remaining thirty per cent of the land is utilised for growing non-foodgrain crops.

(c) Diversity in other Agricultural Spheres

Variation can be seen in agricultural sector in respect to ownership of land, methods of irrigation, size of landholdings, system of agriculture, crop rotation etc. Such variations occur not only between regions but even within regions owing to their social, cultural, political and economic reasons. In such situation no uniform agriculture policy can fit in or can be effectively implemented throughout the country.

(d) Disparity in Size of Holdings

Rapidly growing population has led to the subdivision and fragmentation of holdings. Not only this, there are many who do not own any land and rather work as tenants on lands belonging to others. Indian agriculture suffers from the predominance of small farmers as they are not in a condition to make worthwhile investments in land or agricultural operations. This negatively affects the agricultural output. Small holdings hampers agriculture to be carried on as a business. On the contrary, it serves merely as a source of subsistence.

Disparity has also been observed with respect to the size of holdings. In ratio to population, the small and marginal farmers who constitute majority of the landholders operate less per cent of the total land while the large holders who constitute a very small proportion of the total landholders cultivate on greater area of the total land.

(e) Semi-Commercialised Agriculture

In India, farming is done not for the solo purpose of self-consumption nor for sale only. As such it is said that India has semi-commercialized agriculture. While the bulk of foodgrains produced are consumed by farmers and their families, the major portion of non-foodgrains are marketed.

(f) Low Productivity Level

Indian agriculture has a very low level of productivity. In comparison to developed countries, India lags far behind in terms of output per hectare of land or per workers. Technical, economic and social factors are the causes that hinders agricultural progress. Most of the farmers make use of either primitive implements or inferior modern inputs, and practice the outdated ways of organising agriculture. Many of them are simply ignorant of the latest discoveries in the arena of agriculture which could have boosted the low level of agricultural productivity.

(g) Massive Underemployment

Except for few places which enjoy adequate irrigation, underemployment prevails all over the country. Proper irrigation facilitates double cropping. Hence, those areas where double cropping is possible, farmers are engaged in work throughout the year. But these areas that lack in such facility, a large number of farmers remains without employment for an average 4-5 months. Even those apparently engaged in agricultural activities in fact are not so occupied, rather their unemployment is disguised. Unfortunately, number of such persons are extensively multiplying owing to the rapid growth of population on the one hand and faint expansion of job opportunities in non-agricultural sectors on the other.

Progress of Agriculture

With considerable dependence on monsoon and steady decline in investments in irrigation—particularly public investment, agriculture has on average been a stagnant sector for a decade except in years of bumper harvests helped by adequate rainfall. However, its share at over 50 per cent of national output in the 1950s has declined through the subsequent decades as the country focused on industrial transformation while services, like trades, financial, transport, community and social, began assuming a larger dimension in the economy with a relatively faster growth record of average 8 per cent since mid-1990s. The share of industry and services in GDP was 26.4 and 55.1 per cent respectively as against 18.5 per cent for agriculture in 2006-07. From 9.6 per cent in 2003-04, growth in agriculture declined by 1.1 per cent in 2004-05 because of the weak monsoon. Table 7.3 clearly shows the growth of the agricultural sector since 1950-51.

Table 7.3: Growth of Agricultural Sector

Period	Agriculture and Allied Sector	Overall GDP Growth Rate
1951-61	3.3	3.8
1961-71	2.2	3.7
1971-81	1.7	3.3
1981-91	3.9	5.7
1991.01	2.8	6.7
2002-03	–7.0	3.8
2003-04	10.0	8.5
2004-05 (P)	0.0	7.5
2005-06 (Q)	6.0	9
2006-07 (A)	2.7	9.2

P: Provisional; Q: Quick estimates; A: Advance estimates
Note: Growth rates from 2000-01 onwards based on 1999-2000 prices.
Source: CSO.

Emerging Areas in Agriculture

The emerging areas in agriculture like horticulture, floriculture, organic farming, genetic engineering, food processing, branding and packaging, and futures trading have high potential of growth.

(a) Horticulture

The importance of horticulture in improving the productivity of land, generating employment, augmenting income of farmers and entrepreneurs, enhancing export and, more importantly, providing nutritional security to the people is widely acknowledged. Acreage under horticulture that includes fruits, vegetables, spices, floriculture and coconut, has shown an increasing trend in recent years. As per the latest data, area under horticulture crops contributed about 10 per cent of gross cropped area of the country in 2004-05 and its contribution to GDP from agriculture was 28 per cent. In 2003-04 India was the second largest producer of both fruits and vegetables in the world. Vast areas of India have tropical and agro-climatic conditions which are well suited for cultivation of horticulture and plantation crops. They are also ideal substitutes for marginal and degraded lands which are unsuitable for crop husbandry. Besides, horticulture helps in diversification of agriculture. The changing scenario encourages private investment to go for hi-tech horticulture with micro-propagation, protected cultivation, drip irrigation, fertigation, and integrated nutrients and pest management, besides making use of latest post-harvest measures, particularly in the case of perishable commodities. Consequently, horticulture crop production has moved from rural confines to commercial ventures.

Floriculture

Though flower cultivation has been practiced in India since time immemorial, floriculture has blossomed into a viable business only in recent years. Considering the potential that this sector has in generating income and employment opportunities, promoting greater involvement of women and enhancement of exports, it has been identified as an Extreme Focus Area for exports by the Government of India.

Plantation Crops

Tea, coffee and rubber are traditional plantation crops in the country. These are mostly grown in the southern and north-eastern states. Apart from meeting indigenous consumption demand, these crops also make significant contribution to the country's export basket. India is the largest producer and consumer of tea in the world, accounting for around 27 per cent of world production and 13 per cent of the world trade. Coffee has made significant contribution to the Indian economy during the last 50 years. Although India contributes only 4 per cent of the world production, Indian coffee has created a niche for itself in the international market. Rubber plantations are spread over 5.7 lakh hectares in 16 states of India. Production is dominated by small holdings which accounts for 88 per cent of the production as well as area with an average holding size of 0.5 hectare. Overall, the plantation sector suffers high cost of production and stagnant productivity.

Livestock, Poultry and Fisheries

The entire livestock sector plays an important role in the national economy and the socio-economic development of the country by contributing significantly to not only value added in allied sectors and providing employment and incomes to millions of people in both urban and rural areas but also nutritional security to the people. According to the 17th Livestock Census, 2005, India owns one of the largest livestock populations in the world. While it ranks first in respect of cattle and buffalo population, it is among the top six egg producing countries in the world. In fact, poultry today is one of the fastest growing segments in the economy. The fisheries sector is a source of livelihood of over 11 million people engaged fully, partially or in subsidiary activities pertaining to the sector. Marine Fishing Policy (2004) laid the foundation for a sustainable level of marine fish production keeping in view ecological and biodiversity considerations. The Table 7.4 clearly indicates the growth in production of some of these areas of agricultural sector.

Table 7.4: Production of Major Livestock Products and Fish

Year	Milk (Million tonnes)	Eggs (Million nos.)	Fish (Thousand tonnes)
1950-51	17.0	1832	752
1960-61	20.0	2881	1160
1970-71	22.0	6172	1756
1980-81	31.6	10060	2442
1981-82	34.3	10876	2444
1982-83	35.8	11454	2367
1983-84	38.8	12792	2506
1984-85	41.5	14252	2801
1985-86	44.0	16128	2876
1986-87	46.1	17310	2942
1987-88	46.7	17795	2959
1988-89	48.4	18980	3152
1989-90	51.4	20204	3677
1990-91	53.9	21101	3836
1991-92	55.7	21963	4157
1992-93	58.0	22929	4365
1993-94	60.6	24167	4644
1994-95	63.8	25975	4789
1995-96	66.2	27198	4949
1996-97	69.1	27496	5348
1997-98	72.1	28689	5383
1998-99	75.4	29476	5298
1999-00	78.3	30449	5675
2000-01	80.6	36632	5656
2001-02	84.4	38729	5956
2002-03	86.2	39823	6200
2003-04*	88.1	40403	6399
2004-05	90.7	45201	6304

* Provisional

Source: Department of Animal Husbandry & Dairying.

Brief Study of Agricultural Growth Since the First Plan

Actual glimpse of agricultural growth can be obtained by evaluating the agricultural performance since the beginning of planning in 1951. Accordingly, an attempt is being made here to deal with the subject in terms of the planned efforts made on the part of the government to boost agriculture in the past five decades and more, the actual improvements in the various areas of agriculture, and the shortcomings that hinder the agricultural growth.

During the First Plan (1951-56), agriculture was in a deplorable condition. Farmers who were usually owner of the small and scattered holdings entirely depended on uncertain monsoon for irrigation. They were in dire need of money and simply lacked in knowledge of using proper equipment, good seeds and chemical manures. Productivity level was one of the lowest in the world and as such the country had to depend on imports of foodgrains. In other words, the problem of food insufficiency was acute at the time of independence.

It can be well said that such prevailing situation forced the government to improve the agricultural sector on priority basis. Adequate strategies were adopted to increase agricultural productuion as well as rural employment. Appropriate objectives have been laid down in the various plans, some of which may be enumerated as under:

1. Increase agricultural production through acquisition of more land for cultivation.
2. Application of adequate agricultural inputs like irrigation, fertilizers, seeds etc. that would considerably result in increase in per hectare yield.
3. Generation of additional employment opportunities in agricultural sector and thereby raising the living standard of villagers.
4. Engagement of surplus labour on land to secondary and tertiary sectors in rural or semi-urban areas.
5. Distribution of surplus land among small and marginal farmers so as to reduce inequality of incomes to some extent in the rural areas.

Generally speaking, all the above-mentioned objectives have been followed in all the Five-Year Plans. To achieve these objectives, the government has made concerted efforts and the thrusts in the government's approach have changed from time to time depending upon the prevailing requirements.

Keeping in view the large-scale import of foodgrains in 1951 and inflationary pressures on the economy, the First Plan (1951-56) accorded the highest priority to agriculture including irrigation and power projects. The Plan allotted 31 per cent of total outlay on agriculture.

The Second Five-Year Plan (1956-61) sought to promote a pattern of development that would ultimately result in the establishment of a socialistic pattern of society in India. It aimed at rapid industrialization, increased production of iron and steel, heavy chemicals including nitrogeneous fertilizers and development of heavy engineering and machine building industry. Out of a total outlay of Rs. 4,600 crore, a sum of Rs. 950 crore—*i.e.* 20 per cent, was spent on agriculture. Overall, there was a significant progress on agricultural front despite the reduction in outlay on agriculture.

One of the objectives of the Third Plan (1961-66) was to achieve self-sufficiency in foodgrains and increase agricultural production to meet the needs of industry and exports. Under this Plan, the government launched the new agricultural technology called Intensive Agricultural District Programme (IADP) and High Yielding Varieties Programme (HYVP). The Third Plan allotted 21 per cent of total outlay on agriculture. But unfortunately, the target for agriculture could not be achieved because of the extensive and serious drought conditions for two successive years.

As a consequence to the failure of the Third Plan, the Fourth Plan (1969-74) aimed at creating favourable economic conditions for the promotion of agriculture and reducing fluctuations in agricultural production. It emphasized to take effective measures to extend the application of science and technology to improve the prevailing agricultural practices. It is a matter of fact, however, that none of the agricultural targets fixed in the Fourth Plan were achieved.

The Fifth Plan (1974-79) was formulated against the backdrop of severe inflationary pressures. It gave high priority to bringing inflation under control and to achieving stability in the economic situation. Of the total plan outlay at Rs. 39,430 crore, an outlay amounting to Rs. 8,740 crore was allotted to agriculture. In terms of percentage, it is 22 per cent of the total Plan outlay. Because of the inflationary situation during 1973-74 and declaration of emergency in 1975, all the financial calculations proved wrong. Yet, the progress in agricultural sector was steady and Plan targets were also achieved.

The foremost objective of the Sixth Plan (1980-85) was the removal of poverty through the strategy of strengthening infrastructure for both agriculture and industry. This Plan is considered the most successful of all the Plans, especially on the agricultural front owing to its achievement of growth rate of 4.3 per cent against the targeted 3.8 per cent for agriculture. The Indian Government called it the Second Green Revolution. While the introduction of new high yielding varieties of Mexican wheat and dwarf rich varieties brought about First Green Revolution during 1967-68, the expansion in supplies of inputs and services to farmers, agricultural extension and better management brought about Second Green Revolution from 1983-84. It is to be noted here that the First Green Revolution was restricted mainly to Punjab, Haryana, and Western U.P. The Second Green Revolution spread to West Bengal, Orissa, Bihar, eastern Uttar Pradesh and Madhya Pradesh.

The Seventh Plan (1985-90) emphasized policies and programmes, which aimed at rapid growth in foodgrains production, increased employment opportunities and productivity within the framework of basic tenets of planning, namely growth, modernization, self-reliance and social justice. Foodgrains production during the plan period grew by 3.23 per cent against 2.68 per cent and agricultural growth rate of 2.55 per cent was also achieved owing to the favourable weather conditions of eighties.

During the Eighth Plan (1992-97), an average annual growth rate of 6.8 per cent was achieved above the envisaged target of 5.6 per cent. Even in agricultural and allied sectors, several targets were met. Not only this, the actual outputs of oilseeds, sugar cane, cotton and jute were even higher than the set targets.

The specific objectives of the Ninth Plan (1997-2000) included priority to agriculture and rural development with a view to generating adequate productive employment and eradication of poverty. It focused on ensuring food and nutritional security for all. Of the total Plan outlay of Rs. 8,59,200, a sum of Rs. 1,70, 230, *i.e.* 20 per cent of the total outlay, was allotted to agriculture.

The Tenth Five-Year Plan (2002-07) aims at doubling per capita income in ten years and achieving a growth rate of 11 per cent of GDP per annum. Agriculture forms the core element of the Tenth Plan. Key reforms for the agriculture include: Eliminating inter-state barriers to trade and commerce; Amendment of Essential Commodities Act and Agriculture Produce Marketing Act; Liberalising agri-trading, agri-industry and exports; Encouraging contract farming and permitting leasing in and leasing out of agricultural lands; Replacement of various acts dealing with food by one "Food Act"; Permit futures trading in all commodities; Removal of restrictions on financing of stocking and trading.

As against the target of annual growth rate of 4 per cent during the Tenth Plan (2002-07), agricultural growth rate in the first year (2002-03) was negative (–6.9 per cent) due to a severe drought of 2002. But in the following year (2003-04), owing to favourable monsoon, growth was an impressive 10.0 per cent. Again, the year 2004-05 witnessed a decline of foodgrains production as well as rate of growth of agriculture and allied sectors to 0.7 per cent. However, an average annual growth rate in agriculture in the Tenth Plan has been 2.3 per cent against the target of 4 per cent.

A look to the Tables 7.5 and 7.6 would acquaint the readers well with the trend of progress of agriculture sector under various plans.

From the Tables 7.5 and 7.6, it can be inferred that despite the fact that each Plan did not necessarily met the target, in the last five decades (1951-2002) the production of foodgrains, oilseeds, sugarcane and cotton has gradually increased. It is to

Table 7.5: Plan-wise Government Outlay on Agriculture

Plan	Period	Total Plan Outlay	Outlay on Agriculture & Irrigation	Per cent of Total Outlay
First Plan	1951-56	1,960	600	31
Second Plan	1956-61	4,600	950	20
Third Plan	1961-66	8,600	1,750	21
Fourth Plan	1969-74	15,780	3,670	23
Fifth Plan	1974-79	39,430	8,740	22
Sixth Plan	1980-85	1,09,290	26,130	24
Seventh Plan	1985-90	2,18,729	48,100	22
Eighth Plan	1992-97	4,34,10	1,02,730	21
Ninth Plan	1997-2002	8,59,200	1,70,230	20
Tenth Plan	2002-07	15,25,639	3,05,060	20

Notes: 1. Agricultural sector is composed of agriculture and allied activities, rural development, special area programmes and irrigation and flood controls.

2. Figures for all the Plans except the Ninth Plan and Tenth Plan are actual; for the Ninth and Tenth Plan, figures are projected outlays.

Source: Various Five-Year Plan Documents.

be noted here that the Tenth Plan has fixed a target rate of growth of 4 per cent in agriculture to achieve 8 per cent rate of growth in GDP.

Although Indian agricultural productivity apparently appears to be growing, it is yet not on par with many other countries of the world. For example, though India accounted for 21.8 per cent of global paddy production, the yield per hectare in 2002 was less than that in neighbouring Bangladesh and Myanmar, and only about a third of that in Egypt, which had the highest yield level in the reference year. While accounting for 12 per cent of global production in wheat, India had average yield levels higher than the global average, but only a third of the highest level achieved in the UK in 2002. However, in maize and groundnut, while accounting for 2 per cent and 18 per cent of global output, yield levels were only 39 per cent and 57 per cent of the global levels. In sugarcane, yield was in excess of average global levels.

Table 7.6: Performance of Various Crops under Five-Year Plans

Plan	Foodgrains		Oilseeds		Sugarcane		Cotton		Jute	
	Target	Achievement	Target	Achievement	Target	Achievement	Target	Achievement	Target	Achievement
First Plan	62	67	5.5	5.6	63	60	4.2	4.0	5.4	4.2
Second Plan	81	80	7.6	6.5	78	104	6.5	5.4	6.5	4.0
Third Plan	100	72	9.8	6.4	100	127	7.0	4.6	6.2	4.5
Fourth Plan	129	104	10.5	8.7	150	140	8.0	5.8	7.4	6.2
Fifth Plan	125	126	12.0	8.9	165	165	8.0	7.1	7.7	7.1
Sixth Plan	154	146	11.1	13.0	215	170	9.2	8.5	9.1	7.8
Seventh Plan	180	172	18.0	17.0	217	210	9.5	10.5	9.5	7.9
Eighth Plan	210	191	23.0	25.0	275	277	14.0	14.3	9.5	11.0
Ninth Plan	234	211	30.0	20.7	336	300	15.7	10.1	—	11.6
Tenth Plan										
2003-04		213		25.3		237		13.9		11.2
2004-05		204		26.1		232		17.0		10.5
2005-06		—		14.6		257		—		—

Notes : 1. Production of foodgrains, oilseeds and sugarcane in million tonnes.

2. Production of Cotton in millions of bales of 180 Kgs each.

3. Production of Jute in millions of bales of 170 kgs. each.

Source : Plan documents and *Economic Surveys*.

Table 7.7: International Comparisons of Yield of Selected Commodities: 2002

(Kg/hect)

Rice/paddy		Wheat		Maize	
Bangladesh	3448	Bangladesh	2164	China	5022
Egypt	9135	China	3885	Egypt	7789
India	2915	France	7449	France	8813
Japan	6582	India	2770	India	1705
Myanmar	3532	Iran	1905	Italy	9560
Pakistan	2882	Pakistan	2262	Pakistan	1769
Thailand	2597	U.K.	8043	Philippines	1803
U.S.A.	7372				
World	**3916**	**World**	**2720**	**World**	**43**

Sugarcane		Tobacco Leaves		Groundnut (in shell)	
Bangladesh	39890	Bangladesh	1233	Argentina	2329
China	66353	Canada	2600	Brazil	2043
Colombia	94789	France	2778	China	2986
Egypt	119893	India	1353	India	794
Guatemala	94032	Indonesia	829	Sudan	630
India	68049	Italy	3333	U.S.A.	2869
Pakistan	48042	Pakistan	1848	Uganda	701
World	**65802**	**World**	**1589**	**World**	**1381**

Source: Ministry of Agriculture and Cooperation.

FACTORS RESPONSIBLE FOR SLOW GROWTH RATE IN AGRICULTURE

1. Dependence on Monsoon for Irrigation

As already said, even after five decades of planning, Indian farmers are still subject to the vagaries of monsoon. It is unfortunate that none of the Plans have fulfilled the targets for irrigation nor the irrigation potential have been utilised to its optimum.

2. Unsatisfactory Agrarian System

The present agrarian system of the country offers little incentives to the farmers to make them secure and put in their best. Despite some reforms in the tenurial system, the reforms involving transfer of the ownership of land to the actual cultivators under the policy of ceiling on land and distribution of surplus are far from being implemented. Closely related to this factor that hampers the growth of agricultural progress is the widespread fragmentation of land holdings.

3. Insufficient Use of New Agricultural Technology

In large many areas, the implements used for agricultural operations are inadequate, besides being primitive and totally unsuitable for scientific operations. Not only this, the use of seed-fertiliser-water technology, known as the new agricultural strategy, succeded only in wheat and to a small extent in rice while the other food and non-food crops did not show any considerable improvement in production. So far the dryland cultivation is concerned, it remained far from the new agricultural strategy.

4. Inadequate Credit Facilities

Indian farmers have to often suffer due to inadequacy of credit facilities and organisational drawbacks even in respect of marketing, many of the villages still lack in integration with the urban areas, both in terms of the transactions of agricultural products that the cultivators possess and the consumer goods and many inputs that they need.

5. Low Investment in Agriculture

Government as well as private investment are significant in boosting growth in agriculture. Public investment in irrigation, infrastructure development, research and extension and efficient use of water and plant nutrients are the dominant sources of total factor productivity growth. The sharp deceleration in total investment and more so in public sector investment in agriculture is the main cause for the deceleration. This has resulted in the slow-down in the growth of irrigated area and a sharp deceleration in the rate of growth of fertilizer consumption. It also adversely affects the agricultural research and extension. Although in the early years of green revolution and technology breakthrough, improvement in private investment in farm assets like irrigation pumps, wells, tractors etc. was perceptible, in the recent years such investment has declined. Moreover, private investment is generally confined to northern states like Punjab, Haryana and Western UP.

Except for the seventies, public investment on the other hand has significantly declined in recent times. The most disturbing element is the decline in the share of the agricultural sector's capital formation in GDP from 2.2 per cent in the late 1990s to 1.7 per cent in 2004-05. This declining share was mainly due to the stagnation or fall in public investment in irrigation, particularly since the mid-1990s. However, there is indication of a reversal of this trend with public sector investment in agriculture reaching its highest level of Rs. 12,591 crore in 2004-05 since the early nineties. The share of public investment in gross investment increased by over 11 percentage points to reach 29.2 per cent in 2004-05 relative to 1999-2000.

6. Failure in Implementation of Land Reforms

The government has failed to implement land reforms measures and only a meagre land distribution in favour of marginal farmers and landless labourers or protection of tenants from eviction has been made possible. For instance, under the land ceiling policy, so far only 7.6 million acres of land have been considered surplus as against significantly larger estimates of surplus land. Out of the total declared surplus land; it is only the 5.6 million acres of land that have been taken possession of land only 4.5 million acres distributed. Under the Bhoodan programme, 1.4 million acres of land have been distributed out of the 4.3 million acres of land received. Above all, it is only the 15 states that have enacted laws in this regard and of which only two states have yet able to complete the process of consolidation fully.

7. Failure in Curbing Population Growth

The Planning Commission has failed to realize the hard truth that the process of agricultural transformation needs to emphasise not only higher growth rate in agriculture but also the decentralized industrial pattern of growth with greater emphasis on labour intensive technology. Curbing of population growth and adequate generation of non-agricultural employment in the rural sector could help reduce the excessive pressure on land.

8. Lack of Integrated Nutrient Management

Phosphorus deficiency is presently the most widespread soil fertility problem in both irrigated and unirrigated areas. Attention needs to be given to balanced use of nutrients. Correcting the distortion in relative prices of primary fertilizers could help correct the imbalances in the use of primary plant nutrients—nitrogen, phosphorus and potash, and use of bio-fertilizers. Enhanced location-specific research on efficient fertilizer practices such as balanced use of nutrients, correct timing and placement of fertilizers, and wherever required, use of micronutrient and soil amendments; improvement in soil testing services; development of improved fertiliser supply and distribution systems; and development of physical and institutional infrastructure would help improve the efficiency of fertilizer use which in turn would improve the average yield.

9. Low Literacy Level

Literacy has a positive and significant relation with crop productivity and a strong link exists between literacy and farm modernization. Studies have shown that literacy emerged as an important source of growth in adoption of technology and use of modern inputs like machines, fertilizers, and yield. Literacy level being low in India, particularly in rural areas, a great number of ignorant farmers are still not making use of advanced technology and hence remain deprived of new gains that come through the congruence of gene revolution, informatives revolution, management revolution and eco-technology.

10. Post-Harvest Losses

Post-harvest losses generally range from 5 to 10 per cent for non-perishables and about 30 per cent for perishables. Unless the post-harvest handling, agro-processing, value addition technologies, storage, packaging, handling and transport facilities are adequate and ensured, the agricultural sector will continue to lag behind as it is a matter of fact that a grain saved is a grain produced.

OVERALL ASSESSMENT OF AGRICULTURE SECTOR

Much of the credit for the impressive strides made on the agricultural front in India go to the several million small farming families that form the backbone of Indian agriculture and economy. Policy support, production strategies, public investment in infrastructure, research and extension for crop, livestock and fisheries have significantly helped to increase food production and its availability. Virtually all of the increase in the production resulted from yield gains rather than expansion of cultivated area. Increased agricultural productivity and rapid industrial growth in the recent years have contributed to a significant reduction in poverty level. Yet, India accounts for about one-fifth of the world's poor. Child malnutrition extracts its highest toll in this country. About 25 per cent children suffer from serious malnutrition while more than 50 per cent of the pre-school children and pregnant women are anaemic. Such is the situation mainly because India has high population pressure on land and other resources to meet its food and development needs. The natural resource base of land, water and biodiversity is under severe pressure. Despite the slowing down of the rate of growth, there has been a massive increase in population which, together with substantial income growth, demands an extra about 2.5 mt of foodgrains annually besides significant increases needed in the supply of livestock, fish and horticultural products. In addition, need for future increases in the production of cereals and non-cereal agricultural commodities through increases in productivity cannot be denied owing to the fact that possibilities of expansion of area and livestock population are minimal.

Food demand challenges ahead are formidable considering the non-availability of favourable factors of past growth, fast declining factor productivity in major cropping systems and rapidly shrinking resource base. Even vast uncommon opportunities to harness agricultural potential still remain; there are serious gaps both in yield potential and technology transfer as is evident from the low national average yields of most of the commodities. There is undoubtedly a need to strengthen adaptive research and technology assessment, refinement and transfer capabilities of the country so that the existing wide technology transfer gaps are bridged. Ample scope exists for increasing genetic yield potential of a large number of vegetables, fruits and other food crops along with livestock and fisheries products as well as developing hybrid varieties and other varieties suitable for export purposes.

It is very important for India to maintain a steady growth rate in total factor productivity (TFP). As the TFP increases, the cost of production decreases and the prices also decrease and stabilize. Both producer and consumer share the benefits. The fall in food prices will benefit the urban and rural poor more than the upper income groups as the former spend relatively larger proportion of their income on cereals than the latter. In nutshell, TFP influences the nation's economy to a great extent.

There is strong evidence that technological change has generally pervaded the entire crop sector. In India, however, there are crops and states where technological stagnation or decline is apparent and these are the priorities for present and future agricultural research. Farming system research to develop location specific technologies, strategy to make grey areas green by adopting three-pronged approach—water management, hybrid technology and small farm mechanization, promoting efficient fertilizer practices, and strengthening distribution channel of critical inputs will definitely help resource poor farmers.

It is projected that availability of water for agricultural use in India may be reduced by 21 per cent by 2020, resulting in drop of yields of irrigated crops—especially rice, thus price rise and withdrawal of food from poor masses. Given the ground water depletion and serious environmental and social problems of some of the major irrigation projects on one hand, and the multiple benefits of irrigation water in enhancing production and productivity, food security, poverty alleviation on the other, India will be required to produce more and more from less and less land and water resources. It is to be noted here that water availability per capita was over 5000 cubic metres per annum in 1950. It now stands at around 2000 cubic metres and is projected to decline to 1500 cubic metres by 2025. Further, the quality of available water is deteriorating.

The prevailing agriculture scenario calls for an emphasis on rainfed ecosystem. Resource poor farmers in the rainfed ecosystems practice less intensive agriculture and since their incomes depend on local agriculture, they benefit little from increased food production in irrigated areas. Thus, what is required is the dissemination of available dry land technologies as well as generation of new ones.

Keeping in view the thrust on globalisation and increasing competitiveness, India needs to maintain the quality of the agricultural produce through improving storage, packaging handling and transporting of products so as to enhance the agricultural export contribution of India which is proportionately extremely low.

There is no denying the fact that since nearly 70 per cent of India still lives in villages, agricultural growth will continue to be the engine of broad-based economic growth and development as well as of natural resource conservation, leave alone food security and poverty alleviation. Hence, accelerated investment is indispensable in order to obtain extensive agricultural and rural development. But unfortunately, the public investment in agriculture has been declining and this is one of the main reasons behind the declining productivity and low capital formation in the agriculture sector. Above all, the availability of genetic innovations in developing countries depend on continued high levels of investments in agricultural research, both at the international and the national levels. In addition to investments in research, infrastructure investments, particularly in irrigation, transport, and market infrastructure development are equally important for sustaining the productivity and profitability of food crop production. Given the increasing role of investments, public as well as private investments need to be stimulated.

Against expectation under the liberalised scenario, the non-agriculture employment in rural areas has not improved. The off-farm and non-farm employment opportunities can play an important role in improving the economy of India. Hence, greater emphasis needs to be placed on non-farm employment and appropriate budgetary allocations and rural credit through banking systems should be in place to promote appropriate rural enterprises.

It is a common experience that the frequency and intensity of disasters such as floods, droughts, cyclones and earthquakes have increased in the recent years. For instance, the devastating earthquake in Gujarat that occurred in January 2001 brought untold miseries to the whole state and caused a national disaster. It would not be wrong to say that drought and floods in our country have been a regular periodic occurrence. Hence, effective and reliable information and communication systems, contingency planning, and national and international mobilisation of technologies and resources need to be developed so as to facilitate increasing preparedness to predict and to manage the disasters. In this direction, lessons from experiences of other countries in prevention and management of the disasters would prove fruitful.

Information is power and it will underpin future progress and prosperity. Accordingly, the need of the hour is strengthening of informatics in agriculture by developing new databases, linking databases with international databases and adding value to information to facilitate decision-making at various levels.

In nutshell, the following recurring and emerging issues for sustainable agricultural development and poverty alleviation need to be given priority:

(i) Population pressure and demographic transition;
(ii) Resource base degradation and water scarcity;
(iii) Investment in agriculture, structural adjustment and impact on the poor;
(iv) Modern science and technology and support to research and technology development;
(v) Rapid urbanization;
(vi) Conservation of natural resources and protection of environment;
(vii) Tapping potential of soil and water resources;
(viii) Risk management;

(ix) Infrastructure development; and

(x) Exploiting Cyberspace.

SECOND GREEN REVOLUTION

Apart from the Tenth Plan, the necessity of growth in agriculture was explicitly realised at the Agricultural Summit held in New Delhi in April 2005—organised by the Agriculture Ministry and the Federation of Indian Chambers of Commerce & Industry (FICCI). Inaugurating the Summit, Dr. Manmohan Singh stated that the government is committed to reversing the deceleration in agriculture production. In order to sustain seven to eight per cent growth rate of the economy, the growth in agriculture sector needs to be accelerated. For this a Second Green Revolution based on the application of new technologies and modern business practices was required.

The Second Green Revolution needs, *inter alia*, the creation of a single market for agriculture products in the country; catering to the credit needs of the farmers through commercial banks at minimum possible rate of interest; ensuring regular and timely irrigation; developing post-harvest marketing facilities including grading, packaging, transportation and storage; processing and value addition for increasing farm incomes and making agriculture and allied sectors internationally competitive.

Legislative Measures

Some legislative measures also need to be taken in this regard, such as revision of the Agriculture Produce Marketing Committee (APMC) Act to facilitate greater private sector investment in agriculture and open up contract farming, and bringing forward an Integrated Food Law which will assimilate the myriad legislations that are existing at present. This will streamline decision-making on support prices for various types of crops, framing of proper agriculture marketing policies and efficient distribution of foodgrains through the Public Distribution System (PDS).

The Agriculture Summit also called for a proper attention to risk management of agriculture. The new schemes on dryland farming and micro irrigation can reduce our dependence on rain to sustain our agriculture and cut down the risks involved in the rainfed agriculture. The assured irrigation will improve the productivity of marginal land and enhance cropping intensity. Given the limited availability of land, this is crucial for increasing food production.

Genetic Engineering in Agriculture

Initiated by Norman Borlang in 1978, the first Green Revolution depended on an increased use of irrigation, pesticides and fertilizers to boost agriculture growth. The insect-resistent, high yielding varieties of wheat and other cereals helped India embark on the road to achieving self-sustenance.

However, the practices and strategies adopted by the first Green Revolution are no longer sustainable. The increased irrigation has pushed the underground water to an alarmingly low level. The unrestrained usage of fertilizers and pesticides has proved detrimental to our environment. While the old technologies have run their course, the impetus provided by the first Green Revolution has slowed down which is being reflected in the low-key performance of our agriculture sector. There is an urgent need for laying a renewed emphasis on research to increase farm productivity. Indigenous knowledge needs to be blended with advanced science and proper application of biotechnology for the improvement of seeds.

Use of Biotech Seeds

Seeds are critical and basic for agriculture production in different agro-climatic regions. Agriculture scientists have developed biotech seeds which are genetically modified to repel pests, thus cutting down the use of pesticides. Graham Brookes, Director of PG Economics, Britain, and a biotech expert, claims that during the past decade, there has been 14 per cent reduction in environmental hazards with the use of biotech seeds. Some varieties of seeds, so developed, do not require tillage of land. This has reduced the release of smoke in the environment because of lesser use of tractors.

The statistics of earning are also looking up with the use of biotech seeds. The world over farmers, including those in India, have earned US$ 27 billion extra income from genetically modified crops. The UN Millennium Development Goal targets the reduction of world hunger by half by the year 2015. The increased farm productivity as a result of genetically modified crops provides an important means to achieve that target. Application of genetic engineering is imperative to meet the demand of the ever-increasing population.

Since the introduction of biotech crops 10 years ago, it has been found that the cultivation of biotech seeds, such as Bt cotton seeds delivers consistent and long-term agronomic, environmental and health benefits to farmers and to society at large in terms of regular supply of farm products. India is a vast country with variable climate. Its large dryland areas have remained non-arable. With the development of biotech seeds, it has become possible to grow crops on these lands.

Plant biotechnology also provides nutrient enhanced foods and environmental benefits. The introduction of Vitamin A-enhanced Golden Rice would prove to be a medical breakthrough as it provides the essential vitamin in poorer communities in regions where rice is the staple diet. Punjab Agriculture University, Ludhiana, has developed a variety of mustard crop whose oil qualities match those of olive oil that is considered the best edible oil from the health point of view. The researchers have found that genetically modified maize can help tackle the problem of iron deficiency among consumers, particularly in developing nations where people cannot afford to supplement their diet with iron rich intake.

The fertilizers, pesticides and insecticides that are used in the crops are most of the time washed away by rain and find their way into water bodies like ponds, lakes, rivers. These chemicals are not only harmful for aquatic life but also make water unfit for human consumption. Genetically modified crops are insect-resistant and promote a culture of intelligent pesticide usage causing no harm to the water bodies.

Biotechnology allows farmers to produce higher yields on less land. Higher yields are necessary not only to overcome food scarcity but also because of the fact that acceleration in urbanisation is encroaching on agriculture land reducing the area under cultivation. Doubling the farm output using conventional methods would need large scale deforestation to bring more area under farming. Depletion of forests, due to such a measure would lead to long-term harms, like destruction of natural ecosystems, extinction of many species of flora and fauna, floods and soil erosion, etc. Genetic engineering would save us from all these hazards.

The cultivation of biotech crops has resulted in a reduction of greenhouse gas emissions across the world. In the year 2004, 10 billion kg less carbon dioxide was released into the atmosphere as result of use of biotech crops.

However, biotech farming is highly controversial and considered unsafe by the majority of the world's farming community. The experts say that a nomenclature of genetically uniform hybrids could lead to natural crop failure. Diseases could spread faster once the buffer of diversity is removed. We cannot, however, deny the fact that the development of drought-resistant crops can be of great advantage to the farmers in India where monsoon is neither regular nor evenly distributed. The farmers need to be educated to make their own choice as per prevailing conditions.

Farmers in India are recognizing the immediate benefits of cultivating biotech crops—higher yield, more profits, reduction in expenditure on pesticides.

Investment in Agriculture Sector

The Agriculture Summit, highlighting the need for a Second Green Revolution expressed concern over the declining trend in investment in agriculture. There is a good liquidity in the banking sector, yet a large number of farmers are dependent upon informal financial sector for their credit needs. Many of the commercial banks are not able to achieve the target of providing 18 per cent of their credit flow to agriculture sector. Availability of cheap and sufficient credit is crucial for breaking the cycle of low investment in agriculture.

Large investments are needed for irrigation, post-harvest infrastructure, processing and value addition. This is necessary for increasing farm incomes from local sale and also making agriculture and allied sectors internationally competitive. The Agriculture Summit stated that the large investment is also needed for making marginal lands cultivable, increasing cropping intensity and improving water efficiency.

Indo-US Agriculture Knowledge Initiative

The US has launched a Rs. 1000 crore Agriculture Knowledge Initiative with a three-year commitment to link our universities, technical institutions and business to support agriculture education, joint research, and capacity-building projects including those in the area of biotechnology. President Bush and Prime Minister Dr. Manmohan Singh see this as an opportunity to launch the Second Green Revolution to service India's agriculture.

On the threshold of the Second Green Revolution, India needs to bring a qualitative change in agriculture technology—which has the potential to double its present annual output of 200 million tonnes to 400 million tonnes over the next four years. This is necessary to lift millions of marginalised people from poverty and hunger. It is modern technology that will take Indian agriculture from subsistence farming to sustainable and commercial farming. New technologies will enable farmers to make informed choices and undertake product planning in a demand driven rather than supply driven mode. An awareness of the niche markets and export opportunities suited to the new international trade region opening through globalisation and World Trade Organisation is necessary to bring prosperity to the farmers.

Agriculture in the Approach Paper to the Eleventh Five-Year Plan (2007-12)

The transition towards faster and more inclusive growth calls for significant new initiatives in many sectors. In some we need to build on policies that are working well but need further strengthening in critical areas to build the additional momentum needed. In others we need a more comprehensive restructuring since it is evident that business as usual will not do. In this Chapter, and the next, we provide a brief assessment of the broad direction of policy we need to explore in formulating the 11th Plan.

Accelerating Agricultural Growth

Accelerating GDP growth in agriculture to around 4 per cent as envisaged in this Paper, is not an easy task. Actual growth of agricultural GDP, including forestry and fishing, was only 1 per cent per annum in the first three years of 10th Plan and even the most rosy projections for 2005-06 and 2006-07 would limit this below 2 per cent for the full five-year period. The challenge posed is to more than double the growth rate achieved in the 10th Plan. This will require action on both the demand side and the supply side.

(a) *Demand Side Intervention*

On the demand side there is evidence that farmers face adverse demand conditions. Not only has agricultural growth been low in the last decade, the prices received for agricultural products have also failed to keep pace with the costs or the general price level and, as a consequence, profitability has declined. Several modeling exercises suggest that a 4 per cent growth of agriculture will not be sustainable from the demand side unless aggregate GDP growth is much higher than 8 per cent.

Some of the steps already taken, such as the recently introduced National Rural Employment Guarantee Programme, will help the demand side in the 11th Plan. The emphasis on expanding access and improving quality of public sector schools and health facilities may also help by reducing the need for private expenditure on these items by lower income groups and some of this expenditure will be redirected to generate demand for agriculture. Improved rural connectivity envisaged through Bharat Nirman can also trigger growth of an integrated national market where rural people are more able to meet each others demand. In its sheer size and scope, such expanded rural-rural trade is likely to be as important in the initial years as other efforts of demand support such as promoting agricultural exports, or strengthening support to agricultural diversification for domestic processing. The latter of course have the advantage of being able to attract private corporate investment into rural areas once essential infrastructure is in place and their importance is likely to grow over time.

A very large private expenditure shift has occurred over the last decade from food to health, education and conveyance, some of which should be reversible.

(b) *Supply Side Strategy*

The supply side challenge of doubling agricultural growth is also formidable. This is especially so because no dramatic technological breakthrough comparable to the "green revolution" is presently in sight. We are also not exploiting the potential of existing technology. In fact, most of the growth required in cereals, pulses and oilseeds is possible merely through plausible yield increase in currently low yield regions. It is, however, necessary to identify the specific constraints and policy distortions that have produced these yield gaps.

The National Commission on Farmers has drawn attention to the knowledge deficit which constrains agricultural productivity. To overcome this, farmers will need effective links to universities and best practices. A good extension system is the means for achieving this linkage but unfortunately the extension system has virtually collapsed in most states, partly as a result of constraints on non-plan expenditure. Krishi Vigyan Kendras set up by ICAR have very little interaction with the ATMA model of extension being promoted by DAC. The result is that farming practices in large parts of the country are sub-optimal. Soil testing to determine optimal nutrient requirements is hardly practised and fertilizer application is often highly unbalanced with excessive use of nitrogenous fertilisers, often leading to a negative effect on productivity of the soil over time, a consequence that farmers are not fully aware of. These imbalances are themselves to some extent the result of a system of fertiliser subsidy which is irrational and focuses excessively on nitrogenous fertilisers.

Lack of credit at reasonable rates is a persistent problem, in large part, reflecting the collapse of the cooperative credit system. The failure of the organised credit system in extending credit has led to excessive dependence on informal sources usually at exorbitant interest rates. This is at the root of farmer distress reflected in excessive indebtedness.

Accelerated agricultural growth will require diversification into horticulture and floriculture which in turn imply structural changes in the relation between agriculture and non-agriculture. Diversification requires effective marketing linkages, supported by modern marketing practices including introduction of grading, post-harvest management, cold chains, etc. There is a need to encourage the development of modern agricultural markets and for this purpose it is necessary to amend the APMC Acts. Although this has begun, the process needs to be accelerated.

Diversification also means the product must meet the specific requirements of the different markets being serviced, and these requirements vary depending on whether the market is domestic consumption, agro-processing or exports. Contract farming is a potentially effective way of attracting corporate investors to help establish these linkages with markets and also provide farmers with necessary inputs, extension and other advice. Although very limited at present, many states have already taken steps to facilitate this potential to assist the process of diversification. A greater focus is, however, necessary on enabling small farmer participation by encouraging group formation and providing suitable and effective regulatory frameworks. Existing vested interests in traditional trade channels often oppose these changes but they must be overcome.

As farmers adopt new and untried technology, and increase input intensities, they also face larger risks. These risks are often not well understood owing to lack of knowledge of the requirements of new seeds and new technology. All farmers do not have the ability to bear downside risks. Thus, we have seen farmer suicides when new seeds fail to deliver expected output, or when expenditure on bore wells proves infructuous, or when market prices collapse. Farmers should be protected against such risks by appropriate measures. Insurance is one way of doing this, but the financial cost of existing and proposed crop insurance schemes is very considerable, and recurring, so that these are not appropriate as plan schemes. These and related issues of risk management need to be addressed in the 11th Plan.

The agricultural strategy for the 11th Plan must be based on recognition of the need for strategies specific to different agro-climatic zones. The nature of the technical constraints and crop development possibilities vary considerably across zones. Viable policy packages must be devised for each zone keeping these variations in mind. This will need to be incorporated in the design of future plan schemes with corresponding improvements in plan implementation and in administrative structures to optimise region-specific benefits. While the strategies can emerge through consultation between the Centre and the States, the task of implementing these strategies on the ground falls almost wholly on the state governments.

(c) *Agricultural Research*

In the longer run, growth in agricultural productivity can be sustained only through continuous technological progress. This calls for a well considered strategy for prioritised basic research, which is now all the more urgent in view of mounting pressure on scarce natural resources, climate change and also the shrinking availability of spill-overs from international public research. The 11th Plan will have to focus the National Agricultural Research System (NARS) to strengthen its basic research component through properly anticipated identification of strategic research pathways. This must go hand in hand with clearer demarcation of responsibilities within NARS between such basic research, which may not contribute immediately to growth, and the more immediate requirement to adapt and disseminate existing technology and provide region-specific problem-solving capacity. The recently established National Strategic Agricultural Research Fund must be expanded in the 11th Plan and oriented to stimulate research responding to a well defined strategy of prioritisation.

New generation technologies based on rapidly evolving scientific developments will play a pivotal role in achieving new levels of productivity in agriculture. The country's large agricultural research system which successfully launched the green revolution in the past will now be called upon to address newer and more formidable challenges. In this endeavour, business as usual has no place whatsoever. The system needs to be thoroughly revamped and restructured in the light of the advice rendered by the high powered committees chaired respectively by Dr. Swaminathan and Dr. R.A. Mashelkar.

(d) *Water Management and Irrigation*

Water is a critical input for agriculture and this calls for expansion of irrigation, where it is possible and better water management in rainfed areas where assured irrigation is not possible. This is clearly an area where past policies have been inadequate. Performance in expanding irrigation has been disappointing with resources being spread thinly over many projects and a large number of irrigation projects remaining under construction for many years.

The Bharat Nirman programme *inter alia* envisages creation of 10 m.ha. additional assured irrigation during the 4 years period (2005-09). To achieve this, the pace of potential creation will have to be scaled up from 1.42 m.ha. per year in recent years to 2.5 m.ha./year. Of the new potential envisaged under Bharat Nirman, about half is planned for 2007-08 and 2008-09 i.e., first 2 years of the 11th Plan. Assuming the same rate of creation of continues thereafter, a total of about 11 m.ha. of new potential can be expected in the 11th Plan consisting of 5.5 m.ha. in major and medium irrigation, 3.5 m.ha. through minor irrigation and about 2.0 m.ha. through ground water development. In addition, another 3-4 m.ha. of land is to be restored through modernisation of major, medium and minor projects and restoration of tanks.

Investments in the major and medium irrigation sector will require large resources from the state governments supported by Central Assistance under AIBP. However, implementation of these projects by state governments is also important. Monitoring the pace of creation of potential assumes special importance. Besides regular monitoring by Central Water Commission, it is proposed to expand usage of remote sensing techniques for this purpose which has been initiated on a pilot basis in the 10th Plan.

Along with expansion of irrigation facilities, steps need to be taken to ensure that water is distributed equitably and that it is used efficiently. The past pattern where tail enders are denied water because upper end users appropriate it for highly water intensive crops must be avoided. Participatory Irrigation Management (PIM) by democratically organised water user associations empowered to set water charges, collect and retain substantial part of it, would help to maintain field channels, expand irrigated area, distribute water equitably and provide the tail enders their just share of water. Experience in Gujarat has shown the effectiveness of such PIM. The 11th Plan must expand reliance on PIM on a large scale.

Water is also critical for the more than 60 per cent of cultivable land that is unirrigated and rainfed. Ground water management is critical for these areas and will, therefore, need much more focused attention in the 11th Plan. Unless this is done we run the risk of a deepening agricultural crisis in dryland areas. Water must be recognised as a scarce resource and every drop needs to be used efficiently. In this context, it must be recognised that some existing policies followed by state governments contribute to the problem. Continued provision of free power by some states and highly subsidised power by all states is leading to an increase in semi-critical, critical and over exploited areas of ground water use, which already cover 29 per cent of the blocks in the country.

Watershed management, rainwater harvesting and ground water recharge can help augment water availability in rainfed areas. Building structures for water management and managing them also provides opportunities for employment generation in rural areas. In addition the enhanced productivity of land will generate its own employment. The National Rainfed Areas Authority to be set up in the current year provides a vehicle for developing concerted action plans for rainfed areas in close consultation with state governments.

With an estimated 80 million hectares needing treatment, and average expenditure of Rs. 10,000 per hectare, the total requirement of funds is about Rs. 80,000 crore. For this magnitude of funding to be feasible during the 11th Plan, it is absolutely essential that these programmes be converged with or at least supplemented by the Employment Guarantee programme funding local level schemes which conserve moisture and recharge ground water.

(e) *Animal Husbandry and Fishery*

The livestock and fisheries sectors together account for about 30 per cent of the value of the output of Agriculture & Allied Sector and provide full time and part time employment to 5.5 per cent of the total working population. Their contribution to total GDP in 2003-04 was 6.3 per cent. The 11th Plan must evolve viable strategies for these sectors to expand rapidly. The effort to revive agricultural dynamism must, therefore, pay sufficient attention to this sector.

India continues to be the largest producer of milk in the World with a total production of 91 million tonnes in 2005-06 and the contribution of milk alone was higher than paddy, wheat and sugarcane in the year 2003-04. Yet the per capita availability of milk at 231 gm. per day during 2003-04 is still very low. Matters are even worse regarding meat, with abattoir conditions pathetic and utilisation of by-products inefficient. Poultry development in the country has shown better progress over the years, primarily because research and development schemes of the government have been complemented with effective management and marketing by an organised private sector.

Some of the important initiatives that are needed are:

- Promotion of appropriate crossbreeds while conserving indigenous breeds of livestock.
- Establishment of livestock marketing system.
- Promotion of rural backyard poultry in a cooperative marketing set-up.
- Development of cooperative dairy firms.
- Enhancing livestock extension services.
- Encouraging private veterinary clinic.
- Institutionalising a framework for utilising synergy between restoration and creation of water bodies for water harvesting and fishery.
- Provision of an insurance package to avoid distress.

The survival of pastoralism is crucial for sustainable land use. Besides conserving domestic biodiversity, it is a means of producing food in drylands without depleting groundwater resources. However, there are many constraints on expansion in this area Grazing permits are denied in traditional grazing sites that have been converted into protected areas/wildlife sanctuaries, national parks/Joint Forest Management (JFM) programme. Original pasture lands or stipulated animal drinking water ponds are encroached upon, or used for other purposes. Bio-diesel (Jatropha) planting is being promoted through state agencies without seeing all the consequences such as blocking the migration routes of animals and encroaching upon herd-passing pathways.

Recent Initiatives by Government for Growth of Agriculture Sector

- Irrigation is one of the six components for development of rural infrastructure under Bharat Nirman programme of the government. The irrigation component of this programme aims at creation of irrigation potential of 10 million hectare in the four years from 2005-06 to 2008-09. Under the Bharat Nirman programme, the government also envisages to develop new projects of minor irrigation to cater to the requirement of specific areas, particularly to provide benefit to small and marginal farmers and dalits and tribals.
- Under the Kisan Credit Card (KCC) scheme of the government which was introduced in 1998-99, more than 556 lakh cards have been issued until November 2005 so as to enable farmers to cater with the investment needs. The scheme, needless to mention, has remarkably helped in augmenting the flow of short-term crop loans for seasonal agricultural operations to farmers. Besides the prevailing facilities of providing crop loan, the scope of KCC scheme has been enlarged to include term loans for agriculture and allied activities along with a component to meet the consumption needs.

- The Self-Help Groups (SHG) Bank Linkages Programme has emerged as the major micro finance programme in the country. The focus under the SHG bank linkage programme is largely on those rural poor who have no sustained access to the formal banking system.
- The National Agricultural Insurance Scheme (NAIS) is being implemented from 1999-2000 rabi reason. The scheme is available to all farmers, making no distinction between loanee or non-loanee as well as irrespective of their size of holdings. The objective of the scheme is to provide insurance coverage and financial support to the farmers in the event of failure of any of the notified crops as a result of natural calamities, pests and diseases, and to help to stabilise farm incomes, particularly in disaster years. At present, 23 states and 2 Union Territories are implementing the scheme.
- Quality seed is the most critical and basic input for agricultural output, and accounts for 25-30 per cent of yield increase. Since eighty per cent of the Indian farmers rely on farm-saved seed and the low seed replacement rate results in low yields, the seed export and import regime have been simplified to facilitate availability of quality seed to Indian farmers and help India emerge as a global hub for seed production.
- Four Central Sector Schemes have been introduced for development of marketing infrastructutre: (i) development of Marketing Research and Information Network (MRIN), (ii) a scheme with 25 per cent back ended subsidy component for construction of rural godowns, (iii) strengthening of agricultural marketing infrastructure, grading and standardization in those states that have amended the APMC Act on the lines of Model Act, and (iv) Venture Capital Assistance scheme by Small Farmers' Agri-Business Consortium to promote agri-business projects.
- Under the Vishesh Krishi Upaj Yojana, introduced in 2004, exporters of fruits, vegetables, flowers, minor

forest produce, dairy, poultry and their value added products have been made entitled to duty credit scrip equivalent to 5 per cent of the FOB value of exports for each licensing year with a view to promote agricultural export.

- Farmers obtain short–term credit from the cooperative credit structure and Regional Rural Banks, with refinance from NABARD. Given the prevailing market conditions, Government has decided to ensure that the farmers receive short-terms credit at 7 per cent with an upper limit of Rs. 300,000 on the principal amount from kharif 2006-07.
- Under the National Horticulture Mission, the government proposes to set up model terminal markets in different parts of the country.
- Initiatives taken to boost the plantation sector include:
    - Withdrawal of the additional excise duty of Re. 1 per kg on tea.
    - Sanctioning of two schemes, viz. grant of subsidy for production of orthodox tea and assistance to the two R & D Institutions, viz. Tea Research Association at Tocklei (Assam) and United Planters' Association for Southern India.
    - Sharing the total interest burden of Rs. 287.10 crore on Special Coffee Term Loan (SCTL) for the three-year moratorium period equally amongst the banks, the Government and the power loanees.
    - Continuing the interest subsidy scheme on working capital loans for small growers (below 10 ha.) at the rate of 5 per cent and large growers at the rate of 3 per cent for the remaining period of the Tenth Plan. The interest subsidy would be reduced by 1 per cent for a period of 3 years in the case of those growers who received the benefit of reduced interest burden on SCTL during the moratorium period. The package will reduce the debt burden of a large number of coffee growers.

Cess on coffee exports which was levied @ Rs. 500/tonne has been brought down to zero level.

For promoting coffee export to Russia and CIS countries, Government has approved a proposal at a total cost of Rs. 15.32 crore under Market Access Initiative (MAI) scheme.

— The Government through Rubber Board is implementing seven Plan Schemes for development of rubber plantations during the plan period with an outlay of Rs. 415 crore.

The objective of the Price Stabilisation Fund is to provide relief to the growers of tea, coffee and rubber when the prices of these commodities fall below a specified level, without resorting to the practice of procurement operations by the Government agencies. The Price Stabilisation Fund was established with a corpus of Rs. 500 crore, which includes Rs. 482.88 crore by the Central Government and Rs. 17.12 crore as a non-refundable initial contribution by the participating growers @ Rs. 500 per grower.

India Agriculture and WTO

India is a founding member of the World Trade Organisation formerly GATT. Under WTO, India has been amending patent laws, curbing trade barriers, facing foreign competition on a more equal footing and showing dramatic economic growth. But agriculture remains a divisive issue at the WTO, and recent negotiations have stalled because of conflicts over agricultural subsidies. A central conflict is with the United States, where big corporations corner a majority of its $ 19 billion farm subsidy and want to bring down tariff barriers in the Indian market. The EU has also been challenging India to further open its market to agricultural imports. India's position is that subsistence farmers are not traders and cannot compete with the heavily subsidized agricultural industry of the United States and European Union. Agricultural subsidy in which countries amounts to 80 per cent of India's national income. International intellectual property rights also favour corporations at the expense of small farmers. Thus, Indian agriculture has been facing external challenges under the WTO regime in addition to the domestic concerns such as decline in productivity, high input-cost, stagnated net sown area, declining public sector investment, inadequate availability of institutional credit, and rising agricultural imports. Accordingly, the country needs to evolve a more conducive policy regime, facilitating all sort of bottlenecks in this sector, and also there is an emergent need to develop a team of experts comprising eminent trade economists, policy analysts, scientists, legal experts and political scientists so as to best avail the opportunity that may arise after successful implementation of Agreement on Agriculture (AoA). The AoA aims to eliminate distortions in agricultural trade through reducing export and production subsidies and import barriers including non-tariff barriers. It was expected that implementation of AoA would raise international prices of agricultural commodities and would improve export prospects for developing countries like India. However, even after completion of few years of WTO, world trade in agriculture is yet highly distorted due to heavy export and domestic subsidies provided by industrialised countries and little market access offered by them to the agricultural products of developing countries.

The main provisions of AoA are as under:

(i) Non-tariff barriers such as quantitative restrictions and export and import licensing etc., are to be replaced by tariffs to provide the same level of protection. Tariffs thus obtained together with other tariffs on agriculture products, were to be reduced by an average of 36 per cent over 6 years in the case of developed countries and 24 per cent over 10 years in the case of developing countries.

(ii) Setting up of a minimum level for imports of agricultural products by member countries as a share of domestic consumption. Countries are required to maintain current level (1986-88) of access for each individual product.

While the current level of import is negligible, the minimum access should not be less than 3 per cent of the domestic consumptions during the base period and tariff quotas are to be established when imports constitute less than 3 per cent of domestic consumption.

(iii) Member countries are required to compute an Aggregate Measure of Support (AMS) for the base period (1986-88). All payments deemed to be decoupled (green box measures) together with those so-called blue box measures and other de minimis payments are deducted from the AMS. The residual has been placed in the amber box. Domestic supports that come under 'green box', 'blue box' and 'de minimis' categories are exempted from requirement of reductions. Other significant exemptions include the domestic supports in developing country that meets requisites set out in paragraph 2 of Article 6 of the Agreement, for instance, investment subsidies which are usually available to agriculture in developing countries, and agricultural input services available to low income and resource poor producers in developing countries are exempted from reduction commitment.

Under the AoA, reduction commitment in the AMS for developed countries was 20 per cent by 2000 and for developing countries it was 13.5 per cent by 2004 while de minimis level for the developed countries and developing countries is fixed at 5 per cent of the value of agricultural products and 10 per cent of the total agricultural production respectively.

Green Box subsidies include amount spent on government services such as agricultural research, disease control infrastructure, extension and buffer stocks for food security purposes, domestic food aid, direct payments to producers, decoupled income support, government assistance in income insurance and income safety net programmes, payment under environmental and regional assistance programmes, payments for relief from natural disasters, aid to help farmers restructure agriculture, marketing and promotion services.

Blue Box subsidies are certain direct payments made to farmers under production limiting programme. It is government assistance programmes to encourage agriculture and rural development in developing countries, and other support on a small scale when compared with the total value of the products supported—15 per cent or less in the case of developed countries and 10 per cent or less for developing countries.

(iv) Close to domestic support subsidies is the export subsidy, which is on two counts: (a) reduction in the total budgetary outlays on export subsidies, and (b) reduction in the total quantity of export covered by the subsidy. Developed countries were required to reduce the volume of subsidised export and expenditure on subsidies by 21 per cent and 36 per cent respectively by 2000, while developing countries had to reduce by 14 per cent and 24 per cent respectively by 2004.

Implications of AoA

Although effective implementation of the AoA, *prima facie*, appears to be the most significant factor for ensuring a transparent trade in agriculture, in reality the prospects are bleak owing to loopholes in the AoA that provide enough space for developed countries to heavily subsidize their agricultural products. Consequently, its achievement in terms of market opening has been limited while the anticipated gains from agricultural trade liberalisation have eluded the developing nations as yet. The fixing up of very high level of minimum access tariff quota and unweighted average reduction commitment have facilitated the developed countries in maintaining a high level of protection to their agriculture.

One of the most controversial issues in the WTO conferences has been the apparent distinction created between price support and input subsidies on the one hand and 'green box' and 'blue box' subsidies on the other, and excluding the later from subsidy cuts. It is altogether an unfair discrimination against developing countries like India as subsidies directly linked to production (amber box support) or having indirect production effects (blue and green boxes support) distort trade. During the Uruguay

Round, it was expected that the contemplated fair trade regime would enable the efficient producers in realizing higher prices for their products. But in reality the prices of most of the agricultural commodities are declining in the world markets. It was also assumed that as a consequence of reduction in domestic support in developed countries, cereal production would shift from developed to developing countries. On the contrary, there has not been any remarkable change in the trend of world cereals production and exports.

Export subsidies of developed countries significantly constrain the export potential of developing countries. The developed countries like those of EU and USA plead for better market access to their agricultural products in the developing countries by negotiating on tariff reduction and raising in-tariff quota and avoiding reduction of domestic support and elimination of export subsidies. The heavy subsidies have adversely affected the export of agricultural products.

Assessing on the basis of market access, domestic support, and export subsidies—the three components of the AoA, it can be well said that India would stand to gain in the world market of agricultural products provided the domestic support and export subsidies are substantially reduced by the developed countries and market access is enhanced through reducing quota tariffs.

In India, market support to agricultural crops is negative in almost all the cases. The country has already removed quantitative restrictions for agricultural products. The tariff levels in India have been bounded at 100 per cent for primary agricultural products and 150 per cent for processed products. In all other products, except for rice, basic duties are relatively much lesser than bound duties. For cereal products, the basic duty is 35 per cent. So far the export subsidies are concerned, India does not provide any such subsidy to the agricultural products listed for reduction commitments. However, the exporters do receive subsidies only in the form of exemption of profits from export sales in income tax, and subsides on cost of freight, marketing and shipments of livestock products.

It is generally believed that reduction in three components of the AoA may push up international prices of agricultural products. Whether a country would gain or lose in case of specific product due to trade liberalisation is largely determined by its status as to whether it is a net exporter or net importer of that product. Since India is a net exporter of agricultural products, India would stand to gain in her share in the agricultural exports provided all trade related distortions are removed. Besides, India needs to mobilise support of developing countries in various WTO forums to put pressure on industrialised countries for reducing production and export subsidies. After the removal of QRs, the main problem for India is from the heavily subsidized exports of industrialised countries. With the greater volatility in the global market of agricultural products, huge decline in international prices can be disastrous for farmers in India. The producers of oilseeds are already facing hardships due to price volatility. Hence, ample actions need to be taken to safeguard the farmers from the onslaughts of foreign producers.

Rich countries promised nearly five years ago to make the global trade system fairer for poor countries, changing rules to help them reap the rewards of international commerce. But, unfortunately, the negotiations launched then are reaching a do-or-die stage, and after the Ministerial Meet at Geneva in June 2006, the prospects are rather bleak for a deal that would bestow much benefit on the poor. Farmers in rich countries continue to receive billions of dollars as subsidies from the government which encourage them for excess production of crops that result in gluts on world markets of depressing prices. However, India is committed to providing support prices to farmers and ensuring cheap supplies to the public distribution system.

Conclusion

Prospects of agricultural production in the coming years are estimated to be progressive as considerable initiatives are and will be taken further, by the government as it has been generally recognised that country cannot progress without attaining not only food sufficiency but a remarkable increase in agricultural exports. The emerging areas in agriculture like horticulture, floriculture, organic farming, genetic engineering, food processing, branding and packaging, and futures trading have high potential of growth. For harnessing this potential, development of rural infrastructure, rural extension services and agro-based as well as food processing industries are indispensable. Problems of low yields per hectare, volatility in production, wide disparities of productivity over regions and crops, insufficient production of pulses and oilseeds are to be resolved on top priority. Similarly, the distorted cropping pattern and input usage resulting from the inadequate agriculture price support policies of the government adopted in the past have to be corrected. Market for farm output still depends heavily on expensive government procurement and distribution systems. A shift from the prevailing MSP and public procurement system and developing alternative product markets are essential for crop diversification and broad-based agricultural progress.

Food Security and Public Distribution System

8

It is very surprising that after more than half decade of independence and all-around development in various fields of life, food security is one of the most significant forms of material insecurity in India. It remains a major policy challenge, despite the fact that food production has increased manifold during this period and the country do not have any shortage of foodgrains at macro level. The inadequate aggregate nutrition and food insecurity is most starkly reflected in declining per capita calorie consumption among the poorest section of the population. According to National Sample Survey data per capita foodgrain consumption in India declined from 476 gms per day in 1990 to only 418 gms per day in 2001. Aggregate calorie consumption per capita declined from just over 2,200 calories per day in 1987-88 to about 2,150 in 1999-2000.

Nutritional deficiencies remain a big problem. At least half the children in India are born with protein deficiency. Anaemia and iron deficiency are still widespread and continue to be severe problems. According to World Bank estimates about 25 per cent population in India is undernourished. This presents a paradoxical picture. India which was a food-deficit country in the 1960s and 70s turned to food-surplus country in the 1980s and 1990s.

The problem of chronic food insecurity is primarily associated with poverty. Some 200 million people in India are still denied access to sufficient quantities of food. This food insecurity is not a result of the shortage of food, but lack of economic access. The policy related forces have played a substantial and indirect role in declining food security. The misguided policies have also directly damaged food security in India since the mid-1990s.

Attempts to reduce the central government's food subsidy by increasing the price of foodgrains in public distribution system led to declining in sales and access holding of food stocks. This meant more losses and a larger level of food subsidy, even as more people in the country went hungry. Ultimately, several million tonnes of foodgrains were exported at ridiculously low prices despite widespread hunger and malnutrition in the country.

CONCEPT OF FOOD SECURITY

Food security means availability of food to all at all the times. World Development Report (1986) defines food security as, "access by all people at all times to enough food for an active, healthy life".

Food and Agriculture Organisation (FAO, 1983) defines food security as, "ensuring that all people at all times have both physical and economic access to basic food they need".

Other useful definition of the food security is "that every individual has the physical economic, social and environmental access to a balanced diet that includes the necessary macro- and micro-nutrients, safe drinking water, sanitation, environmental hygiene, primary health care and education so as to lead a healthy and productive life".

From the analysis of the above definitions, the following points emerge:

- Food security means availability of food to the entire population of the country.
- The available food should be adequate in quantity as well as quality so as to ensure the nutritional requirements of the people.
- The purchasing power of the people should be so strong that they may acquire foodgrains to fulfill their minimum basic requirements.
- The concept of food security means to ensure timely, reliable and nutritionally adequate supply of food on the long-term basis. It means that a nation needs to ensure and maintain the growth rate in food supply so that it may be able to make available sufficient foodgrains

to the increased population also fulfilling the increase in demand resulting from increase in the income of the people.

Thus, food and nutrition security involves concurrent attention to both food and non-food factors. Cutting across all these issues is the overriding need for ensuring the stabilization of the human population. India is likely to overtake China by 2030 in the size of population. Human numbers even now are far in excess of the population supporting capacity of the ecosystem. In addition, restructuring the delivery system relating to all nutrition support programmes particularly covering the weaker sections of society may help in achieving the target of food security in India.

SELF-SUFFICIENCY AND FOOD SECURITY IN INDIA

Food security was one of the major problems faced by the independent India. It was the cause of concern for the country. India has to depend largely on foreign countries for this minimum requirements. The first Prime Minister Pandit Jawaharlal Nehru expressed this concern in one of his broadcasts to the nation, "We have sought help from abroad...and we shall continue to do so under pressure of necessity, but the conviction is growing upon me more forcefully than ever. How dangerous it is for us to depend for this prime necessity of life on foreign countries. It is only when we obtain self-sufficiency in food that we can progress and develop ourselves. Otherwise there is the continuous pressure of circumstances, there is misery and trouble and there is sometimes shame and humiliations."

Thus the problem of food security was realised in the early days of planning. The policy-makers of the country realised the need to attain self-sufficiency in the field of foodgrains and it was set as one of the prime goals of planning. Agriculture sector was given priority in the five-year plans. The surplus food countries used their surplus as a tool to force the food deficient countries to submit to their dictates. For example, when India suffered severe drought in 1965 and 1966, the then American President, Lyndon Johnson restricted food aid to monthly basis under the PL 480 Programme as a punishment to India for condemning American aggression to Vietnam.

It was under the tremendous pressures of import that India under the Prime Ministership of Indira Gandhi went in seed-water-fertiliser policy which is popularly known as the Green Revolution. This policy brought about a revolution in the field of foodgrains production in India and dispensed it with foodgrains imports altogether. Within ten years of the adoption of this policy, India gained self-sufficiency in food production. Hence, its foodgrains imports declined to almost negligible. Undoubtedly, this is a great achievement for India.

As a result of the Green Revolution India's foodgrains production rose manifold. The foodgrains production which was 51 million tonnes in 1950-51 rose to 209.2 MT in 2006-07 as per the advance estimates.

The various components of cereals production indicate that whereas the cereals which accounted for 84 per cent of foodgrains in 1950-51, their share has increased to 94 per cent in 2003-04, but interestingly, against them the share of pulses has declined from 16 per cent to just 6 per cent during the same period. The production of pulses in 1970-71 was around 12 million tonnes. In 1990-91, the peak year of foodgrains production, production of pulses was 14 million tonnes. In most years, however, production has been stagnant around 13 to 14 million tonnes. The per capita consumption of pulses, which was 69 gm per day in 1971 has come down to 36 to 37 gm. This sharp decrease in the consumption of pulses is a cause of serious concern, more so for the poor for whom pulses are the major source of protein.

Table 8.1: Percentage Distribution of Cereals and Pulses in Foodgrains output

Year	Cereals	Pulses	Total
1950-51	84	16	100
1960-61	84	16	100
1990-91	92	8	100
2003-04	94	6	100

Source: *Economic Survey*, 2004-05.

The share of two prominent cereals—rice and wheat—which was only 53 per cent in 1950-51 had improved to 78 per cent in 2001-02. But the share of coarse cereals had declined from 37 per cent to 18 per cent during the same period. This indicates a marked change in the consumption pattern of the weaker section of society in favour of rice and wheat as against coarse cereals consumed by them earlier.

Table 8.2: Percentage Distribution of Cereals Output

Year	Rice	Wheat	Coarse	Total
1950-51	48	15	37	100
1960-61	50	16	34	100
1990-91	46	34	20	100
2003-04	44	37	19	100

Source: *Economic Survey*, 2004-05.

Population Growth and Availability of Cereals and Pulses

Table 8.3 interestingly shows that with the steady rise in population growth, the production of foodgrains, cereals and pulses, also rose equally. Naturally, net availability of cereals also went up. Despite the improvement in population growth, the government had to import large quantity of cereals from other countries to improve the net availability in the country.

This is clear from the available data that the annual net imports which were 4.1 million tonnes during 1950-51, rose to 10.3 million tonnes during 1965-66. But after the Green Revolution of the mid-1960s the imports declined and since 1976, food imports were almost negligible. By the year 1995-96, India became an important exporter of cereals in the world. India's exports of cereals during 2001-02 rose to a record 8.5 million tonnes. The proportion of agri exports to total exports was 11.9 per cent in 2003-04 but there was a slight decline during 2004-05 and it came down to 10.2 per cent.

Table 8.3: Net Availability of Cereals and Pulses (5-Yearly Annual Average)

Year	Population (millions) (1)	Cereals (million tonnes) Net Production (2)	Net Imports	Net Availability	Pulses Net Availability (million tonnes)	Per Capita Net Availability per day (gram) Cereals	Pulses	Total
1950-51	363	40.1	4.1	44.3	8.0	334.2	60.7	394.9
1960-61	442	60.9	3.5	64.6	11.1	399.7	69.0	468.7
1970-71	551	84.5	2.0	84.0	10.3	417.6	51.2	468.8
1980-81	689	104.1	0.5	104.8	9.4	417.3	37.5	454.8
1990-91	851	141.9	-0.6	145.7	12.9	468.5	41.6	510.1
2000-01	1,033	162.5	-4.5	145.6	11.3	366.2	30.0	416.2
2002-03	1,068	142.7	-7.1	158.7	11.4	407.1	29.1	436.3

Notes: 1. Population figure relates to mid-year.

2. Net availability of cereals = Net production + net imports – changes in government stock of cereals.

Sources: *Economic Survey* (2004-2005).

From the Table 8.3 it is clear that the per capita availability of foodgrains also improved from 394.9 gms per day in 1951 to 451 gms in 2001. It rose to 463.3 gms in 2004. This indicates an improvement of nearly 15 per cent in per capita availability during the 50 years period. Foodgrains has two components—cereals and pulses. The per capita availability of cereals increased from 334 gms to 407 gms during the same period. This is an increase of 9 per cent in per capita availability of cereals during the same period. But the picture is not encouraging in case of pulses. Its per capita availability was 65 gms per day in 1950 which declined to 29 gms in 2001. This indicates a sharp decline of 55 per cent in the per capita availability of pulses. This point finds appropriate mention in the Ninth Five-Year Plan, "Reduction in per capita pulse availability may adversely affect protein intake. Coarse grains that are inexpensive can provide substantially higher calories for the same cost. If made available through PDS at subsidised rates, there will be self-targeting and improve calorie intake and reduce 'hunger' among the poorest segments of population."

Thus, India's growth in foodgrains production is consistent with the growing population and is steadily moving towards foodgrains security, but it has miserably failed to increase the production of cereals and fulfill the demand of its rising population. It still has to depend on import for its requirements.

National Agricultural Policy, 2000

The National Agricultural Policy, 2000 was presented in the Parliament on July 28, 2000, in the context of relatively poor growth of agriculture during the nineties. It covers the various aspects of agricultural sector which finds obvious mention in the official document. It states, "The national policy on agriculture seeks to actualise the most untapped growth potential of Indian agriculture, strengthen rural infrastructure, to support faster agricultural development, promote value addition, accelerate the growth of agro-business, create employment in rural areas, secure a fair standard of living for the farmers and the agricultural labourers and their families, discourage migration to urban areas and face the challenges arising out of economic liberalisation and globalisation." On the performance of agricultural sector, the Policy document mentions, "Capital inadequacy, lack of infrastructural support and demand side constraints such as controls on movement, storage and sale of agricultural products, etc. have continued to affect the economic viability of agriculture sector. Consequently, growth has also tended to slacken during the nineties."

The Policy envisages to establish an agrarian economy that can ensure the fulfillment of food and nutrition requirements of its population as well as supply the raw materials to industries. The Policy seek to promote technically sound, economically viable and socially acceptable use of country's natural resources to promote sustainable agriculture. The main objectives envisaged in the Policy are as follows:

- An annual growth rate of over 4 per cent in agriculture sector;
- Growth that is based on efficient use of resources and conservation of soil, water and biodiversity;
- Growth with equity, which is widespread across regions and farmers;
- Growth that is demand driven and caters to domestic markets and maximises benefits from exports of agricultural products in face of the challenges arising from economic liberalisation and globalisation;
- Growth that is technologically, environmentally and economically sustainable.

National Nutrition Policy (1993)

National Nutrition Policy (NNP), which was adopted in 1993, envisages the following goals, sought to be achieved by 2000 AD:

1. Reduction in the incidence of moderate and severe malnutrition among pre-school children by 50 per cent.
2. Reduction in chronic under-nutrition and reduction in incidence of low birth weight children to 10 per cent.
3. Elimination of micro-nutrient deficiencies, namely blindness caused due to deficiency of Vitamin 'A',

anaemia caused due to iron deficiency, goitre caused due to iodine deficiency. The Policy through the universal iodisation of salt envisages to eliminate goitre.

4. Emphasis to geriatric nutrition.
5. Production of 250 million tonnes of foodgrains per annum.
6. Improving household security through poverty alleviation programmes and promoting appropriate diets and healthy lifestyles.

Obviously, the Policy primarily emphasises on the promotion of nutrition through several poverty alleviation programmes so as to eliminate many deficiency disease and contain the spread of other diseases as well as ensuring food security to its population.

Main Components of Food Security System

The food security system has several components. Some major components of it are as follows:

- Promoting domestic production so as to meet the demands of growing production also reducing under-nutrition;
- Providing minimum support prices for procurement and storage of food items;
- Operating a public distribution system;
- Maintaining buffer stock in case of natural calamities resulting in temporary shortages of food, and also provides a mechanism against the traders and businessmen who cause to rise in prices particularly at a time when there is shortage of it.

Thrust Areas of the Nutrition Policy

The Indian Prime Minister on 15th August 2001 announced to set up a National Nutrition Mission to improve the nutritional status of the population. The Mission has been launched in selected nutritionally backward districts of the country to further carry toward the goals of National Nutrition Policy. The major thrust areas of the Policy are as follows:

- Reduction in under-nutrition;

- Reduction or elimination of micro-nutrient deficiencies, namely iron, iodine, vitamin A deficiency;
- Reduction in chronic energy deficiency.

Carrying forward the objectives of the National Nutrition Mission, the Tenth Five-Year Plan emphasises the nutrition goals to be achieved by 2007. These are as follows:

Intensify nutrition and health education to improve infant mortality and child feeding and caring practices so as to bring down the prevalence of under-weight children below the age of three from the current level of 47 per cent to 40 per cent; reduce prevalence of severe under-nutrition in children in the 0-6 years age group by 50 per cent; reduce prevalence of anaemia by 25 per cent and that of moderate or severe anaemia by 50 per cent and eliminate vitamin A deficiency as a public health problem and reduce prevalence of Iodine deficiency disorders to less than 10 per cent by 2010.

Food Security in Tenth Plan

The remarkable change in the consumption pattern of the population taken place in the Post-Green Revolution era has been prominently discussed in the Tenth Plan. It states, "Between 1972-73 and 1993-94, the food basket has become much more diversified, with the share of cereals seeing a dramatic decline of ten percentage points in most regions. At the all India level, cereal consumption in the rural areas declined from 15.3 kg per capita per month in 1972-73 to 13.4 kg per capita per month in 1993-94. The corresponding decline in the urban area was more modest—from 11.3 kg to 10.6 kg over the same period. At the same time, consumption of milk and meat products as well as vegetables and fruits has increased. Such changes are the natural outcome of economic development."

CURRENT AGRICULTURE SCENARIO

Agriculture is the backbone of Indian economy. Despite great industrialisation during the last five decades, agriculture remains one of the major sectors of economy. It still occupies a place of pride in India. It is the largest occupation in the country which provides employment to three-fourth of the total workforce of the country. The Table 8.4 presents a clear picture of agriculture in India.

Table 8.4: Share of Agricultural Sector in Total Gross Domestic Product at Factor Cost

(At 1993-94 prices) (Rs. crores)

Year	GDP at Factor cost	Agriculture	3 as % of 2
(1)	(2)	(3)	(4)
1950-51	1,40,470	83,150	55.4
1970-71	2,96,280	1,42,580	44.5
1990-91	6,92,870	2,42,010	30.9
2003-04*	14,30,550	3,43,810	24.1

Note: Agricultural includes agriculture, forestry and fishing.

* Quick Estimates.

Source: Compiles *Economic Survey 2004-05* Table 1.3.

This is clear from table 8.4 that the share of agriculture in GDP, which was 50-55 per cent in 1950-51 declined to 24.1 per cent, however, it contributes a major share of the national income. In a developing country like India this is a good sign as it marks the increasing growth of manufacturing and service sectors.

India's Social Development Report released in January 2006 says about 260 million Indians which constitute 26 per cent of the total population, continue to live below poverty line. This section of the population is the worst affected by the problem of food insecurity in India. M.S. Swaminathan, the Father of Green Revolution and Chairman of the National Commission on Farmers says, "Maintaining a balance between population and the capacity to produce is becoming more and more challenging." He further adds, "About 70 per cent of India's population comprises farmers and those engaged in farming. So, farmers are also the largest chunk of consumers of agriculture produce." With production down, they are the ones most affected, both as producers and consumers. Today, even the heartland of Green Revolution—Punjab, Haryana and Western

Uttar Pradesh—is facing economic and ecological problems. He adds, "Wheat production, which would have closed to about 90 million tonnes had agricultural policies been environmentally friendly and small farmer-oriented, is estimated to be less than 70 million tonnes this year." According to him, increased wheat production is synonymous to food security in India. R.S. Paroda, Director General of Indian Council of Agriculture Research, says, "Currently at second position after China, it can become the largest wheat producer in five to 10 years if we adopt an aggressive and well-planned strategy with greater emphasis on eastern and north-eastern region."

During the five decades of planning, the percentage of people involved with agricultural activities also came down from 70 to 59 per cent. According to Tenth Plan, it is 57 per cent. It means that still more than half of the population depends on agriculture for their livelihood. In brief, the prosperity of Indian agriculture can largely stand for the prosperity of Indian economy. In other words, general economic development would require rapid agricultural development either to precede or go hand in hand with it. Failure of the agricultural sector can be disastrous for the entire process of planning. The Tenth Plan, keeping in view the crucial role of this sector, has emphasised that "agricultural development is central to rapid economic development of the country".

In the first three years of the Tenth Plan, GDP growth in agriculture and allied sectors averages only 1 per cent per annum abysmally against the target of 4 per cent. The advance estimates of National Income for 2005-06, released by the CSO on Feb. 7, 2006 has estimated a growth rate of 2.3 per cent based on New Series (at 1999-2000 prices). Tenth Plan expenditure of the Ministry of Agriculture during 2002-03 and 2003-04 was 27 per cent of the total Tenth Plan outlay. In 2006-07 the foodgrains target in the Tenth Plan is 230 million tonnes. Its production was 212.9 million tonnes in 2001-02 and since then it has been declining. Large exports at below domestic prices and subsequent poor monsoons have now reduced the stocks to a low level. These all combine to add to problem of food insecurity in India.

Food Insecurity is a major problem in India. The following measures could be of great help in this regard:

- Increased capital investment in agriculture to at least 15 per cent;
- Supply of growth-oriented inputs, such as quality seeds and fertilisers at farmers' doorsteps;
- Improving wheat, rice, groundnut, rapeseed, mustard, vegetable and fruits productivity;
- Making gray areas green with emphasis on rain-fed agriculture;
- Emphasis on new area approach;
- Promoting inland agriculture;
- Capitalising on livestock sector. India having the largest cattle and buffalo population, second largest goat population and the third largest population of sheep in the world;
- Improved on-farm efficiency and precision farming;
- Critical policy interventions.

FOOD SECURITY AND GOVERNMENT SCHEMES

Food security has always been a matter of concern for the government. For this various food and security programmes have been launched by the Government time to time. Some of such programmes are as follows:

Integrated Child Development Services Scheme (ICDS)

The Integrated Child Development Services Scheme was started in 1975 with an objective to provide food supplementation to children and pregnant nursing women. The ICDS programme covers 4,200 blocks with 5.92 lakh *anganwadis* in the country as in 1996. By 1996, the number of beneficiaries rose up to 18.5 million children and 3.7 million mothers. Reviewing ICDS, the Ninth Plan mentions, "Experience gained during the last two decades indicates that the most needy may not access to the facility and even when they do, the food provided acts more as a substitute than as a supplement." A review of the ICDS programme reveals, "While 25 per cent of the nursing mothers in ICDS areas introduced semi-solid supplements to their breast-fed infants at 6 months. Only 19 per cent did so in non-ICDS areas. These evaluations have shown the gains in terms of improvement in nutritional status from the ICDS programme have not been impressive."

Mid-Day Meal Programme

The Mid-Day Programme was started for the children between age groups of 2-14, attending *balwadis*/schools at the expense of Re. 0.44 to 0.90 per beneficiary have been covered. Under the programme the children who are not attending schools are not covered under. This programme has been renamed as Nutritional Support to Primary Education. It was implemented in 1975 to universalise primary education. By March 1997, the programme covered 5.57 crore children in 4.426 blocks.

National Food for Work Programme (NFFWP)

The National Food for Work Programme (NFFWP) was launched in November 2004 as a centrally sponsored scheme in the 150 most backward districts to generate additional supplementary wage employment with food security. Under the programme states receive foodgrains free of cost. The programme focuses on works relating to water conservation, drought proofing (including aforestation/tree plantation), land development, flood control/protection (including drainage in waterlogged areas), and rural connectivity in terms of all-weather roads. In 2004-05, allocation of Rs. 2,020 crore and 20 lakh tonnes of foodgrains generated 7.85 crore person days of employment. In 2005-06, of the allocation of Rs. 4,500 crore and 15 lakh tonnes of foodgrains (revised) Rs. 2,219 crore and 11.58 lakh metric tonnes of foodgrains had been released up to January 27, 2006. About 17.03 lakh person days were generated up to December 2005.

Sampoorna Grameen Rozgar Yojana (SGRY)

Launched on September 25, 2001, the Sampoorna Grameen Rozgar Yojana aims to provide additional wage employment in the rural areas. The Yojana has a cash and foodgrains components. The Centre bears 75 per cent and 100 per cent of the cost of the two with the balance borne by the States/UTs. In the year 2004-05, 82.23 crore person days were generated with the Centre releasing Rs. 4,496 crore as cash component of the SGRY, with the States and UTs meeting the cash components. Centre released 26 lakh tonnes of foodgrains to the 13 calamity affected states. In 2006-07, up to November, 2006, the number of person-days generated under SGRY was 18.71 crore, while the Centre's contributions in terms of the cash and foodgrains components up to December 31, 2006 were Rs. 2,762 crore and 16.67 lakh tonnes respectively. Under the special component, about 4.44 lakh tonnes of foodgrains have been released to the calamity-hit states in the current year up to December 2006.

Wheat-based Nutrition Programme

Launched by the Ministry of Human Resource Development, the Programme intends to provide food security to children below six years of age and expectant lactating mother. The foodgrains allotted under this scheme are utilised by the States/ UTs under Integrated Child Development Scheme (ICDS). Foodgrains are supplied to States and UTs at BPL rates under the scheme.

Nutrition Programme for Adolescent Girl

This pilot project, launched by the Planning Commission, provides foodgrains to the families of the identified under-nourished adolescent girls, pregnant and lactating mothers at the rate of six kg of foodgrains per head per month in two of the backward districts in each of the fifteen major states and most populous districts (excluding the capital districts in remaining) smaller states and union territories.

Emergency Feeding Programme

This is a food-based programme, being implemented in eight KBK districts of Orissa, namely Kalahandi, Bolangir, Koraput, Malkangiri, Nawarangpur, Naupada, Rayagada and Sonepur. The Programme, which covers two lakh beneficiaries, provides foodgrains at BPL rates to old, infirm and destitute persons belonging to BPL households. It intends to provide them food security in their distress situation.

Annapurna Scheme

Launched by the Ministry of Rural Development in 2000-01, the scheme provides food security to the indigent senior citizens of 65 years of age or above who despite being eligible for the old-age pension under the National Old Age Pension Scheme (NOAPS), but were not getting the pension. Under this scheme they are supplied ten kgs of foodgrains free of cost per person per month.

From 2002-03 it has been transferred to state plan along with the National Social Assistance Programme comprising the National Old Age Pension Scheme and the National Family Benefit Scheme. The funds for the transferred scheme are being released by the Ministry of Finance as Additional Central Assistance to the State Plan. The state has the flexibility in choice of beneficiaries and implementation of the scheme. The implementation of the scheme at the ground level rests with the States/UTs.

Antyodaya Anna Yojana

Launched on 25 December 2000, the Antyodaya Anna Yojana provides food security to the poorest of the poor. Under this scheme, 25 kg of foodgrains was made available to each eligible family at highly subsidised rates of Rs. two per kg for wheat and Rs. three per kg for rice. From 1 April 2002, this quantity has been raised from 25 kg to 35 kg. The families are identified by the States/UT Governments from among the BPL families. The coverage of the Yojana has been expanded to cover an additional 50 lakh BPL families giving priority to people belonging to the households headed by widows or terminally-ill persons or disabled persons or persons aged 60 years or more with no assured means of subsistence or societal support and households of widows or terminally ill persons or disabled persons or persons aged 60 years or more or single women or single men with no family or societal support or assured means of subsistence as well as all primitive tribal households. The Yojana was further expanded in 2004-05 to include another 50 lakh BPL families. Thus under the Yojana 1.5 to two crore BPL families have been covered.

FOOD PROBLEM IN INDIA

India has made striking agricultural progress since independence. Agricultural products has increased manifold. It has become self-reliant in the field of foodgrains. But a large number of people in the country still find it difficult to meet their requirements. Their diet is also deficient in respect of nutritious elements. Poverty and poverty-induced undernutrition and malnutrition are widespread. International and national media refer to this situation as the co-existence of "grain mountains and hunger millions". India is still the home of the largest number of under-fed children, men and women.

In its present form, it has been the problem of the poor, largely attributed to the inadequacy of food articles as also of the lack of purchasing power. Several other factors have also contributed to the problem. This problem can be conceived in its threefold aspects, namely the quantitative inadequacy, the nutrition deficiency and the poverty of the poor.

Quantitative Inadequacy

This aspect of the food problem is directly related to the supply of foodgrains. The quantity required has very often fallen short of that needed for a minimum calorie intake. The overall per capita per day requirement of foodgrains has been put by FAO (Food and Agriculture Organisation) at 440 gms. But to a large number of people, the actual availability has been less than that, although the food production position has considerably improved because in quite many years the availability has been higher. However, this aspect has some disquieting features. Firstly, the growth rate in the production of foodgrains in comparison to large population growth is not yet satisfactory. Secondly, there have been great fluctuations in the output of foodgrains, which were filled by imports, hence causing instability in the availability. Thirdly, the improvement has been confined to certain foodgrains, namely wheat, rice and not every items of foodgrains. For example, there has been large gap between production and requirement of pulses and its per capita availability has been low. Fourthly, the large income inequality, the per capita availability among the poor is much less than the average for the entire population.

Deficient in Nutrition

The food taken by most of the Indians are deficient in terms of nutritive elements. It lacks the important elements of a balanced diet, namely protein, vitamins and minerals. It affects their health which ultimately results in fall of the efficiency of the working people. Many people suffer from various deficient diseases like beriberi, scurvy, pellagra, goitre, blindness, etc. Although the country has to some extent been able to eliminate nutritional deficiency, yet chronic energy deficiency among adults, under-nutrition among children, micro-nutrient deficiencies and anaemia are still prevalent across all sections of the population. One half of the children under the age of five years in India are moderately or severely malnourished, 30 per cent of new born children are significantly underweight and nearly 60 per cent of women are anaemic. The problem may aggravate in future as our population is continuously rising.

In the livestock sector the success in the area of dairying is well-known. Production of milk has gone up more than five-fold since independence, resulting in near doubling of per capita milk availability. The entire livestock sector plays an important role in the national economy and the socio-economic development of the country by contributing significantly to not only value adding in allied sectors and providing employment and incomes to millions of people in both urban and rural areas but also nutritional security to the people.

But a matter of concern is the lack of sufficient focus and thrust in horticulture as the importance of horticulture in improving the productivity of land, generating employment, improving economic conditions of the farmers and entrepreneurs, enhancing export and above all providing nutritional security to the people is widely acknowledged. Despite being the second largest producer of fruits and vegetables in the world, the availability of vegetables especially green leafy vegetables and yellow, red vegetables throughout the year at affordable cost both in urban and rural areas has remained an unfulfilled dream.

The availability of pulses, which is a great source of nutrition, is also below the recommended quantity. The intake of pulses is recommended 40 gms per day. Even the national average is 34 gms in 1996-97 and thus the conditions of the poor in intake of pulses has become worse. But the situation is not the same all across the country. While in Karnataka, Madhya Pradesh, Uttar Pradesh and Rajasthan, the per capita per day pulse intake is above the recommended level of 40 gms while the situation is different in other parts of the country.

According to the National Nutrition Monitoring Board (NNMB) in 1975-80, in 31 per cent of households energy consumption was adequate in all members of the family. In 19 per cent of the households, the energy consumption was inadequate in all members of the family. It is noteworthy that in 25 per cent of households energy consumption was adequate among adults, but not among the school children.

Nutrition education can be of great help in this regard. It can improve the intra-familial distribution of food thus contributing to the nutrition level of the members. It can help to direct the available resources to use green and leafy vegetables and also such commodities as iodised salt, which contributes in reducing iodine deficiency.

Enhancing the income status of a person has a direct bearing on the improvement of the nutritional level. It bears a close relationship with the consumption of pulses, milk, fruits, fresh food, oil, sugar and other things.

This deficiency is obvious from the preponderance of foodgrains and the inadequacy of nutritive foods like milk in the diet of the people. For instance, the per capita daily intake of protein is much lower in India. In 1991 it was 59 gms which is almost half of that in countries like France, Italy and the USA. Though the protein needs vary in terms of body-built and climate but the difference is much wider in case of India. The picture is equally dismal in case of the availability of fat. India's daily per capita intake of 45 gms is much lower in comparison to many developed countries where it is three times more than it. The picture is not very different in case of foodgrains. The availability of the nutritive food to the poor is far less. In brief, it presents a grim picture.

Poverty and Unemployment

The widespread poverty and unemployment make the situation all the more miserable. A wide gap between various income groups and large unemployment and underemployment have caused a decline in the purchasing power of the poor. Their condition has become so miserable that it has become difficult for them to buy food for their physical existence. They do not have regular employment. Whenever they get a job they are underpaid, even lower than the minimum wages fixed by the government. They are too poor to earn their livelihood on their own. They neither possess productive assets nor do they have adequate skills. All these combine to present all the more dismal scenario which is that even when at sometimes in a year, when the supply of goodgrains is adequate, the poor are even then not in a position to fully meet their own minimum requirements.

Detailed analysis of various factors responsible for the food insecurity in India reveal that the problem is thus a threefold one. First is the insufficiency of foodgrains which constitutes a major part of most of the Indians. Second is that the diet of most of the Indians are deficient in nutritive elements which are almost absent in the food of the poor people. Third one is the inadequate purchasing power of the people due to lack of job or livelihood opportunities, which is now the primary cause of endemic or chronic hunger in the country. When news of deaths from hunger catches the headlines of the newspapers all the achievements made by the country in various fields of life seem to appear worthless and our heads are hung in shame.

Causes and Remedies

To solve the problem of food insecurity in India, it is necessary to first reach at the root of problem and only then it would be easier to suggest measures to overcome this problem. Some of the causes along with measures are discussed below:

1. Farm families in India constitute over two-thirds of the total population of the country. The detailed analyses of the causes of food insecurity in rural and urban India have revealed that the major cause of food insecurity is due to lack of adequate purchasing power

to permit access to balanced diets and clean drinking water. Therefore, a three-pronged strategy needs to be introduced to ensure the economic well-being and nutrition security of the poor families. First, families possessing assets like land, livestock or fish ponds will have to be assisted to enhance the productivity of their resource endowment in an environmentally and economically sustainable manner. Emphasis has to be made on increasing outputs per units of land, water, nutrients and labour based on technologies which are ecologically and economically sound. This needs a great deal of research and development in the field of eco-technologies based on blending traditional ecological prudence with technologies like information and biotechnology and space and renewable energy technologies.

2. One third of the rural population and a large proportion of women earn their livelihood through wage employment. They have no assets like land or livestock and such other assets. They are also often illiterate. This poses a big challenge. A massive effort in the field of knowledge and skill empowerment of the women and men constituting the landless labour workforce is essential so as to ensure the value of their time and labour. They need to be trained in a way that they may take to skilled non-farm employment through market-driven micro-enterprises supported by micro-credit. Common property resources need to be developed and managed in a way that they can provide essential support system in area such as fodder and feed for stall-fed animal husbandry as well as fuel wood. Besides, the unfinished segments of land reform including the distribution of ceiling surplus land to asset-less families should be added to with great sincerity and commitment. At the same time the interests of unregistered cultivators as well as tribal cultivators have to be safeguarded.

Rural artisans working in the secondary and tertiary sectors of the economy constitute the third group. Their skills need to be groomed and mobilized to enhance the competitiveness of agriculture through value addition to primary products and diversification of livelihood opportunities. The technological upgradation of rural profession based on the social inclusion needs to be promoted. However, the lasting solution to the food insecurity in India lies in poverty alleviation. Since they are the most affected section of society, upliftment of their economic status would help in overcoming the problem of food insecurity in India. For this they need to be given employment-orientation training so as to ensure the productive use of their time and labour. This means the use of labour-intensive techniques, consistent with efficiency. Besides, equal distribution of resources will also help in the upliftment of the economic status of the poor. It implies redistribution of assets such as, for example, the distribution of surplus land among the poor under the policy of ceiling on land. This will improve their purchasing power.

An efficient public distribution system constitutes an essential requirement of the problem of food insecurity in India since agricultural prices and output are subject to large fluctuations in India. Through it supply of essential foodgrains at reasonable prices to the weaker sections of society can be ensured. For the efficient management of public distribution system, several interrelated measures have to become a part of the overall policy of price-stability, output increase and equitable distribution of food articles that include stocking, transportation, fair price shops, etc. The supply of food items should be made on permanent basis so as to ensure them the food security. This will ensure the solution of foodgrains shortages and inadequacies.

A loss of livelihood is typically the key shock factor that generates a process that culminates in greater malnutrition in India. This explains the coexistence of higher production and lower prices of food with the continued, widespread and even increasing incidence of hunger. As world trade prices of food have fallen, incomes of the poor especially the rural poor have fallen even further, which reflects the general stagnation of productive employment opportunities and the worsening of livelihood conditions.

Ironically, cultivators are suffering from the increase in food insecurity just as much as or even more than other groups. This probably is the most significant cause of the continued prevalence of widespread malnourishment. The macroeconomic causes of livelihood insecurity arise primarily from the effects of deregulating the market and reducing the subsidy.

Thus, the three-pronged strategy aims at improving the productivity of land, water, livestock and labour in the case of asset owning farm families, converting unskilled agricultural labourer into skilled entrepreneurs engaged in organising market-driven non-farm enterprises and shaping and enhancing the skills of families involved in the secondary and tertiary sectors of the rural economy. All these are motivated to make them skilled enough to contribute in agricultural efficiency and bridging the prevailing gap between production and post-harvest technologies.

The strategy to overcome this problem includes short-term interventions to raise the purchasing power of the poor through endowments of land and non-land assets by generating employment opportunities and long-term growth-mediated interventions to improve food availability and raise incomes. By implementing the policies with full sincerity, the goal of a hunger-free India by 2007 could be achieved.

FOOD INSECURITY AND FARMERS' SUICIDE

Farmers' suicide is the latest distressing phenomenon of the problem of food insecurity in India. The news of farmers' suicide are catching the headlines of the newspapers. The number of farmers' suicide are on the rise in the country. It is an outcome of price rise in the last 15 years, crop fluctuations and accumulated debts. The wide gap between the input costs and output is also one of the factors responsible for rising cases of farmers' suicide in the country. Maharashtra's cotton belt has already seen 1,006 farmer deaths since June 2005. Across India, the figure has crossed a thousand this year alone.

At least 31 districts across the country have been identified by the Government as the 'suicide-prone' districts in the country. Sixteen of the suicide-prone districts are: one in Andhra Pradesh, six each in Maharashtra and Karnataka and three in Kerala. According to official sources, between 2001 and 2006 as many as 5,910 farmers committed suicides in Karnataka, 1,835 in Andhra Pradesh, 981 in Maharashtra and 201 in Kerala. Countrywide, between 1995 and 2003, 9.26 lakh farmers are reported to have committed suicide, according to the statistics put out by the Home Ministry. The main causes are attributed to indebtedness, crop failure and other economic and psychological reasons.

Special relief packages are being worked out for farmers in these areas. Indian Finance Minister P. Chidambaram announced in Parliament in July 2006 that the government would make short-term farm credit at 7 per cent from the kharif season of the year 2006 and action would be taken against those banks found violating this order within 48 hours of receiving a complaint.

Keeping in view the rising farmers' suicide and falling agricultural growth rate, which are becoming issues of national concern, the Indian Government has taken several fiscal decisions which are intended to give a fillip to the farm sector.

As a part of the relief packages provided to the farmers, the Indian Government plans to release 1600 crore to provide subsidies on interest rates to ensure that the farmers have to pay only 7 per cent interest on short-term agricultural loans. Thus the government keeps up his budget 2006-07 promise to lend farmers at soft interest rates. The move comes even as the government contemplates interest waivers on past loans for small farmers across the country. The ministries of agriculture and finance are also working on extending the interest waiver offered to farmers in four Indian states to the entire country, but limited to "farmers in distress" who either produce one crop a year or have been hit by repeated crop failure. The lending is aimed at farm boosting in food production.

PUBLIC DISTRIBUTION SYSTEM (PDS)

The Public Distribution System (PDS) in India was started as a part of the strategy for poverty alleviation. It was one of the main constituents of government's strategy aiming to enhance food security particularly to the economically weaker sections of the society. The PDS ensures the availability of the essential commodities like wheat, rice, sugar, edible oil and kerosene through a wide network of outlets or Fair Price Shops (FPS). At present there is a wide network of 4.6 lakh PDS retail outlets in the country. The Centre procures and supplies commodities to States and Union Territories, who are directly involved with the distribution through the state-organised wide network of Fair Price Shops.

The PDS has crossed 64 years of working as a public policy in a welfare state like India but the problem of hunger, starvation, malnutrition, poverty and food security of the poor and the vulnerable sections of the society remains a question. The PDS which was started in the early years of independence to solve the rampant poverty in the country by maintaining price stability of food and food products in the market and at the same time provide food security to the poor through Fair Price Shops, failed to provide the umbrella of food security to the poor now. This is attributed to some extent to the fact that the policy of PDS is regarded as the financial burden for the Central Government, the reduction of food subsidy became the primary motive that led the government to target the system with less food subsidy in budgetary allocation. Thus, the government is trying to dismantle the system, ignoring the problem of food insecurity.

The shift from a food deficient economy to a food surplus one has been the cause for complacence in official circles. Yet, the absolute number of people living in impoverishment and the number of hungry and malnourished are on the rise. India's foodgrains production has risen four-fold in the last 50 years, from 51 million tonnes in 1950 to 210 million tonnes in 2000. The Green Revolution brought about the multiplication of food production, but even after its four decades, the goals of food security remains elusive.

Meaning of Food Security

Food security means the availability of food at all the times, access to all the persons in terms of quantity and quality which should be nutritionally adequate, that should be acceptable within the given culture and food habit. It is indicated by physical and economic accessibility of food. The physical access to food depends on procurement, storage, buffer stock and supply of food whereas the economic access to food demands purchasing power of the consumer. The PDS in the early days of Independence was started to cover all the above items necessary for food security. The policy of PDS has been drawn primarily with the objective of providing food security to the poor and simultaneously fixing remunerative prices to the producers. In fact the latter function was better served in course of implementation of the PDS. This aimed to ensure the fact that the farmers may not resort to distress sale due to weak bargaining power and monopoly of market functionaries and also to their demands. The government through procurement operation provided Minimum Support Price to the producers to save them from market exploitation and to boost production as well. It also aims to build buffer stocks to ensure food security in case of scarcity situation.

The wide network of PDS is a major instrument of government, with the help of which it tries to implement food and economic policies for ensuring food security particularly to the poor. This system largely aims to help the producers and consumers of foodgrains. It provides the Minimum Support Price (MSP) to the farmers as well as ensures the distribution of foodgrains to the consumers at affordable and subsidized prices throughout the country.

In the 1990s, when India adopted the policy of liberalisation and globalisation, the objective of expenditure reductions took priority over the welfare objectives, including the objective of providing food security to the poor. The existing PDS was characterized as inefficient, having more leakages, less benefit to the poor and maladministration. The government shifted its operation to target-orientation and revamped orientation of PDS.

Origin of PDS and Food Security

The PDS in the field of foodgrains in India dates back to the early years of World War and the Great Famine in India. It was started as an emotional issue with an objective to help the common people. It was introduced as a measure to maintain the morale of the people in the context of war mobilization and foodgrains scarcity. Later it became an integral constituent of food and economic policy of the government that aimed to protect the vulnerable section of the society from the rising prices of essential commodities.

The PDS continues to be an essential plank of economic policy of the country even after independence. The policy on the food security of the fledgling Indian state had two essential components, namely the policy of increased agricultural production and the policy of food distribution system. The first one was clearly a vital component of the modernization of the Indian state. The second was more unambiguously a part of its welfarist orientation. It is to achieve this goal that the system was assigned a significant role in the beginning of the planning era in India and to ensure efficient and equitable distribution of available foodgrains at reasonable prices. Over a period of time, the system evolved many measures regarding the procurement that include foodgrains price control, their procurement, building of buffer stocks that is carried on by the Food Corporation of India (FCI) for stabilizing foodgrains prices and an even below of the supplies movement control through zonal system, fixation of producers price to support their income. It with the help of a wide network of Fair Price Shops (FPS) provides protective umbrella to the vulnerable sections of the society by distributing foodgrains at concessional rate.

The Food Corporation of India, purchases foodgrains for the Central Pool at minimum support prices announced by the government and then it is released for Public Distribution System and other schemes at issue prices fixed by the government. The difference between issue prices and procurement prices constitutes the food subsidy. Handling, storage, interest, and administrative charges are also reimbursed to the Corporation.

The PDS in India has been working efficiently for more than half decade only because of the huge subsidy that is borne by the Government of India. While the food subsidy was negligible until the end of the 1960s, but later it increased steadily. By the end of the mid-1990s, it rose to 50,000 millions which constitutes 3 per cent of the total expenditure of the Central Government budget and about 0.5 per cent of the Gross Domestic Product (GDP).

Phases of its Development

The development of PDS in India regarding its organisation, coverage and structure can be divided into following phases:

Phase I – Origin to 1960

Phase II – 1960 to 1978

Phase III – 1978 to 1991

Phase IV – 1991 to present day

During its first phase PDS had a restricted and limited coverage. The second phase of PDS is marked for major organisational changes and expansion of coverage while the third phase is characterized for its sustained expansion and coverage propelled by the influence of growth of domestic production. During this period it acquired the status of a welfare programme. The PDS in India is perhaps the largest distribution network of its kind in the world. Under several employment generation programmes, subsidised foodgrains are provided as a part of wages. The fourth phase of PDS is marked as the weakening of PDS with the rhetoric of cutting down subsidies and major changes in food policy motivated by the target of expenditure reduction. The Government of India's Economic Survey (1992-93) stated, "It was decided to have a phased withdrawal of food subsidies by targeting PDS." Later, several committees also advocated for even total abolition of food subsidies. The growth of food subsidy components of the Central Government, its annual growth and per cent of GDP during the last decade is given in the Table 8.5 below:

It is clear from the following table that food subsidies have been continuously increasing rising from 2450 crore in 1990-91 to 26200 crore in 2005-06 showing an increase of above 27 per cent during each of the three years, namely 2000-01, 2001-02 and 2002-03. The annual increase came down to 4.1 per cent during 2003-04 and is expected to further decelerate to 2.54 per

Table 8.5: Growth of Food Subsidies

Year	Food subsidy* (Rs. crore)	Annual growth (per cent)	As per cent of GDP
1990-91	2450	-	0.43
1991-92	2850	16.33	0.44
1992-93	2800	-1.75	0.37
1993-94	5537	97.75	0.64
1994-95	5100	-7.89	0.50
1995-96	5377	5.43	0.45
1996-97	6066	12.81	0.44
1997-98	7900	30.23	0.52
1998-99	9100	15.19	0.52
1999-00	9434	3.67	0.48$
2000-01	12060	27.84	0.57$
2001-02	17499	45.10	0.77$
2002-03	24176	38.16	0.98$
2003-04	25160	4.07	0.91$
2004-05(RE)	25800	2.54	0.83$
2005-06(BE)	26200	1.55	

$ As per cent of GDP (new series base on 1999-2000).

* Other than that on sugar.

Source: *Economic Survey*, 2005-06.

cent in 2004-05. The food subsidy which was 0.43 per cent of GDP in 1990-91 shoot up to 0.98 per cent of GDP in 2002-03. As a proportion of Central Government expenditure, it was in the range of 2.9 to 3.2 per cent during 1980s and 1990s. Since 1997-98 the PDS expenditure sharply rose from 7900 crore to 25800 crore in 2004-05. But under popular pressure to continue the scheme as a welfare measure along with a price stabilization instrument, food subsidies went up sharply to 3.6 per cent in 2000-01 and 5.2 per cent in 2003-04.

Provision of minimum nutritional support to the poor through subsidized foodgrains and ensuring price stability are the major objectives of the food security system.

Significance of PDS in India

The role and importance of PDS was realised as far back as the First Plan of 1951-56. The Public Distribution System in India was introduced with an objective to act as price support programme for the consumer during the food shortage of 1960s. As the food-items constitute a major portion of the consumption of workers, PDS helps in supplying wage-goods at prices lower than the market prices. At the same time the real wages of the workers are protected. The price level of several consumption goods is kept stable. Besides, the supply of foodgrains is also regulated by the PDS. The PDS helps in overcoming the regional disparities in respect of foodgrains production which creates regional imbalances. For example, rice which is the staple diet of the major proportion of the population, the difference in growth rates have often been very large indeed as the Northern Region (Punjab, Haryana and Western Uttar Pradesh) achieved a growth rate as high as 10.9 per cent during 1970-71 to 1980-81 while the Southern Region Andhra Pradesh, Karnataka, Tamil Nadu and Kerala) recorded a growth of as low as 2.0 per cent. The Eastern Region (Eastern UP, Bihar, West Bengal, Orissa and Assam) is almost a non-growth region with the rate at 0.8 per cent. The Public Distribution System helps in bridging this gap prevailing in various regions of the country. Thus, it maintains a balance between supply and demand as well as provides the non-inflationary way to development.

The PDS helps in reducing the food insecurity of the poor which is caused by the very low incomes of the poor, particularly those who are destitutes with very little employment. The PDS which ensures the supply of foodgrains at cheap rates, provides a means of security to the poor when the PDS is made an integral part of some of the employment schemes of the poor, it becomes all the more important as payment of the workers in some of such schemes are made partly or wholly in foodgrains, thus protect their consumption level. Thus, the PDS is one of the important tools to combat prevailing poverty and food insecurity in the country.

The PDS is of great help in providing security to the weaker sections of society who are vulnerable to the structural changes in the economy initiated in the 1990s. The changes which promote an open and market-oriented economy may cause harm to the poor because a number of traditional occupations have been left open to the market forces. Undoubtedly, the economic reforms will create new opportunities, but the poor who are not well-trained or educated may not be able to take the advantage of the new policies of the Government. The opening up of the economy under the new policy may cause a rise in the domestic prices of the essential goods, thus will make the situation for them all the more difficult. Thus, the PDS is of immense help in protecting the poor from the adverse consequences of the reform policies.

Coverage of PDS

The Public Distribution System (PDS) ensures the distribution of essential items such as selected cereals, sugar, edible oils and kerosene at subsidized prices to holders of ration cards. It ensures the availability of essential commodities through its wide network. Through the PDS Government regulates supply and distribution of essential commodities with a view to secure their equitable distribution and availability at fair prices. People living under Integrated Tribal Development Project (ITDP) are supplied foodgrains (wheat and rice) at special low prices. Rice, wheat, sugar and kerosene account for 86 per cent of the total PDS sales, sugar alone accounts for 35 per cent followed by rice 27 per cent, wheat 10 per cent and kerosene 15 per cent. Coarse cereals like jowar, bajra and others, which are largely consumed by the poor, account for less than one per cent of total PDS sales. The share of pulses which is the major source of protein for the poor is even lowest which is less than 0.2 per cent.

An overview of the commodity-wise composition of market dependent population reveals that in rural areas 44 per cent of the population is dependent on PDS for kerosene, 36 per cent for sugar, 26 per cent for wheat and 14 per cent for rice. Obviously, it implies that this relates to the poor who would like to purchase subsidised sugar and kerosene. Since the poor are directly or indirectly involved with agricultural activities, they get their part in kind (since most of them are landless labourers), hence their dependence on wheat and rice is relatively low. But when wholly or partially market dependent population together is taken into account, then the PDS purchasers constitute 68 per cent in case of sugar, 51 per cent for kerosene, 40 per cent for rice and 31 per cent for wheat in rural areas. This shows that the non-poor also take advantage of PDS commodities particularly in sugar and kerosene.

The situation is not very different in urban areas where wholly or partially dependents on PDS was 76 per cent in case of sugar, 64 per cent for kerosene, 39 per cent for rice and about 37 per cent in wheat. It may be noted that about 27 per cent of market dependents were either wholly or partially dependent on PDS for edible oils and for pulses this percentage was 23. If it is conceded that sugar and edible oils are not consumed by the poor, then it becomes clear that bulk of the PDS purchases of these commodities go to benefit the non-poor.

The Central Government is the pivot of the PDS. It procures and allocates or supplies the commodities to the states and the union territories, who are responsible for the allocation and distribution of foodgrains in their territories. Out of more than four and a half lakh Fair Price Shops in the country more than third-fourth are in rural areas and one-fourth in urban areas. On an average one Fair Price Shop is required to cover a population of 2000. The access to the system is universal that is both the poor and the non-poor can draw rations from these shops. The rationing system is in fact an informal one. One can also buy from the free market any required quantity of the goods supplied from Fair Price Shop. The total of foodgrains supplied through PDS constitute 9 to 10 per cent of the total production in the country. The food subsidy for the year 2005-06 is Rs. 26200 crore.

PDS and the Poor

One of the important questions which needs to be probed is whether PDS has been successful in achieving its objectives. The history of PDS of the country reveals that its performance varies state to state. Equally, the PDS is grossly uneven in respect of its distribution of foodgrains across classes and regions. The socially and economically backward states of Bihar, Uttar Pradesh, Madhya Pradesh, Rajasthan and Orissa account for as much as 52 per cent of the population as well as the large proportion of the country's poor population, but these states receive only 20 per cent of central allocations of foodgrains. Thus, there is no relation between the incidence of poverty in a state and the scale of PDS supplies. Again, the PDS has evolved in a way that the regional variations in it have nothing to do with the foodgrains deficits of the states or with the requirements of states. A study conducted by E.K. Rao reveals that "in general states with larger urban population get larger PDS supplies". When the PDS was restricted to the urban and food deficit areas, the PDS did serve the deficit areas, but with the extension of the coverage to the entire country, this aspect was lost in priority.

This is evident from the studies conducted by Radhakrishna et. al. on the basis of 42nd NSS round which reveals mistargeting in the distribution of foodgrains. In Kerala and Andhra Pradesh, PDS purchases were relatively high in all expenditure groups. The PDS purchases constituted 40-58 per cent of cereal consumption. Although the very dependency of the very poor on PDS was as high as 58 per cent but the beneficiary in the non-poor group constituted 40 per cent of the population in 1986-87 as a result of the generalisation of the scheme. The poor purchased 4.3 kg per month while the non-poor purchased 4.5 kg. Almost similar pattern could be observed in the urban areas. The same year monthly per capita purchases by the very poor and the non-poor in Andhra Pradesh were 2.3 to 2.5 kg and 2.2 to 2.6 kg in rural areas and urban areas respectively. In case of poor it constituted 22 per cent of the total cereal consumption of the poor in rural areas which was 17 per cent in the non-poor population. In urban areas, the PDS cereal purchases for the poor was 25 per cent against that of the 19 per cent of the non-poor in urban areas during the same period.

But the all India coverage of PDS was very low. In rural areas the monthly per capita purchase was 0.9 kg and 1.3 kg in urban areas. The low PDS cereal purchase in all India can be attributed to the extremely low cereal purchase from PDS in prosperous states like Punjab and Haryana as well as states having high poor population such as Bihar, Orissa, Madhya Pradesh and Uttar Pradesh. Thus, it is clear that monthly purchase from PDS was the lowest for the very poor uniformly across all the states.

Despite big claims of surplus food, the food availability condition in the country has not improved. The food availability in India claimed to be sufficient, but the news of death from starvation proves that we are still far from fulfilling our commitment of 'food for all'. Production surplus does not necessarily indicate equitable availability of foodgrains, as a large number of people here have not too money to buy food. According to FAO (Food and Agriculture Organisation) over 225 million Indians are chronically undernourished. Alarmingly with the beginning of reforms processes in India, in the 1990s, it increased by 5 per cent. As a whole, there is a steady decline in per capita food availability in the country and surprisingly the rural population is the worst affected despite being the producer of foodgrains. In the year 1999-2000, out of total 0.26 billion living below the poverty line, about 74.25 people live in rural areas while in urban areas the percentage is just 25.75. Even the per capita food consumption is lower in India. It is 150 kg/annum which is far less than that of an American where it is 850 kg/annum, in case of Russia, it is 1,000 kg/annum.

Thus, it is evident that per capita foodgrains consumption is high in the countries with higher per capita income. This is also reflected in the country itself. Similarly per capita food consumption varies state to state. Affluent states like Punjab and Haryana have high per capita per day food consumption. The National Sample Survey (NSS) data reveals that per capita consumption of foograins is declining over time for all income groups. Situation is equally dismal in case of per capita calories intake which experienced a drastic decline of 13 per cent for rural India as against 1.5 per cent in urban India.

Regional Difference in the Off-take of PDS Foodgrains

The off-take of PDS foodgrains varies state to state. In some state it is even lower than the central allocation. In fact, it is the consequence of the upward revision of issue price which has caused narrowing down of the gap between subsidised issue price and open market price. To some extent it is attributed to the State Government's persistence to implement subsidised PDS which is evident in case of Kerala and Andhra Pradesh where the governments are very enthusiastic regarding the implementation of subsidised foodgrains. According to World Bank Report, the off-take in poorer states like Bihar, Orissa and Madhya Pradesh was substantially lower than central allocations, partly due to the narrow difference between the central issue price and open market price and partly because of weak fiscal capacity of the state in financing any additional subsidy in form of lowering of issue prices. Besides, theses states have not yet built up effective institutional mechanisms to lift the quotas from FCI depots to fair price shops. Ironically, the incidence of poverty is high precisely in the states with the lowest off-take of FCI grains.

The studies conducted by Radhakrishna et al. states, "The per capita off-take was low in food surplus states with low incidence of poverty such as Punjab, Haryana, as well as in poorer state, with low fiscal capacity such as Bihar, Orissa, Madhya Pradesh and Uttar Pradesh. The off-take was high in food deficit but relatively richer states such as Gujarat and Maharashtra.

The higher per capita off-take of foodgrains reflects the social commitment of the states which is evident in case of Kerala and Andhra Pradesh. While the most poor states of India, namely Bihar, Orissa and Madhya Pradesh have weak commitment to the programme. The commitment to PDS is equally low in case of affluent states like Punjab and Haryana.

Foodgrains Allocation and Off-take under Public Distribution System

Table 8.6: Foodgrains Allocation and Off-take under Public Distribution System

(Million tonnes)

	Wheat		Rice	
Year	Allocation	Offtake	Allocation	Offtake
1991-92	10.36	8.83	11.36	10.17
1992-93	9.25	7.85	11.48	9.69
1993-94	9.56	5.91	12.41	8.87
1994-95	10.80	4.83	13.32	8.03
1995-96	11.31	5.29	14.62	9.46
1996-97	10.72	8.52	15.16	11.14
1997-98	10.11	7.08	12.83	9.90
1998-99	10.11	7.95	12.93	10.74
1999-2000*	7.81	2.66	10.33	5.49
2000-01	11.5	4.0	16.3	7.9
2001-02	13.1	5.6	17.2	8.1
2002-03	29.4	6.1	27.3	7.3

* Allocation up to December 1999, Off-take up to September, 1999.

The Table 8.6 reveals that there is variation in the off-take and allocation of foodgrains meant for PDS by the states ranging from 53 per cent to 87 per cent. Sharp fluctuations in PDS off-take is attributed to low margin between open market price and issue price or low releases of PDS supplies by the Government to dealers, low commitment to PDS programme, which was evident in case of some of fiscally weak states, namely Bihar, Madhya Pradesh, Orissa and Uttar Pradesh. But it was equally lacking on the part of richer states like Punjab and Haryana.

Subsidies to the foodgrains are provided by the government by using APL (Above Poverty Line) and BPL (Below Poverty Line) as cut-off marks. As per 1993-94 poverty lines, expenditure per head of Rs. 205-84 in rural areas and Rs. 281.35 for urban areas was used to determine the population below the poverty line. For 1998-99 this works out in the range of Rs. 300 per head in rural areas and Rs. 400 per head in urban areas. Taking into account an average family of 5 members means that families earning approximately Rs. 1,500 per month in the rural areas and Rs. 2,000 in the urban areas come under the category of BPL. On this criterion, even the class IV employees in the public as well as the private sector are not eligible for the benefit of the PDS foodgrains. It is really difficult for the Government to identify the population below poverty line because only 9 per cent of the total labour force works in the organised sector while in unorganised sector it constitutes 91 per cent. Thus, to restrict the benefit of the PDS to the population below the poverty line is almost impossible. The Government maintains a huge stock of foodgrains to meet the requirements of the poor.

Targeted Public Distribution System (TPDS)

The resolve of the government to reform and improve the PDS by focusing the poor and needy sections of the society resulted in the launching of the Targeted Public Distribution System in June 1997. The revised system follows a two-tier subsidised pricing structure—families Below Poverty Line (BPL) and those Above Poverty Line (APL)—the former represent the poorest of the poor. The objective was to identify the persons/ families living below the poverty line and issue a distinct ration card for selling specified cereal items through PDS outlets at specially subsidized rates, i.e. half the normal price under PDS. It was intended to benefit about six crore poor families in the country for whom a quantum of 72 lakh tonnes of foodgrains was earmarked annually at the rate of 25 kg per family per month. In fact it was started to make PDS more responsive to the needs of the poor. The Targeted Public Distribution System has a dual price system—heavily subsidised rates for families below the poverty line (BPL) and somewhat less subsidised rates for families above the poverty line (APL).

A quantity of 103 lakh tonnes of foodgrains per annum is earmarked for the population above poverty line (APL) for distribution under PDS at a price which as per Government policy should be close to 90 per cent of the economic cost.

The Centre guarantees the supply of foodgrains to the states for the BPL families. In case of additional demand from the states, it depends on the availability of stocks in the Central Pool and are made available at a price which is almost very close to FCI's economic cost. The Central Issue Price (CIP) for BPL families is Rs. 4.15 per kg for wheat and Rs. 5.65 per kg for rice, which is about 45 per cent of the economic cost of the Food Corporation of India (FCI). During 2004-05, 346.23 lakh tonnes of rice and 374.33 lakh tonnes of wheat have been allotted under TPDS. A quantity of 163.95 lakh tonnes of rice and 130.28 lakh tonnes of wheat were lifted against this allocation.

Under this scheme, the Antyodaya Anna Yojana was launched for the poorest of the poor on December 25, 2000. The Scheme provides 25 kg of foodgrains to the poorest of the poor families at a highly subsidised rates of Rs. 2 per kg for wheat and Rs. three per kg for rice. This quantity has been enhanced from 25 kg to 35 kg from April 1, 2002. About one crore families are getting benefited from this scheme. In June 2003, the scheme was expanded to cover an additional 50 lakh BPL families from among the poorest of the poor families. Again, in August 2004 the Government expanded the scheme to cover another 50 lakh BPL families by including, *inter alia*, all household at the risks of hunger. An announcement has been made in the Union Budget 2005-06 to expand the scheme to cover another 50 lakh BPL households, thus increasing its coverage to 2.5 lakh household. In this expansion, the main thrust will be on the BPL households in the poorest and backward blocks and/or where nutritional deficiency is more widespread.

According to the current Buffer Stocking Policy of foodgrains, the total minimum stock in the central pool held by public agencies was 20 million tonnes as on January 1, 2006. The minimum buffer stock required in India is now fixed around 16 to 17 million tonnes of foodgrains. The off-take of foodgrains (wheat and rice) from the central pool by various States/UTs and others for distribution through fair prices shops and for various welfare and employment programmes in 2004-05 was 400.33 lakh tonnes as against 376.93 lakh tonnes during

2003-04. The total off-take of foodgrains under Targeted Public Distribution System during April 2004 to March 2005 is above 294.24 lakh tonnes.

Suggested Measures

The public distribution system should be efficient enough to achieve its objective of ensuring an equitable distribution of essential goods at the cost which could be affordable to the poorest section of society. Its primary aim should be to provide a security net for the poor only, excluding the non-poor from the system. This feature needs to be built into the system itself so that it ceases to be pro-rich or urban biased. The items meant to be distributed through the PDS should also be increased to cover all the essential goods required for the physical well-being. In addition, it should expand its coverage so as to include all the poor in all the regions.

Besides, the public distribution system needs to be well-integrated and well-coordinated. A proper coordination is required in the process of production, procurement, transportation, storage and distribution of selected items, which needs an infrastructural changes as well as the strengthening of the infrastructure in the backward, remote and inaccessible areas. The working of the system also needs to be improved so as to make it more cost-effective. For instance, the timely procurement, transportation and storage of foodgrains will reduce the need of buffer stock. Thus, the carrying cost of the goods to be distributed through the system would also reduced. The leakages in the movement of foodgrains need to be plugged. Proper checking of the fair price shops, godowns, etc. would also be of great help in this regard. But the greatest success of the system lies in it that it enables the poor to buy a consumption basket, nutritionally so sufficient that it ensures the well-being of the poor. The prices of these items are required to be fixed so as to ensures its easy availability to them. To help the effective transfer of income to the poor, the gap between the issue prices of essential commodities and their market prices should be sufficient to attract the poor to buy the PDS commodities. In addition, the PDS should be implemented through various employment generation schemes because it ensures the double benefit to the poor. Firstly, the possibility of the inclusion of the non-poor is minimised because they generally don't undertake employment under such schemes, namely, Jawahar Rozgar Yojana (JRY) or Employment Assurance Scheme (EAS) or other such schemes. Secondly, it helps in enhancing the purchasing power of the poor. Thus the PDS which evolves would be a powerful policy instrument, efficient enough to provide a much-needed food security net to the poor in the country. To sum up, the strategies which reduce poverty need to be emphasised to ensure enduring food security to the poor.

Industry

9

Industrialisation has a predominant role in the economic development of a nation, more particularly the underdeveloped countries like India. To quote Pt. Jawaharlal Nehru, "It is only when India has acquired the ability to design, fabricate and erect its own plants without foreign assistance that it will have become a truly advanced and industrialised country." In fact, material riches and industry go together. This is amply demonstrated in the gap in per capita incomes between the developed and developing countries. While the former is largely industrial economies, the latter is confined to mainly agriculture. No doubt, countries like Saudi Arabia, Kuwait and UAR have achieved considerably higher per capita income owing to their natural resource—petroleum. These countries enjoy monopoly in the export of petroleum and hence have achieved higher per capita income. But these countries are a rather exceptional case. In general, industrial development alone can provide a secure basis for a rapid growth of income. The scope for internal as well as external economies is much greater in industrial sector than in other sector including agriculture. With the proceed in industrialization, the economies of scale and inter-industrial linkage become more assertive. As against agriculture where man's efforts and hard work is restricted by the limitations of Nature, in the industrial sector man can by putting in additional effort and employing advance technologies push on the total production. This provides for a relatively high marginal propensity to save and invest and thus a self-sustaining economy can be eventually achieved. In other words, industrialisation is the basis for substantial, sustained economic development as it is both a consequence of higher incomes and a means of higher productivity. The close correlation between the high level of income and industrial development is evident if we have a look at the per capita income of the developed countries. While the per capita income of USA is $ 34,260, Belgium—$ 24,630, UK—$ 24,500 and Japan—$ 34,210, the per capita income of developing countries like China and India is $ 840 and $ 460 respectively (World Development Report, 2002). Besides, industrialization enables for employing excess labour power and catering for the diversification of the market required at higher stages of economic development.

India started her quest for industrial development after independence in 1947. The Industrial Policy Resolution of 1948 marked the beginning of the evolution of the Indian Industrial Policy. The vast manpower, large and varied resources, and continental dimensions are strong cases for industrialisation of India. With the introduction of the New Industrial Policy (NIP) in 1991, the Indian Government aimed at providing the competitive stimulus to the industrial sector for higher growth. The thrust of the Industrial Policy initiatives has been to increase the domestic and external competition through extensive application of market mechanisms and facilitating forging of dynamic relationships with foreign investors and suppliers of technology. On the eve of independence, the industrial pattern of India was marked by high concentration of employment in small factories and household enterprises. While the medium sized factories did not exist then, the foreign firms and those owned by big businessmen were quite prominent. A structural imbalance was the another feature of the prevailing industrial pattern. In case of consumer goods, domestic supply was more than the demand while in case of producer goods the domestic supplies in relation to demand fall short, thereby adding to our dependence on other countries. Besides, the general low level of wages and the small size of the home market in view of the low per capita income and less use of production techniques resulting in low capital intensity mark the industrial pattern in India on the eve of planning.

Economic Development since Independence

India has made tremendous progress in the industrial sector since independence. During 1951-65 it had a steady growth rate of about 8 per cent. Although little was provided in the First Plan (1951-56) for industries, there was much by way of industrial development in the Second Plan and the Third Plan during 1956-61 and 1961-66, respectively. In addition to setting up several industries, the government took initiatives to provide resources and facilities for the private sector so as to enable them to start industries on their own or jointly with the government in the arena earmarked for the private sector. The other important factors that led to industrial development during this period were: firstly the existing entrepreneurial class invested considerably in establishing new set-ups as they realized better opportunities in the post-independence circumstances; secondly, restrictions on import, imposed by the government, helped remove the fear of foreign competition among the private entrepreneurs; thirdly, Indian industrial policy permitting, although conditionally, the entry of private foreign capital further helped in receiving foreign aid as loans on concessional terms. Such large funds in the form of foreign exchange enabled the country not only to face to an extent the balance of payments constraints on development but also helped in purchasing equipments, machines and other inputs.

The period between 1965-76 however witnessed a slow growth in the industrial sector. In the sixties (1960-70) the average growth rate of industrial output was put at 5.5 per cent and in the seventies (1971-80) the average growth rate was about 4 per cent per annum. Thereafter, during 1980-85 the growth rate of industrial production was 5.5 per cent per annum. The above data reveal that the industrial sector showed a declining trend. Later, during the Seventh Plan (1985-90), the growth rate however picked up to an average of over 8 per cent per annum while in the Eighth Plan (1992-97) it again declined to 7.3 per cent per annum. In order to increase industrial production, the industrial policy was made more liberal and globalised and privatization was increased. The main objectives of the New Industrial Policy, 1991 were to increase industrial production, to improve disequilibrium in balance of payments, to get rid of the sick units of public or private sectors and to control inflation by increasing production and regulating money supply, to establish small, medium and large industries, to abolish licensing system for all industries except 18, to permit the use of foreign technology, to modify MRTP and FERA so that entrance asset limit could be abolished. The main focus of the New Industrial Policy, 1991 was to free the Indian industries from unnecessary and disadvantageous restrictions, to free growing entrepreneurial capacity, to provide proper control for market mechanism in resource allocation, to get rid of costlier delays and inefficiency and uneconomical expenses, to develop industrial structure based on technological dynamism and international competition so that India could emerge as a main industrial power by the end of 20th century.

On account of industrial policy, structural changes in industrial production have taken place which is shown in Table 8.1.

Table 9.1: Index No. of the Structure of Industrial Production

(Base 1960=100)

Industry	1961	1965	1970	1975	1981-82	1987-88	1990-91	1991-92
1. Basic Industries	112.7	164.0	221.7	285.9	431.7	670.4	776.3	805.8 (614.9)
2. Capital Goods Industries	118.0	244.0	224.6	292.2	470.6	850.4	1112.9	1306.5 (1000.2)
3. Intermediate Goods Industries	105.8	140.2	158.8	180.5	235.5	336.8	391.7	415.4 (292.6)
4. Consumer Goods Industries	106.6	127.5	154.7	166.1	236.6	325.6	360.7	398.1 (273.4)

Source: Report on Currency and Finance, Vol. II, Various Issues.

Note:
(i) Figures in brackets are calculated and show percentage figures.
(ii) Figures relating to 1975 onwards are converted with base 1960 = 100.
(iii) Figures upto 1975 are relating to Calendar year and figures after 1975 are relating to financial year. Hence, they are not comparable completely and do not show exact position.

Table 9.1 indicates that in 1961 consumer goods production index was 106.6, while that of intermediate goods was 105.8 which was lower than that of the former, but in 1991-92 this situation changed. Consumer goods production index became lower than that of intermediate goods, *i.e.* consumer goods production index in 1991-92 became 398.1, while that of intermediate goods was 415.4. Highest increase took place in the production of the capital goods. In this case, in 1991-92 as compared to 1961 production increased by 1007.2%. Second place was occupied by the increase in the production of basic goods industries. In 1991-92 its production increased by 614.9 per cent over 1961. During these periods the production of intermediate goods and consumer goods increased by 292.6 per cent and 273.4 per cent, respectively. Thus, it is obvious that due to industrial policy the production of commodities has diversified and quantitative change have taken place. In addition, in industrial policy resolutions the development of basic industries and capital goods industries has always been given priority. Consequently, production has increased favourably in the same direction.

On account of industrialization of economy, trade commodity composition has also changed. In India's imports, share of capital goods has increased. In 1960-61 the import of capital goods amounted to Rs. 356 crore which increased to Rs. 404 crore in 1970-71. Rs. 1,910 crore in 1980-81, Rs. 10,466 crore in 1990-91, Rs. 10,436 crore in 1991-92 and Rs. 13, 123 crore in 1992-93. In India's exports, share of manufactured goods has increased continuously. It was Rs. 291 crore in 1960-61 which increased to Rs. 772 crore in 1970-71, Rs. 3,747 crore in 1980-81, Rs. 23,736 crore in 1990-91, Rs. 32,693 crore in 1991-92 and Rs. 40,835 crore in 1992-93.

Present Scenario

India has attained self-sufficiency in almost all consumer goods. Growth of capital goods production has also been remarkable. A significant industrial capacity has been achieved in mining and metallurgical industries, chemical and petrochemical industries, fertiliser production, capital goods industries including sophisticated equipment for steel mills, fertilizer and chemical plants etc., heavy, medium and light engineering industries, construction industry, power and transportation industry, to name a few. India today is definitely in a position to sustain the future growth of vital sectors of the economy primarily through domestic effort and only with marginal imports. In addition, India has to its credit an impressive record of progress in R & D capability, consultancy and design engineering services, information technology, project management services and innovative capacity to improve and adapt technologies. The Table 9.2 below clearly indicates the growth rate of industrial sector as measured in terms of Index of Industrial Production since 1995-96 to the current year.

Table 9.2: Annual growth rate of industrial production in major sectors of industry (Based on the index of industrial production)
Base: 1993-94=100

(per cent)

Period	Mining & Quarrying	Manufac-turing	Electricity	Overall
Weights	10.47	79.36	10.17	100.00
1995-96	9.7	14.1	8.1	13.0
1996-97	-1.9	7.3	4.0	6.1
1997-98	6.9	6.7	6.6	6.7
1998-99	-0.8	4.4	6.5	4.1
1999-00	1.0	7.1	7.3	6.7
2000-01	2.8	5.3	4.0	5.0
2001-02	1.2	2.9	3.1	2.7
2002-03	5.8	6.0	3.2	5.7
2003-04	5.2	7.4	5.1	7.0
2004-05	4.4	9.2	5.2	8.4
2005-06	1.0	9.1	5.2	8.2
2006-07#	3.8	11.5	7.3	10.6

(April-December)
Source: Central Statistical Organisation.

The target growth of industry during the Tenth Plan (2002-07) was put at 10 per cent consistent with an overall GDP growth of 8 per cent. Notwithstanding a distinct improvement in the manufacturing growth in the last two years, *i.e.* 2004-05 to 2005-06, overall industrial growth so far has remained well short of the target. However, with respect to use based classification of industries, the growth rate in the capital goods sector in April-December 2005 at 15.7 per cent indicate a substantial improvement over the growth of 13.8 per cent during the same period previous year (Table 9.3). Both the durable as well as non-degradable consumer goods also recorded improved performance during the two years, i.e. 2003-05, of the Tenth Plan. Further, growth rate of basic goods remained at 6.0 per cent, showing no change from the corresponding period in the previous year. Intermediate goods, however, witnessed a significant deceleration in growth.

Table 9.3: Growth Rates of Industrial Production by Use-based Classification (Base: 1993-94=100)

(per cent)

Sector	Weight	1998-00	2000-01	2001-02	2002-03	2003-04	2004-05	2005-06	Apr.-Dec.	
									2005-06	2006-07
Basic goods	35.5	5.5	3.7	2.6	4.9	5.4	5.5	6..7	6.1	9.3
Capital goods	9.3	6.9	1.8	-3.4	10.5	13.6	13.9	15.8	16.2	16.1
Intermediate goods	26.5	8.8	4.7	1.5	3.9	6.4	6.1	2.5	2.5	10.9
Consumer goods of which	28.7	5.7	8.0	6.0	7.1	7.1	11.7	12.0	13.3	9.7
Durables	5.4	14.1	14.5	11.5	-6.3	11.6	14.3	15.3	14.2	12.5
Non-durables	23.3	3.2	5.8	4.1	12.0	5.8	10.8	11.0	12.9	8.7
IIP (Index of Industrial Production)	100	6.7	5.0	2.7	5.7	7.0	8.4	8.2	8.3	10.6

Source: Central Statistical Organisation.

Capacity addition and improved productivity are the two sources of industrial growth. From 1993-94 to 2003-04, net capital stock in industries (comprising mining, manufacturing and electricity sectors), which can proxy capacity addition, increased at an average rate of 6.66 per cent per annum. The dominance of the public sector in mining and electricity continued to persist even after industrial liberalization and opening of these sectors to private sector participation. Lower addition to capital stock deprived these sectors of the buoyancy associated with capacity expansion. Table 9.4 shows the net capital stock in industry and the share of public sector.

Table 9.4: Net Capital Stock in Industry and the Share of Public Sector

	1994	2000	2001	2002	2003	2004	CAGR
	in Rupees crore at 1993-94 Prices						in per cent
Mining	75,199	84,061	81,433	80,662	79,351	82,604	0.94
Manufacturing	504,658	956,510	1,001,381	1,031,305	1,070,999	1,123,391	8.33
Electricity, Gas & Water Supply	215,585	277,539	286,758	297,942	303,762	310,832	3.73
Share of the Public Sector (per cent)							
Mining	94.3	93.57	93.13	92.38	92.31	92.77	–0.6
Manufacturing	24.1	14.65	13.73	13.01	12.67	11.72	–6.95
Electricity, Gas & Water Supply	92.8	88.49	87.65	86.28	85.81	85.58	–0.81

PUBLIC AND PRIVATE SECTORS: ITS ROLE

INDUSTRY-WISE CONTRIBUTION

Public Sector

Since independence there has been a progressive expansion in the scope of the public sector owing to the adequate economic planning in India. The passage of Industrial Policy Resolution of 1956 and the adoption of socialist pattern of society as our national goal further added to the deliberate enlargement of the role of public sector.

The significant role of the Public Sector in the Indian economy cannot be overemphasised. In order to assess its role it would be desirable to use a few indicators, like employment, investment, value of output, national income generated, savings, capital formation and capital stock. The share of public sector in these indicators have been discussed individually in the following paragraphs.

Share of Public Sector in Employment

There are two important categories of public sector employment; firstly, government administration, defence and other services like health, education, research etc. and secondly, the economic enterprises owned by the Centre, State and Local Governments. There has been tremendous growth in providing direct employment by the public sector since independence. The total number of workers employed in the public sector in 1971 was 111 lakhs, but by March 2004 it increased to 1.77 million. In the recent years the biggest chunk of employment was in transport, storage and communications while manufacturing remained close to these sectors. Those employed in agriculture and other allied activities reflect employment under Employment Guarantee Scheme rather than any usual productive activity. Overall, the public sector accounts for 69 per cent of the total employment in the organised sector.

Share of Public Sector in Gross Domestic Product

There has been a steady advancement in the share in the public sector in net domestic product in the recent years, more particularly during the ongoing Tenth Plan period. Measured at current prices, public sector accounted for 7.5 per cent of NDP in 1950-51, which later in 1999-2000 raised to 24.0 per cent. In 2002-03 it declined to 23.6 per cent but again during 2004-05 it accounted for about one-fourth of national output.

Share of Public Sector in Saving and Capital Formation

Gross domestic capital formation was 2.8 per cent of GDP during 1950-51 at 1993-94 base year. This share has increased to 7.2 per cent with 1999-2000 as its base year in 2004-05. The Table 9.5 shows the share of public sector Plan-wise.

Table 9.5: Share of Public Sector in Gross Domestic Capital Formation

Plan	Period/year	As percentage of GDP at Market Prices (Base year 1993-94)
First Plan	1951-56	3.5
Second Plan	1956-61	6.6
Third Plan	1961-66	8.4
Fourth Plan	1969-74	7.2
Fifth Plan	1974-79	9.5
Sixth Plan	1980-85	11.1
Seventh Plan	1985-90	10.7
Eighth Plan	1992-97	9.2
Ninth Plan	1997-2002	6.8
Tenth Plan*	2002-03	6.2
—	2003-04	6.5
—	2004-05 (Q)	7.2

Q: Quick estimates; * Base year – 1999-2000

On the contrary to capital formation, the share of savings by the Public Sector has not undergone a similar change. The share of the public sector in gross domestic savings rose from 1.7 per cent of GNP during 1951-56 to merely 4.6 per cent during the Fifth Plan and thereafter during the Eighth Plan declined to more 1.4 per cent. Furthermore, it even became negative during 1999-2000 and 2002-03. However, it improved marginally during 2003-04 and 2004-05. The Table 9.6 gives the data of share of public sector in Gross Domestic Saving.

Table 9.6: Share of Public Sector in Gross Domestic Saving

Plan	Period/year	As percentage of GDP in market prices
First	1951-56	1.7
Second	1956-61	2.0
Third	1961-66	3.4
Fourth	1969-74	3.0
Fifth	1974-79	4.6
Sixth	1980-85	3.6
Seventh	1985-90	2.3
Eighth	1992-97	1.4
Ninth	1997-2002	-2.0
Tenth*	2002-03	-0.7
	2003-04	1.0
	2004-05 (Q)	2.2

Q = Quick estimates * Base year 1999-2000

Share of Public Sector in Gross Fixed Capital Formation

Gross capital formation refers to annual flow of goods partly to meet the needs of depreciation of the capital stock and partly to increase the size of the total capital stock on a net basis. The amount of capital employed per unit of output in the public sector is far greater than in the private sector. It has made a significant contribution in improving gross fixed capital formation (GFCF), more particularly in the capital goods sector. During 2000-01 the growth rate of GFCF in the public sector was 1.3 per cent at 1999-2000 prices increasing to 3.9, 2.2, 13.7 and 8.6 respectively in the following four years consecutively.

Contribution of Public Sector to Export

The export performance of the public sector enterprises has been quite appreciating. Among the items exported from India, metal ores ranks the second position. Even in the export of Indian handicrafts, light engineering goods etc., the public sector has made huge strides. The foreign exchange earnings of the public sector have been rising from Rs. 35 crore in 1965-66 to Rs. 5,830 crore in 1984-85 and finally to Rs. 34,893 crore in 2003-04.

Contribution of Public Sector to Exchequer

Public Sector has been making substantial contribution to the government exchequer in the form of corporate taxes, excise duty, customs duty and the like. While its contribution during the Sixth Plan was Rs. 27,570 crore, in 2003-04 it was Rs. 1,70,891 crore.

The public sector has undoubtedly entered into a wide spectrum of industries and products and its operations extending from basic and capital goods like steel, coal, copper, zinc and other minerals, heavy machinery, etc. to consumer goods like textiles, hotel services, Matches etc. In areas like minerals, coal, petroleum products, hydro and steam turbines its share is 100 per cent while in other products it ranges between 50 to 95 per cent. It significantly mobilize funds to cater the financial needs of the growing economy.

Shortcomings in Public Sector

There is no denying the fact that the public sector has made a tremendous progress but there is yet much scope for improvement in the efficiency and working of this sector. A review of the working of public sector enterprises indicates that the profits in them have been considerably low or they have been making losses. State Electricity Boards and the State Road Transport may be cited in this context. The losses incurred by SEBs in 2003-04 was Rs. 20,380 crore. However, overall this sector shows improvement. It is to be noted here that in the total profit contributed by this sector, the major share has been of petroleum enterprises, that too earned through the rise in oil prices.

It has been noticed that in many cases the public sector projects have not been completed within the stipulated time and estimated expenditure. For instance, Trombay Fertiliser Project took nearly seven years to complete and involved Rs. 40 crore against the estimated 3 years of time and allotted Rs. 27 crore. Thus, in this direction efforts need to be made to avoid delays and increases in costs.

In many of the public enterprises, pricing policies are not rational. Either the prices are very high which adversely affects the overall growth of the economy while in other cases the prices are kept deliberately low even when costs and prices are rising. It is to be realised that profit should be recognised as an index of efficiency on the one hand and that the profit motive is consistent with the broad objective of the socialist pattern of society on the other.

It has also been observed that the labour indiscipline has adversely influenced the performance of public sector enterprises recently. Besides, in many enterprises there has been surplus manpower and inadequate arrangement for training and education of workers as well as poor management-labour relation. More importantly, the unsatisfactory remuneration and incentives has compelled the efficient staff to switch over to private sector. The situation is grim and needs to be handled cautiously.

The public sector enterprises lack in optimum capacity utilisation. As per the latest available data, 87 manufacturing units utilised 75 per cent of its total capacity, 32 units utilised 50 to 75 per cent and 47 functioned below 50 per cent utilisation capacity. Thus, adequate measures must be taken to remove this deficiency.

The performance of public sector is also affected by faulty controls exercised over them. The Ministry of Finance exercises excessive financial control over the operations of public enterprises in India which are obligatory to submit to all the budgetary controls applicable to Government departments. The control over the operations and capital development plans of public enterprises by the Parliament often become rigid, thereby hampering the performance of the public sector. There is thus need to provide greater autonomy to this sector. Close to this aspect is yet another cause that affects the workings of the public sector. This is inefficient management. It is a common experience that the public enterprises are generally governed by bureaucrats who are not genuinely qualified to run industrial enterprises and they often fail to take operational decisions promptly which is one of the crucial factors in improving the overall performance of public sector.

To conclude, the expansion of the public sector was done with the objectives of removal of poverty, attainment of self-reliance, reduction in inequalities of income, expansion of employment opportunities, removal of regional imbalances, acceleration of the pace of agricultural and industrial development, reduction in concentration of ownership and prevention of growth of monopolistic tendencies by being an effective countervailing power to the private sector and making the country self-reliant in modern technology as well as finance. No doubt, the public sector has fulfilled its objectives to some extent but it is equally true that all the public enterprises are not functioning up to the mark. Factors affecting its performance need to be removed.

Private Sector

The private sector has been given sufficient scope to produce intermediate goods and machines since independence. Consequently, a wide range of industries producing chemicals, paints, plastics, machine-tools, ferrous and non-ferrous metals, rubber etc. have come up resulting in self-sufficiency in many consumer goods. The private sector plays a significant role in all important fields, namely agriculture, trade and industry.

Agriculture is the mainstay of the Indian economy, which includes agriculture proper and allied activities such as poultry, animal husbandry, fisheries, dairying etc. In agricultural sector the main dominance is that of private sector as agriculture and its allied activities are exclusively managed by the private enterprises, accounting for 25 per cent of the Gross National Product and 60 per cent employment. However, the private sector in agriculture does not enjoy that concentration and monopoly as in the corporate sector owing to the fact that agriculture is not run on commercial basis rather it is confined to the hands of small and marginal farmers.

The private sector is much more dominant in trading— both retail and wholesale. In the Industrial Policy Resolutions of 1948 and 1956, the Government allotted a specific role to the private sector in the field of industries which enabled the private sector to become more preponderant than public sector. While the public sector was assigned a major role in the planned development of the country with industrial growth in the lead, the private sector too was assigned a definite place in the mixed economy that became the basis of its functioning. An aspect of the growth of the private sector is the large increase in the presence of the foreign private companies with a sizeable segment of industries under their ownership and control. The entry of foreign companies or firms has taken rapid strides. It is either in the form of multinational companies or the Indian subsidiaries of foreign companies. Yet another form is that of collaborations between Indians and the foreigners. Advanced countries like the USA, the UK, Germany, Japan, Italy, etc. have come here and invested huge amount in varied areas like engineering, electronics, chemicals, computers, pharmaceuticals etc. The amount of foreign direct investment has indeed been large, more particularly in the recent years. India has become one of the favourite spots for foreign investors, which is well evident by the latest data available. After exhibiting a downward trend for two years since 2001-02, FDI (net) flows grew by 36 per cent in 2004-05. The increased flows were mainly to the electrical equipment including computer software and electronics and services sectors. India's share in global FDI increased from 0.5 per cent in 2002 to 0.8 per cent in 2004. The Table 9.7 shows the FDI inflows in various sectors during 2002-03 to 2005-06 (April-Nov.).

Table 9.7: Sectors Attracting Highest FDI Inflows

(Amount in Rupees crore and in US$ in million in parentheses)

Ranks	Sector	2003-04	2004-05	2005-06	2006-07 (Apr.-Sept.)	Cumulative inflows (from (Aug. 1991 to Sep. 2006)	Share of FDI inflow (in per cent)
1	Electrical Equipments (including computer software and electronics)	2,449(532)	3,281(721)	6,499(1451)	3,601(778)	27,311(6,272)	17.54
2	Transportation Industry	1,417(308)	815(179)	983(222)	1,187(259)	14,502(3,436)	9.31
3	Services Sector (financial and non-financial)	1,235(269)	2,106(469)	2,565(581)	6,955(1,509)	19,759(4,600)	12.69
4	Telecommunications (radio paging, cellular mobile, basic telephone services)	532(116)	588(129)	3,023(680)	3,835(405)	16,172(3,776)	10.39
5	Fuels (Power+Oil refinery)	521(113)	759(166)	416(94)	632(138)	11,608(2,720)	7.45
6	Chemicals (other than fertilizers)	94(20)	909(198)	1,979(447)	439(95)	9,019(2,238)	5.79
7	Food Processing Industries	511(111)	174(38)	183(42)	150(33)	4,852(1,212)	3.12
8	Drugs and Pharmaceuticals	502(109)	1,343(292)	760(172)	219(48)	4,531(1,055)	2.91
9	Cement and Gypsum Products	44(10)	1(0)	1,970(452)	96(21)	3,327(768)	2.14
10	Metallurgical Industries	146(32)	881(192)	681(153)	511(111)	3,328(766)	2.14

Source: FDI Data Cell, Ministry of Commerce.

The growth of the private sector is also marked by the rapid increase in the diversification of the industrial products. Initially the consumer goods industries were mainly earmarked for the private sector which, however, included a wide range from traditional goods like textiles to the modern products like motor cars, T.V., fridge, etc. But, with the passage of time other types of industries also began to be included in the private sector. These industries include chemicals, engineering, cement, rubber and paper products, printing and publishing etc. In other words, those industries which were earlier reserved for the public sector have been thrown open to the private sector except for a few like those of aircraft manufacture, heavy plant and machinery etc.

In addition to its contribution to the industrial development in terms of output and diversification of products, the private sector has some other plus points to its credit in its operations. This is apparently clear from the working of the public as well as private limited companies in the private corporate sector. IT has exhibited fairly reasonable returns on sales, net assets, and its net worth. The profitability ratios like that of gross profits as percentage of sales, gross profits as percentage of total net assets, and profits after tax as percentage of net worth have been in the range of over 9-10 per cent for a number of years. These profitability ratios also compare well with those of the Indian branches of the MNCs and the Indian subsidiaries of the foreign companies.

The importance of the private sector in the Indian economy can be best assessed in the terms of its contribution to national income and employment. As per the latest data available, the private sector contributed 25 per cent of the net domestic product while the private sector contributed 75 per cent during 2001-02.

So far its contribution to national employment is concerned, it provided employment to 84.21 lakh persons in 2002-03, which is considerably ahead than 73.95 lakh in 1981.

Small and cottage industries which form a part of private sector have an important role to play in industrial development. As these industries are labour intensive, they provide ample opportunities of employment. In addition, they ensure a rather more equitable distribution of income and wealth and assist in the effective mobilisation of human and physical capital. In order to promote these industries the Government has adopted several measures like reservation of certain items for exclusive from production in this sector, freedom licensing procedures, preference to small entrepreneurs etc. It would not be an exaggeration to say that small and cottage industries would continue to remain and develop in the private sector.

Shortcomings in Private Sector

Despite the fact that the private sector contributes significantly to the growth of Indian economy, there are some weaknesses in its functioning and there are some problems that it faces.

(i) *Inadequate Working*: First and foremost, most private enterprises in their lust for profit adopt undesirable practices which are against the consumers on one side and adversely affect the growth of medium and small-scale industrial units on the other. Besides, such practices often result in generation of black money and corrupt business dealings.

Many of the leading business and industrial houses have become monopolistic and got concentration of wealth and economic power in their hands. The sector has also become too much dependent on the government for meeting its import requirements, output sale finances, etc. The private enterprises have been subject to frequent industrial disputes and industrial sickness.

(ii) *High Cost Economy*: Another serious drawback of the private sector is that its costs in general are large and the price of products unduly high, mainly because of the high costs of raw materials and components and the indirect taxes. For instance, in the case of import goods an importer has to pay basic duty, additional duty, and finally excise duty apart from central sales tax on the final ex-factory gate cost and turnover tax.

(iii) *Promotion of Non-priority Industries*: The private corporate sector is charged for expansion of consumer goods industries having low priority such as cosmetics, air conditioners, perfumes, etc., which are mainly consumed by the elite class.

(iv) *Widespread Sickness*: Many sick and weak units constitute the private sector. The growing industrial sickness is evident in many lines of industrial and business activities, notably in textiles, engineering, chemicals, iron and steel, and paper. Factors responsible for the industrial sickness are inefficient and corrupt management, market fluctuations and inadequate marketing strategy, poor labour relations, and improper government policies.

(v) *Monopoly and Concentration of Power*: Some private enterprises have gained monopolistic power after the introduction of economic reforms in 1991. The dominance of some enterprises in terms of capital and assets is an economic and social problem as because such enterprises operates on the principle of maximization of the monopoly profits rather being production oriented. They have been found using the licensing system to prevent rivals from entering the sectors in which they were interested. This implies restriction of production, charging prices than under competition, and making monopoly profits.

(vi) *Industrial Disputes*: The smooth progress of the private sector is hampered by the recurring industrial disputes. Since independence the nation has witnessed several strikes and lockouts that resulted in loss of valuable working days. Industrial disputes have risen mainly due to difference in the interests of capitalists owners and those of the workers. While the private capitalists aim at achieving maximum profits, the workers aim at securing higher wages and incentives. There are ample evidences that industrial relations in the private sector are much disappointing than those in the public sector. The losses caused by lockouts have a strong bearing on the developing economy as it requires optimum capacity utilisation, more production, more employment, and more income.

The expansion of the private sector is being done with a view to giving a market-orientation to the Indian economy. Since the Sixth Plan (1980-85) the private sector has received due importance and has been showing sufficient buoyancy and a fast rate of growth as yet. The private sector has raised increasing amount of funds in the capital market and set up a series of joint ventures in foreign countries.

Engineering Sector

The Engineering Sector is a vast and diverse sector comprising a variety of industries, ranging from low-tech items such as castings, forgings, fasteners to highly sophisticated microprocessors-based processed control equipment and diagnostic medical instruments. Industries like bearings, steel tyres and tubes also come under this sector. The products of this sector are largely used as inputs to the capital goods industry. A few of such industries are as follows:

Cement Industry

Cement makes an integral part of infrastructure industry. It is one of the most advanced industries in the country. Since the decontrol of price and distribution of cement industry and introduction of other policy reforms, this industry has made great progress in terms of capacity, production and technology. There were 128 large cement plants in the country as on 30 April 2005, the installed capacity of which is 152.09 million tonnes and more than 332 mini cement plants with an estimated capacity of 11.10 million tonnes per annum. The production during 2004-05 was 131.56 million tonnes with a growth rate of 6.52 per cent.

The cement industry has made great technological advancement quite in conformity with the technological advancement taking place in various other fields. The industry has made great improvement in quality also and as a result it has found its ready markets in countries like Indonesia, Bangladesh, Malaysia, Nepal, Middle-East countries, Burma, Africa, and South-East Asian countries. It recorded export of cement and clinker of 10.66 million tonnes during 2004-05. In view of the growth trend in the last few years a production target of 142.0 MT was set for the year 2005-06. During the period April to October 2005, production of 82.26 MT was achieved which is 9.39 per cent higher than the production in the corresponding period of the previous year.

Efforts to generate domestic demand to meet the excess production capacity available with the industry are also being made.

Leather Industry

Leather industry is a traditional industry of India. It spreads over both, organised and inorganised sectors. India has been very rich and skilled in this field since olden times. This industry is largely run by small-scale, cottage and artisan sectors which account for over 75 per cent of the total leather production in the country. In this sector, women and people from the weaker strata of society are predominantly involved. Women constitute more than 30 per cent of the total workforce employed in this sector.

Keeping in mind the strength and potentiality of this sector, government has provided an outlay of Rs. 400 crore for implementation of various leather schemes during the Tenth Plan.

Paper and Newsprint Industry

The Indian paper industry, ranked among the 15 top global paper industries, has a prominent role in the socio-economic development of the country. The per capita consumption of paper is considered as a benchmark of modernisation of any country. The century-old paper industry has made great progress with time, at present having an installed capacity of nearly 6.2 million tonnes of paper and paperboard and about 1.24 million tonnes of newsprint. The aggregate installed capacity of the industry is expected to touch 8.3 million tonnes and 1.5 million tonnes for paper and paperboard and newsprint respectively by the year 2010. More than three lakh people are directly and 10 lakh people are indirectly employed in the paper industry.

Rubber Industry

The rubber industry is a goods manufacturing industry. It is a delicensed industry under which major rubber goods such as tyres and tubes of all kinds, surgical gloves, prophylactics, conveyer and V-belts, hose pipes, sports goods etc., are produced. Presently, 32 tyre producing units of the rubber industry are spread in 13 states with about 220 medium-scale units and over 5,500 units are in the small-scale sector, with an equal number in the tiny sector, having an annual turnover of over Rs. 12,000 crore. About 3.5 lakh people are directly employed in the rubber industry.

Man-made Fibre Industry

The man-made fibre industry has a prominent role in the textile industry. The industry comprises fibre and filament yarn manufacturing units of cellulosic origin. About 42 per cent of the total consumed raw material is manufactured by the man-made fibre industry.

Textile industry is a good source of foreign exchange. At present, the export of textiles (including handicrafts, jute and coir) accounts for about 20 per cent of total exports from India.

It is the largest foreign exchange earner for the country as the import content in textile goods is very little. After agriculture, it is the second most important sector in terms of employment generation in India. It contributes about 24.6 per cent to the gross export earnings of the country.

Textile industry contributes about 14 per cent of the value addition in the manufacturing sector, and 4 per cent to the GDP. About 35 million people are employed in this industry. It is estimated that this sector, together with allied agriculture sector, would provide employment to over 91 million people by the end of Tenth Plan (2002-07). It is the only industry which is self-reliant in raw material to the high value added products.

Budgetary concessions, rationalization of duty structure and assistance under the Technology Upgradation Fund Scheme (TUFS) have started paying dividends in the textile sector as is evident from its increased production in the recent years. During 2004-05, production of fabrics touched a peak of 45,378 million sq.m. In the year 2005-06 up to November, such production registered a further growth of a per cent over the corresponding period of the previous year.

Major Industries

In addition to the above mentioned industries, there are a great number of other industries, *viz.* jute, sericulture, handlooms, powerlooms handicrafts which provide employment to millions of people. They also bring foreign exchange for the country.

Jute

The jute sector plays predominant role in the Indian economy in general and for the eastern region in particular. The sector has socio-economic significance not from the point of view of monetary contribution that it makes to the national exchequer through exports, tax and levies but also provides employment in the agriculture and industrial sectors. About four million farmers, most of them small and marginal, are engaged in the cultivation of jute and about 2.6 lakh people are directly employed in the jute industry. Apart from this, a large number of people are indirectly employed in it. India ranks first in the production of raw jute and jute goods while in terms of its export it ranks second.

Handlooms

The handloom industry is a good source of employment in India. More than 65 lakh people are directly or indirectly engaged in handloom weaving and allied activities. Since independence, the handloom production recorded over ten-fold growth. It constitutes nearly 14 per cent of the total cloth produced in the country, contributing substantially to the export earnings of the country. In addition, the Government launches various schemes and programmes to promote handloom. One of the programmes is Deen Dayal Hathkargha Protsahan Yojana. The Government has also set up a National Centre for Textile Design.

Handicrafts

Handicrafts industry enjoys a prominent place in country's economy. It provides employment to a large number of people and is also a great source of foreign exchange earnings.

Powerlooms

Powerloom industry is an integral part of textile industry. Production and employment prospects are rapidly increasing in this sector. The industry has largely developed in the small-scale and inorganised sector. The powerloom sectors is decentralised. During 2003-04, the manufacturing of cloth in the decentralised powerloom sector was 26,947 million sq. m., while the employment generation was 4.58 million. The corresponding figures are estimated 28,526 million sq. m. and 4.76 million respectively for the year 2004-05. The powerloom sector produces cloths of great variety and intricate designs. This sector is a great contributor to the textile industry. During the year 2004-05, its total contribution in the textile industry was 63 per cent. It is also an important source of foreign exchange earnings.

Sericulture

India is a major silk producing country. It has the distinction of being the only country where all the commercial varieties of silk such as Mulberry, Tropical Tussar, Oak Tussar, Eri and Muga are produced. The golden yellow muga silk is unique to India. India next to China is the second largest silk producer in the world, producing about 20 per cent of the total production of world.

Sericulture is a labour intensive industry. Approximately 54 lakh people are directly or indirectly involved in sericulture industry. Most of the people employed in it are small and marginal farmers, engaged in tiny and household industry—largely in hand-weaving and hand-reeling sections.

Heavy Industry

The heavy industry includes heavy electrical industry, automotive industry and others that follows:

Heavy Electrical Industry

The Heavy Electrical Industry comprises industrial units manufacturing large plant and machinery required for power generation, transmission, and distribution. The products of the industry include transformers, switchgears, boilers, turbo-generators, and various types of turbines. These equipments are widely used in a number of sectors of the Indian economy such as multi-purpose power projects including nuclear power stations, petrochemical complexes, chemical plants, integrated steel plants, non-ferrous metal units, etc. The industry has made great technological upgradation and is now ready to take up contracts for export markets.

Iron and Steel Industry

The Iron and Steel industry is the backbone of industrial development. It is an integral part of infrastructural industry. India is the eighth largest steel producing country in the world. The annual growth rate of crude steel production during 2004-05 was 34.821 million tonnes as compared to the production of 34.248 million tonnes in 2003-04.

The production of iron is increasing. The production of sponge iron has been particularly promoted so as to provide an alternative to steel melting scrap which was rapidly becoming scarce. India is, at present, the largest producer of sponge iron in the world. The production of sponge iron has increased greatly. It was 6.44 million tonnes during 2002-03 which increased to

8.085 million tonnes during 2003-04. This has now gone up to 10.0 million tonnes in 2004-05.

All kinds of iron and steel are exported to various countries of the world. Today export items consist of mainly hot rolled coils, cold rolled coils, colour coated spects, GP/GC sheets, pig iron and sponge iron.

However, India has to import finished steel to fulfill its requirements. India annually imports about 1–1.5 million tonnes of finished steel. The imports mainly consist of hot rolled coils, cold rolled coils and semis.

Several measures have been taken by the Government in respect to steel sector. In continuation of the policy thrust to ensure availability of steel and stabilising its price through reduction in customs duty and abolition of special additional duty, Government has reduced the customs duty on non-alloy steel items to 5 per cent and/or alloy/stainless steel to 10 per cent during 2005-06. Besides, the National Steel Policy, 2005, has been approved by the Government which aims at ensuring that India has a modern and efficient steel industry, capable of standing up to international competition and catering to the growing domestic demand for steel.

Automobile Industry

With the liberalisation of economy, the Automobile Industry was delicensed in July 1991 under which Foreign Direct Investment (FDI) is permissible through automatic route in this sector including passenger car segment. Besides, the import of technology for technological upgradation on the royalty payment of 5 per cent without any duration limit and lump sum payment of US$2 million is allowed under automatic route.

Since 1 April 2001 the Quantitative Restrictions (QRs) have been removed and the import of vehicle is freely allowed subject to certain conditions. However, customs duty on import of second-hand vehicles including passenger cars has been raised to 105 per cent so that India may not become the dumping ground for old and used vehicles of other countries.

Owing to the New Industrial Policy, there are 15 manufacturers of passenger cars and multi-utility vehicles,

9 manufacturers of commercial vehicles, 14 of tractors, and 5 manufacturers of engines. The industry has great employment potential and about 4.5 lakh people are directly and more than one crore people are indirectly involved in this sector.

The entrance of foreign companies with their latest models has stimulated the demand for vehicles in the market resulting in the overwhelming growth of the industry. In the last four years, i.e. 2001-05, the industry has maintained a steady annual growth rate of over 15 per cent. During the last couple of years the industry has created great market potentiality across the world. Consequently, the export in this sector has considerably grown largely due to the export of two-wheelers and three-wheelers. Exports of automobiles as a proportion of total production have increased from 2.9 per cent in 1999-2000 to 8.9 per cent in 2005-06. For passenger cars and three-wheelers, exports in 2005-06 accounted for 18-19 per cent of total production.

Chemical Petrochemical and Pharmaceutical Industry

The chemical sector Industry plays a key role in the overall economic development of our country. The chemical sector including basic chemicals and its products, petrochemicals, fertilizers, paints, gases and pharmaceuticals accounts for about 17.6 per cent of the output of the manufacturing sector, and around 13-14 per cent of the total exports of the country. The industry is showing a trend of positive balance of trade for the last few years.

The Chemical Industry in India ranks 12th in terms of volume in chemical production in the world. It contributes to about 20 per cent in the national revenue in the form of customs and excise duties. At present the industry's total turnover is about US$30 billion.

A major portion of chemicals produced in India consists of upstream and intermediate products which are widely used in various downstream industries such as fertilizers, pharmaceuticals, textiles and plastics. These commodities marked for a high degree of price cyclicity, essentially influenced by the international demand and supply dynamics prevailing at the time.

Small-Scale Industries

The small-scale industrial (SSI) sector has a prominent role in the overall socio-economic development of the country. Its contribution to the growth of GDP (Gross Domestic Product) is immense both in terms of employment and exports. According to the Third All India Census of SSIs (Small-scale Industries)—both registered and unregistered—held for the year 2001-02, there were 105.21 lakh SSI units in the country (registered and unregistered) in which 249.09 lakh persons are employed and their contribution to production was Rs. 2,82,270 crore. During the year 2005-06, the number of SSI units is estimated to have increased to 123.42 lakh from 118.59 lakh in the previous year, registering a growth of 4.1 per cent. The value of their production is estimated to have increased by 27.4 per cent to Rs. 4,76,201 crore from Rs. 4,18,263 crore during 2004-05. During the year 2005-06 this sector is said to have grown at the rate of 10.4 per cent at constant prices over the previous year.

The SSIs have recorded a higher growth rate in comparison to the overall industrial growth in the past few years. The SSIs contribute over 39 per cent of the industrial production and nearly 34 per cent of direct exports in the economic growth of the nation. The sector has emerged as an engine of growth in the new millennium. Keeping in view their prominent role this sector has been assigned targets of 12 per cent annual growth in production and creation of 4.4 million additional employment generation in the Tenth Five-Year Plan.

The upper investment limit for the SSI sector continues to be Rs. one crore but in case of hi-tech export-oriented industries, this investment limit has been raised upto Rs. five crore to facilitate technological upgradation so as to make the SSI units to maintain a competitive edge. The exemption from excise duty for SSI continues to be Rs. one crore. The limit for providing guarantee cover to collateral free loans under the Credit Guarantee Scheme has been revised to Rs. 25 lakh. Under the Integrated Infrastructural Development Scheme, 50 per cent reservation for rural areas covering all over the country is provided. The funds available under the non-lapsable pool for the North-East are being used for setting up incubation centers for cluster development and for the Integrated Infrastructural Development Scheme.

As a support to stand for the bitter competition resulting from the globalisation and liberalisation of economy, the Government of India has taken various measures which include:

- Assistance to Industry associations/voluntary agencies to set up testing centers.
- Field Testing Stations provide testing services and services for quality upgradation.
- Under the Integrated Technology Upgradation and Management Programme 59 clusters have been taken up, which include National Programme for the Development of Toy Industry, Stone Industry, Lock Industry, Tool Industry and Hand Tool Industry taken up in collaboration with UNIDO.
- SSI units are given financial support by providing reimbursement of 75 per cent of their expenditure to obtain Certification subject to a maximum of Rs. 75,000, under the scheme for promotion of ISO 9000/14001 Certification.
- 15 per cent is admissible on the loans up to Rs. one crore, advanced by Scheduled Commercial Banks/SFCs/ NSIC for technological upgradation of SSIs, under the Credit Linked Capital Subsidy Scheme for Technology Upgradation.
- Setting up of Biotech Cell in SIDO.

Financial Assistance to SSI Sector

With a view to promoting Small-Scale Industrial Sector, the Government has announced financial assistance to SSI Units, which includes the provisions:

- The composite loan limit has been raised from Rs. 25 lakh to Rs. 50 lakh.
- The limit to collateral free loans has been raised from Rs. 5 lakh to Rs. 15 lakh and up to Rs. 25 lakh in case of SSI units with a good track record.

- Laghu Udyami Credit Card (LUCC) Scheme has been liberalised by enhancing the credit limit from Rs. 2 lakh to Rs. 10 lakh, for borrowers having a satisfactory track record.
- As per the announcement made by the Government Indian Banks Association (IBA) has advised the banks to adopt the interest rate band of two per cent above and below their Prime Lending Rates (PLRs) for the advancement of SSIs.
- The Ministry of SSI has identified 78 clusters for focused development of SE and sent the list to the RBI for incorporating credit requirements of these clusters in the State Credit Plans of the bank.
- Publicise the various schemes facilities of the banks such as collateral free/composite loan extended to the SSI sector.
- To make adequately available financial resources to the SSI sector at competitive rates, the Government announced for the creation of a Small and Medium Enterprises (SME) Fund under SIDBI with a corpus of Rs. 500 crore to provide equity support to small and medium units in knowledge based industries such as pharma, biotechnology and IT sectors.
- To facilitate technology upgradation and enhance competitiveness, the investment limit in plant and machinery raised from Rs. 1 crore to Rs. 5 crore in respect of 69 items reserved for manufacture in the small scale sector.

Agro-based and Non-Farm Industry

Agro-based industry and non-farm industry largely based on local raw material, skills and technology, have been identified as prominent industries having potential for gainful employment in rural areas, and thus, can contribute in the overall growth of the national economy. Taking into account this potentiality of the industries, the Government has launched various policies and programmes, which are being implemented through Khadi and Village Industries Commission (KVIC) and Coir Board, etc.

Industrial Investment

With a perceptible improvement in the investment scenario, both domestic and foreign, together with the policy measures towards further liberalization and simplification of the norms guiding such investment, the overall productive capability of the industrial sector as a whole is expected to increase substantially in the coming years. Buoyant business expectations have been the main factor that lifted the investment tempo in the industrial sector. Filing of investment intentions as reflected in the Industrial Entrepreneur Memorandum (IEMS) for the sectors has picked up again since 2003 after near stagnation in the preceding seven years (see Table 9.8). In the post liberalization period, so far over 66,600 IEMs/LOIs have been filed with investment intentions amounting to Rs. 18,94,202 crore and additional employment potential of 12.0 million.

Table 9.8: Industrial Investment Intentions in Terms of IEMs, LOIs and DILs

Year	Industrial Entrepreneurs' Memorandum (IEMs)			Letters of Intent (LOIs) Direct Industrial Lics(DILs)		
	Number	Proposed Investment (in Rs. Cr.)	Proposed Employment (000's)	Number	Proposed Investment (in Rs. Cr.)	Proposed Employment (000's)
1991*	3,084	76,310	769	195	2,071	34
1992	4,860	115,872,	923	620	13,994	97
1993	4,456	63,976	703	528	12,845	100
1994	4,664	88,771	829	546	17,937	130
1995	6,502	125,509	1,114	355	14,265	91
1996	4,825	73,278	696	522	29,932	181
1997	3,873	52,379	522	321	9,528	96
1998	2,889	57,389	521	145	3,274	27
1999	2,948	128,892	477	132	827	17
2000	3,058	72,332	411	203	1,042	31
2001	2,981	91,234	809	117	1,318	14
2002	3,172	91,291	380	89	649	8
2003	3,875	118,612	833	116	1,395	14
2004	5,118	267,069	856	100	5,265	21
2005	6,203	353,956	1,271	135	2,990	23

* August to December

Source: Department of Industrial Policy & Promotion (DIPP), M/o Commerce & Industry.

The government has taken several measures recently in the area of foreign direct investment (FDI). FDI up to 100 per cent is now permitted on the automatic route in all sectors except for those requiring industrial licence or those proposals where the foreign investors already have a joint venture in the same field of activity or the proposals are for acquisition of shares in an Indian company in the financial services sector or all proposals for such sectors in which FDI is not permitted. Some of the important measures that have been taken by the government are as under:

1. FDI cap in the domestic airlines sector has been enhanced from 40 per cent to 49 per cent and NRI investment is permitted up to 100 per cent.
2. FDI cap has been increased from 49 per cent to 74 per cent in basic and cellular telecom services.
3. Procedures have been simplified and more sectors under the automatic route have been included. This has led to an increase in FDI inflows in India. While it increased by 25 per cent in 2004, in 2005 the increase recorded 33.8 per cent.
4. FDI up to 100 per cent under the automatic route is now permitted for development of township, housing, built-up infrastructure and construction-development projects. The minimum area requirement has been reduced to 10 hectares for serviced housing plots and 50,000 sq. metres built-up area for construction-development projects.

The Indian industry has considerable headway to make before becoming internationally competitive, though it has been going through a process of restructuring with merger and acquisitions and downsizing. Employment generation in the industrial sector has been insignificant in the reform era.

There are recently signs that after more than a decade of liberalisation, the Indian Industry has come to reckon with the reality of international competition, and is trying to put it in order. Many leading corporates are now establishing themselves in both developed and developing countries by setting up subsidiaries or through joint ventures or through acquisitions which would provide them niche markets. Many IT corporations, leading corporates in steel, chemicals, pharmaceuticals and minerals are making a debut in a number of countries. Many of the products have acquired a brand name.

Indian Public Finances

10

INDIAN TAX SYSTEM: SALIENT CHARACTERISTICS

> "Taxes are like hails which destroy the crop.... The best tax system is that which has the least bad economic effects"—J.S. Mill

Thus tax policy of a country must be very sound and in the context of developing countries it must be geared towards accelerating the rate of economic growth. Taxation must raise the level of savings and in the words of Dr. Raja J. Chelliah, it must mobilize the economic surplus. A sound tax system must help in increasing the amount of economic surplus. Therefore, the general emphasis in tax system must be on curtailing the consumption standards. Further, whenever savings are promoted through tax system, they should also be diverted in desired channels.

A necessary feature of all developing countries is that development process is always accompanied by growing inequalities. Therefore, as far as possible, a sound tax system must make an attempt to reduce these inequalities. However, care should be taken that tax rates are not unduly high which discourage the incentives to work, save and invest.

Further, since the development needs of developing countries are unsatiable, therefore, here even the poorest will have to pay some taxes. However, as far as possible, the principle of ability to pay must be observed while collecting taxes from different individuals. A person's ability to pay or (contribute) can be measured in terms of that part of economic surplus accruing to him which he is not utilizing for productive investment. The greater the surplus which a person has above his minimum necessary requirements, the greater should be his contribution.

Another important objective of a sound tax policy in a developing economy is to check inflationary tendencies. Inflation is inherent in all developing countries. In the initial stages of economic development since large investments are undertaken and there is always a time lag between investment and output, the prices rise in the meantime. It is now generally believed that taxation can play a vital role in checking these inflationary tendencies. Taxes, both direct as well as indirect, by reducing the disposable income can exercise restraints on demand. In the words of Taxation Enquiry Commission (1953-54):

> "Taxes that fall directly on the large additional incomes, and commodity taxes that fall on the increase in general purchasing power resulting from inflation have a significant part to play in anti-inflationary policy."

Finally, in a sound tax policy nobody feels that he is being discriminated. Tax evasion is almost non-existent. Tax administrations are very honest and tax system is very simple.

In the light of above discussion we will now examine the salient features of Indian tax system. If we carefully study the Indian tax system, the following features will emerge:

1. Higher Tax Rates in India: Contrary to common belief, India has emerged as one of the highest taxed nations in the world. Ever since the advent of planning, we have been imposing new taxes. The rates of existing taxes are sometimes raised to astronomical figures (97.5 per cent). Consequently, little is left as incentives to work, save and invest. People are now crying under the crushing burden of taxes—both direct and indirect. Realising the fact that in India tax burden is unbearable, in the post-90's period, there is a trend to lower the tax rates—both for direct and indirect taxes.

2. Multiplicity of Taxes/Tax Bases: During the five-year plans taxation has been used in India as one of the main instruments to raise revenue and to achieve the various socio-economic objectives. New taxes have been imposed and tax rates have been increased to mobilize a large part of the income created as a result of economic development. Tax structure in India has been drawn in such a manner that all relevant ability indices are taxed.

All conceivable bases of taxes—both direct and indirect taxes, have been exploited. Direct taxes on income (from various sources including interest and profits), wealth, property, (including land and houses), capital gains, gifts, etc. have been imposed. Then there is a multiplicity of indirect taxes imposed both by the Centre and the States such as export and import (custom) duties, tax on production (Union excise duty), tax on services, tax on the sale and purchase of goods, tax on the movement of goods from one State to another, entry tax on goods entering from one State to another and even entering a particular municipal area within the State, *i.e.* octroi, State excise duty, etc. Recently VAT has been imposed by many States; but all other indirect taxes are still continuing. Apart from these, there are many other levies imposed at the local level.

A taxpayer has to pay income tax when he earns income, he has to pay wealth tax when he holds accumulated income, he has to pay Gift Tax when he transfers that income to others and has to pay Estate Duty (abolished recently) if he dies and leaves his accumulated income to his heirs. During 1957-58 to 1961-62 and 1963-64 to 1965-66, he had to pay Expenditure Tax if he spent more than the specified amount. This might appear taxation with vengeance. In the field of indirect taxes also, duties have been levied on the new items and increased on old items so as to tax more heavily those commodities which are consumed by the relatively well-to-do classes. Even commodities of mass consumption have not been spared.

3. Revenue Surpluses or Deficits: Another noteworthy feature of Indian tax system has been excess of its collections compared with requirements till mid-seventies. To be specific we have been having surpluses on revenue account and these surpluses were partly used to finance capital expenditure. It is only on capital account that our budgets were deficits. On both the accounts taken together, however, our budgets turned out to be deficits. However, since the mid-seventies because of increasing revenue expenditure, a chronic tendency of revenue deficit has been developed.

4. Complicated Tax Structure: As already stated, years after years we have been imposing new taxes and raising the rates of existing taxes. Consequently our tax structure has become very complicated. As compared to this our population is very illiterate. People cannot understand this complicated tax structure. This has led to various malpractices. Tax administration has become dishonest and corrupt. An average taxpayer has fallen victim to the corrupt tax officials who have earned huge amounts of black money. Sometimes tax administration in collusion with the taxpayers exploit the government treasury.

5. Inequitable Tax Structure: Although we impose a large number of taxes yet our tax structure lacks equity. According to Raja J. Chelliah our tax system does not have either horizontal equity or vertical equity. By horizontal equity we mean that all taxpayers with the same level of income, irrespective of the source of income, must pay the same amount of taxes. But we know that our agricultural sector pays less taxes than the industrial sector. In the industrial sector one has to pay direct taxes like income tax, corporation tax, etc., from which the agricultural sector is exempted. Even in case of indirect taxes agricultural sector pays less taxes because it consumes only those commodities which it produces. Naturally, these commodities do not carry any tax burden, since they are not brought into the market.

According to Raja J. Chelliah even vertical equity is conspicuous by its absence from our tax structure. By vertical equity we mean persons having different levels of income must pay differently, *i.e.* persons with higher income must pay higher amount of taxes and persons with low income must pay lower amount of taxes. But this is not the case in India because of the predominance of indirect taxes which are regressive in nature.

6. Imbalance between Direct and Indirect Taxes: The main reason for our inequitable tax structure is the preponderance of indirect taxes. The documents on Long Term Fiscal Policy showed that the proportion of indirect taxes in total tax revenue had increased to as high as 82 per cent in the mid-sixties. Consequently, the ratio of direct taxes has declined to 18 per cent. In developed countries like U.S.A., U.K., Japan, etc.

reverse is the case. The burden of indirect taxes as we know mostly falls on the poor. Consequently, inequality in the distribution of income has increased in India. It is a happy augury that in the post-reform period of 1990s, emphasis is now being shifted to direct taxes. Consequently, the ratio of direct taxes to total tax revenue is on the rise and presently this has reached nearly 24-25 per cent.

7. **Our Tax Structure is not Anti-Inflationary:** As already stated inflation is in-built in the development process in a developing country. An ideal tax structure must cure this evil. Unfortunately, because of preponderance of indirect taxes, our tax structure is not anti-inflationary. Rather it has added fuel to the fire of inflation.

8. **Imbalance in the Tax Sources of States *Vs.* Union:** Another unhealthy feature of our tax system is the increasing dependence of the States on the Union government, for their resource requirements. There is no denying the fact that of all the federations in the world (U.S.A., Australia, Canada, etc.) Indian Federation is the best in the sense that there is clear-cut division of resources between the Centre and the States. But while demarcating these resources, our Constitution makers appeared to have forgotten about the development needs of the States. While the States have to incur increasing amount of expenditure on such items as education, medical and public health, agriculture, industry, etc., they do not have much resources. The elastic sources of revenue like income tax, custom duty, excise duty, corporation tax, etc., are in the hands of the Centre. Consequently, the States have to look towards the Centre for more and more resources. The Central Government often discriminates one State from the other in the matter of allocating funds.

9. **Apathy of the State Government to Exploit Resources:** The fault does not lie entirely with the Centre. Even the State governments do not exploit the tax resources assigned to them in our Constitution. For example, taxes on agricultural income lie in the sphere of State governments. But the State governments do not levy these taxes since agriculturists constitute the biggest vote bank. During elections even many tax concessions are

announced so as to brighten the prospects of winning elections. Thus the State governments too are to be blamed for this failure.

10. Tax Evasion: Last but not the least is the considerable amount of tax evasion generated by our tax system. It is almost impossible to ascertain correctly the extent of tax evasion in the country because of numerous difficulties involved in the process. Any such estimate can only be a guess and would involve an element of subjectivity. However, the Wanchoo Committee estimated that the extent of only income tax evaded was Rs. 470 crore in sixties some conservative estimates show that black money has reached even the level of 25-30 per cent of National Income.

Therefore, there is an urgent need to reform our tax system. Although a number of initiatives to reform both the direct and indirect taxes have been undertaken since 1991, yet much more needs to be done. On direct tax front, tax rates have been slashed. Tax net has been widened by adopting 1/6th criteria (abolished in the budget 2006-07). Tax system has been simplified and rationalized. PAN (Permanent Account Number) for every taxpayer has been made compulsory. Yet measures like taxing agriculture income and wealth, making distinction between earned and unearned income, etc., need to be incorporated. Similarly on indirect taxes' front the adoption of State-VAT and CEN-VAT separately will not serve the purpose. Efforts should be made to have a single VAT-system in the country, wherein service tax is also included. Then keeping in view the growing needs of the States to spend on social sector like education, medical and public health, social security, poverty alleviation programmes, etc., there should be a fair distribution of resources between the Centre and the States.

EXPENDITURE TAX

In a developing economy a direct tax on the basis of aggregate consumption or aggregate expenditure is often recommended in order to promote savings in the economy.

The early advocates of expenditure tax, like J.S. Mill, based their case on the 'double taxation' of savings involved in the levy of income tax. On equity grounds also, the expenditure tax was preferred because the principle of taxing income confers differential benefit on property owners as against those who derive their income from personal labour and who cannot treat the whole of their income as 'spendable' as the capitalists can. Moreover, since taxable income from property can be converted into capital gains in numerous ways, income was considered a defective measure of taxable capacity as it could be manipulated by taxpayers.

Professor Nicholas Kaldor, who vehemently argued of substituting income tax by expenditure tax, favoured it in the context of Keynesian framework also. To him the expenditure tax provides a more efficient instrument for controlling the economy in the interests of economic stability and progress than taxes levied on income. However, this line of thinking has only a limited validity in relation to developing countries like India because economic fluctuations in these countries occur at relatively lower level of output.

The proposal to adopt expenditure tax in India was first made by Professor Kaldor in the mix-1950s when he was invited to suggest some reforms in the Indian tax structure. It was almost at the same time (1955) that he published his book entitled "An Expenditure Tax".[1] His mind was naturally preoccupied with finding a suitable economic environment in which he could test his ideas. Consequently expenditure tax came to be levied in India in 1957 only to be abolished in 1962. It was reintroduced in 1964 and abolished again in 1966.

It will not be out of place to mention here that in the context of British economy Kaldor himself was fully aware of the difficulties inherent in the replacement of personal income tax by expenditure tax. He, therefore, suggested the substitution of expenditure tax in place of surtax—a tax on exceptionally higher incomes. However, surtax was merged with the general income tax with effect from 1970. Thus, it appears that the record of expenditure tax is not very encouraging. As at present, there is only one country in the world (Sri Lanka) that levies a personal expenditure tax. In many developing as well as developed countries Kaldor's work received more attention for its careful analysis of concepts of income than for its arguments in favour of tax on expenditure. In India also, although his personal view for levying an expenditure tax was considered administratively complex, yet the income tax base has been sufficiently widened to include gifts, capital gains, notional income from owner-occupied houses, etc. This has made replacement of personal income tax by expenditure tax almost redundant.

It may be stated that the replacement of income tax base by expenditure base has two constituents: (i) personal income tax, and (ii) corporate tax. As regards replacement of personal income tax, the main task is to make a choice between the two forms of tax so as to step up the rate of savings in the economy. As things are now, there does not appear to be much scope for increasing the aggregate rate of savings. Personal income tax is already sufficiently conducive to savings. Currently, the rate of savings of the upper income groups in the non-corporate sector is quite high. This has been brought about either by direct concessions on current savings or indirect concessions on interest, income and wealth. There are already loud protests that such concessions are promoting inequalities as they act as stimulant for accumulation of wealth by the richer classes who have a higher propensity to save. Thus, total exemption of all savings from income tax would clearly be inequitable.

It may be mentioned here that expenditure tax was suggested for India when there was no tax on capital gains, and when notional income from self-occupied property was excluded from personal taxation. Presently we include not only such gains but also casual earnings like lottery wins within the net of income tax. As such, the need for expenditure tax is less than obvious.

Administratively also, the expenditure tax is too complex to be handled by the country's tax administration and revenue intelligence system. Presently, about 80—90 per cent of income tax revenue is collected by way of advance tax or deduction of tax at source, *i.e.* on the principle of PAYE (pay as you earn). How will the expenditure tax handle this aspect? For the proper administration of expenditure tax, we would need additional data on stocks, opening balances of all types of assets including borrowing, lending, bank accounts, etc. This would create additional problems of an unknown magnitude. Further, expenditure needs of different families are different depending upon such factors as the number of dependents, the number of aged and chronically sick persons, etc. To tackle this issue Kaldor proposed that the tax administration should work out the aggregate family expenditure on per capita basis to be used as some sort of index. The crux of the problem here is, would it not add to the burden of tax administration and make the tax structure still more cumbersome? We had earlier dispensed with such concessions in the 1970s so as to make our tax structure less complicated.

The second constituent in the scheme of replacing income tax by expenditure tax is the corporate tax. It is here that there appears to be some scope for experiment. It is an open secret that the corporate sector of the economy tends to inflate its expenditure in order to reduce the level of corporate as well as personal income. Many perquisites, which do not fall within the purview of their salary, are given to the directors and other executives in order to reduce the level of corporate profits. Often times, even family expenditure on conveyance and entertainment is debited to the firm. Thus expenditure tax on firms—it would be better to call it cost-based tax—may be worth trying. But even here a number of safeguards have to be provided for. In a labour surplus economy, it is just possible that the firms may reduce the use of labour in order to reduce their aggregate cost. Further, industries like mining where labour input is exceptionally high would be discriminated against capital-intensive low-cost industries. Therefore, different yardsticks will have to be applied to arrive at the aggregate taxable expenditure of different firms. Anyway, the problem of reforming corporate tax is a different one and should not be mixed up with that of personal income tax.

The main conclusion that follows is that there is hardly an effective substitute for personal income tax. The objectives which we want to realize through expenditure tax in an indirect manner can be directly achieved through the existing income tax structure. It is only in the case of corporate tax that there is some scope for replacing it with the expenditure tax. The problem is one of reforming the corporate tax and not of levying expenditure tax in lieu of tax on income for all categories of taxpayers.

TAXATION OF AGRICULTURE

Agriculture contributes about one-fourth of the national income and nearly 60-70 per cent of population is engaged in this sector. In the early stages of economic development, other sectors being non-existing, taxation of agriculture, therefore, plays a crucial role. The mobilization of resources from agriculture has come to occupy a place of central importance in the current theory of economic development. In most of the countries the channeling of resources from agriculture has been considered responsible for their take-off. The examples of Japan since 1868, USSR since 1917 and China since 1948 have proved how agriculture plays a dynamic role in economic development.

Japan was the first Asian country, which despite its traditional form of agriculture, primitive methods of cultivation and very small size of landholdings, succeeded in bringing a striking phase of agricultural development with the help of revenue derived from agricultural taxation. In Japan land tax siphoned off much of the surplus generated within agriculture and was the principle source of revenue for the government. Resources extracted by the government by way of land taxes were applied to economic development including the provision for service to the agricultural sector.

In Japan a substantial increase in agricultural production was attained by the adoption of increased irrigation facilities, improved seeds, advanced knowledge, etc. Thus, the dynamic nature of the Japanese society and greater efforts taken to enhance the agricultural production yielded quick results. It was all due to this that the required surpluses from the agricultural sector were siphoned off in an indirect way by the imposition of heavy land tax which amounted to 63.7 per cent of the aggregate tax yield in 1868, 93.2 per cent in 1873 and 83.2 per cent in 1877.

In the erstwhile USSR, inadequate agricultural production was a major impediment in the process of industrialization. But the enforcement of collectivization largely changed the picture. The basic reasons for the introduction of collectivization were political rather than economic. As far as political reasons were concerned, the Soviet Government wanted to set up a socialist society by nationalizing all lands. Insofar as economic reasons were concerned, the transition of the Soviet village to large agricultural farms meant a great revolution in economic relations in the whole way of life of the peasantry. Collectivization put an end for ever to the exploitation of the peasants by large farmers (Kulaks). Also all the advantages of large scale farming could be reaped by the introduction of collective farms, which were required to hand over a significant proposition of their produce to the government at a price which was much below the market price.

Similarly the rate of capital formation in China today was closely related to the extent of tax, primarily in the form of tax in kind, imposed on the peasants. In addition to the taxes payable in kind, the peasants were bound to sell a large quantity of cereals and certain other agricultural goods to the State. This was a form of disguised taxation.

Thus, for promoting economic development in less developed countries heavier taxation of agriculture is generally recommended. Some studies, have used the argument of existence of inter-sectoral inequality as the basis for building a case for additional taxation on Indian agriculture. As Ved P. Gandhi puts it, "There is inter-sectoral inequality in India in favour of the agricultural sector, which must be corrected on grounds of equity between sectors either by additional taxes, on the agricultural sector or by reducing the taxes levied on the non-agricultural sector."[2]

In India land revenue is the major source of agricultural taxation, though a few States also levy a tax on agricultural income. Land revenue is assessed at a flat rate, *i.e.,* the rate of tax does not vary with the area of land or income therefrom. The levy varies with grades of land, as it is related to net produce. But this is not satisfactory as land of equal fertility can be used to raise different crops. The result is that the burden of land revenue could be comparatively heavy in cereal growing tracts than on land where commercial crops are grown. Further the burden of land revenue was comparatively low in the permanently settled areas as the State demand had remained fixed. This led to inequity between permanent and temporary settled areas. In brief, the system of land taxation in India is not based upon any satisfactory criterion of ability.

The Taxation Enquiry Commission (1953-54) has suggested certain steps to improve the system of land revenue:

1. Disparities in the rates of land revenue in different States should be removed and a uniform rate be adopted as a standard method for cultivation in each State.
2. Rate of land revenue should be revised at an interval of time (say 10 years) and the revision should be based on the price-index of agricultural produce.
3. Rates may be revised any time if a situation of exemption occurs.
4. Local bodies such as panchayats and district boards should be authorized to levy surcharges to meet the local financial needs.
5. Fifteen per cent of land revenue collected from each local area should be given to the local bodies of the area.

In 1972, Government of India appointed a committee under the chairmanship of Professor K.N. Raj (commonly known as the Committee on Taxation of Agricultural Wealth and Income) to investigate the question of agricultural wealth and income taxes from all angles.

The main recommendation of the Raj's Committee which received widespread attention was the replacement of land revenue by Agricultural Holding Tax (AHT).

The AHT was to be imposed on the rateable value of land, which was to be determined not on the assessor's actual income, but on what he ought to earn from this operational holding, *i.e.*, on the basis of productivity of land. For the determination of AHT land has to be divided into homogeneous regions according to soil and climate conditions. Norms of output per acre (*i.e.* productivity norm) are to be determined for each year for each such region or district on the basis of actual yields, for the previous 10 years. The value of the output so estimated has to be multiplied by the average harvest prices of the preceding three years. This amount has to be used to calculate the rateable value for the purpose of calculating the AHT. The figure has to be revised every year to account for the changing developments. Further, in order to find out the rateable value for the purpose of tax calculation, costs of cultivation are to be deducted from the gross value of output. On this reduced gross value, a further rebate of 20 per cent, subject to a maximum of Rs. 1000, is to be allowed to account for the vagaries of nature, *i.e.* failure of monsoons. There was a further provision that if the total yield during any year is half of the average yield during the previous 10 years, then the rateable value should be treated as zero or non-taxable.

VALUE ADDED TAX

As part of its ongoing economic reforms, the Central Government has been toeing with the idea of a simple and uniform domestic trade taxation. Value Added Tax (VAT) is considered to be a panacea for all the ills from which our commodity taxation is suffering. We have been hearing the imposition and postponement of VAT since 1 April, 2001. But it was implemented *w.e.f.* 1 April, 2005.

Presently the system of domestic trade taxation is complex and characterized by multiplicity and non-uniformity of rates, increasing compliance cost both on the part of the Government and the taxpayers, and cascading effect of taxes which discourages specialisation.[3]

In the pursuit of resource mobilization both the Centre and States have been taxing different commodities at different rates and even the same commodity at different stages. Then different States try to tax the citizens of other States by exporting tax burden by taxing commodities on the origin principle, which create artificial channel of distribution by sending goods through consignments. Often different States offer large number of incentives to woo the producers and in the process those States, themselves suffer because the moment incentives are withdrawn production is stopped and the allocation of resources again follow the natural economic principles. The present system of trade taxation has also led to an increasing compliance cost for the taxpayers particularly in respect of inter-State trade and even for the Government it does not achieve the principle of economy. However, the greatest drawback of the present system of commodity taxation is that it has cascading effect, *i.e.,* tax on tax, which discourages specialisation by promoting vertical integration of industries and firms. Even the recent Report of the Task Force on Implementation of the Fiscal Responsibility and Budget Management Act, 2003 commonly known as, Kelkar Committee Report II, has remarked that "These difficulties have led to substantial distortions...and the choice of production technologies and inputs in the country has become distorted."[4]

It is not for the first time that these and many other problems have been realized. In the past also many attempts have been made to rectify these ill-effects. As far back as in 1957 the additional excise duties on three key commodities, *viz.,* tobacco, sugar and textiles were imposed in lieu of the sales tax on the pretext of simplicity and uniformity. Later on in 1986 Mr. V.P. Singh, the then Finance Minister tried to extend this list, but he had to retreat before the stiff opposition of the State Governments. However, he succeeded in introducing modified form of VAT (MODVAT) by granting credit on certain central excises already paid on inputs so as to avoid the cascading effect of central excise duty.

VAT is preferred because unlike excise duty it is levied not only production stage but also at different stages of value addition. In the modern days when many durable commodities are sold for prices which include service, warranty and installation charges, VAT would fetch considerable more revenue than general sales tax.[5] Having uniform rate structure throughout the country, it would encourage the free flow of internal and inter-State trade, besides promoting optimum allocation of resources and plugging the artificial channels of distribution of goods which are a consequence of non-uniform commodity taxation. Having no cascading effect of taxes it would improve the production efficiency. Presently more than 100 countries in the world have opted for VAT and European Economic Committee members are the forerunners.

But before we go for a comprehensive VAT in India many issues have to be debated. First of all, it must be borne in mind that there are a number of alternatives to arrive at the value added component on which the tax is to be levied. And each alternative has its own administrative and economic implications.

Almost there are eight forms of VAT. Briefly it is a tax levied on business on the value they add to their purchases of raw materials, and goods and services (leaving aside the problem of capital and stocks). We can represent this by writing value added (V/A), as total output (O) minus total input (I), *i.e.,*

$$V/A = O - I \qquad \text{... (i)}$$

Clearly, the difference between output and the inputs of raw materials, energy interest and rent paid, etc., is the payments of wage and salaries (W), and the residual, which we call profit (P), *i.e.,*

$$O - I = W + P \qquad \text{... (ii)}$$

$$\text{Or } V/A = O - I = W + P \qquad \text{... (iii)}$$

That is value added can be derived either by subtraction (O – I) or by addition (W + P). These forms of calculations sometimes are called subtractive method and additive method.

The tax rate (t) on value added *i.e.* t (V/A) can then be applied in atleast four ways:

$$t\,(V/A) = t\,(W + P) \qquad \text{... (a)}$$

$$t\,(V/A) = tW + tP \qquad \text{... (b)}$$

$$t\,(V/A) = t\,(O - I) \qquad \text{... (c)}$$

$$t\,(V/A) = tO - tI \qquad \text{...(d)}$$

The last one (d) is the most common method used, also called (sometimes) the credit method. MODVAT or CENVAT is based on this principle. According to this method gross tax liability (of business) is calculated by applying the pertinent statutory rate to total sales or output or turnover. From this figure, the amount of tax already paid on the purchase of inputs or intermediate goods is deducted.

Coming back to 'a – d', though they appear mathematically identical, *i.e.,* (a) = (b) and (c) = (d), yet administratively they are not. For example (c) and (d); while in (d) indirect method called invoice method is used to work out the tax liability, in (c) tax is applied directly to the component of (V/A).

The following Table 10.1 will make the distinction between addition and subtraction methods:

Table 10.1: Distinction between Addition and Subtraction Methods

Input	Price (Rs.) excluding any tax	VAT Rate	VAT Paid (Rs.)	Price including tax (Rs.)
Raw Materials	100	20%	20	120
Energy, etc.	100	20%	20	120
Total Input	200		40	240
Value Added (Wages and Profit)	100	20%	20	120
Output	300	20%	60	360

The Table 10.1 shows that the tax liability by additive method t(W+P) or subtractive method t(O – I) and by commonly used invoice or credit method (tO – tI) would be the same, *i.e.* Rs. 20. But the most serious problem arises when VAT is imposed on price of inputs which may include some element of tax. For example, if VAT on various farms products (floor, bread, biscuits, etc.) made from wheat which includes market fee, rural development charges, etc., is imposed, then the effective rate would be different from and higher than the nominal rate (20 per cent). Amongst the EEC members France has adopted this method.[6] Thus the above mentioned four forms of VAT [(a – d)] would give birth to eight forms of VAT.

It may be added that there is no difference of opinion insofar as the subtractive method is concerned and this may be the reason for its widespread acceptability. The only variation is whether to adopt direct approach, *i.e.,* t(O – I) or indirect approach, *i.e.* tO – tI. But while calculating the VAT liability via additive procedure, some fiscal experts prefer to treat sum of the firm's payments to the factors of production used in producing the goods. Under this scheme VAT rate is applied to the firms costs in terms of wages, interest, rent and profits.[7]

Now coming to the various issues which need to be debated in the Indian context. Apart from the form of VAT which we should adopt, in a federal set-up like ours where lies its place? Should it be a Centre's subject? States would not agree to this proposal, as this will deprive them of their legitimate power. If it were a States' subject, it would lead to the similar problems which we have been facing now. It has no place in the concurrent list because the same commodity/service cannot be taxed twice. Then another problem which agriculturally dominated States would be facing is that here value addition component is very small. Therefore, the imposition of VAT would mean an immediate fall in their revenue. Who will compensate such States? Whereas coastal States would gain if import duty is replaced by VAT, which it should be, then there may be a large number of small-scale producers in the unorganised sector who may not be approachable for the levy of VAT. For such producers and the agricultural sector Canada has found a solution where VAT is accompanied by last stage sales tax.

The most important thing to remember is that VAT means there is only one tax on the production, transaction and distribution of goods. In the Indian federal set-up there is a clear-cut division of tax items between the Centre and the States. While commodity taxes like Union excise duty (at the production or manufacturing stage) and import or export duty are levied by the Centre, a large number of taxes at the distribution/sale, entry, entertainment, etc., stages are levied by the States. With effect from 1994, the Centre has also introduced tax on services which has widened its net to cover 58 services (now raised to 71) at the uniform rate of 8 per cent (now raised to 10 per cent in the budget 2004-05). Besides, the inter-State trade is governed by the uniform central sales tax. Thus, there is plethora of taxes on goods and services, which have to be abolished and replaced by VAT. Besides, there is jurisdictional problem, *i.e.*, constitutional bottlenecks, of dividing these taxes between the Centre and the States.

Realising the constitutional bottleneck, the Union government in 1986 introduced MODVAT (later on called CEN-VAT), whereby the credit was given for already paid Union excise duty on selected intermediate goods while calculating the total excise burden of final output. Now the Centre wants that the States should also make a beginning with the introduction of State-VAT in lieu of sales tax. Haryana is said to be the pioneer State in this regard by introducing State-VAT and it is said to have experienced an increase in sales tax revenue, which is inherent in the way Haryana implemented VAT.[8]

The main features of State-VAT in Haryana are:

I. The facility of input credit is granted only in the event of purchases made from within the State from VAT dealers.

II. The manufacturers who earlier could buy most of the capital goods from within the State without payment sales tax would now under the VAT system have to pay tax at the time of their purchase.

III. To bring all kinds of utensils and wares made up of brass, copper and *kanse* under the list of 12.5 per cent tax as against the decades old policy of levying concessional tax rate on these goods.

No other State can afford to go the way Haryana has done it. Moreover it is against the true spirit of VAT. Then it is the problem of integration of goods tax with service tax which is becoming the major source of revenue. The proposed dual model of CEN-VAT and State-VAT would keep out the taxation of services. Thus cascading effect of taxation would continue to operate.[9] A way out has been suggested by the Task Force on Implementation of the Fiscal Responsibility and Budget Management Act,[10] commonly known as Kelkar Committee Report II. The Task Force recommended that both the Central Government and the State Governments should come to an agreement in respect of a comprehensive tax on goods and services. There should be a "concurrent but independent jurisdiction over common or almost common tax bases comprehensively extending over all goods and services and in both cases going up to the final consumer".[11] However, the Task Force suggested the following three *ad valorem* rates, in addition to zero rate on selected key commodities. The proposed rate structure is:

Levels of rate	Centre	State
Floor	6	4
Standard	12	8
Higher	20	14

However, the proposal of the Task force has been criticised on two accounts.[12] First of all, the integration of taxes on goods and services (GST) and its enactment both by the Centre and the States assumes that the States would give up their taxation powers in exchange of taxing services. Secondly, there would be an agreement on the part of all the States to have a uniform rate of taxation. Otherwise, the enactment of different rates by different States, though within the suggested rate structure, would effect our domestic trade with all the ills from which it is suffering now. Then there is problem of double taxation.

It may the concluded that VAT has certain inherent advantages, and in the changed domestic and global economic scenario, we have to adopt it sooner or later. Let the Centre continue to levy VAT up to the production base and manufacturing stage and the States at subsequent stages. But all the States must agree to adopt a uniform VAT policy so that the allocation of resources throughout the country is optimum. All the taxes including service tax have to abolished. Since it is a distant but realizable dream, we should go step by step till a complete switchover to full-fledged VAT is possible. The States are expected to be at the receiving end, therefore, the Centre should adopt a persuasive and pragmatic approach. It is a happy augury that the Centre has already constituted an Experts Panel to draw up a strategy required for education, training and publicity for implementing VAT in the country.

SERVICE TAX

The service tax is important for accelerating the growth process in the economy as it helps agriculture and industry. 'Services' constitute a very heterogeneous spectrum of economic activities. Today services cover wide range of activities such as management, banking, insurance, hospitality, administration, communication, entertainment, wholesale distribution, and retailing including R&D (Research and Development) activities. Service sector is now occupying an important stage of the economy so much so that in the contemporary world, development of service sector has become synonymous with the advancement of the economy.

Broadly defined, the service sector includes all economic activities whose output is not a physical product. This sector encompasses the major areas of trade, finance, insurance, communications, public utilities, transportation, government administration, healthcare, education, business (accountants, consultants) and personal service. There are three sectors in an economy, *viz.* Primary sector, Secondary sector and Tertiary sector or Service sector. Primary sector includes agriculture, forestry and fisheries. Secondary sector includes mining, manufacturing and electric supply and construction. Tertiary sector or Service sector covers trade, transport, communication, finance, real estate and community, social and personal services.

Economists say that as the economy develops, the share of primary sector in GDP declines and that of secondary and tertiary sector increases. The growth of service sector and its contribution to income and employment generation are indicators of economic development.

Table 10.2 gives a cross-section view of the countries ranked in the ascending order of their PCI to reflect the level of development. It depicts the sectoral shares in GDP. It shows

Table 10.2: International Comparison

Country	Share of Different Sectors in GDP (%) in 1990		
	Agriculture	Manufacturing	Services
Bangladesh	38	9	46
India	31	19	40
China	27	38	31
Indonesia	22	20	38
Malaysia	21	19	44
Mexico	9	23	61
Brazil	10	26	51
United States	2	17	69
Japan	3	28	56

clearly that as income rises, the share of agriculture declines, as income increases; further, the share of manufacturing declines and that of services increases.

The service sector in the Indian economy accounted for 29 per cent of the GDP in 1950-51 (Table 10.3). This share increased to around 32 per cent in 1970-71 and to 36 per cent in 1980-81. This is as high as nearly 50 per cent in 1999-2000. The primary sector accounted for around 56 per cent of the GDP in 1950-51. This share decreased to 44.5 per cent in 1970-71 and 38.10 per cent in 1980-81. This was 23.5 per cent in 1999-2000. The secondary sector accounted for around 15 per cent of GDP in 1950-51. This share increased to 23.60 per cent in 1970-71 and to

Table 10.3: Shares of Different Sectors in GDP in India

Year	Primary	Secondary	Tertiary/Services Sector
1950-51	55.80	15.20	29.00
1960-61	45.80	20.70	33.50
1970-71	44.50	23.60	31.90
1980-81	38.10	25.90	36.00
1989-90	32.40	28.10	38.50
1990-91	30.90	30.00	39.10
1997-98	26.74	27.75	45.50
1998-99	26.82	27.01	46.17
1999-2000	23.50	27.40	49.10

Source: Government of India, *Economic Survey*, Various Issues.

around 26 per cent in 1980-81. It became nearer to 28 per cent in 1999-2000. This means that the services sector has been the major beneficiary from the falling share of the agricultural sector.

The service sector as a whole has been growing at more than 7-8 per cent a year during the nineties (Table 10.4). What is more important is the fact that whereas the primary and secondary sectors witnessed a lower growth rate than the overall growth rate, the service sector always outshined the national average growth rate. However, this was never visualized by our Constitution framers and policy-makers with the result that tax on services does not find any place in the Constitution of India. And any tax, which has not been mentioned in the Constitution belongs to the Union government.

Table 10.4: Sectoral Growth Rates

Year	Sectoral Growth Rates			
	Primary	Secondary	Tertiary	GDP
1996-97	9.6	6.8	6.6	7.5
1997-98	1.9	4.9	9.2	5.0
1998-99	6.5	3.3	8.8	6.9
1999-2000	0.7	6.0	9.4	6.4
2000-01	0.9	6.1	8.4	6.0

Source: Government of India, *Economic Survey*, Various Issues.

From a modest beginning in 1994-95, service tax has grown into a significant source of revenue, with Rs. 14,200 crore realised in 2004-05. It was budgeted at Rs. 17,500 crore in 2005-06 (BE).[13] A part of the budgeted growth is attributable to the 2-percentage point increase in the rate of tax. Continuing with the practice of bringing additional services into the tax net, the Budget for 2005-06 added the following 9 items to the list of taxable services: transport of goods through pipeline or other conduit; site preparation and clearance, excavation, earth moving and demolition services other than those provided to agriculture, irrigation and watershed development; dredging services of rivers, ports, harbours, backwaters and map making other than by government departments; cleaning services other than in relation to agriculture, horticulture, animal husbandry or dairying; membership of clubs or association; packaging services; mailing list compilation and mailing; and construction of residential complexes having more than twelve residential units of apartments together with common areas and other apartments.

Besides, the scope of existing services has also been expanded. These were: commercial or industrial construction service to include renovation of such building or civil structure, post construction completion and finishing services for such building or civil structure construction, repair, alteration renovation or restoration of pipeline or conductions; erection, commissioning or installation services to include specified installation services; maintenance or repair services to include maintenance or management of immovable properties, maintenance or repair including reconditioning or restoration undertaken as part of any contract or agreement; broadcasting services to include charges recovered by broadcasting agencies from multi-system operator and provision of direct to home signals to the customers; sound recording to include recording of sound on any media and includes post production services such as sound mixing or re-mixing; video-tape production to include recording of any programme, event or function on any media and includes post production services; taxable services provided by authorized service station to include reconditioning or restoration of motor-cars, two-wheeler and light motor vehicles, beauty parlours service to include all services provided by beauty parlours; manpower recruitment service to include supply of manpower, temporary or otherwise; franchisee service to cover all agreements by which, the franchisor grants representational rights to franchise to sell or manufacture goods or provide services identified with the franchisor; business auxiliary service to include production or processing of goods for or on behalf of the client; and outdoor catering service, to include catering from a place or premises provided, by way of tenancy or otherwise by the person receiving such services. Such measures as widening the tax base and procedures that facilitate voluntary compliance, going forward, would make service tax a buoyant source of revenue commensurate with its high share in GDP. The Budget 2006-07 besides, increasing the rate of service tax from 10 to

12 per cent, brought additional services under the tax net. These services are: ATM operations, maintenance and management, registrars, share transfer agents and bankers to an issue, sale of space or time of other than in the print media, for advertisements, sponsorships of events, other than sports events by companies, international air travel excluding economy class passenger, container services on rail excluding the railway freight charges; business support services, auctioneering; recovery agents, ship management services, travel on cruise ships and public relation management services.[14]

However, considering the growing importance of service tax, the States have started demanding the right to tax the sale and purchase of services just like the sale and purchase of goods. Therefore, there is now a move to impose an integrated tax on goods and services in the country as a whole, which may called Goods and Services Tax (GST).

FINANCES OF THE CENTRAL GOVERNMENT[15]

As Table 10.5 shows, the Central Government revenue as a proportion of GDP, has been on the decline. Although budget estimates for 2004-05 and 2005-06 have put this ratio at 9.9 per cent and 10.0 per cent respectively (compared with 9.7 per cent in 1990-91) yet the actual figures might belie this achievement. The failures on revenue mobilization front are mainly due to shortfall from tax collection. Insofar as non-tax sources are concerned, these appear to perform better than tax resources.

It is unfortunate that the revenue expenditure of the Central Government has as always been more than revenue receipts, with the result that revenue deficit has been on the rise. Expenditure on interest payments and major subsidies are the main villain of revenue deficit. Further, capital receipts of the Central Government have almost been more than capital expenditure, which may have serious implications for social sector and privatization of the economy. Then of the total expenditure, plan expenditure is the major casualty, because non-plan expenditure, being committed in nature, will have to be incurred.

Table 10.5: Finances of the Central Government (Rs. Crore)

	1990-91	2000-01	2001-02	2002-03	2003-04#	2004-05 (B.E) (prov.)@	2004-05	2005-06 (BE)
1. Revenue receipts (a+b)	54954	192605	201306	230834	263878	309322	305187	351200
(a) Tax revenue (net of State's share)	42978	136658	133532	158544	186982	233906	224857	273466
(b) Non-tax revenue	11976	55947	677774	72290	76896	75416	80330	77734
2. Revenue expenditure of which	73516	277838	301468	338713	362140	385493	384745	446512
(a) Interest payments	21498	99314	107460	117804	124088	129500	126540	133945
(b) Major subsidies	9581	25860	30447	40716	43455	42214	44633	46358
(c) Defence expenditure	10874	37238	38059	40709	43203	43517	43967	48625
3. Revenue deficit (2-1)	18562	85233	100162	107879	98262	76171	79558	95312
4. Capital receipts (a+b+c)	31971	132987	161004	182414	207490	168507	193261	163144
(a) Recovery of loans*	5712	12046	16403	34191	67265	27100	60862	12000
(b) Other receipts (mainly PSU disinvestment)	0	2125	3646	3151	16953	4000	4424	0
(c) Borrowings and other liabilities$	26259	118816	140955	145072	123272	137407	127975	151144
5. Capital expenditure	24756	47754	60842	74535**	109228**	92336	113703**	67832
6. Total expenditure [2+5=6(a)+6(b)] of which	98272	325592	362310	413248	471368	477829	498448	514344
(a) Plan expenditure	28365	82669	101194	111470	122280	145590	132160	143497
(b) Primary deficit investment	9750	-3453	-2685	-11339	-25833	11307	131	14239
7. Fiscal deficit [6-1-4(a)-4(b)]	37606	118816	140955	145072	123272	137407	127975	151144
8. Primary deficit [7-2(8)=(a)+8(b)]	16108	19502	33495	27268	-816	7907	1435	17199
(a) Primary deficit consumption	6358	22955	36180	38607	25017	-3400	1304	2960
(b) Primary deficit investment	9750	-3453	-2685	-11339	-25833	11307	131	14239
				(As per cent of GDP)				
1. Revenue receipts (a+b)	9.7	9.1	8.8	9.4	9.6	9.9	9.8	10.0
(a) Tax revenue (net of states' share)	7.6	6.5	5.9	6.5	6.8	7.5	7.2	7.7
(b) Non-tax revenue	2.1	2.7	3.0	3.0	2.8	2.4	2.6	2.2
2. Revenue expenditure	12.9	13.2	13.2	13.8	13.1	12.3	12.3	12.8
3. Revenue deficit (2-1)	3.3	4.0	4.4	4.4	3.6	2.4	2.5	2.7

(Contd...)

	1990-91	2000-01	2001-02	2002-03	2003-04#	2004-05 (BE) (prov.)@	2004-05	2005-06 (BE)
4. Capital receipts (a+b+c)	5.6	6.3	7.1	7.4	7.5	5.4	6.2	4.6
(a) Recovery of loans*	1.0	0.6	0.7	1.4	2.4	0.9	1.9	0.3
(b) Other receipts (mainly PSU disinvestment)	0.0	0.1	0.2	0.1	0.6	0.1	0.1	0.0
(c) Borrowings and other liabilities$	4.6	5.6	6.2	5.9	4.5	4.4	4.1	4.3
5. Capital expenditure	4.4	2.3	2.7	3.0	4.0	3.0	3.6	1.9
6. Total expenditure [2+5=6(a)+6(b)] of which	17.3	15.4	15.9	16.9	17.1	15.3	16.0	14.6
(a) Plan expenditure	5.0	3.9	4.4	4.6	4.4	4.7	4.2	4.1
(b) Non-plan expenditure	12.3	11.5	11.4	12.3	12.6	10.6	11.7	10.5
7. Fiscal deficit [6-1-4 (a)-4(b)]	6.6	5.6	6.2	5.9	4.5	4.4	4.1	4.3
8. Primary deficit [7-2(8)=(a)+8(b)]	2.8	0.9	1.5	1.1	0.0	0.3	0.0	0.0
(a) Primary deficit consumption	1.1	1.1	1.6	1.6	0.9	-0.1	0.0	0.1
(b) Primary deficit investment	1.7	-0.2	-0.1	-0.5	-0.9	0.4	0.0	0.4
Memorandum items								
(a) Interest receipts	8730	32811	35538	37622	38517	36950	32733	25500
(b) Dividend and profit	564	4225	7940	10910	12326	12979	15553	16092
(c) Non-plan revenue expenditure	60896	226762	23811	267144	283502	293650	297249	330530

@ Provisional and unaudited as reported by Controller General of Accounts, Department of Expenditure, Ministry of Finance.

Based on provisional actual for 2003-04.

* Includes receipts from States on account of 'debt swap' scheme for 2002-03, 2003-04 and 2004-05.

** Includes repayment to National Small Savings Fund.

$ Does not include Rs. 60,000 crore for 2004-05 (BE), Rs. 65,481 crore for 2044-05 (RE) and Rs. 80,500 crore for 2005-06(BE) to be raised under Market Stabilization Scheme, which will remain the cash balance of the Central Government and will not be used for expenditure.

Notes:

1. The ratios to GDP for 2005-06 (BE) are based on CSO's Advance Estimates. GDP at current market prices prior to 1999-2000 based on 1993-94 series and from 1999-2000 based on new 1999-2000 series.
2. The figures may not add up to the total because of rounding approximations.
3. Primary deficit consumption = Revenue deficit – interest payments + interest receipts + dividend & profits.
4. Primary deficit investment = capital expenditure – interest receipts – Dividend & profits – recovery of loans – other receipts.

Figures are exclusive of the transfer of State's share in the small savings collections.

Source: Economic Survey, 2005-06.

Coming to the sources of tax revenue of the Central Government (Table 10.6). The most healthy feature of the Central Government tax structure has been the shift from indirect taxes to direct taxes. Direct taxes constituted only 19.1 per cent of total tax revenue in 1990-91. But it has been consistently on the rise and has crossed the 40 per cent limit and is expected to touch the magic figure of 50 per cent. In case of indirect taxes under the pressure of globalization, the excise duty and customs-GDP ratios have been on the decline. But service tax has been emerging as a major source of revenue.

Table 10.6: Sources of Tax Revenue (Rs. Crore)

	1990-91 Actuals	1995-96 Actuals	2000-01 Actuals	2001-02 Actuals	2002-03 Actuals	2003-04 Actuals	2004-05 @(prov.)	2005-06 (BE)
Direct (a) tax	11024	33563	68306	69197	83085	105082	132027	177077
Personal income	5371	15592	31764	32004	36866	41379	48312	66239
Corporation tax	5335	16487	35696	36609	46172	63562	83566	110573
Indirect (b)	45158	76806	118681	116125	131284	147294	171010	192215
Customs	20644	35757	47542	40268	44852	48629	57655	53182
Excise	24514	40187	68526	72555	82310	90774	99155	121533
Service tax	0	862	2613	3302	4122	7891	14200	17500
Gross tax revenue#	57576	111224	188603	187060	216266	254348	304980	370025
			Percentages					
Direct (a)	19.1	30.2	36.2	37.0	38.4	41.3	43.3	47.9
Personal income tax	9.3	14.0	16.8	17.1	17.0	16.3	15.8	17.9
Corporation tax	9.3	14.8	18.9	19.6	21.3	25.0	27.4	29.9
Indirect (b)	78.4	69.1	62.9	62.1	60.7	57.9	56.1	51.9
Customs	35.9	32.1	25.2	21.5	20.7	19.1	18.9	14.4
Excise	42.6	36.1	36.3	38.8	38.1	35.7	32.5	32.8
Service tax	0.0	0.8	1.4	1.8	1.9	3.1	4.7	4.7
			Percentages to GDP*					
Direct (a)	1.9	2.8	3.2	3.0	3.4	3.8	4.2	5.0
Personal income tax	0.9	1.3	1.5	1.4	1.5	1.5	1.5	1.9
Corporation tax	0.9	0.9	1.7	1.6	1.9	2.3	2.7	3.1
Indirect (b)	7.9	7.9	5.6	5.1	5.4	5.3	5.5	5.4
Customs	3.6	3.0	2.3	1.8	1.8	1.8	1.8	1.5
Excise	4.3	3.4	3.3	3.2	3.4	3.3	3.2	3.4
Service tax	1.0	0.1	0.1	0.1	0.2	0.3	0.5	0.5
Total#	10.1	9.4	8.9	8.2	8.8	9.2	9.8	10.5

@ Provisional and unaudited as reported by Controller General of Accounts, Department of Expenditure, Ministry of Finance.

Includes taxes referred in (a) & (b) and taxes of Union Territories and "other" taxes.

* Refers to gross domestic product at current market prices.

Notes:

1. Direct taxes also includes taxes pertaining to expenditure, interest, wealth, gift and estate duty.
2. The ratios to GDP for 2005-06 (BE) based on CSO's Advance Estimates. GDP at current market prices prior to 1999-2000 based on 1993-94 series and from 1999-2000 based on new 1999-2000 series.

Source: *Economic Survey*, 2005-06.

FINANCES OF STATE GOVERNMENTS[16]

The finances of State governments traditionally follow a pattern similar to that of the Centre, albeit with a lag. Recently with States' own tax receipts stagnant at around 5-6 per cent of GDP and declining transfers from Centre on the one hand and high level of growth of total disbursement (around 15–19 per cent of GDP) on the other, the deterioration in revenue and fiscal deficits could not be reversed significantly. As a proportion of GDP, revenue deficit of the States shot up from 0.9 per cent of GDP in 1990-91 to 2.5 per cent in 2000-01 (Table 10.7). The proportion declined to 2.2 per cent in each of the two years 2002-03 and 2003-04 and is placed at 1.4 per cent in 2004-05. Following the TFC award, which includes a quantum jump in grants-in-aid, the position is budgeted to improve to 0.7 per cent of GDP in 2005-06. As a proportion of GDP, fiscal deficit, after increasing from 3.3 per cent in 1990-91 to 4.5 per cent in 2003-04, declined to 4.0 per cent in 2004-05. It is budgeted at 3.1 per cent of GDP in 2005-06. The budgeted revenue and fiscal deficit as proportion of GDP are very proximate to the fiscal consolidation goals enunciated by the TFC. The outstanding liabilities of States were Rs. 10,40,834 crore (33.3 per cent of GDP) in 2004-05 and are placed at Rs. 11,52,530 crore (32.7 per cent of GDP) in 2005-06 (BE) (Table 10.4). With the TFC's debt consolidation and write-off scheme in place, the position might improve further.[17]

While the most recent indicators of State finances show a somewhat improved picture, the causative factors of fiscal deterioration have to be addressed to sustain this progress and keep the balance at the desired level. The causative factors are growing burden of interest payment, pensions liabilities, losses of State PSUs, lack of proper user charges, and lack of buoyancy in taxes. With the successful introduction of VAT by 25 States/UTs and the TFC's incentive to enact State level FRBM legislations, the deepening of State level reforms contributed to the foundation of fiscal reform and their sustainability in the States.

Table 10.7: Receipts and Disbursements of State Government (Rs. Crore)

	1990-91	2000-01	2001-02	2002-03	2003-04	2004-05	2005-06
I. Total receipts (A-B)	91160	349544	373886	425073	527097	588810	581684
A. Revenue receipts (1-2)	66467	237953	255675	280339	316535	384439	430270
1. Tax receipts of which State's own tax revenue	44586	168715	180312	198798	226999	268170	305248
2. Non-tax receipts of	30344	21881	117981	69238	128097	75363	142143
which interest receipts	81541	159921	89536	187415	116269	215245	125022
B. Capital receipts	2403	24693	11438	111591	9205	118211	9502
of which Recovery of	144734	8617	210562	11827	204371	8299	151413
loans & advances	1501	6898	7766	3905	16414	9668	5505
II. Total disbursements (a-b-c)	91088	346971	377311	420461	526023	594129	577986
(a) Revenue	71776	291522	314863	335450	377681	428741	455040
(b) Capital	13556	43717	50145	70664	122429	144616	108904
(c) Loans and advances	5756	11732	12303	14347	25913	20771	14041
III. Revenue deficit	5309	53569	59188	55111	61145	44302	24770
IV. Gross Fiscal deficit	18797	89532	95994	102123	123070	123635	110070
			As per cent of GDP)				
I. Total receipts (A-B)	16.0	16.6	16.4	17.4	19.1	18.0	16.5
A. Revenue receipts (1-2)	11.7	11.3	11.2	11.4	11.5	12..3	12.2
1. Tax recipts of which	7.8	8.0	7.9	8.1	8.2	8.6	8.6
State's own tax revenue	5.3	5.6	5.6	5.8	5.8	6.0	6.1
2. Non-tax receipts of which	3.8	3.3	3.3	3.3	3.2	3.7	3.5
interest receipts	0.4	0.5	0.4	0.4	0.3	0.4	0.2
B. Capital receipts of which	4.3	5.3	5.2	5.9	7.6	6.5	4.3
Recovery of loans & advances	0.3	0.3	0.3	0.2	0.6	0.3	0.2
II. Total disbursements (a-b-c)	16.0	16.5	16.5	17.2	19.1	19.0	16.4
(a) Revenue	12.6	03.8	13.8	13.7	13.7	13.7	12.9
(b) Capital	2.4	2.1	2.2	2.9	4.4	4..6	3.1
(c) Loans and advances	1.0	0.6	0.5	0.6	0.9	0.7	0.4
III. Revenue deficit	0.9	2.5	2.6	2.2	2.2	1.4	0.7
IV. Gross fiscal deficit	3.3	4.2	4.2	4.2	4.5	4.0	3.1

Notes:

1. The ratios to GDP for 2005-06 (BE) are based on CSO's Advance Estimates. GDP at current market prices prior to 1999-2000 based on 1993-94 series and from 1999-2000 based on new 1999-2000 series.
2. Capital receipts (including public account) are on a net basis.
3. Capital disbursements exclude heads of public account.

Source: *Economic Survey*, 2005-06.

Table 10.8: Outstanding Liabilities of States

Year	Total Liabilities (Rs. Crore)	Col. (2) as per cent of GDPs
1990-91	1,28,095	22.5
1991-92	1,46,966	22.5
1992-93	1,68,293	22.5
1993-94	1,87,912	21.9
1994-95	2,17,023	21.4
1995-96	2,50,813	21.1
1996-97	2,86,704	21.0
1997-98	3,36,347	22.1
1998-99	3,97,370	22.8
1999-2000	5,05,009	25.0
2000-01	5,92,743	28.1
2001-02	6,85,474	30.0
2002-03	7,97,684	32.6
2003-04	9,22,263	33.4
2004-05 (RE)	10,40,834	33.3
2005-06 (BE)#	11,52,530	32.7

The ratios to GDP for 2005-06 (BE) are based on CSO's Advance Estimates. GDP at current market prices prior to 1999-2000, based on 1993-94 series and from 1999-2000 based on new 1999-2000 series.

Note: Total liabilities have been revised by broadening its composition to include reserve funds, deposits and advances and contingency funds.

Source: Economic Survey, 2005-06.

State Level Reforms

On the recommendation of the Eleventh Finance Commission (EFC), Government of India implemented a scheme called the 'States Fiscal Reforms Facility (2000-01 to 2004-05)' to incentivise the States to undertake fiscal reforms. Under this scheme, which came to an end on March 31, 2005, all the 28 States had submitted their medium term fiscal reforms programme and all but government of Goa entered into memorandum of understanding with Government of India, individually. As on March 31, 2005, an amount of Rs. 7,217 crore was released to States from incentive fund (Total fund Rs. 10,608 crore) on the basis of improvement in revenue deficit as a proportion of revenue receipts. States (excluding NCT

Delhi), in aggregate, have registered an improvement of 17.95 percentage points in the ratio of revenue deficit to total revenue receipts during EFC award period (2000-01 to 2004-05), over the base year 1999-2000.

As per the latest information available for 2004-05 (pre-Actual), some States, namely Bihar, Chhattisgarh, Jammu and Kashmir, Karnataka, Madhya Pradesh, Manipur, Mizoram, Nagaland and Sikkim, are expected to be revenue surplus. The TFC discontinued this facility beyond March 31, 2005 and suggested a debt consolidation and waiver scheme. The TFC's recommendations for restructuring public finances envisage a positive growth dividend through fall in dissavings. The major reform initiative that underpins the TFC award is this recommendation for a debt consolidation and waiver scheme for States linked to fiscal responsibility. Under the general debt relief scheme applicable to all States during the award of the TFC, all Central loans, contracted till March 31, 2004 and outstanding as on March 31, 2005, get consolidated as loans for a fresh period of 20 years payable in 20 equal annual instalments at reduced interest rate of 7.5 per cent effective from the year in which their FRBM legislation is enacted by the States. TFC has estimated that this would benefit the States in the entire period of its award through lower interest payments of Rs. 21,276 crore and through relief on deferment of principal repayment of Rs. 11,929 crore. A second scheme of debt write-off under the TFC award linked to fiscal performance is calibrated in a manner that incentivises a self-laid down fiscal correction path on a year-on-year basis leading to elimination of revenue deficit by 2008-09 and containing fiscal deficit.

Table 10.9: State Governments—Revenue Deficit as a Proportion of Total Revenue Receipts (RD/TRR)

	1999-2000	2000-01	2001-02	2002-03	2003-04	2004-05
RD/TRR	26.88	23.79	24.22	20.89	20.51	12.29

As on February 2, 2006, 18 State governments had passed their FRBM Acts and 13 States had drawn up their fiscal correction path. States have also strived to explore all possibilities of revenue generation, while at the same time trying to prioritize their expenditure needs. A Central Monitoring Committee, set up for the purpose, has recommended consolidation of Central loans to 12 States, namely Andhra Pradesh, Assam, Haryana, Chhattisgarh, Karnataka, Kerala, Madhya Pradesh, Maharashtra, Manipur, Orissa, Rajasthan and Tamil Nadu. Besides debt liability, there has been a significant increases in the outstanding guarantees given by State governments during the past few years. However, to control the proliferation of State government guarantees, as per the latest information available, nine States have imposed cap on guarantees—six (Goa, Gujarat, Karnataka, Kerala, Sikkim and West Bengal) of the statutory variety, and three (Assam, Orissa and Rajasthan) of the administrative kind in pursuance of the accepted recommendations of the TFC. External loans to State governments are now to be given on a back-to-back basis, *i.e.* on the same terms and conditions (including interest rate maturity commitment charges and foreign exchange variation-risk) as it is received by the Central government.

Value Added Tax (VAT)

Following the June 18, 2004 decision of the Empowered Committee (EC) of State Finance Ministers to implement State-level VAT from April 1, 2005. 25 States/UTs had introduced VAT to replace the sales tax by December 31, 2005. Andaman & Nicobar Islands and Lakshadweep do not have a sales tax. The eight States/UTs yet to introduce the VAT are Chhattisgarh, Gujarat, Jharkhand, Madhya Pradesh, Pondicherry, Rajasthan, Tamil Nadu and Uttar Pradesh. Since sales tax/VAT is essentially a State subject, the Central Government is playing the role of a facilitator for the successful implementation of VAT. A formula has also been finalized in consultation with the States for providing compensation to them, during the first three years, for any loss on account of introduction of VAT. Technical and financial support has also been provided to the States for VAT computerization, publicity and awareness and other related aspects. Despite the initial transitional problems and lack of clarity, the implementation of VAT has been smooth and the results encouraging. The EC constantly review the progress and tries to sort out the difficulties. The EC has advised the States to constantly interact with trade and industry to remove their apprehensions, if any, and to ensure that the benefits of VAT due to input tax credit and reduction in tax rates (wherever applicable) are passed on to the consumers. The EC is also persuading the remaining States/UTs to implement VAT at the earliest.

The initial trend in revenue collection in the VAT implementing States is quite encouraging. During the first 7 months of VAT implementation (April-October 2005), the total revenue (provisional) for VAT implementing States showed an increase of around 14.4 per cent, which is higher than the compound annual growth rate of these States for the last 5 years. Up to January 15, 2006, VAT compensation claims for about Rs. 1,674 crore had been filed by eight States, out of which claims for Rs. 1,317 crore had been settled. Based on trends so far, the compensation liability for the year 2005-06 is likely to be contained within BE. The non-implementation of VAT by eight States/UTs is creating complications and may also lead to undesirable diversion of trade and business from one State to another. Further, the benefits of the VAT system like simple and uniform tax structure all over the country and achieving a common market for goods would not accrue until all the States/UTs implement VAT. In view of this, it is imperative that the remaining eight States/UTs also implement VAT at the earliest. While the VAT Acts of the States follow a broadly uniform pattern, there is a considerable amount of diversity in the VAT rules and procedures. The internationally accepted coding system is the harmonized system of commodity description and coding (HS). While foreign trade and tariffs associated are based on HS, VAT system is not. The EC is looking into this issue of aligning the classification system of VAT with HS.

With input tax credit being allowed in respect of locally purchased inputs involved in inter-State transactions, the Central Sales Tax (CST) reforms have already begun. However, the CST is basically inconsistent with the concept of VAT and needs to be phased out. In fact, it has already been decided, in principle, to phase out the CST. But before doing that, it is essential that the system of information exchange between the States, namely, TINXSYs, is put in place. Further, successful implementation of CST reforms would require that all the States/UTs first successfully implement the State-level VAT. Another critical issue involved in phasing out CST is that of compensating the States, particularly the developed States where a lot of inter-State sales originate, for revenue losses on account of such a phase out. During 2004-05, the total revenue collection from CST for all States was around Rs. 15,100 crore. If CST is phased out, this revenue will be permanently loss and, hence, their insistence on a compensation mechanism on a permanent basis through alternative taxation powers. The Empowered Committee is deliberating on this issue. The EC is expected to finalize its recommendations and place the same before the Central government, after which the Government of India will take an appropriate decision.

Consolidated General Government

The macro-economic impact of the state of public finances are best analysed through the construct 'Consolidated General Government'. With very limited data on local finances and the grant dependent nature of local bodies in India, the aggregation State and Central Government finances poses some problems. After due process of adjustment for the inter-Governmental transfers, the data are usually taken as the General Government Finances. As a proportion of GDP, tax receipts of the General Government fell from 15.4 per cent in 1990-91 to 13.8 per cent in 2001-02. Thereafter the proportion picked up to reach 15.8 per cent in 2004-05 (RE) and is budgeted at 16.4 per cent in 2004-05 (RE) and is budgeted at 16.4 per cent in 2005-06 (Table 10.5). With total expenditure at around 30 per cent of GDP, revenue and fiscal deficit remained intractably high. In the recent years there has been a significant reduction in revenue and fiscal deficits. This reduction was possible through the harmonized fiscal policies being followed by both Central and State Governments. Sustaining this harmony in fiscal balances is critical requirement for reaping the growth dividend through macro-economic linkages.

PUBLIC EXPENDITURE IN INDIA

Public expenditure is an essential part of the welfare states. Since independence public expenditure has gained a significant place in the country to pull the economy out of turmoils. Public expenditure regulates the economic activities and helps to attain the long-run and short-run objectives of economic development. This is the reason that there is a continuous upward trend in both revenue and expenditure of the Indian Government. Actually, the government has been widening its activities in social and economic spheres to bring economic growth as early as possible. Even in the post-reform period public expenditure on social sector has been on the rise. Government cannot leave the provisions like education, medical and public health, social security and poverty alleviation programmes in the hands of the private sector.

Broadly, public expenditure in India can be classified into two parts:

A. Expenditure on Revenue Account.

B. Expenditure on Capital Account.

A. Expenditure on Revenue Account of the Central Government

Generally, major heads of revenue expenditure are being shown in the budget of the Central Government as defence services, civil services, grants-in-aid, interest payments, fiscal services and economic services. Revenue expenditure are generally met out of the revenue receipts of the government like tax revenue and non-tax sources. However, since eighties an unhealthy trend has developed whereby even capital account receipts like borrowings and disinvestment proceeds are used for meeting revenue expenditure needs.

(a) **Defence Expenditure:** According to Adam Smith: "Defence is more important than opulence." Therefore, it is the most important item in the case of every government. For national wealth to save against external aggression and internal disorder, defence expenditure is must. It is constantly increasing as the modern warfare instruments are becoming costlier and more sophisticated.

(b) **Civil Services:** Before independence, the aim of the government was the maintenance of law and order whereas after independence, it was sought to change from "law and order state" to "welfare state". Thus, expenditure in this sector has been rising continuously. It includes expenditure on general administration, justice, election and on the Office of Comptroller and Auditor General. Besides, other types of expenditure are on Secretariat and attached offices of Ministries of Education and Social Welfare, Health and Family Welfare, etc.

(c) **Grants-in-Aid to States:** State governments cannot work properly without the help of Central government as the expenditures of State governments have gone up because of the fact that most of the welfare programmes fall within the jurisdiction of the States, whereas all elastic and growing sources of revenue rest with the Central government.

(d) **Interest Payments:** This includes expenditure on the payment of interest on the outstanding debt. In the recent years, these payments have shown the rising trend on account of the fact that the government borrowed extensively in the past, which has necessitated the interest payment now.

(e) **Fiscal Services:** Collection of taxes and other duties also entail huge public expenditure. Directorate of Customs and Excise Duties, and Directorate of Income Tax are the two major departments of the Central government involved in the collection of taxes.

(f) **Economic Services:** After Independence, it has become the foremost need of the government to spend on economic services to develop the economy at a rapid speed. In includes the expenditure on Department of Commerce, Shipping and Transport, Irrigation, Energy,

Chemicals and Fertiliser, Company Affairs and Electronics, Industry, Agriculture, etc.

(B) Expenditure on Capital Account

Expenditure on capital account consists of expenditure for the acquisition of assets such as land, buildings, machinery, equipments, etc. Expenditure on renewals and repairs of machinery, increase in foodgrain stocks and inventories, commuted pensions, etc. also constitute capital account expenditure.

Here, we must remember that revenue and capital account expenditure is known as economic classification. As already mentioned this economic classification can be converted into economic and functional expenditure depending upon the break-up of total expenditure into various functions like civil, fiscal, economic, etc. performed by the government.

A brief break-up of the data on total public expenditure into revenue account and capital account is given in the Table 10.10.

Table 10.10: Break-up of Public Expenditure of the Central Government

(Rs. Crore)

	Revenue Expenditure					
Years	Interest payments	Major subsidies	Defence expenditure	Total*	Capital Expenditure	Total
1990-91	21498	9581	10874	73516	24756	98272
1999-2000	90294	22678	35216	249078	48975	298053
2000-01	99314	25860	37238	277838	477754	325592
2001-02	107460	30447	38059	301468	60842	362310
2002-03	117804	40716	40709	339628	74534	414162
2003-04 (R.E.)	124261	43569	42597	362887	110628	474255
2004-05 (B.E.)	129500	42214	43517	385493	92336	477829

* This includes other revenue expenditure like salaries, pensions, goods and services, etc.

Source: GOI, *Economic Survey,* 2004-05.

It may also be mentioned that public expenditure in India sometimes is also divided into plan and non-plan expenditure or development and non-developmental expenditure. This has been explained under the heading, "Classification of Public Expenditure".

Expenditure Restructuring

In restructuring expenditures, there is need to make reference to the basic objectives of government intervention in economic activities, as also to the basic objectives for assignment of responsibilities as between Central and sub-national governments. It is also important to relate government expenditures to outcomes in terms of the quality, reach and impact of government services. This would be facilitated if governments focus more on their primary responsibilities rather than spreading resources thinly in many areas where the private sector can provide the necessary services. The primary role of government is to provide public goods like defence, law and order and general administration. This represents one kind of market failure. The role of governments extends to merit goods and services with large positive externalities like education and health. The services should be assigned to the State government if the scope of public goods is limited to regions or if externalities are more local in character like the health services. Admittedly there may be many examples of benefit spillovers, some of which can be internalized to the State level decision-makers by a suitable scheme of grants. There is a felt need to examine whether the Central government is not partaking in many responsibilities that legitimately belong to the domain of the States. Governments at both levels have also stepped into the provision of many private goods, which adversely affects the quantum and quality of service in regard to public and merit goods. Two key elements of restructuring government expenditure relate to public-private partnership in providing infrastructure and a reduction of Central government's expenditures on subjects listed as State responsibilities.[18]

From Expenditure to Outcomes

The conventional budget exercises have focused on allocation of resources to different heads, without taking into account how these government expenditures get translated into outputs and outcomes. Outputs are the direct result of government expenditure and outcomes are the final results. Thus, in the context of education, opening a new school or appointing a new teacher is an output and reduction in the rate of illiteracy is an outcome. Issues of efficiency require consideration whether the same outcome can be achieved at lower costs and whether the same costs can produce better outcomes. A critical part of budgetary reforms must include information on the relationship between expenditures and the corresponding performance in producing real results. As in the past, there have been attempts at introducing performance budgeting; such endeavors have receded in importance. There is need to bring back performance budgeting as an integral part of the preparation and evaluation of budgets, both for the Centre and the States. Thus, the management of public expenditures should be guided by economy, efficiency and effectiveness.

According to Kelkar Committee Report the broad strategy for expenditure reforms may be summarized as comprising of four elements.[19]

1. Public goods versus subsidies: A greater portion of expenditure needs to devoted to legitimate public goods, as opposed to transfers and subsidies. The plan versus non-plan or the capital versus revenue classifications need to be re-examined in this light.

2. Central versus local public goods: In the spirit of the 73rd amendment, resources that are used for the production of local public goods, such as water, sanitation, and primary education, should be transferred to Panchayati Raj Institutions, who have better incentive to spend effectively, and have better knowledge about local preferences, local problems and alternative production technologies.

3. Focus on public goods outcomes: The public finance system in India has traditionally focused on expenditure. There is a need for a greater focus on public goods outcomes.

4. Improvements in institutional mechanisms: The provision of public goods can often be achieved more effectively through the use of the private sector in production. The role of public-private partnerships needs to be extended into a broader range of public goods.

GROWTH IN PUBLIC DEBT: CENTRE AND STATES[20]

The combined debt-GDP ratio of the Central and State governments at the end of 2002-03 was about 76 per cent of GDP, subject to some qualifications. First, the government budget documents give the Centre's external debt as evaluated at the historical exchange rates, *i.e.*, exchange rates in the years in which the debt was incurred. Since the exchange rate has depreciated over the years, it makes a difference if external debt is evaluated at the current exchange rates. This difference was as large as nearly 11 per cent in 1991-92. However, over the years, this difference has steadily come down. In 2002-03 if external debt is evaluated at the current exchange rates, about 5.6 per cent would need to be added to the debt-GDP ratio in 2002-03 to 81.6 per cent. The second qualification is that in accounting for the liabilities of the State governments, certain liabilities of reserve funds and deposits are not included. In 2002-03, about 3.4 percentage points of GDP needs to be added on this account, taking the overall debt-GDP ratio to 85 per cent. These figures do not include contingent liabilities, which amount to more than 11 per cent of GDP.

Even if we focus on the more conventional budgetary figure of debt without these qualifications, it is striking how the growth in debt-GDP ratio has accelerated since 1996-97 when it was 56.3 per cent, which was only marginally above the EFC's stipulated target. During the period of 1995-96 to 2002-03, the combined debt-GDP ratio rose from 56.3 per cent to 76 per cent in 2002-03, *i.e.*, an increase of a little less than 20 percentage points in a span of 6 years. This is an unprecedented increase in the growth of the debt-GDP ratio in such a short span of time. One way of looking at the source of increase in the debt-GDP ratio during this period is to decompose the increase in terms of the contribution of cumulated primary deficits and that of the differential between growth and interest rate. For three consecutive years, *viz.*, 2000-01, 2001-02 and 2002-03, the nominal growth rate fell below the effective interest rate. In these years, instead of absorbing the impact of primary deficits, the growth-interest differential, being negative, worked in the reverse by adding to the debt-GDP ratio. For the period 1996-97 to 2002-03, therefore, the excess of growth over interest could not absorb any part of the impact of cumulated primary deficits, the benefit in the first three years being negated by the opposite effect in the later three years. The entire increase, therefore, was due to accumulation of primary deficits, which remained unabsorbed by any excess of growth over interest rates.

High levels of debt-GDP ratio result in high interest payments relative to revenue receipts. Since interest payments are committed expenditures, revenue deficits are bound to increase when revenue receipts to GDP ratios remain sluggish. This has the effect of lowering the saving rate on the one hand and increasing the fiscal deficit on the other to maintain primary expenditures. Eventually, these changes have the potential of developing into a spiral of rising fiscal deficit. This gives rise to the issue of sustainability of debt.

Government debt is the outcome of accumulation of borrowings which are used to finance fiscal deficits. If the revenue account is balanced, the entire fiscal deficit would be spent on capital expenditures. Such investment can provide direct as well as indirect returns. The direct returns are in the form of interest receipts or dividends. The indirect returns are in the form of returns when government investment stimulates growth, which also results in higher revenue receipts. Debt becomes a problem when the increase in revenue receipts, whether direct or indirect, is not adequate to cover the interest liabilities that are required to service the debt. When large interest payments, remaining uncovered by an increase in revenue receipts, result in growing revenue deficits, the portion of fiscal deficit that is used for revenue expenditures becomes progressively larger and any revenue increases linked with increased expenditures remain small. Eventually, debt becomes unsustainable and the country is said to have entered the stage of debt trap.

Does India Face a Debt Trap?

If we examine the breakdown of public debt into internal and external the country seems to be in comfortable position insofar as the external debt is concerned.

For example, the external public debt of India was $ 101.97 billion in September 2002 which amounted to 20.1 per cent of the GDP. The debt servicing burden was 13.8 per cent of current receipts in 2001-02. This is a comfortable position when compared to countries which have run into debt problems. The component of short-term debt too has been declining, easing the repayment schedule. The external balance has significantly improved and foreign exchange reserves are now nearly more than $ 150 billion or for more than one year import requirements. After 24 years there was a current account surplus in 2001-02. In fact, India has recently become a creditor to the International Monetary Fund. According to all indicators, India does not have any problem with its external public debt. This has been recognized even by credit rating agencies. But it should be mentioned here that India has already entered a debt-trap like situation in 1991, when it accepted the conditional loans from the IMF and World Bank.* However, the country's internal public debt presents a different picture.

A continuous and sharp rise in budgetary deficit and consequently internal public debt poses a serious problem. The size of the Central government's debt was Rs. 2,865 crore at the end of 1950-51, Rs. 1,021,029 crore in 1999-2000 and an estimated Rs. 17,80,063 crore in 2003-04. Adding State governments borrowing, the total debt may exceed the GDP.

The combined budget deficit of the Central and State governments is more than 10 per cent of the GDP.

The debt servicing bill of the Centre in 2003-04 was Rs. 2,88,599 crore and out this, interest payments took away 50 per cent of the revenues.

---

* For detail analysis, see the section on 'Fiscal Crisis of 1991 and Fiscal Sector Reforms' in this Chapter.

A major part of the borrowings go to meet current consumption expenditure such as salaries, pensions and interest payments and do not add to capital assets. This is due to poor revenue collections which are inadequate to cover even routine expenditure.

The combined tax-GDP ratio of the Centre and States shows a declining trend from 16 per cent in 1999-2000 to an estimated 14 per cent in 2005-06, though some improvement were expected in 2006-07.

It is true that the government has not so far defaulted on any of its payment obligations. But the threat of a debt trap is to be examined over the medium and longer time span. All the indicators reveal a trend of growing mismatch between revenue and expenditure and the resultant mismatch between increase in fiscal deficits and the capacity to service the growing debts without jeopardising growth. If the present sluggishness in revenue mobilization and uncontrolled, unproductive and inefficient spending continue, public debt is likely to pose a problem in the medium term. However, the country can still avoid such a contingency if it acts now to correct the fundamental weaknesses in the fiscal policy and management. The recently enacted Fiscal Responsibility and Budget Management Act provides an opportunity to address these issues.

FISCAL CRISIS OF 1991 AND THE FISCAL SECTOR REFORMS[21]

The Structural Adjustment Programme (SAP) or New Economic Policy Reforms (NEP) were adopted in 1991 in response to a severe, unprecedented crisis in the Indian Economy. It was considered basically an external payments crisis. The crisis was reflected in the loss of international investor-financier confidence as India was put on credit watch by several rating agencies. It became more difficult to borrow from the international markets. There was a sharp decline in the foreign exchange reserves, which despite sizeable borrowing from the IMF and World Bank, touched a low of Rs. 3,414 crore in 1991-92 which was barely equal to the import bill for less than a fortnight. The drying up of commercial loans in 1990-91 was accompanied by a net outflow of NRI deposits which began in

October 1990 and was reversed only in January 1992. It was officially recognized that this crisis was not, however, due simply to a deterioration in the trade account, it was accompanied by other adverse developments on the capital account.

As a result of large scale withdrawal of NRI deposits and fall in remittances, the reduced surplus on the invisible account was no longer able to meet India's huge trade deficit. The outflow of Foreign Currency Non-Resident (FCNR) deposits increased from $ 59 million a month in October-December 1990 to $ 76 million in January-March 1991 and $ 310 million in April-June 1991. The Indian exporters were delaying the bringing in of their receipts in expectation of a devaluation. As much as 30 to 40 per cent of India's export earnings during the 1980s had to be earmarked for debt-servicing, while India's exports were able to pay for just a little over 65 per cent of the import bill during 1985-90. In such a situation as fresh borrowing had dried up. India seemed to be heading "for the first time in our history towards default on debt servicing in June 1991". This was considered at the government level an unmitigated disaster as it was believed that its ramifications are never confined to debt alone, leading to a breakdown in credit availability, severe trade disruption and severe and prolonged import compression which results in shortages and industrial dislocation and in very high inflation. Clearly, efforts and methods of avoiding the dreaded default received a high priority for Indian economic management of continued borrowing from the rest of the world.

Related to the BOP crisis India faced a huge fiscal deficit including a large and growing component of deficit on the revenue account. It disturbed the macro-economic balance and crippled state capability to lead and manage the economy. This trend became stronger during mid-1980s and continued unabated as the liberalized, debt-financed growth processes were continued. By 1990-91, the combined fiscal deficit of the Union and States became 10.1 per cent of GDP and the level of the former was 8.2 per cent. Under these conditions price stability was seriously undermined and while the wholesale price index increased by 12.1 per cent in 1990-91, the consumer price index increased at even faster rate of 13.6 per cent. The price situation, eroding people's purchasing power, was putting pressure on the macro-economic stability, public finance and external balance and also posing a political threat to the government.

Faced with this three-pronged crisis, the government went in for frequent borrowing accommodation and withdrawals from the IMF aggregating to $4,366 million or Rs. 9,423 crore during July-September 1990 and March 1992. These borrowings involved the acceptance by the Indian government of the IMF conditionalities, which have broadly been defined as the idea that international public resources should be used to induce policy reform. It is implied that under this kind of policy lending the international institutions have the "ownership of policies". They make the crisis of default-facing countries dependent on continued, growing borrowing to accept these policies. In any case two major lendings by the IMF to India during the 1980s had already made India "dependent on high conditionality borrowing".

There were some other attendant developments in early 1990s, which exacerbated the crisis syndrome. One is the political instability at the Union government level. There was a short-lived minority government, which was followed by a hung parliament leading to another minority government in which both the Prime Minister and the Finance Minister were elected to Parliament after assuming office. Then the imports of petroleum products increased from an average of Rs. 499 crore per month in June-August 1990 to Rs. 1221 crore per month during the rest of 1990. This was in part owing to a sharp rise in world oil prices following the Gulf Crisis. Meanwhile the Soviet collapse removed both a sizeable export market and an ideological prop of the Indian variant of statism. With a sharp fall in the foreign exchange reserves, "emergency action" was mounted to prevent default. The government sold in May 1991, 20 tonnes of gold abroad with an option to repurchase it after six months. In July 1991, another 47 tonnes of gold was shipped to Bank of England in order to raise $600 million. In view of this type of factors, along with the poor prospects for the growth of India's exports and adverse global economic circumstances facing India, India's credit rating was lowered to BA2 in December

1991 and did not change even up to 1994. The external imbalance and crisis have to be seen in the context of the continuous rise in both trade deficit and current account deficit after 1988-89, the disappearance of the cushion of net invisible earnings and increasing the role of external borrowing. But the composition and terms and conditions of external borrowings also contributed to the intensification of the external liquidity crisis. The proportion of short-term loans to long-term loans has reached a very high level during the 1980s, especially in the later half it ranged between 27 per cent and 54 per cent. Similarly, the ratio of undisbursed private debt to disbursed private debt during the period 1985-86 to 1989-90 ranged between 326 per cent to 382 per cent. In addition, interest chargeable went up following her downgrading by the credit rating agencies. So much so that India borrowed from abroad on variable rates of interest as well. Then a good deal of borrowing was done without regard to the impact of this borrowing on the borrower's capacity to repay. As Bimal Jalan, the RBI Governor, brings out that, "External commercial borrowings were permitted liberally to meet foreign exchange requirements of capital intensive investment. Commercial borrowings became a substitute for domestic savings to finance low productivity in investment, with a low export-potential in public and private sector." Clearly, export earnings inadequate to finance imports could hardly provide any means of debt-servicing and necessitated further borrowings. Thus India clearly entered a debt-trap.

These indeed were some really daunting difficulties. The need for continued borrowing was so intense that default would have made the perennially foreign exchange deficient Indian economy face large scale dislocation. More or less inelastic import demand for energy, raw material components, equipment, technology, etc. limited the options available to India. Thus re-opening the blocked channels of borrowing and reestablished the ability to borrow became the major concern of the government. However, it may be noted that the default is as much a matter of concern to the borrowers as it is to lenders, in the sense that the contagion of default spreads and disrupts both financial and real economy in the latter countries as well. Thus the recent experience of Russia, Indonesia, Argentina, etc. discloses the lender too rush in to avoid/reduced the default by rescheduling or fresh large lending with or without conditionality. The question basically boils down to on what terms and who is able to extract what price for the mutually beneficial act to avoiding large scale disruption of international financial markets. The Indian authorities seem to have overlooked this concern and anxiety of the lenders. India accepted in haste the conditionalities of IMF and World Bank and adopted the New Economic Policy (NEP).

Now Coming to Specific Factors which led to the Fiscal Crisis

As already stated the fiscal deterioration had started in 1990 with inadequate nature of tax receipts and almost nil return from public sector investments. However, fiscal consolidations after a promising beginning in the early 1990, started faltering from 1997-98. Fiscal deficit of the Central Government as a proportion of Gross Domestic Product, after its decline from 6.6 per cent in 1990-91 to 4.1 per cent in 1996-97, rose every year to reach 6.2 per cent in 2001-02. Progress in fiscal consolidation resumed in 2002. According to provisional data, in 2003-04, the ratio of fiscal deficit at 4.6 per cent was lower than the budget estimate of 5.6 per cent. A further improvement in this ratio to 4.4 per cent was budgeted for 2004-05.

The fiscal deficit during the 2004-05 period stood at a whopping sum of Rs. 1,51,144 crore, *i.e.* 4.4 per cent of the Gross Domestic Product as on March 2005. The curve has risen sharply from the year 1997-98 and assumed uncontrollable proportions. All economic experts including World Bank, International Monetary Fund, Moody's Standard & Poor's, Fiscal Commission and the Reserve Bank of India agree that high fiscal deficit lowers growth. The Government also believes so and therefore, the parliament adopted the Fiscal Regulation and Budget Management (FRBM) Act in July 2004 which requires the government to try and lower revenue deficit to zero and fiscal deficit to 3.0 per cent by progressively reducing revenue deficit every year by 0.5 per cent and fiscal deficit by 0.3 per cent. However, the 2005-06 budget fell short of FRBM requirement. The revenue deficit remained static at 2.7 per cent though fiscal deficit declined by 0.3 per cent.

Revenue Deficit at the Centre

After witnessing a trend similar to that in fiscal deficit until 1996-97, the deterioration in revenue deficit was much sharper in subsequent years. The rise in revenue deficit continued till 2001-02, when it reached 4.4 per cent of Gross Domestic Product. Revenue deficit declined to 3.6 per cent of Gross Domestic Product in 2003-04, but even at this level, it was higher than the level of 3.3 per cent of Gross Domestic Product observed in the pre-reform year of 1990-91. The increasing share of revenue deficit in fiscal deficit distinctly reveals the deterioration in the composition of the fiscal deficit and in the quality of expenditure. The share of revenue deficit in fiscal deficit had risen from 49.4 per cent in 1990-91 to 78.0 per cent in 2003-04, which was sought to be reversed in 2004-05 by targeting a lower revenue deficit of 2.5 per cent of Gross Domestic Product in the Budget estimates.

The Government had to borrow in order to finance current expenditure which lead to an increase in public debt. Interest payments swallow a major part of the tax revenue. Reduction in revenue deficit increase national savings. When savings are used for investment, it leads to increases in national income.

Fiscal Situation of States

The Gross Fiscal Deficit of States had not assumed alarming proportion till 1989-90. The Gross Fiscal Deficit of States started rising from 1990-91, especially for States like Bihar, Gujarat, Andhra Pradesh, Karnataka, Maharashtra, Uttar Pradesh and West Bengal. The rise was not sharp upto 1997-98 in most of the States except in case of Andhra Pradesh, Madhya Pradesh and Tamil Nadu where it doubled from Rs. 2,427.80 crore, Rs. 1,820.60 crore and Rs. 2,121.70 crore respectively in 1997-98 to Rs. 5,705.60 crore, Rs. 4,126.70 crore and Rs. 4,777.10 crore respectively in 1998-99.

With the combined Gross Fiscal Deficit of States reaching Rs. 74,253.80 crore in 1989-99, the situation called for stringent measures so that the Gross Fiscal Deficit of States is reduced, and does not go beyond control. There was, in fact, a reduction in the Gross Fiscal Deficit of States like Andhra Pradesh, Haryana, Himachal Pradesh, Madhya Pradesh and Punjab from 1998-99 to 1999-2000. But the reduction was marginal and was offset by an increase in other States to take the combined figure from Rs. 74,253.80 crore to Rs. 91,480.30 crore in the said years.

The current position of Gross Fiscal Deficit of States shows an alarming situation. Uttar Pradesh and West Bengal show a Gross Fiscal Deficit of Rs. 19,803.20 crore and Rs. 12,383 crore respectively. Gujarat, Andhra Pradesh, Maharashtra, Karnataka and Tamil Nadu continued to show a high Gross Fiscal Deficit. Even rich states like Punjab and Haryana showed a rising trend in their Gross Fiscal Deficit.

Primary Deficit of States

The primary deficit is the deficit which does not take into account the interest liability. It would be pertinent to mention that primary deficit of most of the States is not very high. In the year 1995-96, only four Indian States, *i.e.*, Maharashtra, Rajasthan, Uttar Pradesh and West Bengal showed a primary deficit of over Rs. 1,000 crore. Six Indian States, *i.e.*, Arunachal Pradesh, Bihar, Jammu & Kashmir, Punjab, Tamil Nadu and Tripura had no primary deficit. The total primary deficit of all the States was Rs. 9,493.20 crore in the said year.

During the year 2003-04 the States of Haryana, Jammu & Kashmir, Sikkim and Uttar Pradesh had a positive primary deficit. The primary deficit in Gujarat, Karnataka, Rajasthan and West Bengal was on the higher side. The combined primary deficit of all the States was Rs. 33,255.40 crore.

It will be noted that the interest component in the gross fiscal deficit is very high. Most of the States are unable to service their debts. The situation calls for a strict fiscal discipline. The States must find ways and means not to let the interest element overburden their Gross Fiscal Deficit.

The average interest cost of States' borrowings which was 9.2 per cent in 1990-91 rose to 13.3 per cent in 1999-2000. The combined effect of growth in debt stock and rise in the cost of borrowing has been the heavy burden of interest. If we calculate the interest liability of all the States put together, we will find that it has increased phenomenally during the last ten years—from less than Rs. 9,000 crore to over Rs. 54,000 crore.

Revenue Deficit of States

The revenue deficit, which accounted for less than 30 per cent of the gross fiscal deficit in the early 1990s, reached a shocking 60 per cent of the gross fiscal deficit by the year 1999-2000. This implied that out of every Rs. 100 borrowed Rs. 60 were being used for meeting current expenditure. The revenue gaps are increasing and so too the gulf between expenditure and revenue receipts. During the year 2004-05, the interest payment accounted for more than 10 per cent of revenue receipts. It was just 3 per cent in 1980.

Then there is no earnings from the PSUs in the States. In an important study made by the Planning Commission on State Public Sector Undertakings (SPSUs), it was pointed out that more than 80 per cent of total SPSUs' losses in 1988-89 were shared by the States of Andhra Pradesh, Uttar Pradesh, West Bengal, Tamil Nadu, Maharashtra, Karnataka, Gujarat, Kerala and Delhi. States of West Bengal, Uttar Pradesh, Tamil Nadu, Maharashtra, Orissa, Karnataka, Kerala, Andhra Pradesh and Delhi account for 90 per cent of the accumulated losses. The RBI Report 2003-04 also spoke with deep concern of the growing interest burden, mounting pension liabilities, alarmingly high increase in administrative expenditure and huge losses by the SPSUs. The situation was reported to aggravate with very low user charges and the progressive decline in Central transfers.

Factors Responsible for Fiscal Deficit

Fiscal deficit has resulted partly in response to external pressure and natural disaster and partly due to policy measures adopted by the Government. The following paragraphs describe the main causes of fiscal deficit.

Government Policies

(i) **Populist Measures:** In the yearly Union Budgets, the Finance Ministers are more concerned about providing a bit of everything for everybody to please the public and satisfy their alliance partners rather than following the prudent principles. No efforts are being made to trim the bourgeoning Fiscal Deficit.

Fiscal Deficit is broadly net borrowings by the Government. It may look harmless like borrowings by companies. But there is a basic difference. Companies borrow to invest productively and earn an income which would be more than the rate of interest they have to pay, Governments, on the other hand, borrow mostly to fund consumption. Consequently, there are no assets against and no income from the outlays. Interest becomes a dead burden. To pay the interest, the Governments have to borrow once again. That is what has blown public debt of the Centre and the States.

The problem affects the whole economy. The diversion of public savings to government consumption reduces private investment and consequently pulls down rate of growth. Had the budgets been balanced, there would have been enough resources for a 10 per cent growth instead of 7 to 8 per cent, which would have generated more employment and improved the income of the people further.

The real cause of the problem lies in the fact that the Central and State Governments are more interested in populist measures than any agenda for economic upliftment of the people. Such measures block many already meager resource. Some examples of populist schemes initiated by some State Governments are enumerated below:

- Free power for farmers has been announced in Andhra Pradesh, Tamil Nadu, Karnataka and Maharashtra. Earlier, Punjab on many occasions had given free electricity to farmers and to even certain sections of the society. Haryana also followed suit for some time.
- The State Electricity Boards (SEBs) which were once reeling under heavy debts of Rs. 40,000 crore, were supposed to become solvent again when their debts were partly written off and partly transferred to the Centre. *The Economic Survey,* 2004-05 estimates that the SEBs will lose another Rs. 21,700 crore this year,

thanks mainly to free supply of electricity to farmers or supply at a nominal-rate.

- The Government subsidies have been rising fast. The rise in subsidy bill in 2002-03 and 2003-04 was on account of higher allocation for food for work programme to soften the adverse impact of drought on the poor and small and marginal farmers. There was also an enhanced coverage under the 'Antyodya Anna Yojana' and other welfare schemes. The undulating pattern observed in the subsidies arises primarily from the expenditure on food subsidies, which is determined increasingly by the minimum support price of food grains, operational efficiency of the Public Distribution System, highly subsidised welfare schemes and special interventions in the drought affected areas. As a proportion of total expenditure, after declining from 12.4 per cent in 1991 to 7.5 per cent in 1995-96, government subsidies maintained a rising trend till 1998-99 when it reached 9.02 per cent of the total expenditure.
- The open-ended subsidy for LPG gas and kerosene could exceed Rs. 10,000. An attempt to recoup some revenue by raising the cooking gas prices by Rs. 5 every month till subsidy was eliminated was rolled back when the Left Front objected to it. It is the height of political jugglery that the Governments announce populist measures to build a sizeable vote bank but when they feel it necessary to take some necessary steps to strengthen the economy or build up resources through taxation or levies; the coalition parties dissuade them from doing so showing their loyalty to masses.
- The Common Minimum Programme (CMP) of the United Progressive Alliance (UPA) Government promises to increase education spending from 3.4 per cent of Gross Domestic Product to 6 per cent of Gross Domestic Product and health spending from 0.9 per cent to 3 per cent of the Gross Domestic Product. The National Employment Guarantee Programme which envisages a

minimum of hundred days employment to at least one member in each family will cost the exchequer at least one per cent of the Gross Domestic Product.

- The price of urea fertilizer is fixed by the Government. In order to ensure adequate availability of fertilizers to farmers at reasonable rates, subsidy is provided by the Government. Urea, the most consumed fertilizer, is subsidized under the New Urea Price Scheme (NUPS), whereas potash and phosphate are decontrolled but covered under the subsidy of Rs. 4,830 per metric tonne. The existing scheme for special freight subsidy has been continued for supplies to the north-eastern states and Jammu & Kashmir.

(ii) Dependence of agriculture on weather and Agriculture Insurance Scheme:

- If the Government goes ahead with the restructuring of National Agricultural Insurance Scheme proposed by the Agriculture Minister, it will have to shell out Rs. 2,000 crore to cover the subsidy component. An equal amount will have to be set aside by the State Governments which would share the burden of subsidy. The amount of subsidy by the States will depend upon the crops, the number of farmers and land acreage covered under the scheme. The subsidy will have to be made available to the Agriculture Insurance Company of India which will underwrite the subsidy scheme and cover the risks hundred per cent. The revamp of the scheme has been pushed in the wake of 13 per cent shortfall in rainfall during 2004-05 which affected the growth of agriculture. The Economic Survey, 2004-05 has shown the growth in Agriculture and Allied Sector at a meagre 1.1 per cent during the year.

The experts, however, feel that instead of propping agriculture, which is the mainstay of Indian economy, on subsidies, we should develop it *per se* and make it as independent of monsoons as far as possible.

Although populist measures are initiated with good intentions yet they may have dubious outcomes. The Government at the Centre should not resort to political jugglery of announcing populist schemes near the elections in some States in order to woo the voters in favour of their political parties. The State Governments should not announce populist schemes with political intentions ignoring the financial health of the State and the adverse impact of such announcements.

For example, there is no need to give free-power to farmers when such an act would push the State Electricity Boards knee deep in the red. Such an act not only blocks a regular revenue channel for the State government but also leads to misallocation of resources and makes it necessary to provide for accumulated losses subsequently divesting the State of its meager resources.

If the Government is that serious about helping the farmers, there are several other ways like developing adequate storage, transportation and marketing facilities, setting up agro-industrial units, freeing them from the stranglehold of private money-lenders, facilitating research to develop high yielding varieties of seeds, providing regular irrigation facilities and developing allied activities in agriculture to supplement the income of the farmers.

To conclude we can say that the fiscal deficits at the Centre as well as in States have reached an alarming level. It is high time that serious thought be given to curtail fiscal deficits by following rational tax and non-tax measures, avoiding populist measures, etc. Further, while increasing salaries in pursuance to the recommendations of the Pay Commission, consideration should also be paid to the productivity of the workers.

UNION BUDGET 2006-07

Even as the economy is projecting to grow at 8.1 per cent in the current fiscal, the 2005-06 Economic Survey cautioned about the risks of inflation, hardening interest rates and fiscal deficit.

The odds are loaded heavily in favour of continuing the growth momentum observed in the last 3 cycles. A virtual cycle of growth and saving rates will increase with accelerating income growth observed in the pre-budget survey.

Giving its empirical strength, the county's per capita income should be four or five times what it is now. The growth prospects are intricately intertwined with the rapid development of physical infrastructure like power, roads, ports and airports.

Growth of service sector continued to be broad-based. Among sub-sectors of services—trade, hotel, transport and communication—continued to lead by growing at double digit rates for the third successive year.

Financial services comprising banking, insurance and real estate services also maintain the momentum with progressive maturing of Indian financial markets and the ongoing construction boom.

Caution against complacency in the face of sustained industrial growth, the survey has asked the Government to 'unburden' industry from high level of taxes to help it become globally competitive and focus on investment in infrastructure sector to sustain high growth of GDP.

Highlights of Budget 2006-07:

- No change in personal income tax.
- Major thrust to agricultural sector.
- Service tax increased to 12 per cent from 10 per cent.
- Defence allocation increased by Rs. 6,000 crore.
- Excise duty on small cars, soft drinks reduced.
- Duty on cigarretes increased.
- Cancer, Aids drugs to become cheaper.
- One by six criteria for filling IT returns abolished.
- Food processing as priority sector for bank credit.
- Limit of FII investment in government securities increased.
- More services brought under service tax net.
- Efforts to create huge job opportunities in manufacturing and services sector.
- Rs. 4,813 crore for mid-day meal scheme.

National Minorities Development and Finance Corporation to intensify efforts to reach to artisans and weavers in urban and peri-urban centres, especially in districts with concentration of minorities: programme to focus on skill enhancement, credit and techno managerial support. Allocation to National Council for Promotion of Under Privilege increased from Rs. 10 crore to Rs. 13 crore. Government to finance 20,000 merit-cum-means based scholarships to encourage students to pursue higher studies.

Kasturba Gandhi Balika Vidyalaya Scheme: 10,000 new residential schools for girls for SC, ST, OBC and minorities communities to be opened in 2006-07, Rs. 128 crore provided and an additional sum of Rs. 172 crore to be provided during the year. As a further incentive to the girl child who passes the VIII standard examination and enrolls in a secondary school a sum of Rs. 3,000 to be deposited in her name, to be withdrawn by her on reaching 18 years of age.

Investment

Government to provide equity support of Rs. 16,901 crore and loans of Rs. 2,789 crore to Central PSEs (including Railways); infusion of Rs. 1,180 crore in cash and non-cash sacrifices of Rs. 2,566 crore in last two years to restructure the PSEs including Indian Telephone Industries Limited and Heavy Engineering Corporation Limited. To develop India as a hub of gems and jewellery, an expert body to be constituted.

Agriculture

Irrigation: Outlay for 2006-07 increased to Rs. 7,121 crore from Rs. 4,500 crore in 2005-06. Command Area Development Programme to be revamped to allow participatory irrigation management through water users' association; 20,000 water bodies with a command area of 1.47 millions hectares identified in first three phase for repair, renovation and restoration, at an estimated cost Rs. 4,481 crore.

Credit: Farm credit increased to Rs. 1,25,309 crore in 2004-05, expected to cross target of Rs. 1,75,000 crore in 2006-07 with addition of 50 lakh farmers, banks asked to open a separate window for self-help groups, a joint liability group of tenant farmers, a one time relief to be granted to farmers who have availed of crop loans from scheduled Commercial Banks, RRBs, PACS for Kharif and Rabi 2005-06, and amount equal to two per cent points of the borrowers' interest liability on the principal amount upto Rs. 1,00,000 to be credited to her/his bank account before March 31, 2006; Rs. 1,700 crore provided for this purpose.

With effect from Kharif 2006-07 farmers to receive limit of Rs. 3,00,000 on the principal amount. It is short-term credit at 7 per cent with an upper limit of Rs. 3,00,000. Supervision of this is given to NABARD.

Sanction under Rural Infrastructure Development Fund (RIDF XI) at Rs. 7,301 crore as on January 31, 2006. Corpus for (RIDF XII) to increase to Rs. 10,000 crore; specified projects under PPP model to be allowed to access RIDF funds, separate window for agricultural rural roads with a corpus of Rs. 40,000 crore during 2006-07.

Agriculture Insurance: National Agriculture Insurance Scheme to continue.

Plantation Sector: A special purpose Tea Fund to be set up, expected contribution of Rs. 100 crore in 2006-07.

Micro Finance: 8,01,000 SHGs credit linked in two years with credit of Rs. 4,863 crore disbursed to these SHGs; another 3,85,000 SHGs to be credit linked in 2006-07; NABARD to open a line of credit for financing farm production and investment activities through SHGs; Committee to be appointed on financial inclusion.

Horticulture and Fisheries: Terminal markets to be set up on PPP model. Rs. 150 crore earmarked for this in 2006-07; under National Horticulture Mission, Central Institute of Horticulture to be established in Nagaland. National Fisheries Development Board to be constituted.

Manufacturing

1. Employment: The industries with employment opportunities are identified in manufacturing sector. These include textiles, food processing, petroleum, chemicals and petrochemicals, leather and automobiles. In service sector tourism and software can offer large number of jobs.

2. Textiles: Allocation for Technology Upgradation Fund (TUF) enhanced from Rs. 435 crore to Rs. 535 crore; Rs. 189 crore to be provided for Scheme for Integrated Textiles Parks (SITP); jute technology mission to be launched and a National Jute Board to be established.

3. Handlooms: Cluster development approach to continue with 100 clusters to be added at a cost of Rs. 50 crore in 2006-07; yarn depots to be established; a 'handloom' mark to be launched, scheme to be introduced to provide interest subsidy on term loans; provision for the handloom sector to be increased from Rs. 195 crore to Rs. 241 crore.

4. Food Processing Industry: Food processing to be a priority sector for bank credit; NABARD to create a refinancing window with a corpus of Rs. 1,000 crore, especially for agro-processing infrastructure and market development; National Institute of Food Technology Entrepreneurship and Management to be set up; Paddy Processing Research to be developed into a National Level Institute.

5. Petroleum, Chemicals and Petro-Chemicals: A taskforce set up to facilitate development of large PC and P Investment Regions; three such Investment Regions expected to be developed by 2006-07.

6. Information Technology: Existing vehicles of viability gap funding and India Infrastructure Finance Company Limited to provide equity and/or viability gap funding to ventures, window to be opened for three years.

Small and Medium Enterprises: 180 items identified for dereservation to give impetus to lending by SIDBI; SMEs to be recognized in the service sector and small sector enterprises in service sector to be treated on par with small-scale enterprises in manufacturing sector; corpus of Credit Guarantee Fund to be raised from Rs. 1,132 crore to Rs. 2,500 crore in five years; Credit Guarantee Trust for Small industries to be advised to reduce guarantee fee from 2.5 per cent to 1.5 per cent for all loans insurance cover to be extended to 30,000 borrowers; ten schemes drawn up under a five-year National Manufacturing Competitiveness Programme including promotion of ICI mini tool rooms, design clinics and marketing support for SMEs; implementation to be in the PPP model.

8. Cluster Development: Empowered groups of Ministers to be constituted to lay down policy and oversee implementation.

Service Sector

1. Tourism: Development of 15 tourist destinations and circuits to be taken up; 50 villages with core competency in handicrafts, handlooms and culture, close to existing destinations and circuits to be identified and developed; 4 new institutes of hotel management to be established in Chhattisgarh, Haryana, Jharkhand and Uttaranchal. Plan allocation increased from Rs. 186 crore to Rs. 830 crore.

2. Foreign Trade: Share in world exports to be doubled by 2008-09.

Infrastructure

1. Telecommunication: To reach 250 million connections by December 2007, provision of Rs. 1,500 crore for Universal Services obligation funds in 2006-07; more than 50 million rural connections to be rolled out in three years.

2. Power: Five ultra mega power projects of 4000 MW each to be awarded before December 31, 2006; framework to carry out reforms an empowered committee of Chief Ministers and Power Ministers to be set up; Tenth Plan target of 3075 MW of installed capacity for non-conventional energy sources exceeded by December 31, 2005 with installation of 3,650 MW capacity; Rs. 597 crore provided for non-conventional energy sources exceeding by December 31, 2005. With Rajiv Gandhi Gram Vidyuti Karan Yojana 10,000 villages in 2005-06 and 40,000 more villages in 2006-07 to be electrified.

3. Coal: Reserves of 20 billion tonnes to be de-blocked for power projects; definition of captive consumption to be amended to allow mining by producers with firm supply contracts with steel, cement and power companies; capacity of Central Liners

Planning and Development Institute Limited to drill in order to preserve reserves to be expanded.

4. Petroleum: Under NELP VI, 55 blocks and area of 3,55,000 sq. kms. offered, investment of Rs. 22,000 crore expected in refinery sector, in the next few years.

5. Road Transport: Budget support for NHDP enhanced in 2006-07; special accelerated Road Development Programme for the North-Eastern Region at an estimated cost of Rs. 4,618 crore approved with allocation of Rs. 550 crore in 2006-07; 1000 km. of access-controlled express-ways to be developed on the Design Build Finance and Operate (DBFO) model.

Maritime Development: National Maritime Development Programme (NMDP), approved work is in progress in 101 projects covering inland waterways, shipping and ports including deepening of channels in Kandla, JND and Paradip; plan allocation for department of shipping increased by 37 per cent to Rs. 735 crore; study to identify a suitable location for a new deep draft part in West Bengal to be carried out, National Institute of Port Management, Chennai, renamed as National Maritime Academy, to be upgraded into a Central University with regional campuses at Mumbai, Kolkata and Vishakhapatnam. India Infrastructure Finance Company Limited incorporated in principle and granted approval for two-three road projects in Gujarat.

Financial Sector

1. Banking Insurance and Pensions: Net capital support to banking sector standing at Rs. 22,808 crore to be restructured to facilitate increased access of banks to additional resources for lending to the productive sectors; Bill on insurance to be introduced in 2006-07.

2. Capital Market: Limit on FII investment in Government securities to be increased from $ 1.75 billion and the limit on FII investment in corporate debt from $0. 5 billion to $ 1.5 billion; ceiling on aggregate investment by mutual funds in overseas instruments to be raised from $ 1 billion to $ 2 billion with removal of requirement of 10 per cent reciprocal shareholding; limited number of qualified Indian Mutual Funds to be allowed to invest, cumulatively upto $ 1 billion, in overseas exchange traded funds; an investor protection fund to be set up under the aegis of SEBI. RBIs anonymous electronic order matching trading module on its Negotiated Dealing System (NDS-OM) to be extended to qualified mutual funds, provident funds and pension funds; steps to be taken to create a single unified exchange traded market for corporate bonds.

Other Proposals

1. **Research and Development:** National Agricultural Innovation Project for research as frontiers of agricultural sciences to be launched in July 2006; National Entrepreneurship Board has set up technology business incubators, enabling concession to be provided to incubate entrepreneurs.

2. **Institutions of Excellence:** Universities of Calcutta, Bombay and Madras to get a grant of Rs. 50 crore each to mark the beginning of their 150th year celebrations, with another Rs. 50 crore each to be given at the conclusion of the year, Punjab Agriculture University, Ludhiana, to get Rs. 100 crore. An autonomous status of National Institute to be accorded to Rajiv Gandhi Centre of Biotechnology, Thiruvanthapuram, Kerala.

3. **Skill Development:** Rs. 97 crore allocated for upgradation of IITs; Skills Development Initiative (SDI) taken up through a PPP scheme with initial provision of 10 crore.

4. **Backward Regions Grant Fund:** Rs. 166 crore disbursed so far in current year and Rs. 15,000 crore allocated in 2006-07.

5. **Jammu & Kashmir:** State plan for 2006-07 fixed at Rs. 2,300 crore, additionally Rs. 848 crore provided for the Jammu & Kashmir reconstruction plan, including Rs. 230 crore for the Baglihar Project, special centre plan assistance of Rs. 1,300 crore provided for regions in power station.

6. **Defence Expenditure:** Increased to Rs. 89,000 crore including Rs. 37,458 crore for capital expenditure.

7. **E-Governance:** National e-governance plan to be approved shortly, 25 projects in mission made, be launched in 2006-07.

8. Celebrating History and Heritage: Rs. 10 crore allocated for celebration of 150th anniversary of the First War of Indian Independence; National Gandhi Museum, Rajghat and the Kasturba Gandhi National Memoriam Fund, Indore to be given Rs. 5 crores each, Rs. 5 crore for safeguarding old art forms and oral traditions.

Fiscal Consolidation

Twelfth Finance Commission's Recommendations: Rs. 94,402 crore to be released as States' share in gross tax revenues in current year compared to Rs. 78,595 crore in 2004-05, grants-in-aid to States are Rs. 25,134 crore in 2005-06 against Rs. 12,081 crore in 2004-05.

Subsidies: Consensus sought on the issue of subsidies.

Gross Budgetary Support and Gross Fiscal Deficit: Gross tax-GDP ratio: 9.2 per cent in 2003-04, 9.8 per cent in 2004-05, 10.5 per cent in 2005-06 (RE), 11.2 per cent in 2006-07 (BE), revenue deficit for 2005-06 to be 2.6 per cent and fiscal deficit 4.1 per cent.

Budget Estimates 2006-07

Plan Expenditure: Estimated at Rs. 1,72,728 crore up by 20.4 per cent.

Non-Plan Expenditure: Rs. 3,91,263 crore up by 5.51 per cent.

Revenue Deficit and Fiscal Deficit: Revenue deficit estimated at Rs. 84,729 crore, *i.e.* 2.1 per cent of the GDP, fiscal deficit estimated at Rs. 1,148,66 crore, *i.e.* 3.8 per cent of GDP.

Tax-Proposals

Indirect Taxes

Customs

- Peak rates for non-agricultural products reduced from 15 per cent to 12.5 per cent duty; on alloy steel and primary and secondary non-ferrous metals reduced from 10 per cent to 7.5 per cent. This will also be the rate of duty for ferrous alloys; on steel melting scrap raised to 5 per cent and brought on par with primary steel.

- Duty on mineral products reduced to 5 per cent with a few exceptions.
- Duty on ores and concentrates reduced from 5 per cent to 2 per cent.
- Duty on refectories reduced to 7.5 per cent.
- Duty to be reduced on basic inorganic chemicals from 15 per cent to 10 per cent; on basic cyclic and acyclic hydrocarbons and their derivates to 5 per cent.
- Duty to be reduced on major bulk plastics like PVC, LDPE, PP from 10 per cent to 5 per cent; on naptha from plastics to nil, on styrene, EDC and VCM which are raw material from plastics to 2 per cent.
- Reduction of custom duty on 10 Anti-aids and 14 anti-cancer drugs to 5 per cent; on certain life saving drugs, kits and equipments from 15 per cent to 5 per cent. These drugs also exempt from excise duty and CVD.
- Duty on packaging machines to be reduced from 15 per cent to 5 per cent.
- Concessional project rates of 10 per cent to be evaluated to pipelines projects for transportation of natural gas, crude, petroleum and petroleum products.
- CVD of 4 per cent to be imposed on all imports with a few exceptions; full credit to be allowed to manufactures of excisable goods.

Excise

- With the intention to coverage all rates at CEN-VAT rate at 16 per cent, duty on aerated drinks and small cars to be reduced to 16 per cent.
- 8.1 per cent duty to be imposed on packaged software, and software packages downloaded from the internet to be exempt; DVD drives, Flash Drives and Combo Drives to be fully exempt from excise duty.
- Condensed milk, ice-cream, preparations of meat, fish and poultry, pasta and yeast to be fully exempt.
- Duty on ready to eat packaged goods and all minerals to be reduced from 16 per cent to 8 per cent.

- Concessional rates of 8 per cent to be extend to all LPG stores.
- Duty on compact florescent lamps to be reduced from 16 per cent to 8 per cent.
- Glassware to attract duty of 16 per cent par with cera microwaves and plasticware.
- Excise duty on specified printing, writing and packing paper to be reduced from 16 per cent to 12 per cent.

Service Tax

- New services to be covered including ATM operations, maintenance and management, registrars, share transfer agents and bankers to an issue, sale of space or time of other than in the print media, for advertisements, sponsorships of events, other than sports events by companies, international air travel excluding economy class passenger, container services on rail excluding the railway freight charges; business support services, auctioneering; recovery agents, ship management services, travel on cruise ships and public relation management services.
- Coverage of certain services now subject to service tax to be expanded.

REFERENCES

1. Kaldor, Nicholas, *An Expenditure Tax,* George Allen and Unwin, London, 1955.
2. Gandhi, Ved P., *Tax Burden on Indian Agriculture*. Harvard Law School, Cambridge, 1966.
3. Bansal, R.K. and J.R. Gupta, *Economic Aspects of Sales Tax,* Atlantic Publishers, 1985.
4. GOI, Ministry of Finance: *Report of the Task Force on Implementation of the Fiscal Responsibility and Budget Management Act 2003,* 16 July 2004.
5. The increasing importance of the service sector and the service tax is now widely acknowledged.
6. Alan, A. Tait, *Value Added Tax,* McGraw-Hill Book Company Limited, U.K., 1972.

7. Richard W. Lindholm, *Value Added Tax Reforms,* Nelson-Hale Chicago, pp. 30-31 as quoted in R.W. Hafer and Michael E. Trebing: '*The Value-Added Tax: A Review of the Issues,*' Federal: Reserve Bank of Louis, January 1980, pp. 3-10.
8. Union Finance Minister, Mr. P. Chidambaram in his budget speech on 8 July 2004, quoted the example of Haryana.
9. Mahesh C. Purohit, 'Is Unified VAT Regime Feasible' (debate), *Economic Times,* 15 June 2004.
10. GOI, Ministry of Finance, *Op. Cit.*
11. *Ibid.*
12. As reported in *The Hindu*, 18 July 2004.
13. Government of India, *Economic Survey,* 2005-06.
14. Government of India, *Budget* 2006-07.
15. Government of India, *Economic Survey,* 2005-06.
16. *Ibid.*
17. Government of India, *Twelfth Finance Commission Report,* 2004.
18. Government of India, *Economic Survey,* 2004-05.
19. Government of India, Ministry of Finance: *Report of the Task Force on Implementation of the Fiscal Responsibility and Budget Management Act 2003,* 16 July 2004.
20. Government of India, *Twelfth Finance Commission Report,* 2004, pp. 64-65.
21. This section draws heavily from (1) Kabra, Kamal Nayan, "A Decade of Reforms: The Unfinished Agenda", The Theme paper for the Member Annual Conference of the IIPA 2002, and (2) Gupta, K.R. (Ed.) "Fiscal Deficits in States" in Studies in Indian Economy, Atlantic Publishers, New Delhi, 2005.